We Decide!

In the series GLOBAL ETHICS AND POLITICS,

edited by Carol Gould

MICHAEL MENSER

We Decide!

Theories and Cases in Participatory Democracy

TEMPLE UNIVERSITY PRESS
Philadelphia • *Rome* • *Tokyo*

TEMPLE UNIVERSITY PRESS
Philadelphia, Pennsylvania 19122
www.temple.edu/tempress

Library of Congress Cataloging-in-Publication Data

Names: Menser, Michael.
Title: We decide! : theories and cases in participatory democracy / Michael
    Menser.
Description: Philadelphia : Temple University Press, 2018. | Series: Global
    ethics and politics | Includes bibliographical references and index.
Identifiers: LCCN 2017018198 (print) | LCCN 2017038960 (ebook) | ISBN
    9781439914199 (e-book) | ISBN 9781439914175 (hardback : alk. paper) | ISBN
    9781439914182 (paper : alk. paper)
Subjects: LCSH: Political participation—Cross-cultural studies. |
    Democracy—Cross-cultural studies. | Politics, Practical—Cross-cultural
    studies. | Social change—Cross-cultural studies. | Political
    science—Philosophy. | BISAC: POLITICAL SCIENCE / Political Ideologies /
    Democracy. | PHILOSOPHY / Political.
Classification: LCC JF799 (ebook) | LCC JF799 .M47 2018 (print) | DDC
    321.8—dc23
LC record available at https://lccn.loc.gov/2017018198

9 8 7 6 5 4 3 2 1

Contents

Acknowledgments

Participatory democracy is an evolving collective enterprise and so was writing this book! Though *We Decide!* is a book of philosophy, it is informed not just by philosophers but by political and social scientists, anthropologists, economists, and historians. And because it is also a book of action, it owes at least as much to nonacademics, including elected officials, government workers, nonprofit members, activists, and committed community members, all of whom show participatory democracy is not just desirable and justifiable but doable.

Over the years I have been fortunate to have had many fine mentors and (public school and university) teachers. But I learned philosophy in the form of deliberative democracy very early, thanks to my family, who loved books and debates. So love and thanks to them all for their support then and to this day: Dave, Laurel, Jalen, Kent, Arlene, Donald, Horty, and Pat Menser and Ed, Julia, and Edward Narkun. And thanks to my partner's family for all their more recent generosity and support, especially John Bell, Carol Rudolph, and of course Clancy and Nat. I learned about participatory democracy (PD) during graduate school at CUNY in the 1990s. The scene in NYC at that time was vibrant and crucial in my own development: thanks to the Autonomedia collective, especially Jim Fleming, Jordan Zinovich, and Jim Feast; Reclaim the Streets and the NYC Direct Action Network, including Brooke Lehman, Dan Vea, and David Graeber. The World and U.S. Social Forum crews and connected movements was my next space of PD learning (again by thinking and doing), thanks here to Premilla Dixit, Thomas Ponniah, Boa Santos, and the U.S. Solidarity Economy Network. As for academic venues, I received critical support and supportive critique from so many at CUNY, including the Found Object and Situations collectives and Stanley Aronowitz, Neil Smith, David Harvey, Omar Dahbour, and the Center for Place, Culture, and Politics, the Center for Global Ethics and Politics, Gary Wilder and the Committee on Globalization and Social Change, and the CUNY Social and Political Philosophy Workshop. And gratitude goes to so many other venues including the Fernand Braudel Center and the Philosophy of the City (APA) Research Group. And at Brooklyn College, Roberta Matthews and the Arts of Democracy and the Whiting Foundation enabled me to undertake this project, and the Wolfe Institute provided essential support for my finishing it. Throughout, at my beloved academic home, the Brooklyn College Philosophy Department, my colleagues were almost always supportive. On a related note, thanks to all of those who fought for me when I was denied tenure. (We won!) Your efforts too inspired me to continue in this work, and the broader project of PD. I also want to thank my union, the Professional Staff Congress, not just for the health care coverage and sabbatical (without which I could not have completed this book), but also for its dedication to the City University of New York and public education. I am truly honored to have been a student and to be faculty at CUNY, one of the most inclusive, vibrant, and impactful public institutions in the country if not the world.

For many significant PD conversations and collaborations, and/or comments on my work thanks to Gianpaolo Baiocchi, Kenneth Edusei, Shane Epting, Ken Estey, Jessica Gordon Nembhard, Andrej Grubacic, David Harvey, Ron Hayduk, Olivia Katz, Shannon Kincaid, Alan Aja, Alex Kolokotronis, Veronica Manlow, Jamie McCallum, Chris Michael, Manny Ness, Laxmi Ramasubramanian, the crews at the Democracy Collaborative and the Science and Resilience Institute at Jamaica Bay, Marina Sitrin, Bill Solecki, Celina Su, Alex Sullivan, Robert Viscusi, Chey Weber, Jocelyn Wills, and Eddie Yuen.

And I would also like to thank the anonymous reviewers; they were exactly what every writer hopes for: thorough, insightful, critical yet encouraging. And to editor Aaron Javsicas, for his guidance and patience. And deep appreciation to Carol Gould. This book would not have been possible without her early and consistent support and encouragement. And her innovative and systematic body of work created a space within philosophy for works such as this one and many others.

And thanks to all those who made PB possible in the United States! Sondra Youdelman and the amazing crew at Community Voices Heard, and all the participants, as well as Chicago Alderman Joe Moore and NYC council member Jumaane Williams. And my deepest gratitude to Josh Lerner and everyone who has worked at the Participatory Budgeting Project. You inspire and teach me so much more than you could ever know: you are participatory democracy in action! And thoughtful, creative, and relentless.

And to my family, Desmond and Vandana, not the least for their efforts at "family meeting time"—our attempt at democracy in action at home!—but more so for their persistent, inquisitive amazingness. And to Nicole, through it all, my true partner.

We Decide!

.

Introduction

We are Everywhere

The time I first heard about "participatory democracy" was in a jam-packed basement at the City University of New York Graduate Center. It was the summer of 2003 and dozens of us were attending a panel on how to make NYC more democratic. The first speaker—a budget expert from a good governance group—described in ruthless detail how the NYC office of the mayor ignored public priorities, intimidated the city council, and manipulated the tax code. We were incensed and depressed. The second speaker shifted the scene to sunny South America and talked about how a town there had solved many of these problems with a process called participatory budgeting (PB).[1] The mood immediately brightened. But then we were stunned, confused, and offended: elected officials in some third-world country turned over millions of dollars to city residents who designed their own process to spend the money in a way that reduced corruption, increased accountability, addressed real community needs, and was creative, efficient, and empowering!? We were stunned because the achievement was so impressive: how could "regular" people set up their own process? But (here was the confusion) why would elected officials help them? Then we were offended: wasn't democracy born in Greece, developed in Europe, and then innovatively scaled up by America's Founding Fathers? How was it that this breakthrough political mechanism was happening in a third-world country amid the shantytowns and rainforests? Our own cultural biases came to the fore.

I became confused (again!), though, because people whom I encountered who praised this participatory democratic process had such different politics and rarely agreed on anything else. Liberals liked it for its transparency and accountability. Libertarians lauded PB for taking money away from the government and giving it back to the people. Socialists commended it as an example of how the state could help the people develop popular power. Even antistate anarchists sometimes said nice things about it because they saw it as a transfer of power from the state to the people, a real example of self-government. As if that ideological range of approval weren't startling enough, others praised PB for embodying the "good governance" paradigm, especially since it led to more efficient public spending (more bang for the buck) and enhanced the legitimacy of the government. Even the World Bank, so despised by the originators of PB, praised it and promoted it (as do the United Nations [UN] and Rockefeller Foundation). Despite all these different perspectives praising PB, when a few of us went down to Porto Alegre to learn more about PB, we were told that such a program would never work in the United States because people here are too lazy (or busy), too stupid (or disinterested), too selfish (or satisfied). I was once more offended: so why then would it work in a country with higher illiteracy, more poverty, and outright civil unrest? But, again, I was hooked and so was the tenacious Josh Lerner, and with the support of the generous Gianpaolo Baiocchi we went on to form an organization to get it started in the United States.[2]

Early on in those efforts we realized we were not alone. There were many others researching and running organizations that were committed to empowering individuals and communities, reducing inequality, and promoting solidarity across borders and sectors, including worker and consumer cooperatives, community land trusts, grassroots health clinics, fair trade alliances, democratic unionists, community development organizations, urban gardens, and public banks.[3] I was stunned (again!): even though participatory democracy seemed so demanding there were examples of it all over the place. But why didn't more people know about it? One reason was lack of a common language. People practicing or praising PD call it by all kinds of names: direct democracy, community control, horizontalism, grassroots democracy, self-determination, commoning, the subsistence perspective, mutual aid, cooperativism, solidarity economy, P2P, the next system, and on and on. This was in part because people from diverse political frameworks praised the same forms but for different reasons and defined key norms such as community, equality, freedom, solidarity, participation, and justice in different ways.

So where were the political philosophers to sort through all these conceptual confusions? The ones that did like PD tended to be ideological and that limited their appeal and the potential for a broader politics since if you didn't subscribe exactly to their political program you were probably excluded or turned off. Second, in the United States at least, there was (and still is?) a real skepticism toward participatory forms that share power. This was/

is true of academics, activists, and "average" people. Influential PD advocate Sherry Arnstein made this point amid the combative cultural politics of the 1960s when she called out the hypocrisy of the racially privileged and elites who praise "participation." She wrote,

> The idea of citizen participation is a little like eating spinach: no one is against it in principle because it is good for you. Participation of the governed in their government is, in theory, the cornerstone of democracy—a revered idea that is vigorously applauded by virtually everyone. The applause is reduced to polite handclaps, however, when this principle is advocated by the have-not blacks, Mexican-Americans, Puerto Ricans, Indians, Eskimos, and whites. And when the have-nots define participation as re-distribution of power, the American consensus on the fundamental principle explodes into many shades of outright racial, ethnic, ideological, and political opposition. (Arnstein 1969, 216)

After the defeat of PD movements in the early 1970s (Katsiaficas 1983), the situation became so bad that even the theorists who professed to be committed to the project of democracy did not believe that creating meaningful venues for popular participation in politics (much less the workplace) was doable *or* desirable. (See my Chapter 1.) Indeed, it could even be dangerous. They argued that "the people" are too lazy, too stupid, too aggressive, too passive, too selfish, too easily misled, too diverse, and/or that there are just too many of them! Far from being anomalous, these arguments became mainstream in political philosophy. Indeed, the project of philosophy begins with Plato and Aristotle *ruling out democracy as a viable political form* and continues into modern politics and philosophy (Dahl 1989, 2, 24–26, 52–55; Keane 2009, 82). But this critique ignores a more pressing difficulty. What about those people who do desire genuine popular power and self-government? What exactly does that look like? And is it doable in today's world of 7 billion people? How would it work in our multicultural cities, racially divided suburbs, and vast rural stretches? Unfortunately, as Macpherson wrote, "realistic works on participatory democracy are scarce" (MacPherson 1977, 117).

The Structure of *We Decide!*: Systematic, Pluralist, Comparative, Critical, and Strategic

There are many different examples of PD succeeding: a federation of worker co-ops in Spain, consumer co-ops in Japan, community gardens in Detroit, and community land trusts in Vermont, but each looks so small, none seems like a vision of the future world, at best a glimpse. What would a PD economy look like? A PD government? To think at this systematic level, we need to stop treating these cases as isolated fragments, or as liberated islands in a sea of despotism, but rather as pieces of a larger puzzle aiming to be interconnected. *We Decide!* develops a framework that is critical and comparative; it seeks to understand the strengths and weaknesses of each model but also looks at the best practices of each model (the best PBs, the best co-ops, the best community-controlled but state-run agencies, etc.). But even the best practices can only solve a limited range of problems; they must be connected with other modes and efforts to complete the picture. *We Decide!* also does this; it is not just case focused but big picture, and it asks how we might work together strategically in order to get there (see Conclusion).

Participatory Democracy Is Maximal Democracy (or MaxD)

We Decide! takes on all of these challenges: first, it takes on the need for a "common language" and develops a conception of participatory democracy that identifies the core principles. Building on my earlier work, I call it "maximal democracy" or maxD. One of the major problems in the literature on PD, even among its advocates, is that there is no concise definition of its core principles, nor is it clear on how to determine whether or not an organization or view is PD. In other words, some organizations and theories seem democratic in some ways but authoritarian or exclusionary in others. How do we decide if they are in or out? MaxD provides a rubric to address such dilemmas by providing an operationalizable framework that can pick out or help inform PD efforts or views across sectors (political, economic, social), cultures, and historical periods. But crucially, maxD is minimal enough to still allow for a pluralism in organizational forms and normative perspectives.

Speaking generally, *participatory democracy* (PD) is that view of politics that calls for the creation and proliferation of practices and institutions that enable individuals and groups to better *determine* the conditions in which they act and relate to others.[4] PD as maximal democracy is defined by four features: (1) collective determination; (2) capacity development and delivery of economic, social, and/or political benefits to members or constituents; (3) the replacement of unequal power relations with relations of shared authority; and (4) the construction, cultivation, proliferation, and interconnection of movements and organizations with overlapping normative frameworks (i.e., those that mostly embody the first three tenets). (These are explained in detail in Chapter 1.)

Maximal democracy is about cooperative power: that is, the ability to act with others to enhance the capacities of and obtain benefits for individuals while reducing inequalities among all. With its focus on power and equality, PD can be contrasted with normative views that are centered upon happiness, rights, and/or freedom as well as political frameworks such as deliberative or representative democracy. To be sure, deliberation and representation have a role to play, but the driving force behind participatory democracy is the creative, collaborative, and constructive power of collective determination.

PD Is Nonideal Philosophy

Another feature that distinguishes PD from so many other ethical and political views is that it operates in the real world. Unlike so many political and ethical views, PD does not presuppose an ideal space where we are all equal. In the uneven playing field of the real world, what use are such "ideal philosophies"? They are either utopian in the sense of being nonrealizable or sophisticated obfuscations that blind us from dealing with the injustices of our time. Because PD rejects the notion of the blank slate—whether the "state of nature" of social contract theory or the "ideal speech situation" of discourse ethics, it is what Charles Mills calls "non-ideal philosophy" (Mills and Pateman 2007, 112–118).

We Decide!'s response to the last challenge makes it not just unique but controversial relative to the field of political philosophy. It is my view that philosophy focuses too much on justification and not enough on illustration. As MacPherson bluntly told us, one of the biggest challenges facing PD advocates is *not to argue that it's just but to show that it's doable. We Decide!* does so in the political arena in the case of participatory budgeting and state agencies, in the economic realm with cooperatives, and in the ecological-social milieu with myriad forms and practices. It draws upon extensive empirical evidence from sociologists, anthropologists, historians, and political scientists both to show how these practices work and to evaluate them. Of the literature that pushes for PD, another weakness is that it often does so uncritically. While I certainly believe that there is far too much critique in political theory (do we really need another book explaining why capitalism is bad?), uncritical praise of PD backfires for two reasons: (1) It makes PD seem "too good to be true" and thus it ends up looking like a false promise. PD cannot solve all the world's problems. It's imperfect and limited. And (2) there are some venues where it will not work. But that's fine. Liberalism, too, has its limits, as do deliberative democracy and socialism. No view is perfect; no view works in all situations for all peoples in all sectors.

There Are No Universal Solutions and No Model Solves All Problems, but We Must Disarticulate the State!

In real life *every* ethical or political model is going to fail on certain counts. Some consumer co-ops may have bad gender dynamics. Worker co-ops in general may not offer enough benefits to address the whole range of needs of those who are discriminated against. And PB in many cases may not adequately address the needs of the poorest of the poor. That does not mean that one gives up on any of them. Liberal states have performed poorly on race, privately owned businesses on gender, and state agencies on preventing too many from falling into poverty. The task is to figure out both the strengths and the weaknesses of each form and how to create an array of them to address the range of problems.[5] PD by itself cannot solve gender inequality. That will require a multidimensional feminist movement. But PD has something to contribute to the effort of remaking the relations between men and women when it comes to care work in the household. The same goes for structural racism. PD in general and PB in particular are not substitutes for critical race theory and the efforts of the Movement for Black Lives (M4BL), but PD has much to offer to those pursuing community power in the environmental justice movement and M4BL has identified PB as a crucial tool for building the capacities of individuals and groups in communities that have suffered long-term structural disadvantages (see Chapter 1).

What we need are comparative and critical examinations of these efforts in order to identify best practices and help improve the weak ones and protect the strong ones, so that, in this moment of global chaos and system change, creating a more democratic, sustainable, and inclusive system is not a speculative fantasy but an engaged and multisector strategy (see Conclusion).

All of the preceding means that PD practitioners and theorists must face up to one of the biggest challenges facing all political theorists in this moment: the role of the state. Too many PD advocates accept the either/or binary not of "smash or seize" but of "ignore or seize" the state and then opt for "ignore." While I accept that "exodus" is an option to be considered (see Chapter 1), it receives too much press and other options should be given more detailed attention (see Chapters 2 and 6). One view I develop is the strategy of fracturing and then reclaiming part of the state, what I have called "disarticulation" (Menser 2009). I call the resulting political form "social-public" to contrast it with the much more common understanding of corporate state as public-private. *We Decide!* raises the issue of the state in every chapter and then builds a more general theory of the social-public governance in Chapter 6.

Description of the Chapters

Chapter 1: Participation and Democracy in History, Theory, and Practice is by far the longest. Why? Because there is no comprehensive treatment of PD in a single volume from any perspective, much less a philosophical one. In this chapter, I lay out the key concepts and principles, construct a PD canon, take a trip through the three waves of participatory democracy theory, and survey the literature of participatory democracy as it operates within the subfields of democratic theory and political philosophy. And I outline my own view of PD as maximal democracy (maxD) that will be utilized throughout the rest of the book. But perhaps the biggest challenge for PD advocates is not so much to explain why it is desirable but to show that it is doable. And this requires revisiting practices in history and the present. I do this in detail with ancient Athens and, with what I argue is an even better and more relevant model, the Haudenosaunee or Iroquois Federation. This first chapter pushes for a political theory that is much more attentive to the mechanics of political practices and shows the importance not only of justification but of illustration. It also aims to show that even though PD has been treated as a minor view with very few examples of it ever occurring much less working, this is false. PD is profusely distributed, in time and space, culture and sector. The history of PD, as more recent histories of democracy show, is incredibly diverse culturally and geographically, and also ideologically and philosophically. Indeed, I argue that there are six different traditions/frameworks that are amenable to and utilize PD: communitarianism, liberalism, associationism, anarchism-autonomism, ecologically oriented feminism, and environmental justice. All of these views endorse PD values and praise PD organizations and practices but for diverse, and sometimes even conflicting, reasons. Debates among these views are played out across the different sectors from the political and economic to the social and ecological.

Chapter 2: Participatory Budgeting, Democratic Theory, and the Disarticulation of the State stays within the confines of the political and focuses in on the case of PB. PB is a process in which some part of a public budget is controlled by those most impacted by that budget. PB is examined in detail with respect to who participates, how they participate, and the impacts on both governance and public service delivery. Detailed case studies are presented on the PB processes in Porto Alegre (Brazil) and NYC and its spread worldwide is also discussed and critically evaluated. Competing normative justifications for PB are analyzed. Difficulties among civil society, the state, and society are noted, "top down" and "bottom up" views of social change are argued against, and PB's impact on the state form is explored, as is the argument that PB articulates a new form of "social-public" governance. Key debates play out between PD and deliberative democracy, and liberal PD and autonomous-anarchist PD (A-PD). An important conclusion is that while there are some very robust models of PB, many PBs are actually not PD, but may still be worth doing because of other benefits. Also, even the best versions are limited.

In Chapter 3: From Corporate Social Responsibility to Economic Democracy: Stakeholder Theory, Civil Society, and Worker Ownership, I bring my empirically oriented pluralist maxD approach to the economic sphere. We begin by discussing just what is the economy and talk about confusions and limitations that result from the either/or binary of capitalism and socialism. Drawing upon the work of Gibson-Graham and a range of economic democracy theorists, we construct an alternative model of economic diversity. However, if the goal is to democratize the economy, this means that we have to transform actual workplaces. And for this we need to engage with business ethics, as both a literature and an audience, not to mention current owners, workers, and customers. In this chapter we do so by engaging with stakeholder theory (ST) and the rubric of corporate social responsibility (CSR). While some may think that ST brings democracy into the workplace, I argue that it does not. Still others argue that a civil society approach made up of independent nonprofit watchdogs engaged in deliberative democracy can do so, but I argue that even in the more successful models of Students against Sweatshops and the Forest Stewardship Council, benefits are too limited. A much more robust approach of the worker cooperative is argued for as exemplified by the Mondragon Corporation in northern Spain.

In Chapter 4: Democracy in the Workplace: Freedom, Equality, and the Sovereignty of Labor, we further explore the normative dimensions of worker cooperatives through three different philosophical views: Robert Dahl's classic *political* work that argues that businesses are not property but minigovernments, Richard Ellerman's contentious and technical *moral* take that argues that wage labor is a modern-day form of slavery, and David Schweickart's *system-level analysis* that makes reference to a pluralistic mix of economic and political arguments but nevertheless considers itself (democratic) market socialist. Critiques of worker co-ops from anti-PD and pro-PD views are then considered with a special focus on A-PD and subsistence perspective or social reproduction participatory democratic (S-PD) views. Even Mondragon gets critiqued, and other forms of cooperatives are explored that include nonworkers as members (e.g., multistakeholder cooperatives). The role of worker co-ops in system-wide change is discussed.

In Chapter 5: From the Culture of Consumption to Democratic Social Reproduction, the discussion of PD in the economy shifts from production to ecologically oriented social reproduction. The main case study is the Seikatsu Club Consumer Cooperative Union founded and run by housewives in Japan. Differences with the worker co-op approach and Mondragon are debated and strategic implications considered.

Chapter 6 is entitled We Administer! From the Public-Private to the Social-Public. One of the most frequent and important critiques of PD is that it cannot be "scaled up." This chapter aims to address that challenge by outlining how PD can collaborate with the state by remaking elements of it (namely the machinery of its bureaucracy). Limits of state socialism and the welfare state are noted as are the failures of the neoliberal "public-private" model. An alternative model is developed, "the social-public," and explained with respect to service delivery and notions of PD and sustainability. Case studies include the 1970s NYC fiscal crisis; water utilities in Brazil, Bolivia, and the United States; and social media and the Internet in terms of "platform cooperativism" and the P2P view of the "partner state." The affinity of the social-public with environmental justice concerns is noted as is the need to better operationalize the conception of the commons for urban areas.

Who will make this happen? In the Conclusion, building on the earlier chapters, I argue that political theory must break its obsession with critique and expand its empirical purview. Future research projects are called to more thoroughly investigate PD histories, key innovations, and best practices. I conclude by discussing four scenarios in which PD could proliferate: a "checkerboard" strategy that remakes local jurisdictions and then interconnects them; economic crisis and major state policy change; civil crisis and massive social movement action; and the ecological crisis and a cross sector multicultural climate justice movement.

1

Participation and Democracy in History, Theory, and Practice

> The struggle for democracy is today above all the struggle for the democratization of democracy. Substantively, democracy concerns the quality of human experience and the social relations that it makes possible. It can be defined as the entire process through which unequal power relations are replaced by relations of shared authority. Liberal democracy confined democracy to the political realm, strictly conceived of as the field that concerns the state's areas of intervention. This rendered the democratic process susceptible to constituting an island of democracy in a wide sea of social despotisms.
>
> —SANTOS AND AVRITZER, *DEMOCRATIZING DEMOCRACY*, LXII

Participatory democracy (PD) is a view about how to collectively share power, whether in government, the economy, or social life. In this chapter, I examine the key concepts of PD (equality, freedom, solidarity, capability development, and collective determination) and (re)construct a multicultural history of PD practices and theory. To do this, I argue there are *two* classical exemplars—not just ancient Greece but the Haudenosaunee or Iroquois Federation—and four key historical views: Jean-Jacques Rousseau's communitarianism, the liberalism of J. S. Mill, Peter Kropotkin's ecosocial anarchism, and G.D.H. Cole's associationism. I then conduct a literature review and construct a taxonomy of the range of six PD views or routes:[1] (1) communitarian PD, (2) liberal PD, (3) associationist PD, (4) anarchist-autonomous or A-PD, (5) (eco)social reproduction oriented or S-PD, and (6) environmental justice or EJ-PD. I develop my own version of PD, which I call maximal democracy (or maxD), and the rules for applying it. What unifies these different views of PD is that they all share the four principles that define PD as maxD. I then distinguish PD/maxD from related views such as deliberative and monitory or watchdog democracy views[2] and set up the more in-depth discussions as they apply to politics (participatory budgeting in Chapter 2), the economy (democratic workplaces in Chapters 3, 4, and 5), and democratic consumption and (eco)social reproduction (in Chapter 5). Throughout, I discuss the limits, contradictions, and possibilities for PD with the state and develop my own theory of such an interaction that I call "the social-public," which is elaborated in depth in Chapter 6. Best practices and possible futures for PD are grouped together in the Conclusion.

A further mission of the present chapter is to reposition political theory, to break free of the cage of critique and move from justification to illustration. Yes, we need to know how to argue for our views and formulate principles. But we also need to take stock of what has happened and what exists and show how and when such models are doable. Indeed, part of what justifies a view is that it is doable (Macpherson 1977, 94). I see this not as being bound to "the real world" but being obligated to be efficacious, to impact and transform. While I am not alone in this pursuit, we are too few.

The history of democracy is so inspiring but its present so precarious. When did it all go wrong? Is it possible that it was (fatally?) flawed from the start? To answer this question honestly, we need to consider the details of the official birthplace of democracy more closely (e.g., ancient Athens) and, I argue, dramatically broaden our conception of its origins to include a very different kind of precursor (e.g., the Iroquois Federation). But first we turn to Athens.

Classical Exemplar 1: Ancient Athens

Democracy: rule by the people. It's a word and concept that almost everyone knows. And most think it is a good idea. But from where did it come? Its English iteration comes into usage in the sixteenth century, just a little modified from the French word *democratie*. But its real origin is the Greek *demokratia*: *kratia* means "rule" and *demos* means "people." In the traditional story of democracy, the first people to have a democracy were the citizens of ancient Athens. After the fall of a power-grabbing tyrant, a wiser patriarch ushered forth a new era of popular power. Although it lasted less than two centuries (506–338 B.C.E.), its impact has been felt for millennia (Keane 2009, 9, 74–75). Indeed, for some, it was one of the most impactful acts in the history of humans, "comparable in importance to the invention of the wheel or the discovery of the New World" (Dahl 1989, 13).

The concept and practice of democracy that emerged in that ancient city diverged from rival forms of rule on two counts: instead of an elite group dictating the laws, all citizens ruled by deliberating with one another. And what bound these persons together was not ancestry in a clan or tribe but membership in a polity in a specific place, collective residence and interdependence—in a word, citizenship.[3]

Athenian democracy had three crucial features: (1) it created mechanisms to actualize *isonomia* (equality before the law) so that all citizens could participate in policy formation and other political decisions; (2) citizens not only were *eligible* to occupy a political or administrative office but in almost all cases actually did serve (*isopoliteía*: the right to hold office and the right to "one person, one vote"; Held 2006, 16–17; Keane 2009, 45–46); and (3) institutions and spaces were created not just for debate and deliberation but also to foster what Aristotle called philia or "friendship."

In the *ekklesia*, those assembled made proposals for laws, discussed and debated them, and then collectively decided which ones to enact. This included decisions about political judgments such as war and peace and what we might consider judicial matters, since they charged and prosecuted fellow citizens (Keane 2009, 33–37). It worked as follows. There were about 30,000 persons in Athens who were eligible to rule,[4] so before each session, slaves (more on that later) would round up adult males (more on that later, too) twenty years or older and bring them to the Pnyx, a kind of amphitheater with steep slopes and steps carved into the stone, surrounded by olive groves and eucalyptus trees. The session began with some prayers and the sacrifice of a lamb or young pig. Then the herald would exclaim: "Citizens! Who has some useful suggestion for the *polis*?"[5] Heralds as well as slaves and archers kept order (Keane 2009, 31–35).

While kings dispensed orders from the throne, ancient Athens created a new seat for popular sovereignty: the assembly, or ekklesia, that convened on the Pnyx, a hill in central Athens (west of the famous Acropolis). The assembly was a place where citizens left behind the particular interests of their private households and met face-to-face in a shared world where each was present and, hence, accountable to all fellow citizens (Mansbridge 1980, 13–14; Dahl 1989, 13–14). In the openness of this commons, the shackles of the particular and the past could be smashed by the will of those present together in the public. Democracy didn't just distinguish itself by who was in charge; it changed what was possible. Tyrants are in essence conservative; the old order of things justifies their place on top. But democracy is dynamic and sometimes unpredictable, as both its critics and supporters note (Keane 2009, 51–53; Santos and Avritzer 2005, xliii).

What happened in the assembly was genuinely participatory governance. Not only did each citizen have the right to speak (*isēgoría*); each had the right to propose a law or bring a charge against a fellow citizen. And each had the right to approve or reject any proposal or prosecution, from going to war to raising taxes. When we think of PD nowadays, we often think of small groups, perhaps seven to nine or dozens at the most, but in Athens the ekklesia's quorum was 6,000. (The Pnyx could hold around 14,000 people.) Think about it: the minimum number required to assemble and carry out this face-to-face democracy was several thousand, and decisions were made by consensus (Mansbridge 1980, 13–15).[6] For such debate and discussion to work, all those participating obviously had to be patient and attentive, but they also had to be of the right mind-set; they had to be disposed to regard their fellow citizens as worthy of being heard even when disagreements arose. They had to be friends. Aristotle himself thought that friendship among citizens was essential to have a just polis. He just did not believe that the masses should rule. (They didn't have the intelligence or the virtues to pull it off.) But the people of Athens believed otherwise.[7]

But to actually work, citizens had to be virtuous and subordinate their private interests to the public good. Indeed, they had to be not just of the right mind but of *one mind* (*homonoia*) (Mansbridge 1980, 13–15). Relatedly, the ekklesia was not just a spot for formal political deliberation; it was a place for fostering a very social and interpersonal education (*paideia*) that was as much ethical as political (Bookchin [1992] 1995, 64). This helped to cultivate the "one mindedness" that Mansbridge calls "unitary democracy." In such a unitary society, it is not enough that we all support some policy; we all have to support it for the same reason. Striving for *homonoia* helps to avoid factions. What unites the polity is the common interest of its members, and this common interest is generated through friendship (philia). Hence, we have Aristotle's maxim: friendship is equality (Mansbridge 1980, 9).[8] Philia is what holds city-states together (Schwarzenbach 2009, 51). And in this originary version of the story, democracy is very much about the participation of a homogeneous community.

Administration by the People

But Athenian democracy wasn't just about debate and lawmaking; it was about running the government and administration. Not only did every Athenian citizen have the right to rule; almost everyone ended up holding office at some time. Governmental functions were many, from military service and tax collection to running festivals and maintaining public spaces. Those positions that required a special skill or talent (e.g., military generals) were elected. The other spots were chosen "blindly" by lot.[9] Citizens were paid for their service. Terms were short, and a citizen could serve only one term. The consequence of this system was that political power did not concentrate in particular individuals or even in a preset group because there was no way for them to hold onto the offices (Held 2006, 16–17).

Could one imagine this happening in the contemporary United States?[10] It would be as if jury duty were extended beyond the courtroom and now included the parks department, public safety, the water utility, and schools. If that were the case, citizens wouldn't be called every couple of years (à la contemporary jury duty); they would be called to serve every couple of weeks. In some ways, it's not that hard to imagine; already many city departments have volunteers who do work (cleaning up parks, assisting seniors), monitor (e.g., serving on civilian review boards for police), and even make policy or control budgets (e.g., serving on school boards) (Dahl 1989, 19). But such citizen duties would have to be systematic and pervasive. The difficulty, of course, is that many Americans would be against it for the simple reason that they don't have enough time. How did the Greeks do it? They had slaves. For the Greeks, work, especially manual labor, was not only time consuming; it was a distraction from the life of the mind, from contemplation, from virtue, and also from politics, discussion, and debate (Bookchin [1992] 1995, 67–69).[11]

The Greatness of the Greeks? Criticisms of Athenian Democracy

In this brief summary, the PD greatness of Athens is evident in four respects. (1) Its norms: it promoted reason, equality, and fairness. Indeed, "the notions of the rule of law, due process and constitutional procedure find their earliest expression in the politics of the Athenian city-state" (Held 2006, 15). Here democracy shows a clear alternative to tyranny and oligopoly. It opposes both the concentration of power and the arbitrary use of it (Held 2006, 14–15). (2) It promoted capacity building and virtue through civic education and learning by doing. (3) It constructed mechanisms for the substantive implementation of these norms. From the rules and procedures for rendering judgments in the assembly, to the drawing of lots to fill government jobs, Athens shows us how substantive political equality can be implemented in terms of policy making *and* administration. Self-rule is not impossible; it happened. (4) Ancient Athens also demonstrates that PD can work at scale with a relatively large population. This is an odd point because oftentimes Athens is used to demonstrate precisely the opposite: that it was a small city. But when we actually get into the details, it involved intense interactions among *thousands* of people on a regular basis and dwarfs what are usually considered to be small-scale venues.[12]

Another weak criticism of the model of Athenian democracy is that it worked only because it occurred in such a unique place. After all, Athens is one of the most famous cities in all of human history. This was a special place not just for political reasons; it was the birthplace of philosophy and tragedy, an incredible space for the arts, and a naval power. We all know that Athens was exceptional, so why think its form of democracy could happen anywhere else; it didn't even last very long there.

Although one would encounter this criticism frequently years ago, in the past couple of decades research has shown that Athens was not alone in its implementation of assembly democracy. Indeed, Athens was not even the first. As we know, the assemblies held on the Pnyx constituted the core of Athenian participatory democratic governance. But other Greek cities had assemblies as well: the Corinthian-founded citizen-state of Ambracia had assemblies dating back to at least in 580 B.C.E., decades before Athens (Keane 2009, 93). Although this may take some of the luster away from Athens as origin, for PD advocates this is very good news. And it gets even better. There is also evidence that assembly democracy did not originate with the Greeks but was invented multiple times throughout the Syrian-Mesopotamian region (Keane 2009, 114–115). The Phoenician cities of Byblos had assemblies that consulted with kings and, argues Keane, introduced the notion to Greeks: "*Ex oriente lux*: The lamp of assembly democracy was first lit in the East" (Keane 2009, 113). This was 200 years before Athens's ekklesia (Keane 2009, 111). What Keane calls the "dogma of Western democracy" has caused us to think of democracy as much more rare than it was. The history of democracy also needs to be democratized. As we are familiar, then, with the Greek ekklesia, we should also talk of the *ukkin* of Sumeria and *puhrum* in Akkadian (Keane 2009, 102–111).

And for Greek and "Western" exceptionalists, the story gets even worse: democracy was born in multiple times on multiple *continents*. There is no single trunk from which the tree of democracy branches out. Instead, there are multiple origins, and rhizomes and root systems that occasionally overlap. Even in those places where democracy arose after Athens, many of the efforts occurred without benefit of knowledge of Athens or even those who were influenced by the Greeks. Indeed, Indian *panchayats*, Balinese *Seka*, Bolivian *ayllu*, and Iroquoian councils emerged from completely separate traditions (Graeber 2013, 184). Even current practices and innovations emerge from non-Greek-inspired spaces and cultures and/or are born of cross-fertilizations or novel recombinations that are quite *distant* from the Greek in all senses of the term.[13] But none of this is really a critique of Athenian democracy; it's just a nod to the fact that it wasn't the first example and, instead, is a critique of the *history* of democracy.

OK, so Athens did not invent democracy. Fine. But the Athenians did it so well. Didn't they? That depends on who you ask. The most stinging critique of Athens is one noted in passing above but not unpacked: *the majority* of the residents of Athens were not able to participate in the democratic governance processes because they were not citizens. How can one call the political system "rule by the people" if most people could not participate in the ekklesia or hold an administrative office? Only some adult males could rule, women could not, and both male and female slaves could not. As if that weren't bad enough, large groups were not only excluded; they were dominated: women lacked public and private power, and thousands of men were slaves. And even worse—yes, it gets worse—some claim those amazing Athenian practices *depended* upon slavery. As Anderson puts it, "It was the formation of a slave economy—in mining, agriculture, and certain craft industries—which, has been remarked, 'permitted the sudden florescence of Greek urban civilization. . . . [T]he free citizen now stood out in full relief, against the background of slave labourers'" (P. Anderson, 1974a, 36–37).[14] Freedom here is "freedom from work" and "freedom for politics" and for a life of the mind, the arts, virtue, and so on—freedom from necessity and for leisure and politics in the deep sense. But it is, of course, absurd to argue that slavery somehow enables PD to come about; most slave societies are not PD. And, thankfully, there are plenty of other forms of PD that did not require such domination and, indeed, tended to do just the opposite: liberate and empower across social groups and sectors.[15]

Classical Exemplar 2: The Iroquois Federation

> In most histories of American thought in general and in histories of American philosophy in particular, people indigenous to America are viewed as having made no contribution to the intellectual, moral, and social progress of immigrant European peoples.
>
> —PRATT, *NATIVE PRAGMATISM*, 1

> In today's search for new human possibilities of self-government, participation, and societal cooperation, we ought to look to Indian governance practices.
>
> —YOUNG, *HYBRID DEMOCRACY*, 24

About 5,000 miles away from Athens, in a land also quite hilly but much more forested and temperate, another powerful people innovated an array of governance processes that enabled participation and implemented a sharing of political power that warrants the title of "PD exemplar."[16] Originally they called themselves *Kanonsionni*; they now call themselves *Haudenosaunee*. However, English speakers are more likely to know them as a federation of peoples called the Iroquois or the Six Nations (Mann 2000, 16–17).[17] The Haudenosaunee are perhaps best known in the United States for their particular dwellings (the longhouses), their use of wampum, and their influence on the U.S. Constitution and its federal structure and the UN (Young 2007 18–23; Manno 2013, 28).[18] But they should also be known for the incredible PD[19] processes and norms they articulated over their hundreds of years of existence.

The Iroquois Federation is one of the most robust instances of PD the Earth has ever known. At its political peak (before contact with Europeans) in the 1600s, the Haudenosaunee had roughly the same amount of people as Athens (about 20,000).[20] And like the Athenians, the Haudenosaunee innovated an array of PD mechanisms anchored by face-to-face assemblies that not only warded off the concentration of political power, hierarchy, and class-based domination but enabled many to participate in policy making, political and legal judgments, and administration. Sadly, even though Athens is discussed routinely by political philosophers and historians of democracy, very few even mention the Iroquois.[21]

However, from a contemporary perspective (PD or otherwise), Iroquoia surpassed Athens in several ways: women were full participants, the majority of its *residents* had what we would regard as citizen status, foreigners were treated with much more respect and could even join the polity, and, oh yeah, they didn't have slaves. Indeed, the values and mechanisms of PD were not confined to politics but also included the economy and households as well. This was in part due to the fact that the Haudenosaunee didn't just foster a democratic "popular sovereignty"; they cultivated a "grassroots economics" system that prevented the accumulation of wealth and property and, instead, circulated economic assets among all groups and promoted an inclusive labor model. As if that weren't good enough—yes, it gets even better!—the Iroquois are well known for their values and practices supporting ecological sustainability—the notion of sustainability as "7 generations" comes from them (Manno 2013, 28–29). And, one last thing, unlike imperial Athens,[22] the whole enterprise started because of the need for a system to end conflicts, promote peace, and create an evolving social dynamic that could respect individual autonomy, promote group rights and powers, and yet remain open and inclusive toward other cultures. In these next sections, we shall briefly discuss their history, the norms and structure of their governance system and culture; contrast it with the case of Athens; and note the inspiring relevance of the Iroquois for PD theorists and efforts now.

The Six Nations and the Great Law of Peace

Several hundred years[23] ago, south of Lake Ontario, five nations came together in order to end a brutal period of war and restore social order (Manno 2013, 27). Living in the lands now known as Ohio, Pennsylvania, New York, and Quebec (Canada), the Mohawk, Oneida, Onondaga, Cayuga, and Seneca formed this agreement called the "Great Law of Peace."[24] Symbolized by the magnificent white pine, the three great laws of peace were popular sovereignty, health, and righteousness.[25]

The main dictate of the Great Law was simple: signers should not kill each other. But the law went on to spell out a system of governance and virtues that provided spiritual and moral guidance as well as institutional regulation of politics, economy, and religious and social life (Manno 2013, 27–31). Like Athens, there was a political and social dimension to this PD system and assemblies were central. But the Great Law spelled out quite different roles and powers for men and women, and the genders, clans, and nations of Iroquoia had a very different standing than the genders and tribes (*demes*) of Athens.

At first the gendered division of space and labor in Iroquoia seems reminiscent of Athens and most patriarchal societies. Women were "keepers of the house" and in charge of the children and cooking, while men were "keepers of the forests" and hunted and traded. But in Iroquoia, the household was not just the longhouse it was more like an *oikos* and included the land around it. So, women did much of the agricultural work. This confused, and offended, the colonizing Europeans who regarded such work as fit only for (male) peasants. For European elites of that time (sixteenth and seventeenth centuries), like the ancient Greeks, manual labor was something to avoid (Mann 2000, 187–188). But even more confounding for the Europeans was that, in Iroquoia, women were not just agricultural workers; they were in *control* of the land and the crops. But this did not make the federation a matriarchy. There was a balance of power between the roles and assets of men and women in their separate spheres. Women then did most of the basic goods production, and they also controlled both much of the means of production and the surpluses. However, it was not the case that men were subordinate in a way that European women were to men. Men also controlled a sector of the means of production (the forest) and were the *main* (but not exclusive) actors in trade, diplomacy, and battle (though women sometimes fought as well). However, the balance tipped toward the women since not only did they control the agricultural surplus and how it was used; the family name came from the women.

Like in many societies of the time, the Iroquoian economy was a mix of agriculture, hunting, and trade, but farming was the core. Three crops were of such significance—corn, beans, and squash—that the Iroquois referred to them as the "three sisters." They were not just agricultural staples but members of the Iroquoian culture that figured in their creation story. They were agents in their own right but also kin to the peoples of the Six Nations. Nature then was not merely a resource for the human economy; it had its own economy and our economy operated within it.[26]

This understanding of nature, as both agent and gift, helps to explain how land and property were viewed in Iroquoia and how their PD grassroots economy functioned. First off, land itself was not the exclusive right of any human or family. Land did not even belong to the people; the people belonged to the land. When it came to farming, parcels of land were divided up by the clan mothers and distributed to particular families. But these women did not distribute the land autocratically; there were three factors that guided them: the size of the family, their agricultural talents, and fairness. In general, families with more mouths to feed received more productive land. But there was also consideration of how good at farming the family was. If some families were particularly skilled, they might be given more land, but less productive land. And if there were particularly choice parcels, they would be rotated so that everyone had a chance to partake of them for reasons of fairness. The details here are important because the distribution was not simply based on need. It also considered skill, which makes it more akin to that classic socialist principle: "from each according to their ability, to each according to their need" (Mann 2000, 217–218).[27] But land rotation also aimed to implement a notion of fairness as equality of opportunity and the de-concentration of power, which reminds one of the lottery for offices in Athens, since it prevented families from accumulating power or privileges with respect to this most valuable economic asset.

Like Athens, assemblies were crucial in Iroquoia, though they were much smaller: forty-nine members not thousands (Mann 2000, 148).[28] Like Athens, gender played a critical role, but, unlike Athens, men and women had assemblies and the latter's were more powerful. In Iroquoia, issues were first taken up at the women's council, which was made up of clan mothers, other women, and run by a speaker, the *Jigonsaseh* (who was not a clan mother). Whatever the issue, like its Athenian counterpart, the council aimed for consensus. If it achieved consensus, the decision went to the men's council where it was discussed and deliberated upon. If the proposal or decision achieved consensus there, it returned to the women's council where it might be reviewed one more time before being implemented (Mann 2000, 162). Like the Greek notion of unanimity, the Iroquois too aspired to what they called "one-mindedness," which was a "functional consensus." Mann writes,

> Achieving **one-mindedness** was the purpose of speaking "the Words Before All Else," known to Euro-American scholars as the "Thanksgiving Address," before important councils. All spirits—from those of Mother Earth, the waters, the plants, and the animals, to those of the Thunderers, Grandmother Moon, and the Milky Way—were called together with the goal of **achieving a perfect consensus of all sentient minds** in a cosmic *Ne" Găshasde^{n'} 'sä'*. (Mann 2000, 166, my emphasis)

The speaker's job was not to debate about what was best for the constituencies from the perspective of her own view, but to articulate the popular will and deal with any differences among other members of the council in accordance with the three great laws (Mann 2000, 166; see also, Mann 2000, 98, on the aim to ensure community-wide consensus).

As we note the pivotal role that women played in this PD system, it is essential to recognize that women's power was anchored in a set of cultural practices that defined gender, family, and marriage quite differently than in patriarchal societies.[29] For example, in Iroquoia, it was not the father-son relation that was central but the mother-daughter nexus. Also, in contrast to Christian cultures where fathers pass on both name and property to sons, in Iroquoia, women were in charge of naming, and names were passed through them. Not only was Iroquoia matrilineal, it was matrilocal (Graeber 2001, 120–122). Men came to live in their spouse's mother's (long)house. And the privileged male-female pairing was brother-sister, not husband-wife. Indeed, women and men often had more than one partner, called "hunting wives" or "seasonal husbands" (Mann 2000, 285–286), and, when raising kids, the brother was more likely to figure as role model than the husband (Mann

2000, 98). And it was female officials, the Gantowisas, who ran the local clan councils, held all the lineage wampum, nomination belts, and titles. They named new citizens to the nation, chose and installed public officials (including the male sachems), and held the power to recall and impeach. Women appointed warriors, negotiated peace, and mediated disputes. And, women controlled the property (Mann 2000, 116–117).

The Six Nations created a participatory democracy that was not based on formal equality in our traditional political sense. Men and women were not entitled to the same roles or powers. Both sexes were formally (and traditionally) restricted in the roles they could take on. But both had considerable private freedom and access to political and economic power, although there were imbalances. But the division of labor goes against current notions of individual choice, equality of opportunity, and equality before the law. We usually think of equality meaning anyone can do anything they are capable of. At the individual level, women, if they are strong enough, can be lumberjacks and men, if they are competent and caring enough, can be nurses. Not so in Iroquoia. Men and women in Iroquoia were not "equal" or "free" in this sense (nor of course were they in ancient Athens).

When looking at the federal structure, it's a similar story. There is no equality among nations as there is supposedly in, say, the interstate system. Roles were fixed (no equality of opportunity), but power was distributed. Each nation had a different role: the Onondaga kept the central fire and hosted the capital of the federation. The Seneca guarded the Western Door (e.g., Ohio). The Mohawks were the nation that had the privilege of beginning the debate in the council, and the Senecas had the power to review the decision to make sure that it was in accordance with the Great Law. (But people from any of the nations could propose laws to the council independent of their nation's representatives.) (Young 2007, 19) The federation, then, like Athens, had all sorts of checks and balances to prevent the concentration of power from occurring whether at the individual, national, or federal level. It would be better described as a radical decentralization of power that distributed particular powers to particular groups. In other words, differentiated responsibilities (Schlosberg 1999). This model of relational and decentered federalism enabled a diverse set of peoples to work together in a way that kept the peace but still preserved collective determination within each nation, and supported collaboration across them.[30]

Comparing the Two Exemplars

From a PD perspective, the Six Nations system of governance and the culture that anchored it were every bit as innovative and participatory as those of ancient Athens. And, Iroquoia was far more inclusive. Like Athens, the League constructed a complex set of mechanisms designed to integrate diverse views, foster discussion and deliberation, and distribute power in a way that prevented its concentration or abuse. Although both were animist or "pagan" and gendered in profound ways, there were significant cultural differences between the two that greatly impacted the kind of PD that emerged. Greece was largely organized around the pair of master and slave so infamously articulated by Aristotle. Thus, although within the ruling class there were neither masters nor slaves, the ruling class itself occupied the position of master. This was not the case in Iroquoia. Though they had significant privileges, the clan mothers and Jigonsaseh were not masters of men as a class or masters of other groups of women.

One of the reasons Iroquoia stands out and inspires to this day in the way that Athens does not is because it fused a PD version of "popular sovereignty" with a democratic model of production and social reproduction. Although the Six Nations were not formally egalitarian, their Gini index so to speak was near zero: that is, the gap between the rich and the poor was so low that there were not classes in any recognizable sense. The Iroquois firmly believed that the economy should be a "grassroots" system with assets and power (and powers) distributed, and hierarchies kept to a minimum (Manno 2013, 26–28). They were shocked by the incredible inequalities in European societies and puzzled as to why the "poor" did not revolt (Mann 2000, 211–212). Their entire conception of economy differed from European ones, especially since it was grounded not upon the notion of competition driven by scarcity but by sharing or "gifting," honoring, and maintaining abundance. (PD economics and the issue of "abundance/scarcity" will return throughout the volume.) This ontology led to a very different conception of popular sovereignty, which could be seen also in the importance of reciprocity and hospitality not only among humans but with nonhumans (Mann 2000, 217, 229–231).

In sum, ancient Athens and Iroquoia give us two very different models of PD. They differed considerably in cultural diversity, duration, geographic spread, and the relation between men and women and classes. Athens was more urban and empire oriented, while Iroquoia was more agricultural. Interestingly, both were formidable fighters, extensive traders, and expansionistic. But while Athenians built an empire and a mighty military machine, the Iroquois were founded on peace and sought to expand relations of reciprocity rather than domination.

PD in the U.S. of A.

One can see elements of both ancient Athens and Iroquoia during the colonial period, particularly in the New England Town Hall meetings that started in 1620 in the Massachusetts Bay Colony.[31] In these assemblies, adult male citizens (they were more Athens than Iroquoia) met face-to-face to decide on matters that impacted everyone's everyday life: from budgets, taxes, and fines to zoning, jury selection, expenditures for schools, fire, police, and administration (Zimmerman 1986, 2). These meetings garnered praise from prestigious commentators for having democracy operate at the intimate level in which people lived, rather than in the distant buildings secluded in state capitals and Washington, DC. Tocqueville said, "Town Meetings are to liberty what primary schools are to science; they bring it within the people's reach, they teach men how to use it and enjoy it" (quoted in Zimmerman 1999, 27). Thoreau called it America's "True Congress" (Zimmerman 1999, 27) and Founding Father Thomas Jefferson called them "little republics and praised these local units of governance for being more intimate, more 'organic' places where capabilities and solidarities could be cultivated" (Zimmerman 1999, 26; see also Cook and Morgan 1971, 28). Ralph Waldo Emerson agreed (Arendt 1963, 235). These units should decide on a significant portion, but not all, of legislation and policy. For Jefferson this included "those portions of self-government for which they are best qualified, by confiding to them the care of their poor, their roads, police, elections, the nomination of jurors, administration of justice in small cases, elementary exercises of militia" (Thomas Jefferson to John Adams, 1813, ME 13:400).

Yet, as is obvious to any student of U.S. political history, the United States did not build upon the PD tradition laid out by ancient Athens and Iroquoia. Like Aristotle, most Founding Fathers (Jefferson notwithstanding) were not fans of democracy. Indeed, they regarded the assembly as the lair of the mob. In the infamous words of James Madison, "In all very numerous assemblies, of whatever characters composed, passion never fails to wrest the scepter from reason. Had every Athenian citizen been a Socrates, every Athenian assembly would still have been a mob" (James Madison quoted in Zimmerman 1999, 6). What's curious though is that the alternative the Founding Founders constructed—a federal system with two houses of Congress and a separation of powers—did draw upon the innovations of the Iroquois (Johansen 1982). But, as Mann notes, they took only *parts* of the popular sovereignty piece and rejected *all* of the economic democracy framework. This selective appropriation produced a very different and much less democratic political-economic system (Mann 2000, 212–213). U.S. federalism was not a popular sovereignty-enhancing one as in Iroquoia. Rather, it was an elitist one that separated the government from the people by taking powers out of the towns and concentrating them in state capitals, and then appropriating other powers for Washington, DC. This system of double distancing is the basis for the U.S. version of *representative* government. At its best, there is democracy, but only for the representatives who *assemble* in the houses of the U.S. Congress (Arendt 1963, 238). The people do not assemble. For this and many other reasons (e.g., the electoral college, limitations on the extension of the franchise), it's misleading to label the United States a democracy. A figure as respected as Dahl states: "Representative government in the nation-state is in many respects so radically—and inescapably—different from democracy in the city-state that it is rather an intellectual handicap to apply the same term, democracy, to both systems, or to believe that in essence they are really the same" (Dahl 1971, 90). For these reasons, I shall refer to the U.S. government (and "liberal democratic states" in general) not as democracies but as representative states.

The United States has a few (participatory) democratic elements (e.g., juries, referenda in some states and municipalities), but these are peripheral at best and do not constitute the essence of the system. And although there are features that do fit the general model of democracy (see above), it is not clear that the United States was at any time a democracy even in that general sense. Many have made this argument, but the quick version is as follows: if we go by the very minimal notion of democracy as rule by the majority through elections, most adult residents could not vote until women were granted the franchise in 1919. But most African Americans could not vote until the Civil Rights voting act of 1965. Although it is possible that the United States could be considered a minimal electoral democracy starting around 1965, the rise of corporate power in politics began around the same time (early 1970s), and, with the Supreme Court ruling in Citizens United (2010) that "money is speech," the dominance of economic power in the political system is practically made law. Because economic power has such an impact politically, and economic power is held by only a few, economic inequality greatly curtails the ability of most sectors of the populace to shape the agenda of the representative state (Gilens and Page 2014). Even worse, since the 2000s, the United States might not even be a *representative* state but a kind of oligopoly.[32]

But there is another U.S. history composed of PD innovators and efforts. It starts with Iroquoia and other indigenous nations and partially continues with the town hall meetings but takes a different route during the colonial period. It is embodied not by the agrarian Jefferson but by a more urban Founding Father, Benjamin Franklin. Franklin was very much driven by an equality promoting liberalism that sought to foster collectives that enhanced economic, epistemic, and social freedoms for both individuals and groups. This can be seen in his helping to form many different kinds of associations that pooled together the resources of individuals to increase access to assets they would not have as separate persons. Examples include the first mutual benefit societies in the United States, a mutual fire insurance company that still exists today, the subscription library, and the Post Office (Howard, Dubb, and McKinley 2014, 234; Estey 2011, 349–350). Franklin's liberalism stands as a great example of how to balance the norms of freedom and equality in a very participatory way that is bottom up but also operates in multiple spheres, from the economic to the sciences, and pushes for what I call the "social public." In these many projects, we see PD not as a formal political mechanism but as a mode of association, a way of being together to promote equality and enhance capabilities. This is the democracy so famously discussed by Tocqueville. In contrast to the aristocratic societies of Europe whose social life was still rigidly class bound, in the United States democracy was a social sensibility that promoted a much more egalitarian way of being together and cultivated individual dignity (Graeber 2013, 171).

Around the same time as Tocqueville's visit to the United States (1831), the word "democracy" is used in a positive sense by a political figure for the first time (Andrew Jackson). This is a pivotal moment because democracy is also deployed to describe not assemblies but the electoral system (Wilentz 2005, 312–330). And from there it spread like wildfire, or, more accurately, like a catchy marketing meme (Graeber 2013, 170). But this is democracy as representation, not participation. However, during this same period (from colonialism to Jackson) for the "popular classes," democracy was not about voting or elections it was much more PD, but as a sensibility. On Graeber's view, then, democracy is a creative process that "is most likely to occur when one has a diverse collection of participants, drawn from very different traditions, with an urgent need to improvise some means to regulate their common affair, free of pre-existing overarching authority" (Graeber 2013, 186). The model here is not Athens or even Iroquoia; it's pirate ships (Graeber 2013, 177–179). This is more akin to the PD of slave burial societies, the one described by Tocqueville in his descriptions of working-class and popular-class associations, of the Knights of Labor,[33] Jane Addam's Hull House (Pratt 2002, 282–283), and W.E.B. Dubois's worker cooperatives (Dubois 1907).[34] This is not so much communitarian PD but libertarian PD, not fixed communities but voluntary associations, part of which would come to be known as "civil society" but another part was more cultural, and another outright economic.

As we move into the late nineteenth century, on the political front, one might have thought that PD flourished in the Progressive Era, but this was not the case. As economic turmoil driven by outright class war forced the U.S. state to become more effectively representative and inclusive, the same state becomes even less (PD) participatory. This combined with numerous changes after both world wars leads to the decline of PD in both practice and theory.[35] It isn't until after World War II that democracy makes a comeback. But the terrain is markedly different after the defeat of fascism, the onset of the Cold War, the development of the modern(izing) nation-state, and the redefinition of liberty and authority.

The Origin of Democratic Theory: Schumpeter's Adversarial Democracy

> The electoral mass is incapable of action other than a stampede.
> —Schumpeter, *Capitalism, Socialism, Democracy*, 283

By the time we get to World War II, the rise of fascism has given popular participation a bad name. And it was in the aftermath of this devastation that contemporary democratic theory was remade in large part by the Austrian economist and political scientist Joseph Schumpeter in his *Capitalism, Socialism and Democracy* (1950; Held 2006, 141–157). Though perhaps best known for his theory of economic growth as "creative destruction," in democratic theory Schumpeter is most famous for his distaste for and fear of mass/popular politics, his incoherent critique of "classical democracy,"[36] and (most important for us) his outlining of a notion of democracy as a process of political competition modeled on the logic of the market (Pateman 1970, 1–6; Shapiro 2003, 6–7).

For Schumpeter, democracy is not a sensibility; it is a procedure or method "that is to say, a certain type of institutional arrangement for arrival at political—legislative and administrative—decisions" (Schumpeter 1950, 242). This method promotes a healthy (nonviolent) competition for leadership where those most equipped to rule battle it out: "Schumpeter compared the political competition for votes to the operation of the (economic) market; voters like consumers choose between the policies (products) offered by competing political entrepreneurs and the parties regulate the competition like trade associations in the economic sphere" (Pateman 1970, 4; see also Shapiro 2003, 66–68).[37] Schumpeter's conception was overtly adversarial, elitist, and anti-PD. The people are not equipped to rule psychologically or intellectually and *should be actively dissuaded from participating*. He even said that the average citizen should not pester his or her representative with letters making all sorts of demands; such protestations were at best a distraction (the unthinking ramblings of the rabble) but at worst they could become mob-like; so then, leave it to the elites to do the leading! On this view, people must choose that which is presented to them, the major structures of the system are not up for debate, and structural injustices (racial, gender, and otherwise) are not subject to change (Pateman 1970, 4–5; Medearis 2004, 464–467).[38] He is worth quoting at length in his own words:

> Party and machine politicians are simply the response to the fact that the electoral mass is incapable of action other than a stampede, and they constitute an attempt to regulate political competition exactly similar to the corresponding practices of a trade association. The psycho-technics of party management and party advertising, slogans and marching tunes, are not accessories. They are of the essence of politics. So is the political boss. (Schumpeter 1950, 283)

As the Cold War hardens, many are dissatisfied with this model and popular movements emerge challenging the basic order of the system as social movements define what comes to be known as the "1960s."

Participatory Democracy in the History of Philosophy

As a view within democratic theory, PD gets going in the 1960s when University of Michigan professor Arnold Kaufman coins the phrase in his "Human Nature and Participatory Democracy" (Kaufman [1960] 1969a). One of his undergraduates was Students for a Democratic Society (SDS) cofounder and Chicago 8 coconspirator Tom Hayden. In the early days of that period of so much social and political tumult, Hayden drafted the original PD manifesto, the Port Huron Statement released in 1962 (Miller 1987, 44, 146; Hilmer 2010, 45). In this work, which is essential reading for all students of PD, Hayden takes on the issues of his time, which are intriguingly different from our own with a few exceptions. Both then and now, racism and the racial divide, are central, as is the military-industrial complex and war machine. And like now, they had serious doubts about the government's ability to solve the problems. Instead, the people must act. They must take on this responsibility and develop their own powers.

But in the 1960s, most activists were not driven by economic insecurity; their problem was more existential. In this early formulation then, PD is as much about the struggle for individual authenticity and social connection (versus corporate America) as it is a struggle against political inequality, racism, and militarism (versus the government and major American social institutions including the political parties, churches, etc.) Here is the view straight from Hayden's teacher:

> A democracy of participation may have many beneficial consequences, but its main justifying function is and always has been, not the extent to which it protects or stabilizes a community, but the contribution it can make to the development of human powers of thought, feeling, and action. In this respect it differs, and differs quite fundamentally, from a representative system incorporating all sorts of institutional features designed to safeguard human rights and ensure social order. *This distinction is all important.* The fundamental error many critics of democracy make consists in failure to recognize that different institutional forms of democracy may be and are defended on the basis of different functional consequences. (Kaufman [1960] 1969a, 184)

On this view, PD is not about fine-tuning the political, economic, and social order of things and people; it is a conception of politics that calls for citizens to seize their collective political fates by reclaiming the public sphere as self-determining agents. This view makes its way into political theory via two different tracks: one is the social revolution frame articulated by anarchists,

New Left Marxists, feminists, black revolutionaries, and others. But the PD view that is consolidated within political theory is a much less contentious version of PD, and one that does value human rights and social order in a manner consistent with the liberal tradition.

Locus Classicus: Carole Pateman's *Participation and Democratic Theory*

The *locus classicus* for PD in the Anglo-American tradition is without question Carole Pateman's *Participation and Democratic Theory*.[39] Published in 1970, the scene has shifted from the 1962 Port Huron statement. In stark contrast to SDS, Pateman takes PD out of the countercultural mix of direct action and contentious politics and instead focuses on PD in political philosophy and the workplace. In this brief tome (based on her dissertation), Pateman unpacks the "classical conception of democracy," harshly critiqued by Schumpeter and others, and shows that it is a straw man view that no figure actually believed but instead makes PD easy to criticize. Then she articulates a view of PD and contrasts it with the liberal view of the representative state. She also (re)constructs a tradition to locate her view in political philosophy. The last chapters focus on the instantiation of PD in the economic sphere, primarily in the case of worker cooperatives. Here we see an empiricism that distinguishes her work from the manifesto approach of the Port Huron Statement and many other writings about PD and much of contemporary democratic theory. The case studies she is most focused on are worker co-ops in England and Yugoslavia. Pateman develops numerous themes that are central to the PD literature and contemporary debate including agency and capacity building and the relationship between freedom and equality. To make her arguments, Pateman draws upon three figures, two from the canon of Western philosophy—Jean-Jacques Rousseau (1712–1778), John Stuart Mill (1806–1873)—and another figure who was a giant in his day, but is less known now, G.D.H. Cole (1889–1959).

After her critiques of Schumpeter and the "classical view of democracy" (Pateman 1970, 1–21) and her reconstruction of the history of PD (Pateman 1970, 22–44), Pateman lays out her own view of PD:

> In the participatory theory "participation" refers to (equal) participation in the making of decisions, and "political equality" refers to equality of power in determining the outcome of decisions [. . .]. [T]he *justification* for a democratic system in the participatory theory of democracy rests primarily on the human *results* that accrue from the participatory process. One might characterise the participatory model as one where maximum input (participation) is required and where

output includes not just policies (decisions) but also the development of the social and political capacities of each individual, so that there is a "feedback" from output to input. (Pateman 1970, 43)

Pateman's definition of PD is simple: it is that process enables individuals to exercise more power over their lives. This is what she calls "political efficacy" (Pateman 1970, 46). The justification for PD is mostly about the results: PD enhances the lives of humans, their capabilities and satisfactions, but, most important, their agency. Here Pateman sounds like SDS and the Kaufman quote above, but she is much more optimistic about the liberal state. The state needs to play a role in this feedback loop: it needs to assist us in creating processes that enhance personal and social capabilities. But we also need social forces to not only demand this of the state but to help make it happen. Society itself needs PD processes to promote equality and cooperation and ward off political despotism and demagoguery. And the state must support PD in order to ward off poverty, alienation, apathy, economic domination, and inequality. Once this feedback loop gets going, we see a cooperative coexistence between the particular and the general, the local and the national, and PD and the representative state. She writes,

The ordinary man might still be more interested in things nearer home, but the existence of a participatory society would mean that he was better able to assess the performance of representatives at the national level, better equipped to take decisions of national scope when the opportunity arose to do so, and better able to weigh up the impact of decisions taken by national representatives on his own life and immediate surroundings. In the context of a participatory society the significance of his vote to the individual would have changed; as well as being a private individual he would have multiple opportunities to become an educated, public citizen. (Pateman 1970, 110)

As she states in this passage and in the earlier arguments for assembly democracy, local PD venues are critical. But this PD form violates the notion of politics that comes from the traditional social contract view.

In the social contract tradition that anchors political philosophy (especially Hobbes and Locke), the dominant view is as follows: states arise because people seeking peace and freedom come together to exit the lawless state of nature and form a pact. In this pact there is a transfer of the powers of legislation and the use of violence from the people, as such, to the state. This transfer is legitimate if there is consent.[40] Once this occurs, each individual is awarded (or guaranteed, depending on the theorist) a sphere of liberty, that is to say, rights and a place to exercise those rights (property). The government is the legislator and protector of the people. And the dividing line between those who govern (the rulers) and those who are governed (the people) is clear (Held 2006, 58–65).

But Pateman opts for another lineage, that of Jean-Jacques Rousseau.[41] Rousseau's scheme is quite different. "The people" do not give up the right to legislate. Rather, they retain it, or even better, develop this capacity when they come together not as members of this or that group or class but as an assembly of citizens. Here they form a political association in which they *will* together not as self-interested individuals but as citizens pursuing what they require to be and to succeed together. The general will can only arise or be obtained when each individual puts aside those particular interests that result from a specific trade or place of residence (e.g., a wheat farmer of this particular stretch of road) and focuses instead on the common interests of everyone, discovering or constructing them. This is where the general will occurs, becomes, and presents itself. *The government's role is to carry out the will.* Whatever elected officials might be called, *they are not representatives* of the people in the usual sense but administrators of the people's will. This is why Rousseau does not call his view "democratic." A democracy is a system of government where all the people execute the political decisions. This is impossible according to Rousseau; there are too many people. So the government is assigned to a subset of these tasks (Pateman 1985, 152, 150–162). For these reasons, it is crucial that the government obey the law. But what is supreme is not the law, as such, but the legislative capacity of the assembled people. Pateman writes, "It is possible to read the Social Contract as an elaboration of the idea that laws, not men, should rule, but an even better formulation of the role of participation is that men are to be ruled by the logic of the operation of the political situation that they had themselves created and that this situation was such that the possibility of the rule of individual men was "automatically' precluded" (Pateman 1970, 23). But this isn't just a procedural democracy. That is, the assemblies in which the general will is able to be discerned require individuals of a particular type, with specific sorts of virtues. On this point, Rousseau articulates a communitarian rather than a liberal view of PD and harks back to the Greeks far more than other social contract theorists.[42] The procedures of the general will are to be "educative." The assemblies enable individuals to learn about one another, to come to understand others' needs as well as their own, and to develop the skills necessary for such exchanges. For Rousseau, perhaps the most crucial skill is for an individual to learn to think "publicly," that is, to distinguish between my own self-interested impulses and the real needs of others that are also mine. When individuals learn how to do this, the general will can be said to be at work. And the development of these traits helps the system to become self-sustaining (Pateman 1970, 25). We shall call this kind of view, communitarian PD. (See taxonomy below.)

What also distinguishes Rousseau's view from many others in the philosophical canon is that the "situation" is not just political in the abstract (citizens in assemblies, government of magistrates, individuals overcoming their selfish and factional groups interests) but it is cultural in the rich sense of both social and physical-geographic.

In these assemblies and related venues, citizens come out of their private abodes and workplaces where they focus on their particular interests and are able to encounter the interests and needs of others. Here they learn about government and issues and develop skills to deliberate and collaborate and form conceptions of the common interests and the public good. In these venues, citizens would decide on particular matters of local consequence that are appropriate to deal with at the local level (schools, local utilities, etc.) This a more pragmatic understanding of the educative aspect of PD and is also held by J. S. Mill who has a more liberal state view of PD.

Pateman is neither a Rousseauian nor a communitarian, her view is much more akin to the second member of her PD canon, John Stuart Mill. Like Rousseau, Mill is in the traditional canon of philosophy and his works in many fields are well known and influential, especially his work on logic and ethics. But it is his lesser known work on politics and economics that puts him in the PD canon.

Crucially, Pateman does not believe all politics should be reduced to the local level. Nor does she believe that national politics should be made PD. Rather, following Mill, she argues that by using PD at the local level, citizens will become more informed and more understanding of their fellow citizens such that the representative state will be able to better respect the rights and meet the needs of the citizenry. In other words, for Pateman, one of the reasons that national politics is so often divisive, ill informed, and inefficient is because the citizenry has not developed the right character nor does it possess the knowledge and skills to foster an effective representative politics. A key reason for the nastiness of national politics and people's lack of interest in it is that not only are there very few local PD venues in which people can learn about politics and exercise their agency but, instead, most people spend much of their time in a venue that is often antidemocratic if not despotic, the workplace. This is also a point she derives from Mill (Pateman 1970, 30–35).

Rather than focus on examples of *political* schemes or mechanisms to institute such political efficacy, Pateman instead focuses (literally half of her book) on the workplace. One might have expected a chapter, or at least a long section, on assemblies like the New England Town Hall meetings noted above, but no such discussion occurs. Let me repeat: THE classic work on participatory democracy in political theory has no discussion on how PD has or could operate in the political realm! While she does praise efforts to democratize schools and families, these remarks are brief and there no real discussion of PD in the social realm either (Pateman 1970, 108–109).

There are good reasons for focusing on the economic realm. First, she argues that political democracy requires a participatory society and the greatest threat to that project in the United States is the economy. The workplace is a source of multiple inequalities: pay and benefits but also class and status. It not only immiserates; it subordinates. It's a place where one learns servitude, so why not make it a place to learn freedom and democracy? Here she draws on Mill's writings on worker cooperatives and economic democracy. For Mill, worker-owned businesses promote dignity at work and thus can promote a moral transformation, and this is crucial because the traits and skills developed there can be applied to larger political venues, such as national representative forums and elections (Pateman 1970, 35, 106–107). PD in the workplace potentially at least attacks all these hierarchies and also gets at those that impair the expectations of persons in the political arena. That is, it makes them less likely to defer to experts or others claiming to know what is best for them or to be captured by the false promises of divisive demagogues.[43]

From the Misrepresentative State to the Partner State: G.D.H. Cole's Associationist PD

> Rousseau's theory provides the starting point and the basic material for any discussion of the participatory democracy and Cole's theory provides one attempt to translate the insights of Rousseau's theory into a modern setting.
>
> —PATEMAN, *PARTICIPATION AND DEMOCRATIC THEORY*, 36

In her PD canon, Rousseau and Mill are the philosophical giants but the figure who has the most consistently PD normative framework and explains the details of how it would happen in the (industrial, urbanized, and populated) contemporary setting is G.D.H. Cole. Though much less well known than Mill now, Cole was famous in his day and was one of the first figures to think of PD through the economy and how to restructure the political realm (Hirst 1994, 102–111; Cole 1920a, 1920b). A major figure in political economy in the late nineteenth and twentieth centuries, like Mill and Pateman, Cole worried that not only was the economic system a source of inequality that led to political inequality, but the workplace was a training ground for servitude that also had negative political effects. Indeed, Cole is famous for his view that the major problem of our society is not poverty but slavery (Pateman 1970, 38). But Cole is much more than a critic, he is a constructive political-economic architect. Although Pateman does not herself give an account of the large-scale transformation of a country's political economy, Cole did, and she outlines his approach.[44]

Cole thought that democracy should be applied to every sphere of social action and the state should step back (which put him at odds with socialists of his era). Cole himself was influenced by and loved to quote Rousseau, as well as Marx and William Morris, and thought that the democratization of industry is key to a PD politics (Pateman 1970, 35–37). Cole, like Rousseau, believed that "will" not force is the basis of social and political organization and argued that the individual is "most free where he cooperates with his equals in the making of laws" (Pateman 1970, 36). What distinguishes Cole's view and associationism is its position that society is a complex of associations held together by the will of its members and that the state shouldn't interfere with associations (Pateman 1970, 36). Here liberalism mixes with the social ontology of some Marxists: what is fundamental is the individual, but the social individual (see also Gould 1994, 283–306). But the primary scene of individual freedom is not the isolated individual with his property in the household. Nor is it the individual in a well-defined Rousseauian community, whether that of the village or the state. In complex industrial modern societies, no single group can satisfy an individual's desires and need for freedom. Freedom means being part of many associations. Associationism then is an alternative to radical individualism and communitarianism.[45] This plays out economically as well. Not surprisingly, associationists favored cooperatives of all types (e.g., worker, consumer) for reasons already noted by Mill: they support the dignity of labor and collective determination over one's working conditions and enable individuals to overcome self-interest and develop a "public spirit" (Pateman 1970, 40–41). However, in contrast to Mill, who even at his most sympathetic subordinated PD to the representative state, Cole was led to a very different view of the role of the state and the nature and limits of representation.[46]

Cole thought that existing parliamentary systems—as well as United States federalism—were *mis*representative states for at least three reasons. First off, no *person* could be represented as such. This was impossible; a category mistake. It was only possible to represent someone's view with respect to some function. Thus, individuals could be represented as workers, parents, sports fans, etc., but not as individuals. Second, existing systems (and again this would include early twentieth-century British Parliament as well as twenty-first-century U.S. Congress) did not make available any sort of mechanism by which citizens could effectively participate with their representatives. Elections are not adequate (Pateman 1970, 37). Third, the political-economic system has become so complex, that it is not intelligible to individuals. Therefore, registering citizens' views on matters is epistemically impossible—they don't have views on most matters.

Cole offers another type of political structure that is reminiscent of both Iroquois and Thomas Jefferson: a horizontal federal one with local "communes" and "wards" as the fundamental unit. Pateman describes it as follows,

> The purpose of the horizontal (political) structure was to give expression to "the communal spirit of the whole society." Each town or country area would have its own commune where the basic unit would be the ward, again to allow maximum individual participation, and representatives would be elected from the guilds, etc., and any other local bodies to the commune on a ward basis. The next horizontal layer was to be composed of regional communes, bringing together both town and country and the regional guilds, and at the apex would be found the National Commune which would, Cole thought, be a purely co-ordinating body neither functionally, historically nor structurally continuous with the existing state. (Pateman 1970, 41)

Cole's proposal then is to restructure the political system so that individuals meet in self-organized associations to decide on matters important to them and/or at the local level. So, for example, in the current system, there are parents and others who are concerned about school lunches and local food options given the prevalence of obesity, type 2 diabetes, and food allergies. While they can exercise some control at the level of the PTA on this issue, much of the budget and regulations guiding operations is at other levels (the school district, state, federal). If they want to change the menu at the local school, they have to lobby at all these other levels to urge elected officials to change the policy. For Cole, such a system is both unfair and doomed to inefficiency. Even if all those elected wanted to change the system, they still have to change the rules in several bureaucracies at various levels. For Cole and associationists, the solution for this is to have the government turn over the power to citizens to do this. The role of the government is to support, coordinate, and act as a watchdog. But the governance should be done by citizens. Citizens would meet at the local level to discuss problems and brainstorm options and send a delegate to the city or state level, which decides on budget matters and regulations for schools statewide. They also send a delegate to the national government insofar as federal funding and regulations are involved. The government's role would be to make moneys available (it, not the associations, does the taxation), and act as a watchdog to make sure one group does not dominate or exclude other groups (Hirst 1994, 56–61). Also, and crucially, at each of these meetings, there would be delegates present from the businesses involved: farmers, food processors and distributors, etc. That is because for associationists, the governance system is not just for "political" actors; it is for all those relevant to the carrying out of the function. All those with knowledge and a stake in the game should have power to set policy (Pateman 1970, 37–38).

Associationism then is not only fairer and more efficient than socialist and liberal states; it also solves an epistemic problem associated with complex, technological societies. It creates a political-economic system that is more intelligible: the system of functional representation implies "the constant participation of the ordinary man in the conduct of those parts of the structure of Society with which he is directly concerned, and which he has therefore the best chance of understanding" (Cole 1920a, 114. Cited in Pateman 1970, 37). In other words, it builds upon some of the insights and aspirations of Jefferson's "ward republic" view by spelling out a more multilayered and multisectored governance apparatus that would shift the governance axis away from politics and Washington, DC, and state capitals to a range of groups across society, who participate because they want to and have knowledge that helps to solve the problems at hand in a way that promotes individual freedom, satisfies particular group needs, and contributes to more general public good (Arendt 1963, 235).

While Paul Hirst picks up the associationist mantle and elucidates it with great rigor in his *Associative Democracy* (1994), few pick up on his insights in the contemporary PD landscape.[47] However, the conception of the "partner state" furthers this cause and has a number of interlocutors who are updating associationism for the twenty-first century by utilizing concepts and practices of networks, multilevel governance, and platform cooperativism (see my Chapter 6).

The Antistate Option: Kropotkin's Social Anarchism

I know that, when reading the associationist section above, some of my PD friends winced. "Functional representation in a bottom-up self-organized commune-anchored federalism sounds great," they say, "but how could Cole be so naive about the state! It's still taxing, coordinating and has a monopoly on violence. Do you really think the state is gonna act on behalf of the people rather than some elite or privileged group? Why does Pateman not consider a nonstatist option?" The complexities of Cole's "national commune" aside, they are right: Pateman does not entertain a nonstate PD option. This is not surprising insofar as most political philosophy does not now nor ever did take anarchism—much less stateless peoples[48]—seriously. Indeed, we might say that *political* philosophy has always been *state* theory, which is to say the view that social order requires political violence (Day 2005, 96–97). However, since the collapse of the Soviet Union, the rise of civil society and the transnational, and the onset of globalization studies in the 1990s, there are many antistate or nonstate forms of political theory currently in play (more below). But the more relevant question for this section is what about the history of philosophy? With Iroquoia we have seen that there are certainly nonstate systems of governance that were PD and did not require a state, but is there any political philosopher who meditates on these modes of governing?

There were certainly antistate political philosophers in the nineteenth century but they do not get much attention in contemporary constructions of the history of philosophy. Nevertheless, the most prominent are often considered anarchist: Proudhon (1809–1865), Mikhail Bakunin (1814–1876), and Prince Peter Kropotkin (1842–1921). Most famous for his slogan "property is theft," Proudhon argued that social order did not require the state monopoly on force but could be established through voluntary cooperation. Bakunin was a strong advocate for self-management, had a major falling out with Marx and authoritarian socialists, and aimed to foment insurrection against the church and state (Day 2005, 112–117). But the one I would nominate for the PD pantheon is Kropotkin, especially because of his work, *Mutual Aid* ([1902] 1976).[49]

Kropotkin lays out a multilayered view akin to Cole's, but one that does so without the machinery of the state. (Like Bakunin, he worked to smash such machinery.) Like Cole, Kropotkin calls for self-organized groups coming together in neighborhoods and workplaces, and both favor forms such as neighborhood assemblies and guilds. But Kropotkin calls for the major political form to be the city, not the state. There is nothing above, or that subsumes, the city in terms of governance. Instead there are associations of cities that come together in what might be called a nonstate, or even an antistate, federalism (Kropotkin [1902] 1976, 154–222). Kropotkin writes,

> The medieval city thus appears as a double federation: of all householders united into small territorial unions—the street, the parish, the section—and of individuals united by oaths unto guilds according to their professions; the former being a produce of village-community origin of the city, while the second is a subsequent growth called to life by new conditions. To guarantee liberty, self-administration, and peace was the chief aim of the city; and labour [. . .] was its chief foundation. (Kropotkin [1902] 1976, 181)

People come together not just for peace and liberty (as in the social contract model) but to rule themselves: "self-administration." The principle of double federation, of territory and labor, is a harbinger of Cole's associationist model, but instead of a national commune or state, Kropotkin calls for a new league of cities. Far from being utopian, there were precursors of such associations, from the Rhenish and Swabian Leagues to the more well-known and long-lasting Hanseatic League (1224–1669). These leagues functioned as federations in ways that Cole and other associationists call for: they regulated taxes and tolls, were venues for solving disputes among member cities, protected minorities within cities, and provided for their common defense.

But they did so without a sovereign body commanding them. Indeed, they even inspired one "people," the Swiss, to opt for a decentralized federal model in lieu of a traditional state (Bookchin 1995, 144–145).[50]

The point in this section is not to argue for anarchism over association-ism. Indeed, when Pateman was writing (1970), one might argue that the radical thing to do was consider in detail a statist form of PD. In the twenty-first century, however, not only have we seen a proliferation of nonstate forms of governance and "governmentality" (Hooghe and Marks 2003); we have seen cities reassert themselves politically and economically as centers of innovation and international cooperation against or despite states and culturally as places of cosmopolitanism and social inclusion. They have even formed alliances and associations to do so. PD advocate Benjamin Barber dedicated an entire book to this theme (Barber 2013). But the more social anarchist articulator of this view who picks up the torch from Kropotkin and avoids the associationist state model is Murray Bookchin who further develops a "libertarian municipalism" and municipal confederalism (Book-chin 1995, 201–269).[51]

Summing Up Pateman (with Critique)

What all these views of PD share is (1) a critique of formal political equality and voting: the latter is not nearly enough and the former is meaningless without more robust mechanisms for popular participation in government, and (2) a call for PD in the economy. As the Iroquois clearly saw and warned the colonists: demanding the right to vote without demanding popular power in the economy is to willingly participate in one's own exploitation (what Charles Mills channeling Rousseau calls the "domination contract") (Mills and Pateman 2007, 79–105). In other words, even liberal political equality requires economic democracy. This view is forcefully argued for by Mill and Cole. As Pateman writes of Cole's view, "Theoretical democrats [who favor abstract political equality of the vote] ignored the fact that vast inequalities of wealth and status, resulting in vast inequalities of education, power, and control of environment, are necessarily fatal to any real democ-racy, whether in politics or any other sphere" (Pateman 1970, 39). However, Pateman's view sides more with Mill than Cole. Although in a more recent essay, she does call for more political PD (e.g., participatory budgeting), it is a modest call and seems to stay at the local level (Pateman 2012) unlike as-sociationists who aim to remake the national state with a more participatory federalism. Pateman also does not go into social PD. Although she address-es the social and political spheres in other works (1989), she doesn't address the household, religion, or other dimensions of social life with respect to PD. This distinguishes her from the originary PD views of Kaufman and Hayden and many of the other PD theorists and practitioners of the 1960s and 1970s.

The obvious drawback to Pateman's exposition[52] is that she does not think about the transformative potential of PD in the political realm. That is, she assumes the dominance of the representative state. In part this makes sense because it makes her view more palatable and relevant to political philosophy. But others writing in the same time period thought more about how PD might be used to eliminate representative structures (e.g., Bookchin) or to displace them (e.g., Cole). And so did one of the other key works about PD at the time, Cook and Morgan's anthology *Participatory Democracy* (1971). As Cook and Morgan eloquently point out in their Introduction to the volume, "There are other proponents of participatory democracy who attack the foundations rather than just the functioning of representative democracy. They may view political participation as a salutary school of subversion rather than as Mill's "school of public spirit" (Cook and Morgan 1971, 11).

Cook and Morgan's anthology is more in the social revolutionary spirit of the Port Huron Manifesto. It details affinity groups and direct action, fights by local communities to democratically control schools and policing, and talks as much of protest and revolution as it does of law and administration (Cook and Morgan 1971). However, despite differences among them, all these works are of the same period, and thus constitute a second wave of PD theory—which follows the first anarchist dominated one.

Periodizing PD: Three Waves of Participatory Democratic Theory

Compared to communitarianism, republicanism, liberalism, libertarianism, feminism, socialism, postsocialism, and multiculturalism, proponents of PD are a minor tradition within political philosophy. Indeed, even within *democratic* theory PD gets far less attention than deliberative, direct, radical, cosmopolitan, and agonistic views.[53] Rousseau notwithstanding, the PD "tradition" is especially sparse until the mid-nineteenth century. But since then there have been three waves of interest in PD approaches. For each wave I note the time frame and select an exemplary theorist and case or two.

1st Wave, 1800s–1959: Rousseau; J. S. Mill; Kropotkin; G.D.H. Cole;—medieval city; guilds and worker cooperatives; federations; Paris Commune

2nd Wave, 1960s–1980s: Kaufman; the Port Huron Manifesto; Pateman; Barber;—Yugoslavian state-sponsored worker co-ops; SDS; "community control"

3rd Wave, 1989–present: C. Gould; Mies et al.; Santos; Holloway; Graeber;—Zapatistas; the Global Justice Movement; participatory budgeting; Mondragon's Federation of Worker Cooperatives; Occupy!

The 1st Wave arises with Rousseau and continues with some socialists and many anarchists in the late 1800s and into the 1900s with the work of syndicalists, council communists (Medearis 2004), and associationists (e.g., G.D.H. Cole 1920a, 1920b) in both Europe and the United States.[54]

The 2nd Wave surfaces amid the tumult of the 1960s and early 1970s, a period marked in the literature by Kaufman's essay ([1960] 1969a), but, as we noted above, really takes shape with the publication of Pateman's monograph (1970).[55] That second wave crashes in the 1980s especially in Anglo-American political theory and philosophy as the global political mood shifts with détente and then socialism in retreat. And, as neoliberalism gains ground, President Ronald Reagan and Prime Minister Margaret Thatcher set the stage for a new anti–welfare state, market-driven politics, PD views nearly vanish from the academic landscape. Margaret Thatcher infamously proclaims that "there is no alternative" to neoliberal capitalism and much of political theory submits. Democratic theory shifts from a focus on power to talk and deliberative democracy grows tremendously, which is not surprising given the "linguistic turn" earlier in the century (Hilmer 2010; Hauptmann 2001, 397; Santos and Avritzer 2005).

Yet, by the mid-1990s, in conjunction with myriad shifts brought about by the forces of economic globalization, a third wave emerges as PD enjoys a resurgence in both practice and theory (but not much in philosophy!) especially because of the failures of socialist states, dissatisfaction with liberal states, and interest in political and economic alternatives to all of the aforementioned (Santos and Avritzer 2005). And this interest was not just theoretical; it was inspired by on-the-ground experiments that actually persisted and proliferated: from the Zapatistas[56] in Mexico who inspired the antiglobalization movement (a key forerunner of Occupy!), to participatory budgeting, which started in Brazil and has now spread to six continents (Menser 2005; and see my Chapter 2). Not only is this latest wave even more multiculturally diverse and geographically dispersed than the first two; it is also increasingly theoretically and ideologically plural.[57] Indeed, contemporary PD approaches are found among anarchist, indigenous, feminist, ecological, liberal, economic democracy, autonomous Marxist, and solidarity economy movements and theorists.[58]

Despite all the dissatisfaction with representative democracy and the interest in more equality-enhancing forms of participation (Santos and Avritzer 2005, xli–xlii), there are only a few volumes, collections, or monographs that systematically present a philosophy of participatory democracy. There have been two anthologies (both called *Participatory Democracy*): Cook and Morgan's (1971) is very much of the 2nd Wave in the 1960s and discusses many of the most contentious issues of that time from student activism to neighborhood control of schools as well as intricate debates about ideology and race.[59] The other anthology solely about PD is from the 3rd Wave: Roussopoulos and Benello's (2005) volume is much more of the global justice movement and discusses corporate power, technology, and new cosmopolitan urban movements. Another volume that has an explicit PD focus and also takes the phrase as its title is Zimmerman 1986. It focuses on the *mechanisms* of PD and explains in detail both their legal structure and how they work, from referenda to elected official recall, New England Town Hall meetings, and procedures for institutionalizing neighborhood government. Berry, Portney, and Thomson's 1993 book has a similar focus but in a later period and with a focus on different cities' experiences with citizen participation programs.

The post-Pateman canon continues with Mansbridge's 1980 book, which develops a theory of PD that harks back to Rousseau that she calls "unitary democracy." This kind of consensus-based politics proliferated thanks to the new social movements of the 1960s but also has an important precursor in the long-standing New England Town Hall meeting discussed earlier. Mansbridge's work is defined by two case studies that she conducted and analyzed: a town hall meeting in Vermont and the participatory workplace of the "Helpline" crisis center.[60] Another PD standout is Bachrach and Botwinick's 1992 book that forwards a class-based analysis of workplace democracy. Like Mansbridge, it is quite empirical but from a wider sociological framework rather than an intimate ethnography. More detailed philosophical approaches are taken up in Barber's *Strong Democracy* ([1984] 2003) and Carol Gould who develops a view of PD from across several works, from the early 1988 book, which places PD within a Marxist social ontology, to the more human rights grounded 2004 and 2014 works. Like Mansbridge and Pateman, Gould also applies her view of PD to both political and economic institutions but extends them the scope of inquiry to social associations and "cross-border" international and global settings, showing that PD is not limited to the culturally homogeneous and geographically limited hyperlocal communities.[61] Indeed, Gould is a transitional figure from the more small-scale and locally focused PD venues studied by 2nd wave theorists such as Mansbridge and Cook and Morgan to the much more globally interconnected efforts of the 3rd wave.[62]

Eric Olin Wright and Boaventura de Sousa Santos are also crucial transition figures who not only moved PD analyses from the second to the third wave but put together international research teams to do the comparative work. Wright's "real utopias" project is exemplary in its multisector analyses of PD: from a basic income guarantee[63] to workplace democracy and participatory governance (Roemer and Wright 1996; Fung and Wright 2003a; Ackermann, Alstott, and van Parijs 2006; Wright 2010). Santos further developed this approach into a large-scale international comparative study of PD efforts both in the political and economic sphere involving women, peasants, and trade union movements in South Africa, Brazil, Colombia,

Mozambique, and India (Santos 2005a, 2005b, 2006a).[64] The last three PD routes as I call them are global as well: the (post)Marxist anarchist inspired autonomous frame (A-PD), the feminist social reproduction focused subsistence perspective (S-PD), and the environmental/climate justice frame (EJ-PD).

Six Routes to Participatory Democracy

With the addition of the antistate Kropotkin to Pateman's PD canon, we now see four different views of PD: first, the communitarian "unitary" model of Rousseau, which, ironically perhaps, is embodied in the "one-mindedness" of both ancient Athens and Iroquoia. The second liberal state PD comes from Mill and is endorsed by Pateman herself. The third, "associationist," route is laid out by Cole and updated by Paul Hirst. And the fourth is the antistate anarchist federalist view of Kropotkin, which is updated by Bookchin. And as we further modify and update Pateman's scheme, I would argue that there are two-and-a-half more routes: four (part 2), a recombinant antistate politics that emerges out of autonomous Marxism; five, a feminist account grounded in an ecological view of social reproduction; and six, an Environmental Justice Movement route that takes race and native peoples as its central categories and is remaking itself to address climate change. The basics of the six views with a few key figures named are as follows:

1. **Communitarian PD** (e.g., Rousseau, Mansbridge) is anchored by a "unitary" governing unit akin to communitarianism or republicanism; the same moral norms structure politics, economy, and social life. (Also, Iroquoia.) (Can overlap with 4. and 5.)
2. **Liberal State PD** (e.g., J. S. Mill, Pateman) PD is deployed to enhance individual and social freedom without a unitary community; mixed landscape of (local) PD with representative state but the former is subordinate to the latter; requires economic democracy.
3. **Associationist PD** (e.g., Cole, Hirst) Most governance is done by voluntary social associations; the state is reconstructed but retained though with far less power than liberal state; requires economic democracy and "partner state."
4. **Anarchist-autonomous PD (or A-PD)** "Anarchist-autonomous" (e.g., Kropotkin, Bookchin, Holloway) Politics is based on local voluntary face-to-face groups combined into federations or networks without a sovereign state; tends to be antistate and anticapitalist, with a reconstruction of politics (and to some extent the economy) that is anchored in the social. (Can overlap with communitarian and S-PD).

5. **Social Reproduction/Subsistence PD (or S-PD)** (e.g., Mies, Benn-holdt-Thomsen, Shiva, Maathai) PD must reconstruct gender relations and social life and democratize not just the economy but social reproduction; ecological systems and nonhumans are part of the community; pluralistic and open relation to state. (Can overlap with all of the other routes.)
6. **Environmental Justice/Climate Justice (or EJ-PD)** (e.g., Schrader-Frechette, Whyte)[65] PD must address racial inequality and settler colonialism; new relations between state and community are necessary as are reparations for past exploitation and destruction. Collaborative relationship with state. (Can overlap with liberal PD.)

We discussed the first four routes in previous sections. The next two-and-a-half are below.

Anarchist/Autonomous PD (or A-PD)

> We start from negation, from dissonance. The dissonance can take many shapes. An inarticulate mumble of discontent, tears of frustration, a scream of rage, a confident roar. An unease, a confusion, a longing, a critical vibration.
> —JOHN HOLLOWAY, *How to Change the World without Taking Power*, 1

> By focusing on doing, we put our own power at the centre of our understanding of society: our power-to-do (and therefore, our power not to do, and our power to do differently). By focusing on doing, we also state clearly that *the argument of this book is not for 'more democracy' but for a radical reorganization of our daily activity*, without which the call for 'more democracy' means nothing at all.
> —HOLLOWAY, *Crack Capitalism*, 85–86 (MY EMPHASIS)

There's a new PD subject on the block and its aspirations are global. It's beyond the working class and workers' parties, even beyond any territorially defined "people." It's the multitude, the 99 percent. It's cross border, precarious,[66] and "screaming," but it's not waiting to be led in a revolution to take over the state. Indeed, it is (ir)resolutely opposed to the state, and aims to be free from it, to go beyond it. Its most recent incarnation is the Occupy Movement (from Occupy Wall Street to Occupy Sandy) but it is inspired by a range of movements, the most exemplary of which are the Paris Commune and the Zapatista Army of National Liberation (EZLN) of southern Mexico. (Think of the EZLN as an Occupy that has lasted for twenty-two years.) We shall call this view autonomous participatory democracy, or A-PD.[67]

Autonomous PD draws upon the antistate views of nineteenth-century anarchism but is deeply informed by Marxism and postcolonial theory mixed in with the antiglobalization movement noted above. A-PD opposes "the global capitalist system" especially multinational corporations but in particular despises two "forms": the state and the commodity. A-PD aspires toward autonomy and dignity and these two values ground its conception of collective determination and solidarity.[68] A-PD can be seen in action in factories taken over by workers in Argentina (Zibechi 2012, 91–108), social centers in Italy (Day 2005, 4–2, 205–206), and women-run community kitchens in Peru (Zibechi 2012, 238). It is practiced by peasant farmers who have reclaimed land and practice agroecology in Brazil (Zibechi 2012, 121–126), indigenous resistance in Chile (Zibechi 2012, 109–120), and trash collectors in Columbia (Zibechi 2012, 171–178). A-PD is, indeed, "everywhere" (Notes from Nowhere 2003).

For A-PD, autonomy in motion is a horizontal power that flattens vertical hierarchies while producing dignity-enhancing power-sharing collectivities. There are four features that define and distinguish such autonomous participatory democracy. A-PD is (1) antagonistic insofar as it aspires to autonomy from the capitalist state system in particular and hierarchical forms in general. (2) It is protagonistic and "prefigurative." We must set the agenda (there is a heavy focus on collective determination and the first person plural). We must lead ourselves and be the change we want to see and that means not just imagining the world we want but making it at whatever level we can. (3) We must not take power but remake power from the coercive and hierarchical to the affective and horizontal. And (4) A-PD requires us to decolonize and decommodify our minds and everyday lives. As in all other PD views, face-to-face assemblies are essential in A-PD, but probably even more so because they occur not just in the political and the economic but in the social. To understand A-PD and in particular how it differs from associationist and liberal PD, we must first unpack its understanding of capitalism and the state.

Crack Capitalism[69]

> How could mutual aid be institutionalized in the state apparatus, separated from the community?
> —RAUL ZIBECHI, *TERRITORIES IN RESISTANCE*, 119

For A-PD, the state has an unjust antidemocratic essence: a procapitalist politics backed by armies and police, separating "the people" (e.g., multitude, or 99%) from their rightful power. The state does this in two ways: through a politics of representation (people don't rule themselves, instead they choose who will do it for them) and the disempowering machinations of bureaucracy. For A-PD, representation is a separation of the body politic from governing and bureaucracy is its concrete realization. Here A-PD channels Rousseau's infamous claim that "sovereignty does not admit of representation [. . .] Every law the people has not ratified in person is null and void . . . The moment the people allows itself to be represented, it is no longer free" (quoted in Mansbridge 1980, 18). We give up power to the legislators, and our ability to govern ourselves atrophies in the process. Holloway writes,

> Representation is part of the general process of separation which is capitalism. It is completely wrong to think of representative government as a challenge to capitalist rule or even as a potential challenge to capital. Representative democracy is not opposed to capital: rather, it is an extension of capital. [. . .] It is built upon the atomization of individuals, the fetishization of time and space, separates leaders from those who are led, and makes possible all sorts of hierarchies. (Holloway [2002] 2005, 229)

Even when the state gives us something good (social security, tax refunds), we are passive recipients of a distribution and rendered dependent (May 2010, 4).[70] This view may be jarring to those in Europe and the United States where the progressive left has fought hard to defend such entitlement programs as the neoliberal right calls for them to be cut. But, then again, this critique of the welfare state might be welcome to libertarians and communitarians who fear the oppression, or simply dread the alienating inefficiency, of big government. In any case, for A-PD, the state is part of capitalism; and it too separates us (Holloway [2002] 2005, 225).[71]

One of the aspects of modern life that makes us scream the most is bureaucracy. The problem with bureaucracy is that it seems to stand in the way of getting things done; it interferes; it prevents things that make sense. It is the classic example of that which separates us from our powers to act. Not content with disempowering, it also humiliates: who among us has not been humiliated by a bureaucrat? Weber recognized this disempowering separation almost 100 years ago. As Santos and Avritzer explain, the

> main reason why Rousseau's conception of participatory management did not prevail was the emergence of complex forms of state administration, which led to the consolidation of specialized bureaucracies in most of the arenas managed by the modern state. For Weber, "the separation of the worker from the material means of production, destruction, administration, academic research and finance in general is the common base of the modern State, in its political, cultural and military spheres". (Santos and Avritzer 2005, xxxix)

A key interlocutor who picks up the Rousseauian spirit here is Castoriadis whose focus on the injustices of state administration led to a split among

Marxists in the 1950s (May 1994, 38–44). State socialists obviously thought the state and its administrative machinery was central to act on behalf of and/or deploy the masses just as a (vanguard) political party was necessary to lead them. On this more traditional socialist-statist model, the state apparatus also possesses the knowledge to teach people (e.g., workers) what is in their own best interest (May 1994, 41). We see this attitude in liberal states too that often regard people as lacking the expertise to know what is best for them, whether having to do with, say, energy policy or education curriculum. And we even see this attitude in corporations that are supposed to be alternatives to government and be all about "customer service" but develop their own "big government" apparatuses and attitudes: cable and health care providers are notorious in this regard (Graeber 2013, 289–291; 2015).[72]

If one insists, à la social contract theory, "But the people agreed to this" then A-PD (channeling Charles Mills who channels Rousseau) calls this "agreement" a domination contract (Mills and Pateman 2007, 92–93). Put in terms of another ontology, the birth of the state is that moment where the people *illegitimately* transfer their own powers of legislation and self-defense to the state.[73] Or, even worse, it is that moment when the state *destroys* your political community and subjects you (if you are still alive) to it, either as a member or as a nonmember. For these reasons, in order to do our politics, we must not collaborate with it, nor treat it as a vehicle for social transformation. We must exit it. Politics means taking our faith out of the state and placing that faith in ourselves. We must change the world without taking (state) power (Holloway 2005, 10–11).

As we split from the state we "crack capitalism." A-PD draws from traditional anarchist and Marxist critiques here as it argues that the problem with capitalism is that it separates us from the land, material resources, and technologies that we need to feed, house, and heal ourselves, and it separates us from each other since we are forced to compete with one another to survive. But it also causes divisions within oneself, this is most overtly seen when we are at work and trade our labor for a wage, we do not control or own that labor, and in that moment our personhood is sundered (Holloway [2002] 2005, 28, 38). But it is also the commodity form that separates and alienates, it "disarticulates the social flow of doing" (Holloway [2002] 2005, 46).

Given all this, we cannot underestimate how deformed we are in the present system. So much so, it causes us to "scream." We are constantly trying to fit into all these forms and spaces and we don't. And we anguish not just because of the bad things that happen to us and our world but because we feel powerless. We don't know what we can do, or where to do it. We can't find the right fit. We are misfits. But this shows that capitalism is full of cracks, so we think of the world through this misfitting in order to find spaces and relationships for affinity and affectivity, for joy and collective determination (Holloway 2010, 9–10).

Exodus and Autogestion. Against and Beyond Capitalism:
"No Matter Who They Elect, We Will Not Be Governed"[74]

> Self determination means the assumption of responsibility for one's own
> participation in the determination of social doing.
> —HOLLOWAY, *How to Change the World without Taking Power*, 229

The consequence of all this critique is that workers (and "the people") don't
just need property, income, and assets to be liberated; they need to manage
their own affairs, collectively and democratically. Castoriadis called this
kind of self-management "autogestion" (May 1994, 40) and this term is commonly used among A-PD advocates. In order to self-manage one has to do
two things: create a process to work together to administer one's affairs with
others, and, also, stop being managed by others! The latter involves the politics of refusal, which is also articulated by Castoriadis and picked up by a
new wave of social and worker movements in the 1970s, including Autono-
mia in Italy, the Autonomen in Germany in the 1980s, and many other
movements throughout Europe. In the workplace, the refusal can be a wild-
cat strike, a work slowdown, or destroying equipment to interfere with the
production process (e.g., monkey wrenching). This refusal also plays out not
just in the workplace, but in politics (Katsiaficas [1997] 2006).

When we say "no," when we refuse, we are "disobedienti,"[75] and the
time-space of authoritarian power loses its functional and ideological integrity. We deterritorialize it. And with exodus, there is crisis. Holloway quotes
the sixteenth-century writer La Boetie: "Resolve to serve no more, and you
are at once freed. I do not ask that you place hands upon the tyrant to topple
him over, but simply that you support him no longer; then you will behold
him, like a great Colossus whose pedestal has been pulled away, fall of his
own weight and break in pieces" (La Boetie 1546, from the Discourse on
Voluntary Servitude, quoted in Holloway 2010, 6). The crisis occurs not because the "powerful" made an error, it's because we stopped participating:
"We are the cause of the crisis" (Holloway 2010, 250–252; Hardt and Negri
2009, 150–164). But leaving (or destroying, negating) is not enough; we must
always create, (re)compose ourselves and our places, our territories and our
subjectivities. A-PD aims to fuse together the acts of opposition and collective determination.

We don't free ourselves from the state to create our own state. We should
not aspire to sit in the seat at the top of some vertical power-over that subordinates. Rather, we should topple such hierarchies and cultivate a horizontal
collaborative power that disperses and interconnects, a power-to and a power-
with in which the social is the interactive ground of the political and economic. It's not perfect, it's prefigurative, and gives a glimpse of both what we
want (potential) and what we can do (capability) (Sitrin 2012, 101–118).

A-PD can be anywhere (except in the state!) at anytime. From the workplace to the school, during lunch or while riding the bus, we can and should always be creating social relations that treat people with dignity, build relations of trust, and cultivate powers for collective determination (Sitrin 2012, 105–107). Holloway writes, "Not all social relations are commodity relations: the commodity form imposes itself, but ordinary life also involves a constant process of establishing non-commodity or even anti-commodity relations. There is not an outside capital, but there is certainly an against-and-beyond" (Holloway [2002] 2005, 222). The goal, then, is not just self-management; it is self-provisioning. Not just to make ourselves, but to do things for ourselves, and in our own way. Collective determination should be done with and in our own style (Hardt and Negri 2004, 213). Holloway calls this the social flow of doing, "Doing is inherently plural, collective, choral, communal. This does not mean that all doing is (or indeed should be) undertaken collectively. It means rather that it is difficult to conceive of a doing that does not have the doing of others as a precondition" (Holloway [2002] 2005, 26). This can be done through seemingly very simple acts of helping to start a garden or fix a bike (Carlsson 2008), or through acts of solidarity on the picket line or through creating neighborhood assemblies to address police violence and pursue restorative justice and alternatives to the prison-industrial complex (Sitrin 2012, 118–123; Zibechi 2012, 225). The best A-PD acts are those where we oppose and remake at the same time; when the scream interconnects horror and hope (Holloway 2005, 8). Exemplary instances of this are the occupied factories movement where workers not only fight for back pay that they are due but take over the factories that were closed and run them collectively (autogestion) without their old bosses (exodus/refusal) (Zibechi 2012, 91–108). Another classic example is of peasants who, after being kicked off their land, don't just fight for jobs on the neighboring plantations but create their own farms, which, again, they manage together (Zibechi 2012, 121–126). Even better is when such movements decommodify and then socially regulate production (see my Chapter 5).

Operationally, A-PD movements and organizations tend to pursue decommodification in some specified way. This desire to make anticapitalist practices present even during/despite neoliberalism is called "prefiguration" (Day 2005, 44–45). Prefigurative politics "is behaving day-to-day as much as possible in the way that you envision new social and economic relationships: the way you would want to be" (Sitrin 2012, 4). Such activities and organizations both decommodify social life and put into place an economy that is framed by anticapitalist norms such as solidarity and reciprocity and actively instantiated (or already embodied) in various customs, institutions, and/or laws. Specific forms include everything from worker-managed firms, food co-ops, community-sponsored agriculture (CSAs), housing collectives, land trusts, indigenous women's collectives, and communitarian agricultural projects. Some produce goods, others are organized around consumption, still others around ownership or political action. Each operates in accordance with norms that foster equality in decision making, accountability in leadership, and, when applicable, the sharing of responsibilities and assets (e.g., wages, use of facilities, garden plots, seeds). What makes them "prefigurative" is that they attempt to insert the future (the widespread realization of the normative framework that we really want) into the present where admittedly our powers are limited in scope. Prefiguration emphasizes the importance of even realizing very small portions of that framework in order to make the alternative seem more concrete and viable. This horizontal politics is an affective politics and also taps the notion of recuperation not just as economic takeover but as sociopsychological healing (Zibechi 2012, 31–36).

Social Reproduction/Subsistence PD (or S-PD)

> We argue that men and women are involved in a set of noncapitalist class processes in the household and that, for the women, this involvement often leads to participation in a set of domestic class struggles.
> —GIBSON-GRAHAM, *THE END OF CAPITALISM (AS WE KNEW IT)*, 209

The fifth tradition/framework we examine continues with many of the themes of 4.: the focus on everyday life; the necessity of antagonistic direct action; the reintegration of politics, economy, and the social sphere; self-management; and decommodification. But its critique is less anarchist-Marxist and more feminist, ecological, and postcolonial. It goes by many names: "earth democracy" (Shiva 2005), the "subsistence perspective" (Bennholdt-Thomsen and Mies 2000), "ecofeminism" (Mies and Shiva 1993), the "living economy" (Shiva 2005, 2), and "feminist ecological economics" (Perkins and Kuiper 2005), and it is also connected to solidarity economy (Allard, Davidson, and Matthaei 2008) and commoning frameworks (Shiva 2005, 2; Federici 2011).[76] Despite its many names, its foundation is crucially different from all of the other forms of PD thus considered: the reproductive labor involved in the production of humans and the maintenance of life in general, or social reproduction (Schwarzenbach 2009, 36–52, 152–158). For this reason, and because the view is often called the *subsistence perspective*, I call it S-PD. S-PD draws upon Kropotkin's ecological-municipal focus and associationism's fondness for social pluralism in the political, economic, and social spheres, but it is not as antistate as anarchism and A-PD. Although it has many of the same norms as A-PD, including mutual aid, reciprocity, and self-provisioning,[77] it diverges from the latter because S-PD argues that patriarchy plays a key role in the environmental and economic crises. Also, S-PD argues ecology is fundamental to the PD project as is having a consistently anticolonial stance, which is not just anticapitalist but anti-imperial.

A good place to start to understand S-PD is in the domestic realm. We begin the explication by revisiting Pateman's feminist critique of PD, including her own work. She writes,

> By failing to take into account the feminist conception of "private" life by ignoring the family, participatory democratic arguments for the democratization of economic life have neglected a crucial dimension of democratic social transformation (and I include my *Participation and Democratic Theory* here). It is difficult to find any appreciation of the significance of the integral relation between the domestic division of labour and economic life, or the sexual division of labour in the workplace. (Pateman 1989, 220–221)

If we believe that men and women should be equal politically, and the sexual division of labor (and/or the related "second shift") interferes with women exercising this right, then we must address this barrier. Even for liberals who are committed to formal political equality but willing to permit much economic inequality, if there is too much of the latter, it undermines the former, and thus has to be restricted for political consequentialist reasons. Liberal feminists make similar arguments.

S-PD acknowledges the injustices of the sexual division of labor, but extends the scope of inquiry into relations among countries and those between humans and nature. This was the aim of the concept of the "subsistence perspective" which

> was first developed to analyze the hidden, unpaid or poorly paid work of housewives, subsistence peasants and small producers in the so-called informal sector, particularly in the South, as the underpinning and foundation of capitalist patriarchy's model of unlimited growth of goods and money. Subsistence work as life-producing work in all these production relations was and is a necessary precondition for survival; and the bulk of this work is done by women. (Mies and Shiva 1993, 297–298)

The sexual division of labor is not just an issue in the home, it impacts on our understanding of the economy, history, the sciences, and law (Mies [1986] 1999, 44–73; Shiva 1989, 14–37; Mies and Shiva 1993, 22–54; Federici 2004, 133–218) and plays a critical part in the global economy and relations among men and women in different countries, particular the "global north" and "global south." This has been true at least since the time of colonialism and slavery, and continues with the proliferation and intensification of the global economy (Federici 2004, 219–243; Mies 1986, 74–144).

Unlike A-PD, S-PD regards the relationship between men and women as fundamental, and a PD politics must reconfigure this relationship (Bennholdt-Thomsen and Mies 2000, 31; Federici 2011, 4). Consistent with the ecofeminist line, the democratization of the relationship between men and women is also required to have an ecological politics. Here Mies and Shiva interconnect not only the view of other S-PD figures, they interconnect the many dimensions that a PD politics requires:

> a non-exploitative relationship to nature cannot be established without a change in human relationships, particularly between *women and men*. This means not only a change in the various divisions of labour (sexual division; manual/mental and urban/rural labour, and so on) but mainly the substitution of money or commodity relationships by such principles as reciprocity, mutuality, solidarity, reliability, sharing and caring, respect for the individual and responsibility for the "whole." The need for *subsistence security* is satisfied not by trust in one's bank account for a social welfare state, but by trust in the reliability of one's community. A subsistence perspective can be realized only within such a network of reliable, stable human relations, it cannot be based on the atomized, self centered [*sic*] individuality of the market economy. (Mies and Shiva 1993, 319)

The "social" then is actually a gendered ecological sphere where the anchoring activity is not production but reproduction. And again, not just of humans, but of ecosystems. (Also, in this passage we again see a critique of the welfare state and commodification, which are central issues for A-PD.)

All human labor presupposes the "productive" activity of nature. Growing food, making goods, building shelter all involves nature not just as resources but as an active partner in the production process. Human labor must then respect these nonhuman processes and treat them as valuable agents. Second, the most important labor done by humans is social reproduction. Social reproduction is the production of persons, of the relations that make persons and develop and cultivate and protect communities. All that everyday labor of preparing meals and cleaning, of teaching morals and telling bedtime stories, of taking care of the sick, maintaining friendships and settling disputes. This is the labor that makes human life not just possible but meaningful. The production of things for use-value is necessary to be sure, but it is secondary to social reproduction in terms of value. Commodity production (e.g., goods produced for exchange value) also has a role to play but is even less significant (Mies [1986] 1999, 44–73; Bennholdt-Thomsen and Mies 2000, 31–35; Shiva 2005, 13–17).

Also, in contrast to all of the PD views discussed above, S-PD in the modality of the "subsistence perspective" comes with a moral view that explicitly defines freedom and happiness in terms of the process of self-determination that maintains the economic and ecological base. It also reintegrates the political, social, and economic spheres in a way that also tries to reterritorialize cultural practices including language. Reminiscent of the social ecology of Kropotkin, its space-time is the ecological region and favors organizations such as communes and cooperatives (Bennholdt-Thomsen and Mies 2000, 19–20). Although S-PD is mildly antiurban, it claims many urban movements, especially the German self-help movements that fight off the encroachment of the state and market, promote the commons and decommodification, are born of affinity and democratically run organizations in media and manufacturing, and are part of communities that barter or use local currencies (Bennholdt-Thomsen and Mies 2000, 129–130, 179–180). A great example of such efforts are the former addicts and homeless who as squatters and garbage pickers organized to form the SSK in Cologne (Mies and Shiva 1993, 312–316). Here we see almost all the dimensions at work: self-provisioning, direct action, a contradictory relationship to the state, radical ecology, and urban subsistence. Mies and Shiva show that the SSK's holism enabled it to flourish by

> combining ecological with social problem-solving; healing the earth as well as people and communities by creating meaningful work, giving a new sense of purpose to socially marginalized women and men; developing a new, appropriate technology out of discarded, obsolete objects; recultivating wasteland; re-establishing a new community-sense among people who are concerned and feel responsible for the future of life on this planet; and finally creating new hope not only for those directly involved in the project but for many who have lost a sense of orientation. (Mies and Shiva 1993, 317–318)

But S-PD is not just anticapitalist, it is anti-imperialist and actively supports, includes, and even partners with movements in former colonies (Dé Ishtar 1994; Mies [1986] 1999, 230–231; Mies and Shiva 1993, 1–21).[78] After all, to make one's own home or town "green" by displacing the polluting industries to somewhere far away is promoting my own collective determination by destroying that of others. The aim of PD—especially in terms of the maximal democracy view that will be argued for in this book (see below)—is to *support* other PD projects not undermine them. Thus, "To live according to the guiding star of subsistence means to no longer to live off the exploitation of the environment or of foreign peoples" (Mies and Shiva 1993, 315). It also means to inhabit a more human and ecological time-space, that of the artisan but integrated with the household and the community

(Bennholdt-Thomsen and Mies 2000, 130). A great setting for understanding the many dimensions of S-PD in action is in Kenya's Greenbelt movement and the work of Wangari Maathai (1940–2011).[79]

Kenya's Greenbelt Movement

One of the most successful PD movements of any period is Kenya's Greenbelt Movement (GBM). Founded in 1977 by Wangari Maathai as a series of tree planting nurseries to foster ecological restoration and employ and empower women, the GBM evolved into a massive multidimensional movement that faced an ecological crisis head on, took on patriarchy and authoritarianism, strengthened the subsistence economy, increased women's participation in the cash economy, and joined with others to end the Moi dictatorship and bring elections to Kenya.

GBM's founder Wangari Maathai was born in 1940 to Kikiyu peasant farmers in a small traditional village while Kenya was still a British colony. Indeed, Maathai started school the year before the Mau Mau uprising against the British occupation (Florence 2014, 12–13).[80] She next went to Catholic school and then studied in the United States, receiving her masters in biology. She returned home to complete her Ph.D. in veterinary anatomy from the University of Nairobi (Maathai [1985] 2006, 9; Florence 2014, 15–35). Upon graduation, she sought to do work that responded to the ecological and economic crisis in her homeland.

In the 1970s, Kenya, like many nations in the global South, faced a triple crisis: ecological degradation, political authoritarianism and corruption, and the social disempowerment leftover from the degradations of colonialism. Rural women faced growing hardships in particular due to deforestation. Because men often worked outside of the village in the new postcolonial cash economy (Turner and Brownhill 2001, 110–114; Maathai [1985] 2006, 17–32), women were in charge of obtaining fuel for cooking and heating and deforestation was causing them to walk farther and get less (Maathai [1985] 2006, 24–25). Deforestation was also degrading the soil used by households and farms, impeding the flow of streams, weakening water supplies, and degrading habitat. However, for the dictator Daniel arap Moi, deforestation was a problem to be ignored, an unfortunate but inevitable consequence of "development," which modernized the landscape and, as it happened, made him and his cronies rich (Taylor 2013, 183–184; Florence 2014, 114–116).

Planting trees and restoring ecosystems was an obvious response to this situation so Maathai formed an organization that established nurseries to cultivate the seedlings necessary for large-scale plantings. Because of the extent of previous cuts, replanting required that trees be rooted in a row of at least 1,000 trees. These rows planted on public lands were called "belts," hence the name of the organization (Maathai [1985] 2006, 9).

Replanting helped to reduce flooding and enable rainwater storage, soil conservation, and habitat restoration. But just as crucially it was a jobs program. But the work wasn't easy. Starting and maintaining successful nurseries to cultivate and then plant and maintain the seedlings required knowledge of forestry and business acumen (Maathai [1985] 2006, 28). By 1999, 6,000 tree nurseries had been established in twenty-six districts throughout Kenya. And, by that time, GBM had established itself not just as an ecologically oriented environmental business that provided a sustainable source of wood and delivered extensive ecosystem services, but as a place for civic education that fostered not just a love for the environment but cultivated the practice of conservation and stewardship (Maathai [1985] 2006, 33–35).

In 1989, the ecological and economic dimensions of stewardship intersected with the political ones in a violent fight against a sixty-story skyscraper with a thirty-foot statue of the dictator Daniel arap Moi in Uhuru Park, a critical green space and public park used by the poor in Nairobi. The protests were homegrown but innovatively forged alliances with international actors (including support from NYC's Bella Abzug!) which further incensed Moi (Florence 2014, 114–115). In the protests, many were killed or severely injured, and Maathai herself was beaten, arrested, and vilified by the government. But the movements won and the park was saved from development.[81] Maathai continued to fuse the antagonistic and protagonistic common to A-PD and S-PD when in 1992 she joined with mothers of political prisoners in the "freedom corner" hunger strike. This action helped to finally bring elections to Kenya and contribute to the establishment of multiparty politics (Florence 2014, 157–159).

The only PD theorist or advocate to win a Nobel Prize, Maathai is an exemplary figure who in a wonderful Hollowayan manner integrated many disparate and contradictory elements that are part of the landscape of our time. Like Kropotkin and Vandana Shiva, she was schooled in the sciences and recognized their importance but also fought for the legitimacy of local knowledge (Taylor 2013). Like Mill, she was an elected official and a bureaucrat who worked for both national governments and international organizations. And again like Kropotkin and Shiva, Maathai was an agitator, beaten and jailed by the state several times, and like them she frequently fought for the release of political prisoners (Florence 2014, 122, 160–172). And her cosmopolitanism was itself manifold: she is a complicated example of the intersection of local traditional knowledge, the global scientific community, and international feminism. She said in an interview:

The United States prepared me to . . . critique what was happening at home, including what women were experiencing. My years in the United States overlapped with the beginnings of the women's movement and even though many women were still bound to traditional ideas about themselves at the time, I came to see that as an African woman I was perhaps even more constrained. . . . It is fair to say that America transformed me: it made me into the person I am today . . . The spirit of freedom and possibility that America nurtured in me made me want to foster the same in Kenya, and it was in this spirit that I returned home. (Quoted in Taylor 2013, 183)

Like Kropotkin, she recognized the ecological and economic dangers of urbanization and pushed for a more integrated regionalism while working to establish S-PD framed transnational networks of solidarity grounded in eco-social reproduction. And like the Iroquois, she saw the link between democracy and peace, between ecological restoration and social harmony; her trees were also trees of peace (Florence 2014, 91).

And throughout, consistent with S-PD, we see in her work an understanding of the devastating intersection of patriarchy, authoritarianism, and ecological destruction, and the power of feminism, ecological restoration, and participatory democratic spaces,[82] which is even more important as we work to tackle climate change and promote climate justice. In sum, in the word of Maathai: "The Green Belt Movement has over the past 30 years shown that sustainable development linked with democratic values promotes human rights, social justice and equity, including the balance of power between women and men" (Maathai [1985] 2006, xii).

Environmental and Climate Justice Participatory Democracy (EJ-PD)

The sixth and last PD approach is also the most recently developed: environmental justice (EJ-PD).[83] Like S-PD, it focuses on the ecological, but unlike all our PD views discussed thus far, the central category for EJ is race and its principal focus (like liberal and associationist PD) is changing state policy. And, as this lengthy quote from the Environmental Protection Agency shows, it has done so.

Environmental Justice is the fair treatment and meaningful involvement of all people regardless of race, color, national origin, culture, education, or income with respect to the development, implementation, and enforcement of environmental laws, regulations, and policies. Fair Treatment means that no group of people, including racial, ethnic, or socio-economic groups, should bear a disproportionate share of the negative environmental consequences resulting from industrial, municipal, and commercial operations or the execution of federal, state, local, and tribal environmental programs and policies.

Meaningful Involvement means that: (1) potentially affected community residents have an appropriate opportunity to participate in decisions about a proposed activity that will affect their environment and/or health; (2) the public's contribution can influence the regulatory agency's decision; (3) the concerns of all participants involved will be considered in the decision-making process; and (4) the decision-makers seek out and facilitate the involvement of those potentially affected.[84]

EJ emerges out of pioneering work done in the 1970s and 1980s by Grossman, Chavis, and others that showed that hazardous waste sites and other environmental "bads" were much more likely to be located in communities that were majority people of color. The groups most likely at risk are Native Americans, African Americans, and Latinos (Dryzek 2005, 210–212). The reasons that this occurred were not so much because of law, though lack of legislation was part of it. It was more about how communities and jurisdictions made decisions about where to site such facilities. In other words, environmental racism is a product of a particular kind of democratic governance process, of majorities overrunning the rights of minorities or not recognizing or valuing the lives of said groups. This logic is put very well, if cynically, by Larry Summers who was chief economist at the World Bank in the 1990s (before becoming head of President Barack Obama's council of economic advisers during his first term). Summers wrote in a memo: "Just between you and me, shouldn't the World Bank encourage MORE migration of dirty industries to the LDCs [less developed countries]? [. . .] I've always thought that under-populated countries in Africa are vastly UNDER-polluted, their air quality is probably vastly inefficiently low compared to Los Angeles or Mexico City" (Quoted in Shrader-Frechette 2002, 11). EJ is born of the realization of environmental racism that principles of distributive justice have failed. Not only must they be reworked, but a democratic decision-making process must be put into place that guarantees that Native American, black, and Latino communities have a real say in policy, in regulation and management, and in the setting the agenda for their communities (Schlosberg and Carruthers 2010, 13).

   EJ was born not of some charismatic figure but from a movement, or really a network of movements, researchers, and organizations that came together in a meeting in 1991 in Washington, DC. There, dozens hashed out a platform of seventeen principles to forward the project of environmental justice (Schlosberg 1999, 13–14).[85] The EJ movement has three main aims: (1) to repair such communities (principles 6, 9, 12), (2) to more fairly distribute environmental bads and goods going forward (principles 3, 4, 6, 8, 11, 12, 13), and (3) to meaningfully involve groups impacted by future decision-making processes (principles 5, 7). And while EJ focuses largely upon the humans most discriminated against, and refers to the rights of especially vulnerable groups including native peoples (#11) and workers (#8), it is also universalist and for all peoples (#2). It also calls for moral consideration for all life (principle #1 regards "mother earth as sacred" and #3 recognizes the moral standing of nonhumans). Finally, being a pragmatic and forward-looking framework it calls for sustainability (#3) in the economy.

The principle that makes EJ a PD view is #7. The platform states: "**Environmental Justice** demands the right to participate as equal partners at every level of decision-making, including needs assessment, planning, implementation, enforcement and evaluation." The justification for this right to participation is both self-determination and, intriguingly, the principle of informed consent.[86] And like all the other PD views, EJ also stresses the importance of developing individual and group agency (#16 and #17).

To promote distributive justice, "participative justice" or "procedural equity" is required. Generally speaking, this means that those communities impacted by some decision are recognized as agents and their concerns and aspirations are given voice in the process (Schlosberg 1999, 13–14; Shrader-Frechette 2002, 11–15).[87] The primary goal of EJ is repaired, sustainable, and healthy communities, democratically governed, with good (green!) jobs. Without the assets, expertise, and regulatory power of the state, the cleanup/restoration and the sustainable development of communities is not possible. The EJ movement has gotten the EPA to include a version of its principles in its policy, but a key problem concerns what counts as "meaningful participation" (Schlosberg 1999, 13–17; Lawson 2008; and see below). That problem notwithstanding, the EJ movement has had a positive impact in a variety of settings and in a range of sectors from improving equity in the siting of toxic sites such as dumps, sewage treatment plants, and waste transfer stations to utilizing government programs to address food deserts, create community run gardens, and promote sustainable urban development in communities that experienced racial discrimination.[88]

While many EJ movements are often more focused on the impact of industrial processes on humans (Schlosberg 1999; Walker 2012), one segment of the EJ movement that is much more ecocentric are Native American communities and indigenous advocates.[89] As we saw with the discussion of the Iroquois, the reasons for this ecocentricity are obvious: such peoples consider specific species to be members of their culture. Fighting for the lives of the Anishnaabe means fighting for the lives of sturgeon and wild rice. These fights are not just for human bodies and the integrity of built environments; they are fights for soil and streams, for ecosystems and habitat, all of which are embedded in ecocultural practices (Corntassel 2008; Whyte 2014). Such tribes and nations have been in the forefront of climate justice politics as well, because of their more global understanding of ecology and because of their position as peoples fighting for their own conception of sovereignty within and beyond the interstate system.[90] Recently, African American and Latino groups have also been moving into this framework, because of both vulnerabilities and aspirations for a green economy that is inclusive (Dawson 2010).

What the Six Views Share: Maximal Democracy

Before detailing the ways in which the six approaches differ, we must delve deeper into what they share. This involves the laying out of a general view of participatory democracy, which I call maximal democracy or maxD (Menser 2008, 2009). MaxD is a view of democracy that treats the economic, political, and social spheres as interwoven along communitarian and/or associational axes (Menser 2005, 2008, 2009). A group or collective is maxD if it abides by and implements the following four tenets:

1. Collective[91] determination
2. Capacity development and delivery of economic, social, and/or political benefits to members or constituents
3. The replacement of unequal power relations with relations of shared authority
4. The construction, cultivation, proliferation, and interconnection of movements and organizations with overlapping normative frameworks (i.e., those that mostly embody the first three tenets)[92]

At the core of the above conception is the principle of democratic collective determination. Collective determination means the right and the ability of a particular group of persons to define, justify, and concretely articulate the normative framework under which they reflect, deliberate, and act with others. For my view a group acting together to carry out some task is a *collective* if the group reflects on and discusses that task within itself. It is *democratic* if each has decisive power with respect to the process. This can happen in an affinity group or small business or an assembly of a dozen people or thousands. Collectives then can be of different sizes and in different sectors. They can also be of different durations: from a few hours (e.g., participatory budgeting assemblies) to years (e.g., indigenous nations, the Mondragon worker cooperatives).

The process of collective determination described here includes not just the activities of norm construction and justification but the relationships involved in institutional design, ownership, management, and labor. To participate effectively in these processes requires capability development or support for members of the group relative to the activity.[93] For collective determination to be democratic, members of the polity (however defined) must be recognized as equal, and there must be mechanisms that aim to render this equality operational. *Because of the impact of changes within or outside the polity and the aspirational nature of such norms, collective determination is best understood as the adaptive evolution of a self-regulating entity seeking to maximize the agency, equality, and the good of its members over time.* Operationally, democratic collective determination goes beyond mere deliberative democracy and like all participatory views tends toward (collective) self-governance but with an eye for creating interconnections with other collectives or polities that share its normative framework (Menser 2005, 2008). For maxD, then, democracy is defined not just as a discursive procedure for justification, but as a set of practices that actualizes collective determination by linking together democratic procedures, capacity development,[94] and material benefits.[95] The robustness of a maxD organization or movement will depend upon the strength and number of the different "collective" forms it can produce and interconnect (Menser 2009, 253). Tenet #4 is my version of the concept of solidarity.

So what makes a particular process or program PD in this maxD sense? And just as important, what factors prevent a process from being PD? A PD process is a procedure by which members of the relevant group directly decide about some issue that impacts them and the members of the group are positioned as equals in the process. A core goal of PD is to cultivate the agency of individuals and collectivities composing the group. A process is *not* PD if it substantially violates these conditions. Therefore, a PD organization or process should make sure that:

1. **Inequalities** within the group do not negatively impact on the result of the process; and that the outcome of the process does not increase but instead decreases inequality in the group.
2. The **size** of the group is such that members have agency in the process, and the outcome of the process addresses the needs of the group. (It has what Pateman called "political efficacy.") A process that is too small or too large in terms of numbers of people participating or geographic scope is likely to violate this goal. For example, Rousseau, Bookchin, and Dahl all argue that for a jurisdiction to be effectively PD it can't be too big. Cities or countries with millions of members are likely too complex and residents are too unfamiliar with one another to effectively join together and deliberate over policy matters. But, on the other hand, Athens required that there be at least 6,000 present in the assembly to make sure it was representative enough of the will of the broader body politic. (See above.) The same sorts of concerns arise in worker cooperatives. Indeed, the Mondragon Federation of cooperatives encourages its businesses to limit their size to 300 worker-owners (see my Chapter 3). Conversely, in EJ, there is often a worry that the unit is too small: when siting a waste or other

kind of hazardous facility, oftentimes the facility is targeted for a small jurisdiction even though it serves a region, thus the wider region is the proper unit for deliberations (Hunold and Young 1998, 91–92).

3. The third parameter to consider is that the **topic or organization** of the process is appropriate for PD. For example, should my church be PD? (Unless you are a Unitarian Universalist, it probably is not.[96]) Also, what topics are appropriate for a PD unit to debate? Should a community collectively decide what sexual practices are appropriate? What about diet?

These kinds of issues will be considered in subsequent chapters.

Participation, Equality, and Power

Given the issues raised by the three parameters just spelled out, there will be many (too many!) processes that are participatory, but not democratic. The two most common factors that prevent a process from being democratic are inequalities among participants and the lack of power possessed by the process with respect to some goal. A PD process is not an "ideal speech situation." It does not assume that everyone in the process comes to the table with the same set of skills and resources. In the real world, the opposite is likely the case. So what does a truly maxD PD process look like? Let's look at a case from the environmental justice literature: the siting of a hazardous waste facility.

For better or worse, our current economic system produces an incredible amount of waste. So where should we put it? Let's imagine a case where a new facility must be built and we are trying to determine what location is best. EJ-PD tells us that it's not enough to have the right law on the books, the decision-making process must include those communities who will be affected. So what does a PD process for "meaningful participation" and "procedural equity" look like? In their 1998 work, Hunold and Young get into the nitty-gritty of such a process (which is usefully summarized by Walker 2012, 48–50).

Phases of a Participation Process
1. Informing exchange and trust formation
2. Discussion and deliberation about values, needs, priorities
3. Proposal generation
4. Proposal selection
5. Plan for implementation[97]

For example, in most actual processes, the first stage is an info session where the situation is explained and the actors involved meet and gain some familiarity and (hopefully!) begin to trust one another. The second stage is often for discussion and deliberation about the needs, values, and priorities of the community. In the third stage, there is discussion and deliberation to generate proposals. If more than one is generated, then there is selection of the proposal. Last is usually a discussion of plans for implementation.

Such a process is EJ-PD if all the relevant groups affected are included in the process and are consulted throughout.[98] This means we have to do outreach to make sure everyone knows about the process, the meetings are accessible both temporally and spatially (e.g., they are not at 6:00 A.M. on a Sunday in a warehouse miles out of town). Given cosmopolitanism and contemporary work patterns and concerns about the unequal distribution of carework, we may have to provide translation and child care. And this has to happen for every phase of the process. Also, and this is often overlooked, all of the crucial variables of the proposal (phases 3 and 4) should be up for discussion: not just the function, for example, but the size of the facility. And, because these issues are complicated and technical, community groups should be assisted in the process so that they have the relevant information and can understand it. This may require support so that impacted groups can retain their own experts or commission their own studies. As far as decision making goes, EJ asks that all affected be "involved" in the final decision, through either negotiation or vote (Hunold and Young 1998, 86, 90; Walker 2012, 49).

Here we see a model of participation that goes beyond simply "being at the table" and actually institutes *informed* consent and procedural equity. (See EJ-PD section above.) Just because one gets a seat at the table does not mean that one is fully informed much less has real power. A just PD process must then assume the unequal position of groups in the process and work to correct it. (Here the other PD "routes" can learn from EJ-PD.) It also must grant members power in the process. But how much? What if all the communities participate in every stage but then have no voting power, is the process PD? Here EJ advocates are less clear.[99]

Throughout this first chapter, we have defined PD as a redistribution of power that promotes the collective determination and capability development of its group's members. But when it comes to an actual process, what does it mean to say that people's participation is "meaningful" in the language of EJ, much less in the mind of the EPA? Here it's helpful to look at the classic essay on participation by Arnstein from 1969 (see quote in the Introduction).[100] In that essay, Arnstein lays out the racialized situation that leads to environmental racism that gives rise to the calls for meaningful participation by EJ in the first place! In general Arnstein distinguishes among three kinds of participation: cynical and/or manipulative; tokenistic; and decisive impact on the process (Arnstein 1969, 216–217).[101] Building upon Arnstein's insights, but modifying and streamlining her categories, I offer the following taxonomy:

Types of Public Participation Processes[102]

0. Manipulation/Silencing: public is included but misled and has no effective voice or power
1. Informing: government *informs* the public about some decision or policy
2. Consultation: government *asks* the public to state their views or concerns
3. Discussion: government and public *deliberate* about some issue or policy
4. Decide together: government and public *share power* and make a decision together
5. Self-rule or direct democracy: public decides, government supports process

0. Manipulation/Silencing. The first type Arnstein names is fake participation. (Which is why I list it as "0".) A typical example is when a governing board that has power adds a community member but that person has no real say on it or no voting power of any consequence. This is manipulation or silencing because when the community member is outvoted, the board can say the "community was represented" (Arnstein 1969, 218–220). This not only is not PD; it's not even really participation.

1. Information Sessions. By themselves these are not PD and may not even really be participation. They can be important, however. For example, a city develops a new evacuation plan and needs to make sure the residents not only know about it but understand it. The session is run to transfer information and the public may be able to ask questions about the plan but they are not there to evaluate much less modify or participate in its formulation. (The session is "after the fact.")

2. Consultation. Unlike 1, where the government is transferring information to the public in consultation, the public transmits information to the ruling body. This can happen through surveys, focus groups, and/or face-to-face meetings. This is usually done when the governing body is developing a plan and needs information. This is done before the plan has been formulated. (If it's done afterward, then it's 0 [manipulation].)

3. Discussion. Building on 1 and 2, the public and governing bodies have a dialogue in which questions and responses are given about the policy or decision to be made. When done well, questions are posed in both directions (the public asks about the details of the policy and the government asks the public about its needs re: the policy) When done poorly, the public asks questions but responses are not forthcoming or there is no follow-up discussion. Town hall meetings are often poor versions of this. (See my Chapter 2.)

4. Decide Together. Residents have formal power to make a decision about some policy or action. Example: an ad hoc committee is formed where voting power is roughly split between public and governing body.

5. Self-Rule or Direct Democracy. Ruling body designates or transfers power to a public body. Example: a policy measure is decided through referendum or a school board vote. Participatory budgeting when done well also embodies this type (see my Chapter 2).

Note that this taxonomy is provisional and tentative. For example, with the exception of 1, any of these processes could be done so well that they accumulate legitimacy so that they have real influence. For example, groups can use consultation to get a particular proposal into the city's plan.[103] That said, there are also cases of processes that were supposed to be robust and participatory but their plans in the end, though initially accepted, never went through. This happens all the time with respect to affordable housing and developers in NYC. The public is invited in and promised x number of jobs, x number of affordable units, x amount of public space, but the agreed upon plans are never fully implemented.

Two of the most common and least effective forms of non-PD participation are the town hall meeting or public hearing and the (powerless) charette. Public hearings are essential to the U.S. republic. They are "one of the ways in which we fulfill the guarantee of due process contained in both the Fifth and Fourteenth amendments to the US Constitution" (Kemmis 1992, 53). At the town hall meeting or hearing, members of the public have an opportunity to speak or testify with respect to some topic. The format is often as follows: in one part of the room sits an audience, in the other, governmental officials or their representatives sit at a table. The government people explain the proposal or policy, then the audience has time to comment and/or ask questions. The government may or may not respond (and they may or may not even listen!).

This kind of public process is often (but not always) unproductive for many reasons: there is no guarantee of discussion between government and the public; it is after all, a "hearing." Nor is there discussion among the public—no real collaboration happens or is fostered. Two, this format does not build an understanding of the issue because there is often no dialogue. Instead, it often encourage divisiveness. And, it's a one-shot opportunity, a few hours at most. Former Montana Mayor Daniel Kemmis writes, "In fact, out of everything that happens at a public hearing—the speaking, the emoting, the efforts to persuade the decision-maker, the presentation of facts—the one element that is almost totally lacking is anything that might be characterized as 'public hearing'" (Kemmis 1992, 53). And all too often, they become venues for berating officials and for blocking proposals. Indeed, this is probably the most "positive" role that they play. They prevent something bad from going through. But they are not scenes for problem solving or collaboration. Instead they favor the shrill, the obstinate, and even turn more people off to the political process. They give us what we've got too much of: bitter partisanship where the competing sides don't listen to each other. And the result: gridlock for the majority, and backdoor deals for the elite minority.[104]

The opposite version of this process is the charette. Here members of the public are encouraged to talk to each other and maybe even with a governmental official or some representative of that official. Here, everyone brainstorms and discusses, some deliberation may even occur. But not only are these bodies powerless; those making the decisions may not even consider their results. These kinds of meetings are particularly common in urban planning (e.g., for a new park or commercial area). In Arnstein's taxonomy, at their best, they are a mix of consultation and discussion, but no power is shared (no citizen control). At their worst, they are a waste of time and misleading (e.g., manipulation) (Reed 2008, 2422).[105]

Returning to the example of EJ and meaningful participation. Unlike most of the other PD views that favor assemblies, EJ's call for "meaningful participation" has a much lower standard. Though it goes beyond "the right to know," it often settles for communication and consultation (Schlosberg 1999, 144–179; though also see Hunold and Young 1998).

Reflections on the Six Routes

The distinctions among the different types of participation not only help to differentiate PD from non-PD participation; it also gets at differences among the PD routes approaches to three different questions: (1) How much of my life needs to be PD? (2) What problems can PD solve and not solve? (3) Can the state be made PD? And/or what is the relationship of PD to the state? In this last section of the chapter, I want to get at these differences and look ahead to the explications and debates of the upcoming chapters.

First, how much of my life needs to be PD? If one believes the private sphere should not be subject to the demands of PD, one could opt for the liberal and EJ-PD models. (Pateman, for example, does not discuss religion or even the family as she admits in later work.) If I want a total PD makeover of my life and community, then communitarian, A-PD, and S-PD are probably the best but there are differences here too. If I want half of my life to be made over, but not the whole thing, then associationist PD is the better option. Whereas S-PD tackles relations among men and women and even humans and nonhumans, A-PD is less demanding on these issues (for better or worse). Indeed, sometimes less is more. By not claiming that PD is the answer to all social problems, liberal PD and associationism put less demand on PD, and, for many, this may make it seem more doable. But for others who believe that we are in a period of system change, the multidimensional holism of A-PD and S-PD might make them seem more attractive and adequate to the moment.

Second, can PD solve all problems? Does every organization need to be PD? Of course not. And, "no." What view can solve all problems? Can human rights solve all problems? Socialism? Neoliberalism? There are no universal remedies, nor does one size (or type) fit all solutions.[106] Should my Environmental Ethics class be PD? What about my local hospital? The police station? In Chapter 4, we will look at a debate between Ellerman and Schweickart on whether or not all businesses should be PD and owned by their workers. While Schweickart permits privately owned corporations in small numbers, Ellerman argues that that's like permitting slavery in small numbers.

Third, what is the relationship between PD and the state? Again, there are options. If you do not like the state, you have S-PD. If you *really* hate the state, go with A-PD. For those who think we absolutely need the state, there is liberal PD. For those who want to remake it, or evolve it, there is associationist PD. Building on insights laid out in Chapter 2 (about participatory budgeting), in Chapter 6 we will push the idea that we can fracture and modify parts of the state and produce a new political configuration, the social-public.

Relatedly, these different PD frames are better or worse at solving different types of political, social, and economic problems. For example, if one believes the ecological crisis is paramount, then routes five (S-PD) and six (EJ-PD) should be consulted, but so should the eco-anarchism of Kropotkin and Bookchin (route four A-PD). And for those with different politics regarding the state, a number of options are available, including two (associationism and social reproduction PD) that refuse the simple "for or against" dichotomy. Also, some forms of PD anchor themselves more so in one sector (social, political, economic) than the others.

To conclude, the social reproduction participatory democracy (S-PD) is the most thoroughgoing of all the PD frameworks, which is to say it seeks to reconstruct the greatest number and types of social relationships. Whereas liberal and associationist PD permit more non-PD spaces, A-PD and S-PD subject much more of one's life to PD because of their intense focus on social life. However, because S-PD focuses more on patriarchy, ecology, and colonialism, it is even more demanding than traditional anarchism or A-PD. To push it even further, in some ways S-PD is more like traditional anarchism than is A-PD. In the long quote above, Mies and Shiva call for a reconstruction of the divide between rural and urban labor as well as manual and intellectual labor, à la Bookchin (see Chapter 4). Indeed, S-PD calls for a reruralizing reconstruction of the urban, again sounding much more like Kropotkin or Bookchin than Holloway or Hirst (see, for example, Bennholdt-Thomsen et al. 2001).

Also, S-PD seems to have a very thick conception of the good (Akhter 2001), going so far as to formulate a conception of happiness that would actually be at odds with the libertarianism of much anarchism and A-PD (Bennholdt-Thomsen and Mies 2000, 250).

Conclusion

In this first chapter we laid out a history of PD in both theory and practice, from the exemplary practices of ancient Athens and the Iroquois Federation to the contemporary Greenbelt Movement of Kenya, and how it is justified and articulated in the political philosophies of Rousseau, Mill, Kropotkin, and G.D.H. Cole. We followed PD as it ebbed and flowed in three historical periods, but our main focus was to lay out the core concepts of PD as maximal democracy and the taxonomy of the six different normative frameworks, which are amenable to and employ PD. This first chapter showed that no single ideology or political philosophy owns this version of maxD; instead we find it in Rousseau's communitarianism, Mill's liberalism, Cole and Hirst's associationism, the work of many anarchists and autonomous Marxists (from Kropotkin and Bookchin to Holloway), the work of feminist theorists of ecological social reproduction such as Mies and Shiva, and the environmental justice movement of Anthony and Eckersley. And, we noted the problems that PD faces in terms of defining what counts as meaningful participation and how different views of PD actually criticize each other with respect to scale, the environment, feminism, the household, and the proper relationship to the state, thereby setting up discussions and debates to come.

2

Participatory Budgeting, Democratic Theory, and the Disarticulation of the State

Introduction

Our first case study is a program operating in the political terrain for more than three decades on six continents and is praised by five and a half of our six PD frameworks. (A-PD is ambivalent.) At its best, this process enables the public to take control over their tax dollars, commands elected officials to serve their constituents, and builds projects that directly serve community needs. At its best, it brings together populations who don't usually talk, increases individual and collective capacity for deliberation, promotes collaborations that increase creativity and efficiency, and shows people that political participation does not have to be boring and pointless but instead can be lively and empowering. It may even lead to a new form of democratic governance that changes our conception of the state and the possible relations among government, civil society, and residents.

At its worst, it entices people to fight over small amounts of money, empowers groups already well positioned, pits residents against the bureaucracy (guess who wins?), and induces community-based organizations to become more subordinate to elected officials. At its worst, it doesn't inspire; it demobilizes.

This pluripotent "it" is participatory budgeting and (thankfully!) the evidence shows that it inspires and empowers far more often than it demobilizes. But even among its advocates, there are very different reasons for praising it.

Participatory budgeting (PB) is a process in which some part of a public budget is controlled by those most impacted by that budget. When done within a governmental jurisdiction,[1] "PB allows the participation of non-elected citizens in the conception and/or allocation of public finances" (Sintomer et al. 2012, 2). And, it is "a vehicle through which participants use deliberation to secure public policies to directly benefit their communities" (Wampler 2007, 266). PB is distinguished by the following features: it is not just consultative but *decisive*—constituents don't just voice their views; they directly decide[2] how to spend the funds. Before proceeding, let me exclaim it again: DEMOCRACY IS NOT JUST ABOUT HAVING A VOICE; IT'S ABOUT EXERCISING POWER. PARTICIPATORY DEMOCRACY IS A PROCESS THAT ENABLES PEOPLE TO EQUITABLY SHARE THAT POWER. Participatory budgeting is an example of a process that attempts to do that. PB is not just a one-time event; rather, it is a multistage process that takes several months and repeats and evolves over years. The point of PB is not just to get more people involved in the business of government; it's to get something out (of it): namely, projects that improve public services and serve people's real needs.

PB started in 1989 in Brazil, in the city of Porto Alegre. Since then it has expanded to more than 1,700 cities across six continents, from the megacities of Chengdu, China, and New York City to small towns such as Nahampoana, Madagascar, and Ilo, Peru (Sintomer et al. 2013, 11; Cabannes 2014).[3] In all these places, PB is a process for allocating funds constituted by some configuration of elected officials, government bureaucrats, civil society organizations, and local residents. The novelty and political potency of PB is that nonelected officials are empowered actors in this process. But the composition of this nonstate agent as well as the norms that structure the process's agenda vary from place to place.

Why have so many places in such a short period of time taken the PB plunge? Over the course of twenty-five years of operations, studies have shown that PB routinely increases civic participation, reduces corruption, makes government more accountable, and implements projects that benefit the public. When done well, PB delivers three distinct types of benefits (and even when done not so well, it delivers at least one): PB enables *empowered participation*—it creates a mechanism for popular involvement in which people have more than just consultative power and exercise and develop agency. PB increases the *access of populations to government* and expands contact of government agencies to the broader public. *PB improves public service provision* and increases the number of people who benefit from city services.

In this chapter, I systematically discuss all three kinds of benefits—most accounts focus only on one or two[4]—and, more uniquely, I look at PB from three different normative perspectives: neoliberal efficiency, good governance, and participatory democracy. Not all actually existing PBs are PD. Indeed, *most* are not. But even though PD PB's are rare, they are doable. And with the right supports, they could spread. Part of the mission of this chapter is to go into the nitty-grity of what a PD PB requires. I then argue for the PD version of PBs and utilize my maximal democracy (or maxD) framework to that end. How does PB enable collective determination (maxD#1) if it requires the support of the state? Does PB really enable people to cultivate capacities such as deliberation (maxD#2)? Are public services actually improved by PB (maxD#2)? Who benefits from them most; do they actually reduce inequality (maxD#2 and 3)? And how does PB relate to other maxD efforts? Does it empower other associations and civil society organizations (maxD#4)? Does it make them more maxD as well? What if, because of political circumstances or lack of resources, a PB cannot fulfill all four? Which norms should be prioritized? Are trade-off's permissible? And how do we avoid the "participation paradox"—where more intensive forms of political participation are only practiced by those with the most resources (Su 2012, 2)? Here are a set of goals for PB that correspond to each maxD principle.

Four MaxD Goals of Participatory Democracy Participatory Budgeting (PD PB)

1. Enable effective and democratic community control of the PB *process* and promote capability development of individuals and group in the process.
2. Promote effective and responsive *governance* to develop, choose, and implement quality *projects* that meet community needs.
3. Reduce political and economic *inequality* in terms of the process and the projects.
4. To strengthen *"civil society"* broadly construed to support associations and community-based organizations to enhance their PD capabilities and impact and increase their numbers.

The originary model of PB developed in Porto Alegre realized all four of these goals. And although most PBs now in existence do not fulfill all of these, many fulfill some. Throughout the rest of this chapter, I articulate this originary, paradigmatic PD model[5] as practiced in Porto Alegre, and how it developed more recently in a much different political and cultural milieu, NYC. I also look at PB's global spread and incredible range of innovations that go beyond both Porto Alegre and NYC. The second half of the chapter looks at how existing PB's fair with respect to each of the goals named above and how the PD approach is different from that found among deliberative democracy views. I also discuss the problem of trade-offs, particularly with respect to deliberation and inclusion. The last sections tear apart traditional understandings of civil society and take on the antistate critique of PB. At this point I get into debates within PD frameworks about PD (especially liberal, associationist, and autonomous versions).[6] I also examine new research regarding the complicated and sometimes counterintuitive relationship between PB and civil society. I conclude by exploring how and why PB gives us a glimpse of a new modality of governance that is not only PD but changes our understanding of the state-form and its relationship with the "social." This helps to set the stage for my Chapter 6 that more fully develops the notion of the "social-public" as a counter to the neoliberal politics behind the public-private partnership that actualizes the general notion of the corporate state.

The Origins of the Paradigmatic Model: Porto Alegre's *Orcamento Participitavo*[7]

> PB represents a pointed and self conscious break from clientilism, bossism, and similar forms of patrimonial intermediation that have long shaped both political and civic forms of representation in Brazil. It seeks to bypass traditional forms of mediation and *create a parallel chain of sovereignty* by creating new spaces and channels of citizen engagement with the local state.
>
> —Baiocchi, Heller, and Silva, *Bootstrapping Democracy*, 162 (my emphasis)

From 1964 to 1985, Brazil was ruled by a military dictatorship. In the mid-1980s, the transition to an open, democratic society faced a double crisis: budget shortfalls and heavy foreign debt, combined with severe public doubt about the legitimacy of the new government. One particular municipality that forged an innovative response to these problems was an epicenter of progressive political activity, Porto Alegre. Although Porto Alegre is the capital of the wealthiest state of Brazil (Rio Grande do Sul), in the 1980s, one-third of its citizens dwelled in shantytowns or slums. In addition, the city as a whole faced a budget shortfall so severe it was unclear how to best spend the funds available (Chavez 2004, 161; Santos 2005c, 327). The post-dictatorship government was looking to legitimize itself in the eyes of the public, and this was especially the case in Porto Alegre because the key opposition party, Worker's Party (*Partido dos Trabalhadores*; PT), just won the mayoralty.

The PT was driven by a provocative mixture of social movement and/or socialist conceptions about how best to pursue social justice, which dramatically changed local politics (Chavez 2004, 160). This transformation was enabled by the new constitution (passed in 1988), which decentralized resources and authority over the provision of basic social services (Wampler 2007, 25). But the PT had not secured an electoral majority; rather, it garnered little more than 30 percent of the total vote (Chavez 2004, 161; Wampler 2007, 28). After an intense debate within the PT, a program was launched to invite participation not just from factory workers (the core constituency of the PT), but the "popular classes"—women, civil society organizations, and lumpenproles. Such an effort at inclusion was driven by the PT's desire to break from more traditional workerist party models that privileged factory—and usually male—labor as *the* subject for revolutionary change (Santos 2005c, 326–328). The issue of the focus on the worker is especially relevant to PB because the previous government had extended some rights to some people, but mostly industrial and public workers. These groups had access to housing, education, and health care, but "the vast majority of the population had limited social rights and few political rights that could be activated to allow them to expand their social and civil rights" (Wampler 2007, 23). Thus, rather than distancing themselves from or subordinating cultural and peasant-communal movements, the PT forged close ties to social movements and community-based politics in pursuit of a "post-authoritarian" democratic politics (Chavez 2004, 57–70; see also Santos 2005c, 311–312). In 1985, as the dictatorship collapsed but before the PT took power, a demand for participatory structure in regard to the municipal budget had been put forward by the Union of Neighborhood Associations of Porto Alegre (UAMPA). The new mayor Olivia Dutra picked up on this proposal and met with associations in the city. Then, through mayoral decree— *no law was ever passed*—the Participatory Budget was created (Baiocchi 2003, 47; Wampler 2007, 113–118).

PB was able to get off the ground because of the shared interests among groups pushing it combined with new institutional possibilities due in part to constitutional changes. Wampler states, "Using the state to promote social justice, opening the decision-making process to ordinary citizens, using the local state to empower individuals to exercise the rights they had won under the 1988 constitution, and subverting the clientilistic relations that have long characterized the distribution of scarce resources" (Wampler 2007, 27). PB's first years suffered from low turnout. But after a few setbacks and much trial and error with mechanisms for participation and criteria for the ranking of needs and projects, Porto Alegre's PB settled into the following formula, which has inspired so many other cities across Brazil and the globe.

PB in Porto Alegre operates as follows.[8] The process begins with neighborhood assemblies in each of the city's sixteen geographic regions—and, since 1994, six nonterritorial thematic assemblies.[9] In the local (i.e., intracity "regional") meetings, any city resident may participate. Sometimes assemblies are attended by more than a thousand participants. The purpose of these meetings is to enable residents to voice their concerns with the local government and to deliberate to determine the top three most pressing needs. Next, there are the Regional Budget Forums where delegates are elected to represent each region at the citywide level in what is called the Council of the Participatory Budgeting (COP). (Delegates serve for one year and can be reelected only once.) Here delegates from across the city's sixteen regions meet to register the needs of all the regions and then to deliberate over what needs are most pressing, *and* what region most lacks the services in question. (Shortly after the onset of the PB process, street paving, sewage infrastructure, and housing were frequently deemed to be the most pressing needs for many of the regions.) These assemblies are conducted in the presence of the mayor and his staff. During this stage of the process, technical experts are made available to the COP by the mayor's office to make sure funding requests and projects are feasible. Delegates take trips to the sites deemed most in need. After completion of the PB budget for the year, it is integrated into the mayor's budget proposal and submitted to the legislature. Because of the popular legitimacy of the PB, the PB section of the budget has for the most part gone unmodified by the legislature.[10] At the beginning of the following fiscal year a review of the past year is taken up and sometimes various procedures or criteria are altered to increase fairness or efficiency. All information about the process is made public through the Internet (Chavez 2004, 183).

Despite potential barriers posed by the technical aspects and time-consuming discussions, large numbers of participants representing broad segments of the population attended once the PD version of the process was consolidated. In 1999, after ten years, 14,000 participated, and by the early 2000s, more than 30,000 were participating (Pateman 2012). But it's not just that more people participate; the process delivers a wider range of benefits to more people. The year before the implementation of PB (1988), 75 percent of households in Porto Alegre had running water. By 2000, 98 percent had it and in that same period access to sewage lines more than doubled (from 46% to 98%). During the pre-PT government from 1986–1988, 1,714 families were provided with housing. Under PB, from 1992–1995, 28,862 were assisted. And, in education, there were twenty-nine functioning public schools in 1988. In 2000, there were eighty-six (Baiocchi 2003, 51). Indeed, as Cabannes puts it, Porto Alegre's success in terms of both the process and the results makes it "paradigmatic":

> 2010 census data indicate that 99.9 per cent of households have domestic energy, 99.35 per cent have adequate water supply, 99.72 per cent adequate domestic waste collection and 93.9 per cent adequate sanitation systems. These impressive results, obtained 20 years after the launching of the first PB in Brazil, owe much to the *priorities* of citizens and to the *mobilisation* of both citizens and local government to comply with these priorities. The results are unique for large cities in Brazil, and for most cities in the global South. (Cabannes 2014, 16, my emphasis)

As PB both increased participation and delivered results, its supporters called for its expansion. At its inception, the Porto Alegre PB was responsible for only 2 percent of the total budget, but in the 2000s it routinely reached 20 percent. And it went beyond water and sanitation, now Porto Alegre's PB handles social services, local school policy, and human rights enforcement as well as the budget of education, culture, health, social services, and sports (Baiocchi 2003).

Not only did PB in Porto Alegre reverse the priorities (see quote above) of the local government by serving the basic needs of those excluded; it inverted the relationship between ruler and ruled; rather than the usual representative model where those elected make decisions on behalf of citizens, in PB the residents make the decisions and those elected carry them out. Crucially, this also means that the expertise and capacity of the city agencies and departments must be deployed to serve the residents. It is this reversal/inversion that defines the PD nature of this paradigmatic PB.

Of course, if this innovation in governance only happened in a single town in Brazil, there wouldn't be much reason for this chapter. For those interested in PD, thankfully that is not the case. The Porto Alegre effort inspired cities across Brazil and Latin America. And now there are more than 1,700 cities doing it across the globe. So how was PB able to spread? And do these thousands of other cities follow the same model, utilize the same mechanisms, and produce the same sort of successes in terms of participation and improvements to public services? We will pick up these questions with a shift in locale, about 5,000 miles to the north, NYC.

In 2005, Participatory Budgeting Project executive director Josh Lerner and I met in Porto Alegre. Both of us were there to attend a huge gathering of activists and researchers called the World Social Forum—over 150,000 people!—to learn about things radical, democratic, and in particular PB. There we met practitioners from Brazil, Seville (Spain), and researchers from Amsterdam to Madison, Wisconsin. We too were inspired. Upon our return, we contemplated how to bring PB to the United States. We gave talks, and got nowhere for years. Then we struck upon an alderman named Joe Moore of Chicago at a related social forum in Atlanta, Georgia. After some nudging, Alderman Moore took the "PB plunge." And within two years, PB spread to the most populous city in the United States (Baez and Hernandez 2012, 319–322; Lerner 2014b).[11] And this latter case sheds some insight into how PD varies from area to area and its potentials and challenges.

NYC PB: *"Revolutionary Civics in Action"*

Like the PB in Porto Alegre, PB in NYC is a multistage process. But it looks a bit different for a few reasons. First, as in Chicago, PB in NYC began not at the citywide level but within a subsection of the city: in Chicago, a single ward (Alderman Joe Moore's forty-ninth ward), and in NYC, it began in

2011 with four city council districts (as of 2016, it's in at least thirty-four).[12] In order to get things prepared for PB at the district level, in NYC, the first stage is to bring together community leaders in the jurisdiction and form a "district committee." "Community leaders" are the persons or organizations that are tapped into the social networks of the jurisdiction and know about the needs, aspirations, and assets of the community. Such leaders are often from religious institutions or block associations or are business owners or activists. The task of the District Committee is *not* to make proposals for how to spend the money. (It often takes some time for the members to process this point!) Rather, its task is to do outreach to the different populations and regions of the jurisdiction—each NYC council district has about 140,000 people—and to set up a process that is equitable, transparent, and inclusive: the three guiding principles of NYC PB. The district committee works with the City Council member's office to do this (Kasdan and Cattell 2012, 9).

The second stage of the process is to spread the word about PB to the general public, and bring people together to discuss the needs of the district and collectively brainstorm about ideas to address these needs. This stage is similar to Porto Alegre and is done through the convening of neighborhood assemblies where dozens of people come to hear about the process and then break out into small groups (5–15 people) with trained facilitators to talk about needs and ideas. Several neighborhood assemblies are held in each district (around 3–5) and reps from the district committee and council member's office also go to already existing organizations (e.g., at a school parent-teacher organization meeting or senior center) and present on the PB process there (Kasdan, Markman, and Convey 2014, 11–12).

Another goal of the neighborhood assemblies is to encourage especially passionate residents to step up to help develop the (usually rough and partial) ideas submitted by the broad public into proposals. This third stage goes from November to February. These folks are called "budget delegates" and receive training in the basics of the budget process and in group facilitation. Budget delegates develop the proposals and then vet them with the help of city officials in accordance with the city's fiscal, technical, and regulatory criteria. All the proposals have to be within a certain price range, meet legal requirements, and get the approval of the relevant agency or agencies.[13] So, for example, a proposal for a school garden must meet the needs of the school and/or local community, be technically feasible at the site (access to sunlight, proper drainage), be within the price range (between $35,000 and $1 million), and be deemed eligible by the Department of Education (Kasdan and Cattell 2012, 7–9).

The proposals that pass these tests are then put onto a ballot. The ballot is presented to the public in February in "expos," to garner publicity and then the vote is held over the course of a week at various sites usually in late March. A *New York Times* article captured one such scene as follows:

> On a weeknight in mid-March, a room in the Park Slope Armory YMCA that is frequently used for children's birthday parties was packed with tables draped in pale yellow, 99-cent-store, vinyl coverings and topped with propped-up tri-fold poster boards. About 100 people bumped and jostled their way to the snack table lined with bowls of popcorn and pretzels. Eager presenters button-holed passersby. It looked like a middle-school science fair. But the buzz in the room wasn't over homemade solar system models or photosynthesis; *it was the sound of revolutionary civics in action.* (Sangha 2011, my emphasis)

To further enable access to the process, people could vote at a range of sites, from the council member's office to schools and churches and tables set up at grocery stores. The last phase of the process involves the formation of a monitoring committee that will follow the projects as they are implemented and go through the various stages in the city bureaucracy. Also, there is a critical review of the process that happens at each district level. That feedback is presented to the citywide steering committee who meets in the summer, in between phases, to make any changes. One change that occurred in year two was the lowering of the voting age from eighteen to sixteen. A major reason for this was lack of youth participation.[14]

NYC PB and Political Equality

In the first year (2011) in four districts, NYC PB engaged over 8,000 people over the course of the entire process. More specifically, 2,400 residents identified 2,000 project ideas to address community needs, over 300 volunteers researched, revised, and developed 78 full project proposals, and 6,000 voters chose 27 winning projects (Kasdan and Catell 2012, 10–11). In year two (2012), 13,889 participated in the allocation of $9.8 million in eight districts, and in year three, 18,184 participated in the allocation of 14.5 million in ten districts (Kasdan, Markman, and Convey 2014, 16). When compared to voting patterns in local elections, PB fared well in terms of turnout and did better from the perspective of inclusion. Overall, people of color and middle to lower income residents were better represented in PB than in the local elections (Su 2012, 10). Also, research found that PB was a site for learning about the political process, social network building, and collaboration that not only built confidence among participants but also had important benefits beyond the PB process itself (Kasdan and Cattell 2012, 18–27). In other words, not only did PB promote collective determination among segments of the community (maxD#1); it also promoted interconnection with other efforts, organizations, and issues outside of PB (maxD#4).

The report released by the research team of NYC PB gives much to ponder about PB and a number of issues already mentioned in Chapter 1. NYC's first year of PB indicated successes from multiple standpoints: in terms of the stated principles (transparency, equity, inclusion) and, PB succeeded with respect to all three, though modestly with respect to inclusion (Kasdan and Cattell 2012, 33, 20–21). Also, there is evidence that, in at least one district, the projects that were funded were more likely to go to residents comparatively lacking services and infrastructure. In other words, the rich (e.g., well served) did not get richer; instead, those with less access to infrastructure got more (Kasdan, Markman, and Convey 2014, 27).

PB reduced alienation with respect to the political process and increased the confidence of those participating as political agents (maxD#1 and maxD#2). PB increased the number of people in contact with the government at the level of elected officials, their offices, and city agencies. Overall, the contact and communications was positive and productive rather than negative and/or confrontational, but there was frustration with specific city agencies especially re: the vetting of proposals (Kasdan, Markman, and Convey 2014, 26, 28). One striking statistic from the perspective of collective determination, capability development and inequality is that 75 percent of budget delegates with a high school diploma reported becoming more comfortable contacting government agencies and officials, and 100 percent "became more comfortable negotiating and building agreement" (Kasdan and Cattell 2012, 24). Relatedly, people talked to their neighbors more about political issues and were more likely to connect with community based organizations (Kasdan and Cattell 2012, 25). Further evidence of this positivity was that more than a few projects that did not win were funded by council members who were motivated to find other sources of funds (Kasdan and Catell 2014, 27, 66).

This development of confidence also played out positively along gender lines. At the beginning of the PB process, women were less likely to be comfortable speaking publicly, but they stayed involved more so than men through the whole process. Indeed, women were overrepresented in every stage of the process, including the budget delegates phase which is where residents exert the most power in the PB process because they shape the ballot itself. When compared to elected officials at the local level, and even more so at the state and national levels, PB has many more women participating. For example, there are twice as many men as women on the NYC council, but in PB processes, more women than men participate as delegates and as voters (Kasdan, Markman, and Convey 2014, 18–19, 121).

PB fostered a more "common good" perspective and brought attention to (infra)structural inequality. As one delegate pithily put it, "People came out with a community agenda rather than a personal agenda" (Kasdan and Cattell 2012, 24). This is a core concern for practically every defender of PD, from Rousseau thru Pateman. (See Chapter 1.) Most winning projects were focused on basic needs and tended to benefit more people than less, for example, public safety infrastructure (lighting, security cameras, traffic improvements) and technology and computer upgrades for schools and libraries. In another case, a proposal was withdrawn from a ballot because it was felt that the school applying for it already had quite a few assets and other schools were in need of much more basic infrastructure. So in this case, the proposer, a teacher at a middle school, withdrew his proposal for a green laboratory and outdoor teaching space and instead his budget delegate committee looked at projects proposed at schools with the highest need. There they found a project for fixing tiles and putting doors on toilets in a children's restroom in PS 124 (Lerner 2014b, 28–30). Cases of this sort occurred in other districts as well (Su 2012, 8; Lerner 2014b, 24–32).

Comparing PB in Porto Alegre and NYC

Overall, PB in Porto Alegre and NYC creates places for democratic community building that are both critical and constructive, agonistic and protagonistic. At its best, PB helps to create an institutional matrix for the production of a democratic culture and sensibility. It does this in a manner that is multifaceted and multidimensional. There is extensive literature that demonstrates this in Porto Alegre. (See above.) In NYC, there are some indications of this happening in some of the districts but it's still very early in the process. Here PB imparts or develops skills that are needed to bring together diverse populations in a jurisdiction. It creates a setting—especially in the neighborhood assemblies—where people from divergent or conflicting social positions can talk about needs and ideas to meet those needs. The assemblies do this by utilizing trained facilitators from the participating communities or from supporting organizations. PB also offers a setting where individuals can develop and exercise deliberative skills and learn about the machinations of the particular political processes (this is especially true for the budget delegates). Indeed, one facet of PB that always pleases the council members and their staff is that residents are exposed to the bureaucratic restrictions that proposals often face. For example, school garden proposals in the forty-fifth district were subject to the jurisdictions of Departments of Transportation, Education, Parks, and the State Dormitory Authority. Residents are also exposed to the costs: yes, a new watering system for a park costs $100,000 and bus location signs screens more than twice that (Kasdan, Markman, and Convey 2014, 26). A related benefit is that residents get a better sense of how much civil servants do (Cabannes 2014, 36).

PB is equipped to aid in the construction of a new kind of institutional engagement. Not only is it a multimonth process in its operation but its track record shows that it often persists over many years. This could help to cultivate a broader democratization since it is not only a funding source for multiple years, but it is a site for the cultivation of relationships among the community, CSOs, NGOs, and local government. It also has a well-defined calendar that allows for regular interaction and long-term planning. In Porto Alegre and NYC, research has shown that PB practitioners do build upon skills and connections developed within PB and then extend them to efforts and projects outside of it (maxD#2 and maxD#4).

PB enables a community to play a role in *defining* its priorities relative to their locale, thereby creating a sense of ownership (e.g., maxD#1). It calls on constituents not just to name problems, critique, or block projects but to actually make the proposals to address these issues. It pollinates and creates cross group collaborations, and reaches the uninitiated and not-usual suspects. It also nicely articulates the core of my definition of PD: "A process by which we try to operationalize the equality of all the members of the group." (See Chapter 1.) By devoting resources to bring in persons and groups normally excluded, PB enables persons and groups without traditional resources or sociopolitical capital to shape the process (maxD#2 and maxD#3). And because it subjects all proposals to public discussion and deliberation, it decreases corruption and patronage and increases the chances that said projects will produce important community benefits. Also, because multiple projects are funded in any given cycle, PB in NYC and Porto Alegre avoid a "winner take all" situation and thus avoid the divisiveness of elections and referenda.

The *differences* between PB in Porto Alegre and NYC are most apparent in terms of who started it, how many participate, and, most important, not just *who* decides which proposals to fund but *how* the who decides what proposals are chosen. In Porto Alegre, and throughout Brazil, the Worker's Party was the key supporter and proliferator of PB. In NYC and the United States, the Participatory Budgeting Project (PBP; a nonprofit NGO) played they key role. In Brazil, PB was driven by a political party in a mix with other social movements as part of a large and comprehensive national political movement (Touchton and Wampler 2014, 1447). In the United States, PB also was tied to a larger national framework, the U.S. Social Forum, but was not supported by a major political party. Also, the spread of PB in the United States was due to the efforts of PBP working with relatively isolated elected officials, and the different cities that chose to do it had no real political connections beforehand.

The spread of PB in the United States is indicative of the "network" politics model, which is driven more by NGOs than political parties. Operationally, network politics functions in a much more decentralized and horizontal manner than hierarchical political parties with their central committees disseminating platforms and talking points. And while political parties operate in terms of nation-states and their subunits (states, cities, counties, etc.), network politics is more local and transnational and stretches across multiple layers of a fragmented landscape, more so in terms of affinity than territory or jurisdiction. Indeed, PBP operates in both Canada and the United States and is frequently invited to other countries to advise on starting PB processes. And PBP's board of directors and advisory board, from which it formulates policy and conducts oversight, has members from multiple countries. The staying power and efficacy of these nonprofit networks, however, are limited as they tend to be especially underresourced relative to the political parties.[15]

A second difference concerns how many participate. In Porto Alegre, a city of 1.4 million, 30,000 participated in the annual cycle in the 2000s (see also Sintomer et al. 2012, 5–6). In NYC, a city of 8 million, more than 50,000 participated in its fourth year (Community Development Project 2015). Crucially, there are also some key differences in the structures of the processes. Many PB programs in Brazil adopt a "quality of life index," which allocates greater resources on a per capita basis to poorer neighborhoods (Wampler 2007, 2012). This creates a bias in favor of the poor, thereby encouraging poor citizens to participate. It is also designed to encourage greater spending on the types of policy problems that most strongly affect poor neighborhoods (e.g., access to public health care and public housing, building basic infrastructure) (Sintomer et al. 2013, 27). Research on PB in Brazil has demonstrated that majorities of participants and elected PB delegates are low income, have low levels of education, and are often women, thus confirming that PB rules have successfully expanded public venues to include poor and traditionally excluded sectors (Touchton and Wampler 2014, 1447). However, research has also shown that the most vulnerable, the poorest of the poor, are usually not effectively integrated into the process (Pateman 2012, 11–12).

The most tangible difference between NYC and Porto Alegre is in regard to who votes and how they vote. In NYC, *residents* choose the proposals. In Porto Alegre, *delegates* elected by the residents in the assemblies choose the proposals in the COP. The other difference, though, is that in Porto Alegre, the ballot of proposals to be voted on is in part structured by need. That is, those neighborhoods with greater need are much more likely to have their proposals on the ballot and have an increased chance of winning the vote (Wampler 2007, 52–53). In NYC, no formal measures like this are in place, and, although budget delegates are urged to consider need, there is no mechanism to formally favor the least advantaged areas (Kasdan, Markman, and Convey 2014, 73). Despite their differences, it is my view that both Porto Alegre and NYC PBs are maximally democratic. Each has fulfilled all four norms although Porto Alegre on a scale and with a history that dwarfs that of NYC.[16] But what about the 1,000s of other PBs? Are they of the same PD/maxD type?

PB Spreads! Numbers, Types, and Best Practices

> [PB] is a mechanism (or a process) by which the population define [*sic*] the destination of part or the totality of public resources. The participatory budgeting is a process of direct democracy, universal and voluntary, through which the population can discuss and define the public budget and policies. PB combines direct democracy and representative democracy.
>
> —YVES CABANNES, "20 CITIES," 8[17]

For many years, my view was that what makes a budget allocation process PB is that residents have control over, and play a role in, *every* stage in the process. As such, if residents are excluded from some part of the process (proposal generation, proposal selection, etc.), that might be an improvement on the previous situation, but it's not a PB. But reading the analyses of Sintomer et al. and Cabannes has convinced me that I am being too strict for at least two reasons. Sintomer et al. define PB as a process that "allows the participation of non-elected citizens in the conception and/or allocation of public finances." Five other criteria must be met for Sintomer et al.: a finite budget is at issue, the city level is involved (not just a neighborhood), it has to be repeated for multiple years, there must be some form of public deliberation, and there is accountability with respect to the proposals generated and the funds allocated (Sintomer et al. 2012, 2–3). Cabannes's definition is similar; for him, PB is a practice where "citizens meet to agree on priorities for part of the local government budget for their neighborhood or the city as a whole and oversee the project implementation" (Cabannes 2014, 3). In other words, for Cabannes, it's about having communities set the *priorities* and government acting on these priorities. Even if a community doesn't have formal power in the project selection phase, if their priorities are driving the selection process, then it is still worth designating the budget allocation a PB. According to this measure, there are at least 1,700 PBs in the world. However, I still would not necessarily deem these PD PBs because some fail to meet maxD#1, the collective determination requirement.

The other reason for including these non-PD attempts to democratize budget allocations and manage public resources within the PB rubric is because political conditions vary so much. In authoritarian China, what would be denigrated as a mere "consultation" process in Brazil can be quite remarkable and impactful (Cabannes and Ming 2013; Sintomer et al. 2012, 65–67). In Africa, where states lack capacity if not always resources, a PB opened a budget line for social services that previously did not exist. In other words, it was not about communities "reclaiming" public services; it was about communities using the government to *create* them! Relatedly, in at least three other cities studied by Cabannes, PB helped to increase fiscal and tax revenues (Cabannes 2014, 6, 26). In some municipalities, PB generated financial and nonfinancial resources beyond the strictly defined public budget—including community resources and voluntary work. In others, matching funds were negotiated from other tiers of government: for example, some popular projects that lacked PB funding in NYC were funded by other agencies (Kasdan, Markman, and Convey 2014, 35). Still other cities received funds from private sources or international aid agencies (Cabannes 2014, 6). In other words, what happens in PB does not always stay within PB; demands originating in a PB occasionally pressure other parts of government to act. And a process that seems like a pretty watered-down PB can actually make a big impact on the tax base or governmental priorities.

This brings us to another point about the different types of PB: all PBs should not be judged relative to the model and successes of Porto Alegre. On the one hand, yes, there are some well-done PD PBs such as NYC that we value, but still, they are not nearly as robust as Porto Alegre's PB (especially because of size of the budget allocated). But again, we admire them because they are done in different sorts of political circumstances, without support from a political party, or without major CSOs, etc. But then there are PBs that have innovated a different model of PD; they have invented other mechanisms and frameworks that have benefited populations not served in Porto Alegre. For example, youth PB and gender budgeting (Cabannes 2014). Indeed, when one looks at the current landscape of PB, the sheer number of cities is remarkable as are the different sizes of these cities and jurisdictions: from Rheinstetten, a German municipality with 20,529 inhabitants, to Chengdu, China, an urban-rural regional jurisdiction of more than 14 million. And there are starkly different cultural contexts: from Chicago to Madagascar, the Dominican Republic to South Korea, Long Beach (California) to Kerala, India. And there are different types of budgets: in Brazil, there is a PB for home ownership (Belo Horizonte) and another is linked with strategic planning and finance (Santo Andre), a serious limitation of PB in Porto Alegre in the early years.[18] In the technological center of Campinas (969,396 inhabitants), the PB process controls *all* of the investment budget of the city! In Alvorada—a poor municipality (183,968 inhabitants) in the state of Rio Grande do Sul—PB has increased tax revenue growth.[19] Outside of Brazil, there are PBs for financial planning and financing small businesses and households, the aforementioned Rheinstetten and Chengdu (Cabannes 2004, 30; Cabannes and Ming 2013). And, in Chengdu, as in the state level

PB in Rio Grand do Sul (Brazil), PB is used, quite unusually, to address urban-rural problems (Cabannes 2014, 13–20; Cabannes and Ming 2013; Sintomer, Herzberg, and Allegretti 2013, 28–29). Other innovative PBs are in Ilo (Peru) and Nahampoana (Madagascar), where PB is carried out with royalties paid by mining companies. Indeed, Cabannes considers Ilo to be the most complex and novel governance process of all the cities he has studied (Cabannes 2014, 21, 31).

Countries with the most PBs relative to the size of the population are the Dominican Republic, Peru, and Poland (Sintomer, Herzberg, and Allegretti 2013, 33). The cities that use the highest percentage of their budget for PB include the aforementioned Ilo, Peru, and Campinas, Brazil. Others that rank high include Ampasy Nahampona in Madagascar, Seville (Spain), and Santiago de los Caballeros, Dominican Republic (population 678,300), where the figure was 44.3 percent (Cabannes 2014, 22, 33).[20] And the best PBs? For Cabannes, Porto Alegre, Guarulhos, and Ilo stand out for their remarkable improvements in basic service provision (Cabannes 2014, 24). For Sintomer et al., the top PBs are Porto Alegre, Fissel (Senegal), Villa El Salvador (Peru), and, to a lesser extent, but still very good, Seville (Spain), Dong-ku (South Korea), and Catachi (Ecuador).[21] In sum, the diversity of places using PB on the lists above shows that, despite much skepticism early on, PB can flourish in very different cultural and demographic contexts,[22] at different scales, with different types of funds. How far we have come from ancient Athens! (See Chapter 1.)

Praising and Criticizing PB: Good Governance or Participatory Democracy?

At the beginning of this book, I noted that my initial exposure with PB was mired in confusion. Although not many had heard of it, those that had praised it for different reasons. From the sketch so far, it is easy to see why. PB delivers measurable benefits on many different registers.[23] As noted at the beginning of the chapter, there are three types of general benefits of PB: *PB improves public service provision and increases the number of people who benefit from city services. PB expands access of populations to government processes and expands contact of government agencies to the broader public. PB enables empowered participation: it creates a new avenue for popular participation in which people have decisive (rather than consultative) power and develop agency.* But each of these benefits can be characterized in different ways and have different political perspectives attached to them. Indeed, even among PB advocates, there is a tension among those who praise it. The preeminent PD scholar Carole Pateman articulates this split among PB advocates nicely in a close reading of a World Bank report. She notes that the World Bank praises

PB for improving the performance and accountability of the bureaucracy. However, she praises it for different reasons. She writes, "While bureaucratic accountability and increased performance are all to the good—they are a necessary condition for democracy and participatory budgeting—they are not what PB is about, not, at least, if one is interested in participatory democracy and democratization" (Pateman 2012, 13). Indeed, another preeminent PD scholar, Boa Santos, made the same point several years before in a landmark essay (Santos 2005c). The title of the anthology in which his article appears sums up his view of PB quite nicely, "Democratizing Democracy." But the juxtaposition of "good governance" with "democratizing democracy" is too either/or. The problem with this dichotomy is that, in my view, "good governance" is fairly neutral; so it doesn't actually address the ways in which PB can play into a positive or negative politics. In other words, it's not just that PB is either good or a harmless waste of time; it can also have negative political repercussions. Or, more accurately, there are fears that it can promote a (neoliberal) politics that further erodes state capacity to promote the broad public good, and instead it creates state partnerships with private actors in which the state "withers" and inequality is intensified. This is what I call "neoliberal efficiency," and while it overlaps in some ways with "good governance," it is distinct from it, just as it is opposed to the politics of participatory democracy, and the ways in which it understands and deploys PB.

Three Frames for Praising PB
1. **Neoliberal Efficiency:** Public helps the government do more with less; efficiency of government is increased.
2. **Good Governance:** Those elected and agencies are more accountable and political process is more transparent *for* the public; reduces government corruption and patronage; legitimacy of government is enhanced.
3. **Participatory Democracy:** Public helps the government do more with more (i.e., PB increases the range of resources available for public control and benefit); government supports individual and collective agency.

When we look at each "general benefit" of PB (first laid out in this chapter's Introduction), the different frameworks characterize the benefits in divergent and sometimes conflicting ways.

Benefit 1: PB Increases the Quality and Quantity of Public Services

This consequentialist focus on results can play out in different ways. The PT developed PB in Brazil as part of a broader "popular administration" platform. Santos calls PB a "redistributive" democratic mechanism since it gets goods to those who most need it and connects them to the broader city (Santos 2005c; Harvey 2012, 4). In Porto Alegre, PB benefited mostly working- and lower-class members; for example, neighborhoods without sewers now have them. When such benefits flow to those most in need, PB embodies what is called the "right to the city" frame. But in other cases (e.g., Germany), PB's benefits go to the middle class more so than the poor (Sintomer et al. 2013, 48–49). Also, when projects focus not on basic needs but on less vital services—dog parks are a notorious example in the United States—PB might not be said to fulfill its paradigmatic "right to the city" frame.

The negative version of the above is that PB could enable further budget cuts because it more effectively spends public money and/or benefits more people but does not reduce class or racial inequality. This might be called the neoliberal justification of PB that some believe motivates the World Bank to endorse it. Relatedly, but less harshly, PB is criticized by some members of the "radical left" for being too "bread and butter": for installing street lights and sewers but not taking on the deeper issues of structural inequality in terms of class, race, and gender. That is, it's too "rice and beans" oriented (Santos 2005c, 337), or more cynically, rearranging the deck chairs on a sinking ship (Lerner 2014b, 28). Here the justification for PB is not neoliberal, but more likely the good governance frame. But critics maintain that this good governance justification permits PB to modify pieces of infrastructure but doesn't change the logic of the city. The big money still goes to sports stadiums and business districts rather than, say, affordable housing and public schools. Because the amount of money in PB is limited, it also encourages a "more bang for the buck" mentality that aims for efficiency and/or resource maximization. And this is why the World Bank has praised it, along with other more business-oriented and traditional economic development organizations. Indeed, because of the way it improves infrastructure for everyday life and the economy, it also is favored by those fond of quality-of-life frameworks. Since the advent of PB, Porto Alegre has made incredible improvements on this front. Indeed, the influential business journal *Exame* has designated Porto Alegre to be the Brazilian city with the best quality of life based on the following criteria: literacy, enrollment in elementary and secondary education, quality of higher and postgraduate education, per capita consumption, employment, child mortality, life expectancy, number of hospital beds, housing, sewage, airports, highways, crime rate, restaurants, and climate (Santos 2005c, 310). The "neutral" version of efficacy is the good governance framework: service delivery is improved, but again there is little attention to whether or not it reduces inequality. The positive (PD) version of benefit 1 is that it reduces inequality and fosters an inclusive right to the city framework.

Benefit 2: PB Brings More People into the Governance
Process and Gives Them Access to Power

> There is extensive literature that has shown that traditional policy-
> making venues in Brazil are primarily open to small numbers of elected
> officials and appointed government officials. If Nylen's arguments can be
> substantiated, then it will be plausible to assert that PB is helping to
> transform political life in Brazil. Avritzer and I argue that one of the
> primary effects of PB is that it is helping to change the basic processes
> through which citizens gain access to resources.
> —BRIAN WAMPLER, *PARTICIPATORY BUDGETING IN BRAZIL*, 34

And PB does so in a way that enables government resources to better meet
people's needs as defined by the people, in concert with city agencies and
experts (that is, produce more of benefit 1 above).

Here the negative neoliberal version is that the government enhances its
legitimacy by opening its doors and increasing transparency—"look how we
listen to and give power to the people!"—but the *scope* of the budget is severely limited so, even if many participate, they have very little impact on
public service provision overall. The neutral good governance version just
looks at the numbers participating, and the size of the budgets, but doesn't
consider whose agenda is driving the process (e.g., which community, the
agencies, a political party?) and is less concerned with inclusion. Participating in PB renders the governance process more transparent: elected officials
and government bureaucrats are put into direct contact with residents.
Residents learn about the budget process, who has what power and expertise,
and what things cost. Good governance advocates like PB because more
people are involved in "politics." This makes the government more responsive to people's needs, and it increases the government's legitimacy. This
means that the budget process is less corrupt: the moneys are better tracked
to prevent mismanagement, and patronage is reduced because there must be
public justification of the proposals rather than backroom deals. The positive
PD version is that not only do more people participate and the size of the pots
of money increase but power shifts to communities and inclusion increases,
inequality decreases, and the capacity of the community is enhanced and
influences other non-PB parts of the governance process and administration.

Benefit 3: PB Enables Empowered Participation
and Capability Development (Political Agency)

As argued in Chapter 1, collective determination as political agency is at the
core of the participatory democracy frame and distinguishes it from other
views. From the PD perspective, there are two ways of understanding benefit
3. Some praise PB for developing the capacities of those participating even if

the benefits of the service provision are unclear or not pronounced.[24] In other words, for some PD advocates, a major reason for praising PB has little to do with the *results* of the process. Yes, better services are great, but the uniqueness of PB is that people are not just passive recipients of benefits; they develop their own capabilities (maxD#2) in an empowering group setting (maxD#1) that reduces inequality and creates relations of shared authority (maxD#3). They discuss with each other their needs and develop the proposals themselves. And they have access to resources to develop their capabilities and the knowledge base to do so. When done well, this increases the deliberative skills and social capital of those participating, which increases individual agency as well as social solidarity and collective power. Furthermore, the development of agency can have benefits outside of PB: it can help residents act with better intelligence and efficacy in other political matters—whether at the local community or national election levels. As noted in Chapter 1, Mill and liberal PD stressed these sorts of benefits: having small-scale local democracy, even if it doesn't deliver much direct benefit, creates better citizens for the more important venues. Others report that PB develops forms of collective agency that have enabled groups to pursue democratic forms outside of politics, for example, collective housing (Baiocchi 2003, 58–59).

In other words, for many the power of PB is less about the projects and more about the process; PB is significant because it develops the deliberative capabilities of the individuals in a community and fosters cooperation without eliminating contestation. It is a training ground for deliberative democracy, community building, and community empowerment, since these communities not only enter the political process but also become accountable to it because they are making decisions (Santos 2005c, 310). In sum, the good governance paradigm does not adequately capture what PB does so well in so many of the cities named above. These PDs are more about agency, and the good governance frame at best does not care, or, at worst, is opposed to such a power transfer and capability development.

From Deliberation to Empowered Participatory Governance

> The fundamental idea of democratic legitimacy is that the authorization to exercise state power must arise from the collective decisions of the members of a society who are governed by that power.
> —JOSHUA COHEN, "PROCEDURE AND SUBSTANCE IN DELIBERATIVE DEMOCRACY," 95

Based on this last section, some might say that PB is a very rich form of deliberative democracy insofar as it is fosters reasoned debate and exchange.

But PB goes further. Its mission is not just deliberation about priorities and policies. It is about the formulation, implementation, and monitoring of projects. Put simply, deliberative democracy is about authorization. PD is about governance. In addition, PB has innovated mechanisms to address some of the critiques of deliberative views: that it reinforces existing hierarchies, empowers the best speakers, and so on (Baiocchi 2003, 52–57). In this sense, PB addresses worries of deliberative democrats who are critical of privileging some forms of deliberation but are nevertheless sympathetic to the deliberative view.

Why PB is not just about deliberation can perhaps best be seen when comparing it to forums promoted by deliberative democrats such as citizen assemblies, citizen juries, deliberation days, and deliberative polling. Many of these "minipublics" seem like PB: they involve nonelected "regular" people and get them together to debate and brainstorm about important topics. But the details of their operations reveal crucial differences.

Citizen assemblies and citizen juries are specially commissioned forums—usually hosted by a government, agency, or nongovernmental organization—where persons deliberate about subject matter chosen not by them but by a "commissioning body." Such forums are inclusive because the commissioning bodies select those who can participate (unlike PB, it's invitation only). Like PB, the facilitation is guided, and expertise is brought to the table (by the sponsoring organization). At the end of their deliberations, the participants prepare a report and recommendations (Pateman 2012, 8; Gilman 2012, 3; Van Reybrouck 2017, chapter 4). Such a process goes hand in hand with the major principles of the deliberative democratic view: (1) an arena is constructed for discussion to produce more inclusive and rational judgments; (2) individual's preferences are subject to criticism and individuals are exposed to multiple viewpoints, expertise, and information (Cohen 1996; Young 2000, 21–27); and (3) the forums aim to impact policy making or improve some institution's problem-solving capability. And all these norms are important for PD as well. These minipublics could certainly constitute an improvement on the existing representative state system; they may even contribute to good governance. But as Pateman notes, "PB is not a specially commissioned event for which a few citizens are chosen, but a regular part of a vital area of municipal government" (Pateman 2012, 11). If the deliberative minipublics operate without any transfer of power, and if there is no empowering of the group deliberating, then it is not a PB. What these forums do is construct a new information input into a governance process, but they do not change the logic or the power relations of the decision makers in the process. As Pateman states, "Deliberative democracy still leaves intact the conventional institutional structures and political meaning of 'democracy.'" (Pateman 2012, 10). It does not give deliberators decisive power, nor does it put them in relation to elected officials or city agencies.

Indeed, many deliberative democrats explicitly avoid such power-laden settings, since they could interfere with the deliberators' ability to make rational informed judgments.

With respect to established models in democratic theory, I would argue that PB is better understood as a form of empowered participatory governance (EPG) as laid out by Fung and Wright and others (Fung and Wright 2003b; see also Sintomer, Herzberg, and Allegretti 2013, 40). The difference in the names reveals much: PB is not just about deliberation; it's about governance. Deliberative democracy struggles to create a rational discursive setting; this means striving for a diverse group but also keeping the space from being corrupted. EPG also stresses the importance of deliberation not just for big policy issues but "tangible problems" that enter into a much messier dynamic that requires three *institutional* features: (1) devolution to local empowered unit; (2) "creation of formal linkages of responsibility, resource distribution, and communication that connect these units to each other and to superordinate, centralized authorities; and (3) the creation of new institutional forms for interface (Fung and Wright 2003b, 15–16). Again, PB pursues all of these; minipublics do not. Once we enter the terrain of the institutional changes that PB requires, the divide between legislation and administration is breached. PB is not just about formulating priorities; it's about realizing projects. This requires bringing the popular into the administrative, the people into the government agencies. This is again something that PD frequently requires but deliberative democracy does not.[25]

Evaluating the Impacts of PB (and More Criticisms)

One of the biggest difficulties facing participatory democratic views like PB is not justifying them; it's showing that they are doable. (See my Chapter 1.) How effective is it in the real world? In this section, we will delve more into the particulars about the ability of actually existing PBs to realize their myriad norms and goals.[26] How should we measure PB's successes and failures? Building on the previous discussions of Porto Alegre and NYC and the benefits, norms, and the principles of PD and maxD, I offer the following re-articulations[27] of each MaxD principle in order to operationalize PB's norms and evaluate its impact.

Measuring the Success of PD PB (Four Goals)

maxD#1*: Enable effective and democratic community control of the
    PB *process* and promote capability development: this requires
    securing state support for a community-driven process and creating a space where persons may enhance individual and collective capacities in order to gain knowledge of the political process
    and community needs, deliberate over priorities, integrate

diverse constituencies, mediate conflict, and creatively collaborate to formulate projects.

maxD#2*: Promote effective and responsive *governance* to develop, choose, and implement quality projects that meet community needs.[28]

maxD#3*: Reduce political and economic *inequality* in terms of the process and the projects.

maxD#4*: Strengthen "civil society" broadly construed: to support associations, civil society organizations (CSOs), and community-based organizations (CBOs) to enhance their PD capabilities and increase their impact and numbers.

So how does PB play out with respect to these four? As one might expect, the results are mixed. For each category, I note PB successes, failures (or "flaws"), and limitations.

For maxD#1*, there seems to be a range of evidence that PD PB often has positive impacts. Again, this is a requirement for a PB to be considered PD PB, but we should note that, for example, in NYC, increases in individual and collective PD skills will come primarily, if at all, to budget delegates, not, for example, to voters. That is, NYC PB is truly PD only for a very few.[29] And even for delegates, it may not be as intensive as one would hope. And although it is possible that voters were at assemblies, and did debate about proposals with their neighbors, there is little evidence to support this one way or another. Intriguingly, some have contemplated requiring participation in deliberative venues for voting eligibility. This leads to a PD trade-off question: the more requirements you place on participants, the fewer will partake of the process. And for those who do want to participate, increasing capability development requires more material support for the process, for example, more funding. Asking those elected for more resources often turns them off or excludes locales with fewer resources. In NYC, turnout has been relatively low, and there is pressure to shorten the PB calendar—too many events and meetings—but such a shortening could decrease the amount of 1*.

PB and Deliberation: Lessons from NYC

This leads to another question: what is the minimum standard of deliberation? And, how does an actually existing PB deal with the trade-offs issue? Above, I emphasized that PB is more than deliberative democracy because it involves a level of agency and power sharing not mandated by deliberative models. Yet any PD view requires deliberation to occur. But what counts as "deliberation" in the real-world PB context? It's fairly easy to define: deliberation entails giving reasons for one's view, facing questions and criticisms from others, considering other views, and unpacking the values and interests driving a particular position or proposal. But in public discussions of issues and proposals over many months, this is not so easy to assess. For example, deliberation is supposed to occur in NYC PB at the "assemblies" but more so when the budget delegates are developing the proposals that will be put on the ballot for the community to vote upon. Research on the NYC process questions how much deliberation took place in some meetings in some districts. Gilman notes that, in particular, there is a tension, and a trade-off, between the norms of inclusion and efficiency (Gilman 2012, 2).

Because PB is part of the NYC budget allocation process, it is in some ways "results driven" since it aims to deliver quality proposals in a time-restricted environment. This need for efficiency brings with it trade-offs. Gilman writes,

> The results-driven model mitigated the strong opinions of budget delegates. One consequence of heavy-handed, stern facilitation was fewer opportunities for heated disagreement between participants. The absence of serious moral disagreement, in turn, short-circuited the exchange of reasoning that forms the core of the deliberative democratic ideal. Where citizens cannot disagree, they cannot learn from one another, nor can they learn to accept the validity of other ideological and moral points of view. (Gilman 2012, 10)

But in other discussions in NYC PB, the process model included diverse views, enabled debate and deliberation, and promoted creative problem solving. Why such successes in some meetings but not in others? Sometimes success was a result of the facilitator's ability to implement the process. Yet the composition of the neighborhood was also a factor, "Especially in more heterogeneous districts, with more avenues for disagreement, results-structured deliberation opened up spaces for genuine deliberation and discussion. In more homogenous and less conflict-prone districts, the results-driven model runs the risk of dissuading innovative proposals and leading to greater disillusionment" (Gilman 2012, 14). Other groups and facilitators opted for more of a process model and understood the benefits of deliberation from a more long-term perspective. Gilman notes,

> When given the option to make a results-based decision they decided to prize deliberation above all. Ultimately, their project was put on the ballot, received a low number of votes, and was not chosen by the residents. Yet, all the participants were still confident in their decisions. "Even though our project was not chosen, we began the process to put forth the type of proposal we want to better our neighborhood. This is just the beginning," one delegate recounted. (Gilman 2012, 12)

According to Gilman, PB NYC was able to integrate both norms, though unevenly at times. The difficulties of the NYC process noted, many PBs don't even approach the richness of its deliberations however variable. In Europe, many PBs (e.g., Lisbon, Rome) have lower-quality deliberation than NYC due to both the structure of the process and the quality of facilitation (Sintomer et al. 2012, 19–21). Indeed, in some PB's, the agenda is predetermined. Some are neoliberal; others progressive. Sometimes it's a state-party led agenda ("neo-corporatist"); other times NGO driven.[30] For example, there are PB's that focus on making budgets more responsive to consumer demands with respect to some government service. Sintomer et al. name PBs in Zeguo (China), Bukavu (Congo), and Cologne (Germany) as examples of this approach (Sintomer et al. 2012, 23). Whoever is driving the agenda, whatever the politics, from a PD perspective, democratic ownership of the process ("maxD#1*") suffers. And this impairs the scope of deliberation far more than the trade-offs faced by NYC PB.

MaxD#2*: **Promote effective and responsive *governance* to develop, choose, and implement quality projects that meet community needs.** PB is not only more likely to address real basic needs than traditional budget processes, but it gets more bang for the buck since "popular" oversight allows for a degree of vetting and supervision that reduces corruption and makes sure that projects are not full of expensive bells and whistles that do not directly address needs. Also, PB allocations can "have a strong catalytic effect and channel both monetary and non-monetary resources" (Cabannes 2014, 9). The PB in Chengdu has been exemplary in this regard. PB also reduces the number of projects built that have little public benefit (Cabannes 2014, 25–27).

A weakness here is that PB can be too short term in its focus and fragmented in its vision. In other words, focusing on immediate and basic needs at the local level can backfire because many needs cannot be met by simply upgrading existing services within a neighborhood. Having better water pipes and drainage means little if the water treatment plant across town is substandard. "Safer streets" presupposes that those same streets actually take you somewhere you want to go. PB needs to be much more engaged in large-scale infrastructure debates and the envisioning of the city's future. And this means connecting PB to participatory planning bodies. In the abstract, this sounds doable. There are many examples of participatory planning procedures and PB would seem a well suited to help foster a more robust planning process. But here the problem is not imagination; it's politics. Since the 1970s, much large-scale urban planning has been driven by a private investment model of economic growth that caters to high-end residential development and services oriented toward the same such residents and consumers and tourists with much disposable income. (See Chapter 6.) And, as if breaking with that model were not difficult enough, a PD planning process would require obtaining long-term financing as well (Cabannes 2014, 7).

A few cities have made strides in this regard (Porto Alegre, Ilo), but, even in those cities, it would be tough to argue that PB had led cities themselves to a "reversal of priorities" at the level of planning and urban development. No city has been remade by PB, yet. Indeed, such a shift would entail a multidimensional reorganization of city agencies and their relationship to financing as well as public participation.[31]

MaxD#3*: Reduce political and economic *inequality* in terms of the process and the projects. The most overt way in which PB reduces inequality in the city is by obtaining improvements that give lower-income communities better basic services. Belo Horizonte is exemplary in this regard (Pateman 2012, 12). But PB doesn't usually raise people's income or enable them to obtain property (Belo Horizonte and Chengdu are exceptions) (Cabannes and Ming 2013, 263–270). PB oftentimes improves their basic services, especially in terms of water/sewage/sanitation, public safety, transportation and roads, and energy and electricity. To a lesser extent, PB often delivers benefits with respect to basic health services, education, and parks (Cabannes 2014, 8–9). However, there are those projects that are born of special interests that actually exacerbate inequalities in the community through what is sometimes called "resource hoarding": for example, an already comparatively advantaged school or park gets an upgrade, the poorly maintained ones get nothing. Porto Alegre's PB has built in checks preventing this sort of situation, but U.S. PBs do not. Although there are many cases where PB has been shown to improve the situation of the working-class and low-income populations, I am not aware of any PBs that have exacerbated inequalities, although there are anecdotal examples of projects of PB that are "frivolous" or serve better off residents.[32]

MaxD#4*: Strengthen "civil society" broadly construed. Does PB strengthen civil society or allow powerful actors to co-opt it? One of the best ways for PB to maximize or democratize democracy is by empowering those groups and organizations that support maxD#1. This increases the chances that communities can obtain maxD#2* in a way that reduces political and economic inequality (maxD#3*). The development of nonstate, nonbusiness associations and organizations are often thought to play this role. Indeed, Porto Alegre's PB was initiated for precisely these reasons: to support civil society and make government more responsive to it. Most of the literature about PB and "empowerment" is not on the more liberal PD, J. S. Mill–oriented individual and collective capability development but on the relationship between (the more Tocquevillean) associationist PD and the connections between associations and civil society (which also could be A-PD or S-PD). Many claim that PB has numerous positive effects on civil society, and, overall, it is a mechanism that strengthens it. However, it is misleading to talk in terms of "PB and civil society" because there are three different modalities of civil society and some of them work *against* PD. Put another way, from a PD perspective, civil society is not always something to be supported. Indeed, some of its forms should be undermined or eliminated.

Tocqueville Was Wrong?

Early on in the debates about PB, a key question was the following: does PB *require* a strong civil society to work? The answer—after decades of experiments and research—is a qualified, "no." Tocqueville was wrong (Baiocchi, Heller, and Silva 2011, 142).[33] There are some very effective PBs that succeeded in locales *without* a strong civil society. A second question travels in the opposite direction: does PB strengthen civil society? This can happen through increasing the number of CSOs, or through the generation of social capital. In a large case study by Touchton and Wampler of PBs in Brazil, they found that PB often does both (Touchton and Wampler 2014, 1456). They then proceed to detail a very specific list of the ways in which PB strengthens civil society and in a PD manner (which I highlight in the text):

> several key rules associated with PB promote the strengthening of civil society. These rules include internal vote aggregation, which encourages individuals to form groups and for groups to forge alliances with other stable groups; a preferential bias in favor of poor groups, which encourages poor citizens and communities to participate in policy making; citizen mobilization supported by government funds but organized by groups (i.e., transportation to distant meetings); and, finally, increased ease of oversight of policy implementation. Therefore, the institutional rules of this new democratic institution promote new organizations because the rules favor collective action via community groups. *A more mobilized citizenry then has greater opportunities to pressure government officials to fund public goods that correspond to their interests* while also decreasing the cost for citizens to monitor state action (see Table 2). (Touchton and Wampler 2014, 1457, my emphasis)

This passage touches on core principles of maxD and PD: PB promotes collective determination (e.g., from vote aggregation to group agenda setting), capability development (e.g., skills for policy making), and the active interconnection of groups sharing these norms (it encourages the formation of groups and "alliances" among them and a "mobilized citizenry" acting to actualize the public good). And it does this in a manner that addresses inequality ("favors poor groups") and replaces relations of inequality with those of shared authority (maxD#3). In Touchton and Wampler's survey, PB processes also address a key weakness cited above regarding PB's fragmentation and short-term focus: "*Our results imply PB is associated with long-term institutional and political change—not just short-term shifts in funding priorities.* PB is an important proxy that captures shifts in basic governance arrangements" (Touchton and Wampler 2014, 1458). In these Brazilian cases, then, PB seems to both democratize democracy and strengthen civil society. But in another major study by Baiocchi, Heller, and Silva, a subtly different set of lessons emerged as they looked at PB's impact on populations who are outside of (organized) civil society (Baiocchi, Heller, and Silva 2011, 114).

First off, Baiocchi, Heller, and Silva differentiate between social capital and CSOs. PB does and has increased the number of *individuals* in interaction with one another and the government. But, sometimes PB increases the number of interactions they have with one another and the government *without* increasing the number of CSOs. That is, PB mattered more for improving *engagement*, not for improving the self-organizing capacity of the CSOs (Baiocchi, Heller, and Silva 2011, 111). This poses a problem for Touchton and Wampler's findings because increasing the number of CSOs might be different than "strengthening civil society." For Baiocchi, Heller, and Silva (2011), civil society is "strengthened" not because the number of CSOs increases, but because the CSO's autonomy is increased. PB might lead to new CSOs, but if they are captured by the state, this does not strengthen civil society in the sense that PD advocates require—nor in the way that Tocqueville understood the benefits of associationism (Baiocchi, Heller, and Silva 2011, 144–145). This is not a mere theoretical problem. In Sintomer et al.'s reviews of the state of PB across the globe, they note many processes where civil society is "active," but still subordinate to the state. But again, even here there is a complication. Some active civil societies are dominated by groups that are not inclusive and/or are exclusionary in ways that conflict with social justice norms. This could and does happen with religion, political parties, immigration and citizenship, LGBT rights, as well as along class, gender, and/or race lines. Second, and more controversially, even the justice or rights promoting CSOs (the "good" ones!) are frequently *not* democratic in a general sense much less PD! Indeed, there are numerous critiques of CSOs and NGOs, about their failures in terms of inclusion and community participation in their governance. As theorist and PB researcher Celina Su argues,

> Social movement organizations appear to also provide fewer opportunities for meaningful participation when they become hierarchical, professionalized, and divorced from the grassroots [. . .] Ordinary members can do little but send in their membership fees or make donations each year, while paid lobbyists from Political Action Committees form the core of these organizations. While these social

movement organizations play an important role in politics, they hardly contribute to a deep, healthy democracy at the local level. (Su 2012, 3)

Put another way, many CSOs improve service delivery without building community power or even individual capabilities. CSOs and social movement organizations are often guilty of using too much of their moneys for salaries, and the professionalization of the operations can be off putting to community members, and indeed, even foster an elitist approach that prevents the community from determining its own agenda—which is essential for a PD PB.[34] We are now entering a familiar terrain of debate for those on the left, particularly in Latin America.[35] *In many situations, strong CSOs are part of the problem.* That is, they are antidemocratic and foster relations of dependency (Baiocchi, Heller, and Silva 2011, 163–165). They can be as bad as political parties with their patronage and stifling of dissent and their unwillingness to build capacities of individuals in communities. For example, in NYC, and so many other places around the neoliberal globe, developers have tremendous power. And many residents and CSOs get into contentious relationships with them with respect to differing views of what constitutes just and fair economic development. Some CSOs whose members are negatively impacted by economic development plans have squelched their members' antagonistic dissent. Why? Because these organizations are often dependent upon city funds for their operations or particular projects. If they publicly oppose the developer, the elected official who supports the plan may cut their funding. From the PD perspective, this violates the autonomy of the CSO. That is, the CSO is dependent on an external organization—in this case a city agency or elected official—in a way that undermines the CSO's core agenda. This is a reason why some "autonomous"-PD CSOs refuse government funding, because they fear losing this kind of autonomy. (More below.) Because of the scarcity of resources available in NYC, few opt for this route, but, in other locales, this debate is intense.[36]

The Autonomous PD Critique of PB

For Holloway and autonomous PD (A-PD), it is in the nature of the state to interfere with the collective determination of groups (Holloway 2002, 26–36; 2010, 56–63; Zibechi 2010, 65, 88–90). In other words, on Holloway's view, the state always seek to foster dependence with CSOs and undermine their ability to pursue the project of collective determination. This does not mean that states always successfully co-opt movements or impose their logic upon them. Again, research shows that there are autonomous (PD) PBs. A-PD can accept this since no entity, states included, are omnipotent. So yes, sometimes a PB will achieve some real autonomy because states have to give in sometimes, or they mistakenly believe that they could appropriate a CSO but then were not able to. Or, perhaps, the local government just does not see the effort as a threat. But for antistatists such as Holloway, at best, there are a few exceptions, but overall PD PBs will remain marginal.

As I argued in Chapter 1, most PD views disagree with Holloway and A-PD about PB. For some, this is similar to the difference between PD and most traditions of anarchism. Anarchism also regards the state as essentially coercive and hierarchical, and Holloway's view gives a very sophisticated articulation of that position. But most PD views do not have such a view of the state. Far from being naive, I think the reasons for this is that such views are less essentialist and more empiricist, pluralist, context-sensitive, and functionalist. For example, integrating the most marginalized is a goal of both PD views and Holloway. What organizational form is best at that? Baiocchi, Heller, and Silva (2011) argue that when it comes to integrating the most marginalized in the context of PB, *states are better at this than CSOs*. Also, too many locales have very weak civil societies, much less autonomous organizations. What are we to do in such places, wait for movements to arise? For how long should we wait? Baiocchi, Heller, and Silva show that in the venue of PB, so-called top-down state interventions can lead to real social justice benefits. But that's in part because these state interventions are not really "top down." They confound the top-down/bottom-up distinction. States are acting decisively here, but they, in the best cases, are not imposing an agenda but instead standing alongside and supporting the community's agenda.[37]

But note, this is not any old state, this is the Brazilian state that has been dominated by a pro-PD political party for more than a decade in the 2000s. Even if one bemoans the trajectory of the PT since Lula was elected, and the impeachment of Dilma Rousseff in 2016, and plenty do, comparatively, it is (was?!) a uniquely progressive party, especially for such a large state.[38] And, in this specific case, at the local level, the government is (was!) better than the CSOs at bringing in marginalized groups. Indeed, Touchton and Wampler show that PB performs best when the supervising city has a mayor that is a PT member (Touchton and Wampler 2014, 1444). These mayors have resources. The government also has the power to bypass or break through patronage patterns or relations of dominance within civil society. If this is the case, then it supports the liberal PD view (PD route #2) that the state is necessary, or better positioned, to protect the rights of vulnerable groups and assist them than CSOs or PD.

But PB's achievement turns the traditional liberal critique of PD on its head. (See my Chapter 1.) This can be seen in the debates with Iris Young who is sympathetic to PD but more so a critic. Young argues that PD has an important political role to play but only in very limited circumstances. Part of the reason for that is that it lacks the expertise to formulate policy and is often exclusionary. Young's solution to these flaws and limitations of PD is to only permit it in narrow arenas: at the very local level or as consultation (Young 2000, 177–195). But PB's demonstrated success changes the equation. Yes, PD efforts can be exclusionary or lack expertise. But the solution to this is to demand that states deploy resources to support the PD processes to overcome these limits. PB has shown how to do this: bring in the agencies and state outreach resources and put them at the service of the PD process (e.g., PB).

The danger with such an associationist (route 3) or "partner state" approach is obvious: it is all too easy (or tempting) for the state to cross the line and go from supportive partner enabling the collective determination of a social group to being an antidemocratic predator imposing its agenda (the Hollowayan fear). Baiocchi, Heller, and Silva note these sorts of situations. They write,

> The subordination of social organizations was a curse for the participatory democracy model. I think the agenda of involvement is an agenda that has to come from the people. And today, this agenda is the government. The popular movement, I think, has lost its autonomy. We see this in the PB of Camaragibe. It's not co-opted, but it is the logic of the government . . . . The participation of the popular movement in institutional spaces does the following: the governmental agenda is imposed on the popular movement. (Baiocchi, Heller, and Silva 2011, 125)

So even when an allied political party is in power, a PD PB is not guaranteed.

PB and Trade-Offs

Perhaps the biggest dilemma for organizers and participants of PB interested in PD is the following: in the places where a PD PB did take root, trade-off's emerged among the norms. We saw this with respect to NYC and deliberation and autonomy, and Baiocchi, Heller, and Silva. discuss it with respect to inclusion and autonomy in the town of Gravataí. From the autonomy perspective, its PB had the least, yet it was the most inclusive in terms of subordinate and marginalized groups. Which value is more important to maximize? Because the government led the process, it also delivered resources to do outreach and mobilized heretofore excluded groups. But because the government set the agenda, and its "logic" dominated the PB setting, it was the least open to "societal innovation in claims-making." Baiocchi, Heller, and Silva write, "In this institutional environment, the associative fabric of Gravataí revolved around a logic of organizations attaching themselves to political mediators who monopolized access to public projects and services" (Baiocchi, Heller, and Silva

2011, 121). (The projects that won were additional police patrols, day care, and classrooms [Baiocchi, Heller, and Silva 2011, 121].) This is consistent with the Hollowayan A-PD fear/prediction.

Speaking generally, one might say the major drawback was the "colonization of life world" by the government and the lack of autonomy of "civil society." But Baiocchi, Heller, and Silva reject such characterizations. Intriguingly, they do not argue that the state co-opted the movements of Gravataí because there were no "right to the city" social justice–oriented movements to co-opt! (Baiocchi, Heller, and Silva 2011, 34–38). On the contrary, the civil society groups that were present were hierarchical and created their own relations of dependence with various social groups. The Gravataí PB made an extreme break with such clientelism by enlisting the power of the state and "designing" CSO participation out of the process (Baiocchi, Heller, and Silva 2011, 120, 123). Gravataí then did well on the social justice criteria for inclusion and diversity as well as projects that benefited those with least access to the city and its goods and infrastructure. In other words, it did well in a more robust version of the good governance frame especially in terms of the *presence* of the public, but poorly from a PD *procedural* perspective: "The absence of mediators, and most notably organized civil society, was compensated for by a proactive government. As a result, civil society did not develop a preference formation capacity of its own outside of the actual deliberative fora" (Baiocchi, Heller, and Silva 2011, 139). The deliberations were also "compressed" and the "chain of preference formation and sovereignty" was short (not much mediated) but inclusive from a class composition perspective (Baiocchi, Heller, and Silva 2011, 139). From the maxD perspective, however, Gravataí PB was weak since participating groups had little control over the structure of the process and its agenda (they lacked maxD#1: collective determination). Nor did groups develop the capabilities to create projects outside of PB or forge alliances with other groups (maxD#2 and maxD#4).

On the other side of the PB spectrum were Diadema and Joao Monlevade. In these cities, groups had considerable autonomy and were the most open to societal innovation in claims making. Indeed, for Baiocchi, Heller, and Silva, both are best practice or "prototype" PBs (Baiocchi, Heller, and Silva 2011, 125). Joao Monlevade's associations were careful to retain their autonomy, which meant not becoming subordinate to the government, the political party, or other CSOs. Evidence of the autonomy of civil society in terms of agenda setting was that Joao Monlevade's PB went beyond focusing just on annual budget cycles and led to thematic discussions about the city's long-term development goals and a conference on regional development. Associations also exercised collective determination in terms of the PB process, and even remained a little bit contentious (Baiocchi, Heller, and Silva 2011, 126). Indeed, Joao Monlevade's PB goes beyond the more reformist "good governance" frame and instead appears to be a comparatively robust expression of the "disarticulate the state" framework. Baiocchi, Heller, and Silva write, "In contrast to much of the governance literature which tends to presume that 'good governance' is only possible when administrations are insulated from politics, in this case it is clear that *contention and institution-building reinforced each other. A second point, however, is that social movements, or an active civil society, can hardly be transformative on their own*" (Baiocchi, Heller, and Silva 2011, 130, my emphasis). However—and this is crucial—because they were "more free" from the state (Baiocchi, Heller, and Silva 2011, 138), associations had less state assistance and were less inclusive than Gravataí in terms of class and race and reaching the unaffiliated (Baiocchi, Heller, and Silva 2011, 163).[39] There was no transcending the trade-off.

Critical Summary of PB and Civil Society

When PB is successful in a PD manner, it enables participating groups and persons to formulate their own agenda (collective determination) (Baiocchi, Heller, and Silva 2011, 162). The city then supports this process by helping to provide resources for the development of the capabilities to do this (maxD#2) and moneys are available in the PB process that address these needs and reduce inequality (maxD#3). Also of concern for Baiocchi, Heller, and Silva is whether the CSOs participating are strengthened with respect to their other projects outside of PB. In three of their four cases, "PB was implemented in cities with weak civil society, and with clientilistic pasts and oligarchical elites for two (Camaragibe and Gravataí). These cities were not likely sites of broad-based participation, but this is precisely what PB achieved" (Baiocchi, Heller, and Silva 2011, 157). The degree of impact on residents can depend upon CSO strength or local government interest and discretion. This is the basis for the autonomy/dependence equation for Baiocchi, Heller, and Silva (2011, 124). But the counterintuitive insight—especially from the vantage of the PD literature—is that a top-down PB can increase *PD*. Indeed, this phenomenon is so counterintuitive the description seems a contradiction. (More below.) The converse is a locale where PD is so strong already that PB isn't needed so much. For Baiocchi, Heller, and Silva, the ideal type of such a *movement* democracy is Diadema. There, a well-organized civil society had few avenues for participation. So these CSOs used contention and used it very effectively to win services, housing, and other improvements. Here, in a sense, was a place that didn't need PB so much. But of course such sites are rare (Baiocchi, Heller, and Silva 2011, 113–114).

From a PD perspective, increasing the number of CSOs is not, in itself, "good." Nor is "empowering civil society." Many CSOs and civil societies are antidemocratic, disempowering of certain groups, and exclusionary in myriad ways. The point of a PD PB is to further the *PD* process. *Thus, the state must be democratized, and, in many places, so must civil society: the maximization of democracy requires not just the democratization of the state, but the democratization of civil society.*[40] The nitty-gritty of this, however, exposes more splits among PD views.

Above, we noted the A-PD view that argues that the state CANNOT be a consistently effectively vehicle for PD. It may seem like a "partner" for a time but this is at best an exceptional circumstance and at worse a lure to trap groups and co-opt them. The very astute antistate PD view of Zibechi makes the same sort of claim with respect to civil society. He distinguishes between two types of NGOs: the first are those aligned with the state. They are either formally part of it or are part of the machinery of political parties or political NGOs. These organizations have a state-led agenda, are hierarchical in their operation, and promote a "professionalization" that is expert driven and not empowering of communities. Instead, "average citizens" are to be informed and led. Examples include political party groups, unions, and single-issue advocacy NGOs.[41] However, there is another class of organizations; these are led by regular residents, have memberships organized more by territory or neighborhood than by sector (e.g., housing, transportation), are run more informally (less professional), and are more horizontal (less hierarchical). This type is funded primarily by its members, unlike the NGOs who are funded by business, foundations, and/or the state. But the key difference between the two for Zibechi is that the second type is driven and organized in terms of the everyday needs of its members. That is, they prevent the separation politics from the everyday life of the social; they preserve "the social flow of doing" in Holloway's lexicon. Examples of such organizations are those that organize festivals and community events, athletic clubs, and musical associations (Zibechi 2010, 43–63; 2012, 205–239). Indeed, they are so "social" that they often seem "apolitical." But it is these organizations that for Zibechi are truly PD in Holloway's sense; they promote the popular and antihierarchical control of the "social flow of doing." They are grassroots, meaning that they develop the capacities of the members, not just in a formal bureaucratic sense (improve literacy or graduation rates) but in the context of the culture and desires of their communities.[42] From the perspective of Zibechi and the Hollowayans, PB in most cases is likely to be a lure, a new form of co-optation and domination (Zibechi 2012, 303–306). Ask yourself: why would a government use PB? Either to demobilize a contentious civil society (Baiocchi, Heller, and Silva 2011, 140) or increase its legitimacy relative to a frustrated and/or apathetic populace. But while the first reason is "bad" from the PD perspective, the second cuts both ways. In a sense, the second means that the state too can be "lured" into transferring assets and resources in order to increase its legitimacy. But once this transfer occurs and is institutionalized, contra Zibechi and Holloway, in my view, "disarticulation" may commence.[43]

And the Economy?

However, one of the problems with the focus on PB's relationship with civil society is that such a framework reinforces the divide between the political and the economic realms. While it is certainly worthwhile to explore the impact of PB on CSOs, it is my view that it is just as important to study PB's impact on the economy and businesses, especially at the level of economic development. Baiocchi et al. and Touchton and Wampler—along with the great majority of analysts of PB—do not look at these relationships and impacts.[44] To be sure, one can only study so much, but from a PD frame, part of the project is to reconnect the social with both the political and the economic realms. And even from the perspective of CSOs themselves, political inequality and human rights are as tied to economic structures as they are to political institutions. For many CSOs, it's not just about getting out the vote; it's about creating jobs or securing or improving benefits. And it's about getting access to all those basic goods that stand at the intersection of the political and the economic realms: housing, health care, education as well as access to effective public services (e.g., transportation, water, electricity). For all six PD routes, inclusion and participation is not just about discussion and deliberation, it's about access to and control over resources. Thus, the ideal PD PB doesn't just produce more venues for political access, it supports the democratic management of economic activities. Examples of locales where PB has helped to inspire or support economic democracy efforts such as worker co-ops, land trusts, and community housing in particular and democratic CSO driven community development in general include Kerala (India), Cotacachi, (Ecuador), Toronto Housing Authority (Canada), Fissel section of M' bour (Senegal), Villa El Salvador (Peru), and in a more complicated way Seville (Spain) and the larger scale efforts in the state of Rio Grande du Sol (Brazil) (Sintomer et al. 2012, 26; Sintomer, Herzberg, and Allegretti 2013, 36–37). We return to this discussion of the intersection of the social-political with the economic especially in my Chapter 6 on the social-public.

PB, Political Theory, and the Disarticulation of the State

PD PBs don't "deepen" democracy, they redefine it. In this section I will consider the argument that PD PBs are producing a new form of governance that I call "social-public." This new form of governance is not adequately described by "governmentality" frameworks, and it is misunderstood by views that are for OR against the state, or discretely demarcate between the state and civil society. This new form of governance is also missed by those who claim there is a deep disjunction between participatory democracy and representative views of governance.[45]

So how is it that PB doesn't just improve or "deepen" democracy but actually produces a new mode of governance? A first insight comes from those who argue that PB breaks the state's monopoly on the legislative function, and does so without seizing the state (Chavez 2004, 170–177, 184; see also Hilmer 2010, 60; Menser 2009). Further buttressing of this idea can be found in Baiocchi, Heller and Silva's (2011) claim that PB constructs a "parallel chain of sovereignty" connecting rulers to ruled in a way that may actually scramble if not reverse the distinction. As Touchton and Wampler argue, "Governments adopting PB produce new forms of governance, which are based on the direct incorporation of citizens and CSOs into incremental policy-making processes. This requires reforming how the local state (municipality) is organized internally as well as broadening the surface area of the state through an increase in public venues and access points" (Touchton and Wampler 2014, 1444). Because PB breaks the monopoly of state power on the budget process it disrupts the usual channels of power *and* legitimacy. In the usual (idealized!) representative government model, citizens present their interests to those elected, who sort through them and make decisions about how to best serve those interests. Bureaucracy is supposed to assist those elected in forming policies or proposals to satisfy those interests. In PB, the "people" meet (without the electeds!) to discuss their interests, debate them among themselves, and make proposals. The role of those elected is to be supportive watchdogs, to make sure some groups don't dominate others in the process, and to use their assets to support PD goals such as inclusion and equity. Bureaucratic authority and expertise are brought into play to help people further develop the proposals. The role of those elected then is to obey "the people" and submit proposals without modification to the machinery of state. Both elected and PB participants supervise implementation, which alters the machinery of the state (see Chapter 6).

But others would disagree. Couldn't one argue from a more liberal PD perspective that PB *deepens* representative democracy insofar as the elected officials still have to submit the proposals? Consider this characterization of PB from a World Bank report:

> This arrangement [PB] is clearly a step beyond both the traditional watchdog or society-driven horizontal role of civil society as well as protest or referendum based direct vertical roles for social actors. Instead of trying to influence policy from the outside, the citizens [. . .] are invited inside the governmental apparatus itself, thus confusing the neat horizontal-vertical framework for understanding accountability mechanisms. (World Bank 2004, 14)

On this view, people are brought into the space of representative state. Not surprisingly, the World Bank stresses the accountability aspect of PB, not the (community) empowerment one. But one could argue the other way since PB grants decisive power to nonelected officials, it enables a nonstate source of power. "In this sense, then, PB seems to challenge the theoretical basis of representative democracy, especially the actors and the institutional arrangement. But it does it in a constructive way, showing a valid alternative which could outline a new concept of state and democracy" (Stortone 2010, 18). One could see this tension at work in popular reactions to PB in NYC. Oftentimes I would hear people say that PB is a "no brainer": "it's the people's money, let them decide." Others, nervously, would ask, "isn't this the government's job? Don't we pay them to do this for us?"

When one breaks up a monopoly, a decentralizing splitting occurs. When done well, what PD PB does is fracture the governance apparatus of the municipality in a way that creates an internal rift and destabilization that enables a nonstate PD social grouping to appropriate a part of the function normally carried out by the bureaucratic apparatus. For example, in a PD PB (whether Porto Alegre or NYC or Spain), bureaucratic staff are made available to the PB council and serve them. While some welcome the opportunity to interact more directly with the public, many of these staff are uncooperative at the start (and afterward!) Why? They have to answer to a new authority. But unlike an elected official, this authority is not a boss; it's more akin to a partner or client. PB not only producers a power shift (from elected to community), but a different logic comes into play; *a different form of power is constructed and deployed*. This is the logic of cooperation and support, not subordination. And the two logics can obviously conflict with one another. As Stortone notes, "On the one hand, the scope of PB is to empower civil society to be able to come up with autonomous and agreed-upon decisions. This fosters the growth of self-organizational skills and thus a competitive power which is not necessarily in tune with the state" (Stortone 2010, 14).

Building on the conceptual frame of Baiocchi, Heller, and Silva, PB should not be described as "bottom up," because decisive state action is what makes it possible and can help to promote it. Yet when the state supports PB in a PD manner it is not "top down"—that's when the state imposes its agenda on PB. So how to describe state-supported PD PB? Perhaps the most apt spatial metaphor is "standing alongside" or "diagonal" (World Bank 2004, 14). Standing alongside captures the horizontal nature of the relation, as if it were among equals or partners. Standing alongside even suggests the side-by-side of solidarity and helps to illustrate the idea of a "partner state." But standing alongside is too static and naive. First off, it's not that the entire local government is supporting the PB process. What happens is that particular parts of the government come into contact with specific segments of the public through mechanisms controlled by the community. In this encounter is a reorganization. The "diagonal" (of the World Bank citation above) is then better than standing alongside because there is an internal reconfiguration that occurs as the interrelationship develops between, say, the executive or legislative branches and a specific segment of civil society.[46] Sintomer et al. push the conceptualization even further:

> This model is mainly characterized by the simultaneous emergence of a "fourth power" (participants have a real decision-making power, different from the judiciary, the legislative and the executive) and a "countervailing power" (the autonomous mobilization of civil society within the process leads to the empowerment of the people and the promotion of cooperative conflict resolution). (Sintomer et al. 2012, 20)

Cabannes also calls this novel governance node a "fourth power" that emerges alongside the other three powers of the executive, legislative, and the courts (Cabannes 2014, 29). This fourth power (PB) is a nonstate space that is dominated by the community and driven by its agenda. But this "nonstate" space is plugged into the state.[47] And this "plugging into" changes or rewires a segment of the state space. I call the configuration of this rewiring that shifts and anchors decisive power in the community "social-public."

This nonstate space is supported by (some part of) the state, but it is also in contention with (others parts of) it. This fourth power then is both a (cooperative) governance node and a (contestatory) counterpower (Cabannes 2014, 29). Because this rewiring involves contestation and a *fracturing and reorganization* of the previous internal organization of the state (say, the mayor's office or city agency), I call it "disarticulation." Cabannes calls this new relation an "inversion." Again, this resonates with the "diagonal" metaphor since one could imagine a line from the top of the state where power flows downward (diagonally) to the community (the base or ground at the bottom). Following this diagonal directionality, PBs greatest strength, most simply stated, is that it inverts the priorities of the government and sets in motion the realization of the right to the city (Cabannes 2014, 24) or the city as commons (Foster and Iaione 2016). From the perspective of the traditional capitalist state: PB threatens to turn the world, that is, *their* world, upside down; the people gain control over the state's resources; the community defines the public good; and the bureaucracy lends it authority and expertise to implement the specifics of the community-driven agenda. From the PD perspective, the world is turned "right [to the city] side up."

PD tries to have it "both ways." PD in general, and PD PBs in particular, are both protagonists and antagonists. If they are only the former, then the critics are probably right, co-option is inevitable. To avoid co-option, PD PBs must create and maintain the internal organization (collective determination of the PB process); create and expand alliances and strengthen partners (specific CSOs and agencies or departments); and combat opponents (e.g., certain political parties, recalcitrant agencies, local elites). Again, the fusion of the contestatory and the transformative is what I call the "disarticulation of the state" and the production of the new governance configuration is social-public. (See my Chapter 6.)

Of course, disarticulating the state is easier said than done (and it's not so easy to say!). In the real world, there are tensions among "the people" and between the residents and the government (elected officials and agencies). Consider the below report from a PB in NYC:

> "Sometimes the discussions got uncomfortable," Ms. Tobin said, adding that she often bit her lip to keep from screaming. "It seemed like our group was torn between form over function or function over form." Though they couldn't always see eye to eye, they [the residents] united over a common bond: a feeling that government agencies—in this case, the Transportation Department—weren't really interested in their ideas. (Sangha 2012)

Even when those elected support residents in the PB space, the agencies aren't always so cooperative. Again, this is part of the heterogeneity of the state thesis (noted above and below and explained more in Chapters 3 and 6). Some agencies and those elected don't have cooperative relationships for all sorts of reasons. And some agencies do not get along with other agencies. One simple reason is territoriality: not only does PB take power away from legislators; it also threatens agencies and departments.

Also, these actors create a process where the decisions are based on a different normative framework and, again, when done well, creates a different sort of relations among the actors in the process: budget delegates don't have the same kind of power as council members, the proposals are subject to review in a much more public manner, and overall the process is much more horizontal and less hierarchical. A most overt difference is that PB diminishes the importance of political parties, they play no official role and indeed are banned from playing such a role within the PB process: usually CSOs play that role. Stortone again emphasizes the different logic at play: "From this analytical perspective, PB would represent a very radical impact on the traditional idea of politics: it raises an alternative source of political power, which is no longer concentrated on a specific elite, but is fragmented and spread into multiple social spheres and actors which represent the contemporary 'molecular' or 'issue-based ideologies'" (Stortone 2010, 17).

Conclusion

The evolution and proliferation of participatory democratic PB shows that two of the most common criticisms of participatory democracy are wrong. PB as a form of PD can flourish in very different cultural contexts with diverse populations and at different scales (including units with millions of people). PB is worth doing from a PD perspective for three sets of reasons: (1) it empowers communities through the development of knowledges (of government, infrastructure) and skill sets (deliberation, conflict resolution) that enable individual and community capacity development and relationship building that enhance social capital and even inspire solidarity; (2) the presence of PB often leads to programs that benefit broad sections of the public especially in terms of basic services and public goods; and (3) PB promotes an evolution and reorganization of the relations among residents, CSOs, elected officials, and agencies such that a new mode of governance emerges that institutionalizes the benefits by shifting political authority to a nonstate public space that is nevertheless plugged into the state. While it is clear PB does not deliver all of these benefits for every person in every one of the 1,700 plus cities in which it operates, research shows that in those cities where it has been in existence for several years, it frequently delivers benefits especially with respect to public service delivery, and oftentimes with respect to capability development. The jury is still out on whether a new mode of governance is taking over.

The challenge for PB, particularly in its PD form, is to have access to budgets that are large enough to change "business as usual" in the city, and not just be confined to crumbs or on the periphery. For this to occur, the city as a site of capital accumulation must give way to the urban commons. The priorities must be inverted. This means PB must also be connected to the right kind of political milieu and networks of supports for it to flourish, especially to address racial and economic inequality. These efforts may be top-down, bottom-up, and/or, even better, diagonal. Yet, the most effective PD PBs interconnect with organizations that share their normative framework across sectors (political, economic, and social) and across organization types (government agencies, CSOs, social associations, individual residents). And this is why no PB effort by itself is adequate to forward the PD project.

3

From Corporate Social Responsibility to Economic Democracy: Stakeholder Theory, Civil Society, and Worker Ownership

> The Social Responsibility of Business Is to Increase Its Profits.
> —MILTON FRIEDMAN

Introduction

Can participatory democracy work in the real world of capitalist business? How could it possibly balance the demands of stockholders, workers, and customers? Any person who has ever taken a business ethics class knows that a business is a piece of property, and its purpose is to make money for its owner(s). Everything (and everyone) else is secondary. To say otherwise is political correctness, that is, lip service to liberals who know nothing about the principles of economics much less the real time pressures of managing a firm.

Such is the view of Nobel Prize–winning economist Milton Friedman, patron saint of profit maximizing managers everywhere. But since the 1970s, despite the protestations of Friedman and his ideological kin, more and more *moral* demands are being voluntarily taken up by businesses both small and large. The movement is called "corporate social responsibility" or CSR. And although profits still matter, so do people, and the environment. CSR is most often justified by the stakeholder theory framework, and it claims to bring democracy into the realm of the capitalist workplace. I will argue that it fails. Especially for workers. And this is true if business managers inside the firm do it, or watchdog organizations in civil society take up the cause. Is all hope for economic democracy then lost? Not at all. Luckily there is a range of alternative traditions and frameworks that both justify and illustrate how the project of economic democracy is not only moral and just; it is doable, even profitable.

In this chapter, first we define economic democracy and consider economic diversity both among states and within them and the strengths and limits of the market. We then raise the question of democracy in the economy from the perspective of business ethics and corporate social responsibility and stakeholder theory. We look at this view and the case study of McDonald's CSR program. It is found wanting on most counts. We then explore a CSR view grounded in a civil society approach made up of independent nonprofit watchdogs engaged in deliberative democracy. There are theoretical heavy-weights and famous organizations, such as Students against Sweatshops and the Forest Stewardship Council, behind this view. And this civil society view also enjoys considerable popularity not just in business but in the political and social sciences and among good governance advocates. But, we argue, it too is not able to deliver consistent benefits to workers, communities, and the environment. As a result of these inadequacies, we explore a much more PD framework, the worker cooperative model as exemplified by the well-studied Mondragon Corporation located in Basque Country in northern Spain. This sets us up for more thoroughgoing debates about how to justify and implement economic democracy and worker co-ops in the next chapter and critiques of both are taken up in the second half of Chapter 4 and Chapter 5.

What's *in* a Name? Defining Economic Democracy

Economic democracy (econD) is the idea that the principles of popular sovereignty and the values of freedom, solidarity, and equality should be applied to the economic system in a way that empowers all stakeholders from workers and owners to residents and customers. EconD practices do this by promoting inclusive and meaningful participation in terms of financing, ownership, management, regulation, waste disposal, and/or consumption. Pluralistic in its origins and history, econD projects vary in their relationships to states, markets, communities, and individuals. Though some regard themselves as liberal capitalists and others as state socialists, many others eschew such categories (associationists, anarchists) or aspire to more experimental and pluralistic frames (e.g., solidarity economy, social economy, sharing economy). Still others root themselves in dissimilar ethical or cultural traditions (religious communitarianism, indigenous philosophy). EconD projects occur in multiple sectors including banking and finance (e.g., divided sharing, credit unions), the workplace (ESOPs, worker co-ops), consumption (buying clubs, consumer co-ops), landownership (community land trusts), and service delivery (public utilities).

For the purposes of this chapter, and this book, econD is a broad category meant to include all those economic projects or business forms that promote collective determination (maxD#1) and capability development (maxD#2) while replacing relationships of inequality with those of shared authority (maxD#3). Even if success in isolation was possible, econD efforts choose to link up with other forms that share their values in order to increase their own chances of success while also proliferating econD (maxD#4). And just as political PD is focused on sharing power, econD is focused on sharing wealth.

This conceptual frame puts econD at odds with standard forms of state socialism and corporation-led capitalism. I think it is fair to say, following the conceptualization of Howard, Dubb, and McKinley, that econD

"differs from state socialism in that it favors democratic (and often decentralized) planning over former communist-style central planning and makes considerable use of market mechanisms." [. . .] And that econD splits from "corporate capitalism in that it favors public or community forms of ownership as opposed to stock ownership, and favors worker self management over top down corporate management." (Howard, Dubb, and McKinley 2014, 231)[1]

In the English-speaking realm, economic democracy becomes a *phrase* around the turn of the twentieth century with G.D.H. Cole (1889–1959) and C. H. Douglas (1879–1952) (Howard, Dubb, and McKinley 2014, 231). This phrase expressed the emergence of a framework often regarded as a path between or around state socialism and corporate capitalism. As Ellerman puts it, "Economic democracy is a genuine third way that is structurally different from classical capitalism and socialism. It can be viewed as an outcome of evolution starting *either* from capitalism or from socialism" (Ellerman 1990, 104). Precursors include solidarism (Kohn 2016, 13–31), anarcho-syndicalism, and other bottom up and participatory socialist and anarchist hybrids (Ness and Azzellini 2013). Another precursor is "associationism," which gets going around the turn of the twentieth century, peaks with the work of Cole, but wanes with Hirst by the 1990s—though it persists as a view to this day. (See Chapter 1.)

Although the 1890s–1920s is a fertile period for econD views (e.g., Cole 1889–1959, Douglas 1879–1952, Dubois 1868–1963), debates, and projects, the literature is rather thin from the 1930s–1980s.[2] In the 1980s, econD reemerges as a more defined project—though some might even say an unfortunately *confined* and siloed one, especially in academia. The most visible early work is done by one of the most influential political scientists of the twentieth century, Robert Dahl (1985). Other key works include Ellerman 1990, Fotopoulos 1998, Schweickart 2002, Eric Olin Wright 2010, and more recently Malleson 2014. In the 1990s, after the collapse of the Soviet Union and the rise of the antiglobalization movement, econD makes a comeback, oftentimes under the more movement-oriented label called "the solidarity economy" (see Allard, Davidson, and Matthaei 2008).[3] Fellow travelers Michael Albert and Robin Hahnel use the closely related phrase "participatory economics" and Eric Olin Wright's Real Utopias crew deploy a different nomenclature but are still very much a part of econD's project and resurgence.[4] I would also include Paul Hirst (1994) whose work is very much in the spirit of an (updated) G.D.H. Cole.

EconD then includes efforts that are state-based and civil society based but also those that are antistate and communitarian and others that are associationist and/or liberal capitalist. EconD also includes related political projects such as social economy, solidarity economy, subsistence economy, feminist economics, living democracy, earth democracy, and bioregionalism.[5] On my view, econD, like the solidarity economy framework, is and should continue to be pluralistic and for more than one reason. First off, the world is too large, diverse, and complex to be fixed by some magic "one size fits all" solution. A state takeover and nationalization of all industries won't solve all the problems, nor will converting all multinationals into privately owned worker cooperatives. Each and every model is limited and contexts vary in terms of needs and potentials (Cumbers 2012, 79). EconD's endorsement of multiple models and methods is also an expression of epistemic humility: with so many different traditions, peoples, knowledges, and organizational forms, who knows which will work and for whom (Santos 2004, 237–243)? Last, amid so much tumult and crisis, and so much system change, an open-mindedness makes sense for reasons of urgency: let's throw as many darts at the board as is humanly possible (and ecologically desirable) and see which ones stick (take root and grow).

Just as there is a distinction between the broad category "democracy" and the particular view of participatory democracy, in this chapter, consistent with the mission of this book, I will focus on those econD views that are animated by a **PD perspective** and fall within a political philosophical approach in the broad sense. To understand how PD plays out in the economy, however, it helps to first examine what is currently out there in terms of the array of existing economic systems and the commonly invoked but confusingly deployed concepts of capitalism and socialism.

Economic Diversity: Capitalism, Socialism, and the Global Economy

The question is, how do we begin to see this monolithic and homogeneous Capitalism not as our "reality" but as a fantasy of wholeness, one that operates to obscure diversity and disunity in the economy and society alike?
—Gibson-Graham, *The End of Capitalism (As We Knew It)*, 260

There are many "socialisms" and there are many "capitalisms."
—David Ellerman, *The Democratic Corporation*, 91

By portraying the economy as multiple, or as a site of difference, we are placing another nail in the coffin of the capitalist totality.
—Gibson-Graham, *The End of Capitalism (As We Knew It)*, 207

A simple means of defining and contrasting capitalism and socialism hinges on their differing stances on property, labor, markets, and the role of the state. In a capitalist economy, most of the land, resources, and equipment used for production—the "means of production"—is owned by individuals, or by organizations (often corporations) that are, in turn, owned by individuals. Goods are exchanged in a market where prices are largely set by the forces of supply and demand. Most workers don't own the means of production and instead are wage laborers: that is, they exchange their labor for a wage. The state plays a regulatory role in this scheme and may even own some land and run a business or two (e.g., public utilities). In capitalist countries, most employment is private, although the state certainly is a major employer in many European countries as well as in the United States. But the key difference is that the surplus, the profits that result from all that production, are not possessed or managed by the producers. Instead, the surplus is controlled by a different group: investors or "appropriators" depending on one's view (Wolff 2012, 82). And in a capitalist society, this group is made up of private individuals.

In socialist countries like the USSR and China before the 1990s, the council of ministers and state officials functioned as employers and managed the surplus. In a socialist economy, most of the "means of production" is owned by the state. In the Soviet model of socialism, goods were distributed not by buyers and sellers in the marketplace but by a ruling party that formulated a plan and used the state to implement it. Such a scheme is often called a "centrally planned economy" (Schweickart 2011, 49).[6] Interestingly, workers are still paid a wage, but this time by the state. In this model, many basic goods and social services are also supplied by the state, from housing to health care. The last crucial difference between the two is what happens to the profits or "surplus." In a socialist scheme, because the state is the primary owner of the means of production, whoever controls the state manages the surplus. In a capitalist scheme, private individuals own most productive property and thus manage most of the surplus. This means that financing and investment in a capitalist state is mostly in the hands of private individuals in contrast to socialism where it's controlled by government bureaucrats and/or the political party that controls the state (Wolff 2012, 99–114).[7]

When this binary taxonomy is applied to the actual history and present reality of economies of planet Earth, no past or current state is fully capitalist or socialist (Gibson-Graham 1996, 5–23).[8] Even in a country like the United States, which claims to be dedicated to private ownership and free markets, many assets are owned and/or controlled by the state. For example, the federal government owns vast amounts of land (over 30% in the United States is "public") and a variety of other jurisdictional levels (e.g., state, county, city) own not only land but infrastructure from harbors to airports, powerlines to airspace, not to mention schools and hospitals (Wolff 2012, 20). The U.S. Army Corps of Engineers has jurisdiction over all the coasts. Additionally, in "capitalist" states around the world, many services are not exchanged on the market but instead delivered by the government to citizens (and sometimes noncitizens) including fire and police protection, education, electricity, water, and the mail. Generally speaking, these services are delivered not to make profits but based on residents' needs. In the United States, federal, state, and local governments own and operate a variety of service providers from schools and hospitals to ports, pipelines, and methane capture facilities to hotels, mines, and even a bank or two. Last, even in *market* capitalist states, the government provides a range of subsidies to private enterprises in the form of tax breaks, grants, support services, and the leasing of facilities below market rate. The point is, that even in the United States, the government is active on many fronts not just to regulate business but as a partner supporting business. Some (parts of) governments might even be understood as savvy investors (Mazzucato 2014, 15–28)!

Such messy hybridity also occurs on the other side of the ideological fence.[9] In socialist countries, private ownership of a variety of personal goods is the norm, and not just personal items like toothbrushes but tools, equipment, cars, and even homes. And there may be markets permitted in specific sectors such as food, media, and clothing. Also, although most people do not have access to markets and capital to use as investment, elites were often granted a range of economic privileges associated with market capitalism. This is particularly the case in China, which now has the second largest economy on the planet and is run by the communist party (Schweickart 2011, 59, 175–179). And then there was the socialist state of Yugoslavia, which under Tito created an economy that was largely organized around a form of worker management[10] (Pateman 1970, 85–102; Cumbers 2012, 32–36).

Even if one ignored the massive anomaly that is China and claimed that capitalism has gone global and is the reigning economic-political regime, there are still nontrivial political and functional variations among the economic practices of existing states. Although global capitalism with its free markets and its accompanying gang of institutions has been said to place states in a "straitjacket" (T. Friedman 1999, 101–111), there is still considerable variation in the attire, particularly in regard to where the straps are placed—that is, what parts of the "body" are permitted to move freely and which are not.

First off, there are countries that call themselves socialist or communist. There are currently four: Laos, China, Vietnam, and Cuba.[11] Even if one doubts the designation, the relationship between the state and the economy and the role of private property and job markets function quite different in these four than those in, say, South Korea, Mexico, Nigeria, and Canada. Furthermore, although (socialist) Laos is regarded as having one of the worst performing economies and ranks quite low in the UN human development index, (socialist) China's gains over the past couple decades are on a scale never before witnessed with respect to the number of people lifted out of poverty, the size of its middle class, and the overall growth of the economy (Schweickart 2011, 14, 174–179). Some might say, but China is not REALLY socialist anymore: it has stock markets and private investment in urban real estate, etc. OK, fine, let's say China and all the rest are in some sense neoliberal or capitalist, but what does that even mean? In the oft-cited left critique of this model, David Harvey admits that there is no single of model of the "neoliberal state." Different states have quite different setups, and, although many are responding to similar pressures, because of their internal diversity and different histories, geographic positions, etc., they construct quite different models (Harvey 2005, 70).[12]

The point here is that not only are there many different ways of organizing an economy; there are many different ways of being successful according to mainstream capitalist measures (GDP, average income, productivity, etc.). For example, Denmark is one of the most competitive economies in the world. Its workers are also among the world's most educated and productive in terms of GDP per hours worked, and employers regard its labor laws to be among the most "flexible" in the world, similar to the United States. Yet, Denmark also has universal social services, including health care, and a very high income tax rate in order to fund it. It also has the highest minimum wage, the lowest income inequality, and the best protections of worker rights.[13] If Denmark became the dominant model of a capitalist state, think of the difference it would make to wage workers in terms of pay, security, and benefits in the United States and so many other capitalist states!

A very different model is in play in another country that has done very well for itself economically, the United Arab Emirates (UAE). Considered to be the twenty-second best country in the world for doing business (out of more than 200), it has the world's tallest building and busiest airport and is now a regional military power as well. Unlike Denmark, which is a multiparty democracy, the UAE is a federation of principalities, each of which is an absolute hereditary monarchy. That's right; Dubai, that Mideast mecca of capitalist business and finance, is a principality ruled by a family (of the Al Maktoum lineage since 1833). Not surprisingly, the situation is quite different from Denmark with respect to workers. In the UAE, the majority of the labor force are not citizens and have few rights. Indeed, if they try to organize or unionize they can be deported. UAE has one of the worst worker rights records in the world but it also has one of the richest cities, Abu Dhabi.[14]

Even using traditional capitalist business criteria, in the top ten of World Bank favorites are places with, again, very different economic systems: from the liberal and well-developed welfare state of Denmark to the more authoritarian city-state of Singapore. Then there are the countries at the bottom, only one flirts with socialism (Venezuela), the others are intensely capitalist.[15] Whether one is an advocate or critic, from the perspective of the norms discussed above, there are meaningful existing differences among countries with respect to equality, inclusion, channels for democratic participation, management and ownership, and access to basic goods and other services.[16] From the perspective of human rights, needs, and well-being, this is especially true.

Internal Economic Diversity: Different Economies within the Economy

In the above we focused on the economic differences among existing states.[17] But the heterogeneity of existing states hints at another manifestation of economic diversity: one that expresses itself *within* a single country. Even in quintessentially capitalist states that worship Hayek and relentlessly extol the virtues of the market—what used to be called capitalist liberal democratic states—there are the private and public sectors and they are structured by different principles (Cumbers 2012, 48–50). In the private sector, "Ownership is determined by the private control of capital. The primary purpose is to maximize returns on investment to shareholders. Capital controls labor. The key aim of the commercial exchange is the economic principle of efficiency" (Lewis and Swinney 2008, 31). In the public sector, the aim is to distribute a good so as to meet a basic need or right to some service: water, electricity, mail, health care. "The operations of the public sector focus on the redistribution of wealth and the provision of public goods for the purpose of promoting the economic principle of equality" (Lewis and Swinney 2008, 31). This is decidedly not the rationale of a capitalist market economy, which is oriented around the individual freedom of buyers and sellers (more below).

The other sector, which gets much less attention from economists (especially in the United States), is what is sometimes called the "social economy." Diverging from both the private property–controlled profit-oriented sector and the planned-provision public sector, this third sector is made up of voluntary associations and the household or family economy. This sector often gets lost in the talk about "privatization." There are also many government services that are contracted out not to businesses but to nonprofits, from religious organizations like the Catholic Church to secular institutions such as the American Red Cross to more local service providers like University Settlement House in NYC. The driving principles of these organizations are self-help and reciprocity, and the goal is to realize "social purpose through various types of organization and association" (Lewis and Swinney 2008, 29; M. Bouchard 2013, 5–7). Thus, even in hypercapitalist states that worship the market and praise the private control of profits, there are multiple economies at work and some employ nonmarket mechanisms that serve ends other than the private accumulation of wealth. A key reason for this is that *markets were never intended to serve all human needs*. Indeed, these limits are not controversial, they are well understood.

Market Failure(s)

Supply and demand. That's the essence of the market in the popular economic understanding. In many cases, it seems to work great: take shoes. Feet come in all shapes and sizes: so we have different lines for kids and adults, men and women. There are some for wide feet, others for narrow ones. People like to do all sorts of activities with them in different types of terrain and weather: so we have hiking boots for high-altitude jaunts and flip-flops for the hot sandy beach. Bank accounts, too, for better or worse, come in all shapes and sizes, so there is an incredible price range: literally from two bucks to $10,000. And we haven't even broached the issue of style and material and brand: Gore-Tex rain boots, leather dress shoes, cork high heels, canvas low tops, there are even "barefoot" and vegan shoes! In a "planned" or subsistence economy, it's hard to imagine such a variety.

But there are other sorts of goods that are not available in such mesmerizing variety, despite demand for them: affordable housing, quality health care, decent K-12 education, renewable energy. For the most part, it's not that any of these goods are "scarce." It's that the market doesn't make them accessible to those who most need them. Why are markets so good at delivering some goods rather than others? And why do they seem to be so bad at delivering quality versions of many of the most basic goods (Panayotakis 2011, 10–56)?

Limit 1. Markets respond to dollars, not people. The first point about contemporary markets is that they don't respond to "demand"; they respond to *consumer* demand. In a just political system, we like to think that all members of that community are at least formally equal. A billionaire and an unemployed person each get one vote. But in the economic system, nobody argues that consumers are equal. Dollars, as we all know, are not distributed equally; Bill Gates has much more purchasing power than the average American worker, who is more and more likely to be working part-time and without benefits. And since markets respond to money, markets are much better at serving the rich than the rest of us. For example, the pharmaceutical Pfizer's slogan is not "drugs to serve human need." Hence, there are no products for those with tuberculosis (which kills 2 million mostly poor people a year) but there are eight new drugs for impotence and seven for balding (Malleson 2014, 96). This failure of markets to serve basic human need is even more egregious in the food system where new product development is oriented around about a billion wealthy consumers many of whom are already obese while close to 2 billion who are food insecure if not starving do not have their needs met with respect to nutritious, affordable, and culturally appropriate food (Patel 2007).[18]

Limit 2. Markets don't deliver all the goods. There are some critical goods that markets do not deliver. It's not because those goods are not scarce (such as air); it's because the delivery of those goods is not profitable.[19] The classic, and oldest, example of this is water.[20] But this is also true of very different kinds of places and institutions from temples for rituals, to infrastructure for dwelling and commerce. From the Great Wall of China to the Cathedral of Notre Dame, the Golden Gate Bridge and the U.S. electrical grid, none were built by markets or private investors. Indeed, we form cities or states to deliver basic goods, and even in times of neoliberal "privatization," many goods are still delivered via states including security, K-12 education, water, and mail. Then there are other goods that are exchanged on the market and are privately owned but are heavily subsidized including (some) food, housing, energy, transportation, and health care.[21]

Limit 3. Monopolies, oligopolies, and cartels. *Ideally* capitalist markets are radically democratic arenas where each individual preference has an opportunity to be satisfied in the dialogue between producers and consumers. Unfortunately, in actually existing capitalism, this space isn't a "level playing field." As noted above, consumers with more resources tend to bring the action toward them. And on the other side of field, producers with more resources (or market share) have the power to constrain consumer choice because of their ability to curtail competition. This is most obvious in a situation where there is just one major player, but market failures can also occur when a sector is dominated by just a few players. Examples here can be seen in lack of options for consumers with cell phone contracts, food labeling (e.g., GMOs), and tech companies, hence the antitrust suits brought against major firms such as Google (Malleson 2014, 96).

Limit 4. Externalities. Market transactions are deemed moral because each person ideally is consenting to the transfer. But sometimes there are side consequences of a transaction that significantly impact a third party who is not part of the exchange. These are called "externalities." The textbook case is of a firm that pollutes the local river. The firm reaps the benefits (profits) but is able to avoid the cost associated with a negative side consequences of the process by sending those "negatives" downstream so it isn't impacted by them nor does it have to cover the costs of being impacted by them. Some argue that global warming is a consequence of this type of market failure (Malleson 2014, 97). Additional externality issues come up with accounting (see Trucost 2013).[22]

Limit 5. Long-term planning and investment. Markets are all about existing people and their present needs. But some goods require long-term planning for their effective provision (Malleson 2014, 97). Markets themselves are literally built upon infrastructure—power plants, roads, ports— that result from long-term planning and investment. And if we want to address large-scale problems such as affordable housing or climate change, the arrangement of financing and administrative coordination requires a multiyear planning process that goes against the short-term considerations of so many buyers and sellers. Global warming is a prime example: developing technologies that will reduce greenhouse gases and not pollute water and air takes dedicated spending for research and development even if there is no current "market" for the product. Also, even if the product makes it to market, it doesn't mean that consumers will adopt it. Price could be an obstacle as well as nonfinancial aspects driving preference (Sachs 2008, 32–33).

A recent case of such market limitations is the once ubiquitous incandescent lightbulb. From an ecological and economic perspective, it is incredibly wasteful of energy and phasing it out is a critical component to creating a more sustainable system. But the market alone was not able to solve this problem. Although competitors emerged (e.g., compact fluorescent lights), because of price and aesthetics, many did not make the switch. So the government moved in and has banned their sale; and much more efficient options have emerged that will meet the goal of reducing energy consumption but also led to a range of alternatives that gives consumer's options ("freedom"). An earlier favorite, the CFC, proved problematic (mercury contamination especially), but the LED has survived testing and usage thus far and other options are becoming available. When there are market failures with respect to basic goods such as a safe and healthy environment or affordable housing, not only must the financing be set up for multiple years and for multiple phases but a number of different regulatory agencies and jurisdictions must be coordinated. One need only look at the difficulties of health care reform at the federal level or affordable housing in major urban areas.

In sum, even the most promarket capitalist recognizes that some goods and services are not adequately delivered through market exchange and some nonmarket form is preferable (planned provision through the state or nonprofits, etc.). What all this means is that there is no one economy. That is, there is no single system that structures all economic activities according to one principle (e.g., profit, the public good, private property, the market, capital, human need). Instead, there is a diversity of economies structured by different principles run by different organizational types operating within nearly every existing state. The challenge, then, from the econD perspective, is not to wait for the demise of the present economy and then build a new one. (There is no [one] "economy"!) The task is to understand this diverse landscape of activity and strengthen the ones that contribute to the norms of maxD. The challenge is to (re)structure economic activity to expand the sustainable, equality-enhancing, need satisfying, democratic ones and weaken the unsustainable, exploitative, and/or authoritarian ones. Now we can turn to the question of organizational types: which is capable of moving the project of econD forward? What are our options?

Business Structure and the Rights of Workers

Macrosystem-level considerations are crucial for thinking through the prospects for econD, but without a reconstruction of the workplace, such efforts are doomed. Indeed, the notion that there could be a democratic economy but no democracy in the workplace is an offense. If workers don't have real power in the place where they make their living, if they don't control the conditions in which they work, if they don't control the profits that they generate, then how is that democracy? Under capitalism we constantly hear about two types of firms, corporations, and small businesses. But how are they actually organized? A small business is intelligible: there is an owner, he or she is often the manager as well, and there are a couple of employees. But what about a corporation? If we want to remake them, or even better, perhaps, replace them, we need to know how they work in order to create a better alternative.

A corporation is a legal entity chartered in some state and owned by shareholders. Yet it is independent in the sense that it is an artificial "person" and thus "it"—not the shareholders—is responsible for its own actions and debts (Kelly 2001, 12, 89–90, 163–165). In the modern publicly held capitalist corporation, the owners are the shareholders and they choose the board of directors responsible for the financial health of the firm. Ellerman explains, "The usual governance structure in a corporation is for the shareholders to elect the board of directors (there are usually 9–20 members) and then for the board to appoint the general manager and possibly other members of the top management team. Top management then appoints the middle managers who, in turn, select the low-level managers or foremen at the shop floor level" (Ellerman 1990, 87). But shareholders are not equal; it's not one person, one vote. It's one share, one vote. A shareholder's number of votes is determined by the number of shares that he or she owns.

The board hires the managers and the latter usually hire the workers. In the United States (unlike in Japan, for example), it is rare for a worker to be on the board, though sometimes board members are high-ranking managers in the firm. (One can already sense the distance between the board and the workers, and it will become even more so.) Another critical function of the board is to decide what to do with the surplus or profits. They decide how much will go to owners as dividends for example. The function of managers is to "monitor, supervise, and control both the production of commodities inside capitalist enterprises and all of the ancillary nonproduction tasks needed to achieve profits and growth (purchasing of inputs, sales of outputs, legal counsel, advertising, lobbying, and so on)" (Wolff 2012, 117–121). On this standard model, the workers have no power within the firm, although they do have the right to leave it (more on this below). But they do not possess any governing authority, nor do they even have a voice in the firm in any structural sense. Sure, managers may ask workers for advice or recommendations, but they don't have to, nor are they required to abide by the recommendations. The workplace is not a democracy. Indeed, most don't even pretend to be, the popularity of "corporate social responsibility" notwithstanding (more below).

On the contrary, the lack of democracy is sometimes even celebrated. For some, the corporate hierarchy is explicitly a virtue: those who earned it, the most talented, the best, they are in charge. Hierarchy leads to game changing innovation and large-scale efficiencies, from Thomas Edison and electric power and light to the accessible-to-the-masses automobiles of Henry Ford to the computers of Bill Gates and phones of Steve Jobs. In each of these cases, genius thrived because it was in charge, the public benefited, and, oh yes, investors made some money. It even makes employment look like a privilege afforded to workers: "Come and work **for me**!" So what's not to like?

From the workers' perspective, a lot. The wage labor relationship introduces three levels of alienation: (1) the worker doesn't control the conditions of his or her work (the manager does), thus one is alienated from one's labor and one's self. It's as if you are not "you" at work. (2) The wage laborer does not decide what to do with the product and the profits (surplus); the owner does. Thus one is separated from what one produces and its benefits. (3) The worker is alienated from his or her fellow workers because she is competing with the others, trying to outdo them, to avoid being laid off, to move up the corporate ladder, etc. (Marcuse 1941, 276–282). How is it possible to develop real relationships of trust and support if each has to try to outdo the others. I have to put me and my family first, right?

The Right to Exit: Employment at Will

Part of the justification for wage labor is that it increases people's freedom of choice, to leave or choose another job. In business ethics and legal circles, this is called "employment at will." A job is based on a contract, and you are not forced to sign it. When viewed in the abstract, this sounds like freedom, but when these contracts are negotiated within the context of the present system, a pronounced asymmetry of power leads to a very uneven playing field when it come to workers and employers. Because most people don't own much, the bargaining power of most workers is quite limited. In the United States, 8 percent of the working age population are owners defined as having "the ability to live off their income generated by their private property," 25 percent are professional workers, 60 percent are average workers, and 7 percent are self-employed (they "work for themselves"; Malleson 2014, 29–30). In this reality, for most people (85%!), refusing wage labor would make it impossible to live. Yes, there is the romantic image of the lotto winner who hits the big jackpot and keeps his job. And if the boss messes with him, he says, "see ya!" But the chances of that are, well, low.

OK, so maybe we don't really "choose" to work. Still, work can be rewarding for a variety of reasons. Even when the work itself is not so meaningful or enjoyable, there may be camaraderie with fellow workers, or the location might offer adventure or amenities, or the relationship with customers might be a source of pleasure. Sure all of these can be nightmares—especially the customers if you work in retail!—but people make friends at work. Some are fortunate enough to obtain a mentor who can really teach them something. Others meet their life partners. But even in these workplaces where there are real rewards, there is an undercurrent of vulnerability. You are not in charge. Your boss may value you tremendously, but, if sales plummet, you may "have to go." Even worse, even if sales don't plummet, you may be asked to go. In others words, while you can't be fired for any reason (antidiscrimination laws in many sectors), you can be fired for no reason. Again, if you just won the lotto, or you have a trust fund, or an inheritance, or really nice parents with a big house, you will be all right. But if you don't, you could literally lose everything. For many, the situation is so uncertain a new term to describe workers has emerged: the "precariat" (Hardt and Negri 2009, 146–147).

If you are "lucky" enough to have lost a full-time job, then you are likely able to collect unemployment insurance, and that will help, but depending on your needs and the size of your household, it may not be enough to "make ends meet." Indeed, in some countries there are a variety of kinds of "insurance" to protect workers, and nonworkers, when they enter, or are pushed, into dire economic straights. Social security for the aged, housing assistance, free college for one's children, all these reduce the job pressure for many. There are also even more robust econD measures such as "guaranteed" or "basic" income (Ackerman, Alstott, and van Parijs 2006) and "dividends for all" (Barnes 2014). But in the United States, for a family of four, a living wage is $50,000. The average welfare provision is $17,000 (Malleson 2014, 30). Is that enough? You do the math. (Or skip the math and move to Denmark.)

So the system that claims to promote freedom of choice is for many structured by coercion: if you don't participate you may not die, but you will lose access to many basic goods. This is because in a society like ours, wage labor is the only means to obtain the goods one needs. "Back in the day" maybe you could hunt and fish your way to survival, but now you can't live off the land unless you own it.[23] Maybe you can grow an amazingly productive garden, but you can't pay for the bus with tomatoes, much less make a house payment, nor will bowls of kale put your kids through college. As Carol Gould puts it, "although workers can indeed leave any particular firm (if they can find another job!), they cannot leave all of them, since work is essential for gaining means of subsistence. Indeed, it is tempting to argue that this feature itself introduces a coercive element into the situation of workers, as our economy is presently constituted. It does not suffice, then, to say that workers can leave and find another firm they prefer to work for" (Gould 2014, 9). So even when you have a job, it's not a democratic situation for most (again 85% of us!). Maybe some don't desire such a choice; they are satisfied with a precarious authoritarian workplace. But for those who do prefer one, their freedom is restricted because the option isn't available. Although we live in a republic where the individual is sovereign, you trade away this sovereignty when you go to work. (See the opening quote from Schweickart at beginning of the chapter.) As you enter the terrain of cubicles, self-determination is checked at the door, and you enter the realm of unfreedom, helplessness, and subservience (Malleson 2014, 33), and today, one might add, surveillance. Because of previously noted asymmetries, you can't bargain for democratic rights at the workplace. Nor is there a market for them. It's not that people don't want it; they lack the power to get it.[24]

The Social Responsibility of Business Is (Not Only) to Increase Its Profits: A Stakeholder Theory (ST) Approach to Corporate Social Responsibility (CSR)

So how have businesses responded to the myriad moral challenges posed by the range of issues cited above? Since the post–World War II corporate revolution, many have called for businesses to be more participatory and "socially responsible," not just to their workers and with respect to their rights but to suppliers, customers, the local community, and the environment more broadly. The outcry gained such popular momentum that that staunch defender of free market logic Milton Friedman rose to counter the protest and penned an infamous essay in the *NY Times* magazine read by nearly every business major over the past forty years: "The Social Responsibility of Business Is to Increase Its Profits." In this essay, Friedman famously argued that business should not even pretend to act in terms of the public good or any other social goal for three important reasons: first off, and most important, a business is a piece of property, and the owner of that property should decide how it should be used, and market logic is the most appropriate method for determining said decisions. Second, business managers are not elected by the public, nor is the business theirs, so it is unfair for them to aim for some public good, and even worse, it is undemocratic for them to do so since they were not elected by the public! Third, businesses do not have the knowledge of how to best pursue such public goods or social responsibilities. Public policy makers are better equipped to do so, and they are elected to do so, so they should do so (M. Friedman [1970] 1997).

Interestingly, despite these protestations, businesses have taken on myriad social responsibilities.[25] The moral reasons for this are fairly straightforward: the actions of businesses directly impact on the well-being not just of the owners, but of many groups, from those employed by the business, to those who purchase their products and services to those who live nearby. Managers then should not only consider the interests of owners and maximize profits à la Friedman, they should weigh the interests of workers, suppliers, customers, the local community, even the government and other businesses in their sector. Such is the view of R. Edward Freeman (the similarity of their names has plagued business ethics instructors for decades!). For Freeman, business is not just about maximizing profits for stockholders; it's about generating benefits for multiple stakeholders (R. Freeman 1984a).

Since Freeman's landmark book (1984b), both corporate social responsibility (CSR) and stakeholder theory (ST) have grown tremendously; so much so that not only has ST achieved a dominance within business ethics (R. Freeman et al. 2010), CSR has become commonplace among corporations (Lee 2008). One of the reasons for the increased popularity of the stakeholder theory version of corporate social responsibility (ST CSR) is that much work has been done to operationalize the concept so that corporate managers have guidelines for its implementation in real-time business settings. This proliferation occurred largely because, as Lee argues, ST CSR moved the issue of "social responsibility" from the macrolevel of society to the microlevel of the firm. That is, rather than abstract talk about "improving society" or "solving social problems," ST CSR came to focus on the microlevel of the firm and those who are directly connected to the operations of the business. Thus, rather than tackle "unemployment" as such (for which Milton Friedman [appropriately in my view] made fun of ST CSR) (M. Friedman [1970] 1997, 58–60), more recent versions of ST CSR focus on job security and one's own workers or programs that address a business's needs with respect to the capabilities of the local labor pool. For example, it is common now to see businesses dialogue and sometimes actually partner with local community colleges in order to make sure students are training for jobs for which there is demand.[26] This also enables businesses to know that over the medium and long term there will be a labor pool that can meet their needs as the market shifts or they expand. Such a case illustrates the more robust moral dimensions of ST because fundamental interests of workers and students are considered in a way that have significant benefits for the corporate bottom line *and* the life goals of workers and students (job security, employment opportunities, capability development). This kind of case also shows that ST CSR need not pit the interests of stakeholders against one another: in this case they are mutually supportive: investing in worker capability development enhances company performance and growth and strengthens the local community's tax base. Since Freeman, then, this lineage of ST has made CSR more comprehensible, doable, and measurable.

Furthermore, (and contra Milton Friedman) there are good reasons to believe that ST CSR is not a constraint on profits but can improve a company's *financial* performance and stock value in particular. Indeed, the key economic justification for ST CSR is that by better attending to the needs and interests of all stakeholders, financial performance is improved: thus CSR leads to improvements in "quality of output, customer satisfaction/retention, employee turnover, R and D productivity, new product development, market growth and environmental competitiveness" (Lee 2008, 63). More specifically, it can improve the reputation of the firm, which can attract more talented employees, open new markets for (socially conscious) consumers as well as make boycotts and lawsuits less likely. Indeed, according to Lee's review of the empirical studies, 82 percent of corporations believe that good corporate citizenship helps the bottom line because of the reasons just named.[27]

This Is NOT What Democracy Looks Like: Problems with ST CSR

Among the benefits of grounding CSR in stakeholder theory is that it makes CSR more doable and measurable. It would seem to follow then that the move from the more generalized macro approach to the hands on micro should afford concrete benefits to specific stakeholders. However, this is often not the case. Instead, serious problems result because managers are the adjudicating agents in the deliberative process. Managers are not just a privileged stakeholder; they dictate the logic by which stakeholders are placed and assessed and the process by which stakeholder interests are made intelligible and weighed.

ST CSR is at best a very minimal form of democracy. As we shall see, it's even less democratic than the representative state! ST CSR does not require that all stakeholders have equal power in the management process (the "one person, one vote" of the liberal democratic representative state). Indeed, in many versions, most stakeholders do not have *any power* in the management process. ST CSR requires that managers consider the needs and interests of all stakeholders (and not just stockholders or owners) before wielding decisive power. But, ST CSR does not require that all stakeholders have the right to present their interests to management; it only requires that management *consider* those stakeholder interests. The logic of ST CSR is structured by the goal of "survival of the firm" and management is tasked with interpreting, integrating, weighing, and/or "balancing" stakeholder interests within the confines of that logic. From a moral standpoint, for ST CSR to have a positive impact, it must "discover" that attending to nonstockholder stakeholder interests can both improve the status of said groups AND enhance corporate financial performance. Or, ST CSR must push management to construct and advance a business plan that opts for paths that enhance both. What happens then is CSR is seen as a factor that must be considered for corporations to survive. Lee writes, "The underlying assumption of [ST] was that, if the surrounding society which businesses belong to deteriorates, businesses lose their critical support structure and customer base. Therefore, it is in corporations' long term interests to support the well being of their environment" (Lee 2008, 59). But is this really the case?

ST CSR in the Food Industry: McDonald's

> Aspiring to be the best employer . . . holding ourselves to the highest possible ethical standards and more . . . our commitment to ensuring the integrity of the company in all of its dealings with stakeholders. . . . Managers treat employees as they would want to be treated, employees are respected and valued, all of us act in the best interest of the company, pay is at or above local market, employees value their pay and benefits, restaurants are adequately staffed . . . to allow for work-life balance. (from McDonald's website, quoted in Royle, 2005, 45)

When it comes to customer base, sector dominance, brand familiarity, and visibility in the global marketplace, few firms rival McDonald's. Not only is it in 119 countries; it is the market leader in most (Royle 2005, 45). And unlike high-end darling Apple, it is a product intimately familiar for more than a half century to indefinitely many ("billions and billions served"!). McDonald's is one of the largest employers in the world (1.5 million employees spread across 33,000 franchises), and not only is it a dominant food-industry player; it is one of the largest global toy retailers (Royle 2005, 50).

In terms of its operational setting, each McDonald's franchise has between 35 and 100 employees, with even more working at the larger drive-through operations. According to Royle, a typical outlet has around 50 employees. The benefits package for full-time workers is better than average: private health care, a pension, paid holidays, company car, sick pay, stock options, and a clothing allowance. But the problem is that 90 percent of McDonald's employees are not full-time employees; they are hourly wage earners not eligible for most of those benefits. Indeed, at the typical outlet, only four or five are salaried staff (Royle 2005, 44). (This low percentage of full-time workers is common throughout many of the largest employers in the United States, including Walmart, Home Depot, and the fast-food conglomerate Yum Brands [e.g., Taco Bell, KFC].) One might reply that there is upward mobility at McDonald's, since some workers can and do reach the ranks that access middle-class wages and benefits. This does happen, and there is evidence of this. But such "working one's way up the corporate ladder" is a bit misleading. When an individual purchases a franchise, that owner must work as a shift worker for one year. (After that year he or she moves up, to owner!) What happens to most employees after a year is that they leave. McDonald's turnover rate is between 100 and 300% (Royle 2005, 45).

While some argue that McDonald's is a positive force for local economic development, Royle argues, "While there is no question that McDonald's creates jobs in developing countries and particularly for marginalised sections of the labour market, [. . .] for the vast majority of the workforce, the pay and working conditions in these jobs is far from being 'overwhelmingly positive'" (Royle 2005, 45). The point of all this is not to join the chorus of those condemning McDonald's. But the issue is this: if a seemingly omnipresent multinational corporation (MNC) whose workforce is relatively visible to its customers (as opposed to a factory) cannot be held to a meaningful level of accountability, then what does that say about the efficacy and possibilities of CSR?

What is perhaps most disconcerting about the McDonald's case is the fact that even in developed countries with extensive labor laws and strong unions, McDonald's frequently fails to provide safe working conditions and routinely acts to depress wages and block unions. Indeed, despite its public commitments to ST CSR, minimizing worker presence and power in the managerial process seems to be standard practice, as is the violation of worker rights. Even in countries with extensive hard and soft law protections such as the United States and Europe—and in countries with strong unions such as Germany—workers have suffered from both forms of abuse. Indeed, in Germany, there are worker councils through multiple sectors that seem to instantiate key stakeholder theory demands such as making sure workers are represented in company deliberations. But McDonald's has fought such councils for thirty years. Also, McDonald's, like many firms, hires more and more workers who are exempt from traditional labor law. This includes not just part-time workers, but recent immigrants. In many countries (including Germany), such workers are less likely to file complaints against employers because of the power the employer has over their visas (Royle 2005, 46).

One could argue, however, that this approach does benefit particular stakeholders: costs for consumers are lower and the stock value is higher. From a ST CSR perspective it might seem justifiable insofar as the consumer group of stakeholders is drastically larger than the workforce, as are the class of shareholders. Why not, then, argue that the benefits to those substantial groups outweigh the drawbacks to workers? Because it is done without their consent and violates their basic rights.

In some cases such sacrifices could be justified if there were deliberations and approval by the workers. For example, when faced with plant closings, or even store closings, sometimes workers have agreed to make sacrifices with respect to pay or benefits in order to save their jobs. In such a case, workers would be treated as ends insofar as their views were consulted and management informed them of the options in a reasonable and transparent manner. But this is not the case with McDonald's. Indeed, McDonald's has actively undermined the power and voice of workers and has sought to exempt itself from hard law. Such an approach that not only sacrifices the interests of stakeholders but violates their basic rights in order to enhance financial performance is called a "low road" business model (Lewis and Swinney 2008).

According to Royle's extensive studies, this "low road" business model is made possible and profitable through the firm's use of technology, the labor and consumer market opportunities provided by globalization, and, most crucially for us, its management culture. In economic circles, technology is usually praised for its ability to increase some combination of efficiency, quality, and quantity. This is often achieved through productivity increases that decrease labor costs. What is underappreciated is that reducing labor costs increases management power and intensifies the gap between management and workers (Royle 2005, 43). But the number of persons (e.g., the labor pool) available for such jobs exceeds demand even with the high turnover. And high turnover is possible because so much of the skill set required is lodged in the technologies.

Not only does high turnover help keep wages down; it also enhances the distance between managers (who have much longer average tenures) and workers who come and go much more quickly, are less well known, and are seen as expendable. When combined with stark differences in pay and benefits, this double distancing fosters a management culture that is both separate from and even antagonistic toward its workforce. Royle states, "Managers are under much greater pressure to reduce costs than to act on workers' grievances. The result is that management rarely responds to workers' complaints unless forced to do so by trade unions (where these exist) or bad publicity" (Royle 2005, 47). Indeed, because labor is perceived as a "constraint" on profits (and shareholder value), the reduction of labor costs is pursued by many means. McDonald's management is constantly exploring ways to get employees to work without paying them: favorite strategies include after hours cleaning "parties," and "asking" employees to punch out during slow periods. With respect to worker rights violations, unpaid "off the clock" work seems to be the most persistent abuse (Royle 2005, 46).

To sum up, Royle draws upon the work of Naomi Klein's (2001) which is crucial for understanding the limits of CSR even when CSR is linked to an overtly moral stakeholder view. The situation of workers at McDonald's

> is typical of modern brand management and what Klein (2001) describes as the "discarded factory." Large corporations are less and less interested in manufacturing products, but more interested in developing their brands. Klein (2001) suggests that according to this

logic, corporations should not waste their resources on factories or on employees who will demand better pay and working conditions, but should spend on sponsorships, packaging, expansion, advertising and acquiring distribution, and retail channels. The production of McDonald's toys by others (at mercilessly low prices), its immense advertising speed and the distribution of toys through its outlets is a perfect example of this. (Royle 2005, 51, my emphasis)

In other words, when ST CSR comes to be seen as a route to enhance financial performance in terms of the logic of branding that Klein describes, management privileges the interests of stockholders and consumers and utilizes the public dimension of CSR not to make evident the real interests of all stakeholders, but to make the product more desirable to consumers. Sometimes this involves playing upon their ethical inclinations. CSR is especially subject to the logic of branding (and public relations) because it is in essence a discursive public declaration that is produced and enforced by management. Branding has as its target the consumer, and in a real sense further distances workers from the management process especially when they are contracted out. Workers at McDonald's are not contracted out in the most overt sense of an Apple or Nike, but they are contracted out in two other senses: franchises have relative autonomy from corporate management, and, as noted above, 90 percent of the workforce is part time and thus has a much more precarious contractual relationship with the firm (they are not afforded the same kind of protections and benefits as full-time workers).

This issue goes far beyond McDonald's and the fast-food sector. This kind of labor model has evolved and become so widespread that it has engendered a new name: the precariat (Standing 2014). Over 30 percent of the U.S. workforce is now a day laborer, temp, independent contractor, or freelancer (Scholz 2016, 6). How could ST CSR possibly work in such a situation of the proliferation of part-time workers and the existential condition known as precarity? How could ST CSR possibly work when the bargaining power of workers is significantly weaker than management even in those (few) countries with unions and legal protections? The case of McDonald's shows how difficult it can be for ST CSR to position workers as listened to (much less "equal") stakeholders in the decision-making process. Most troubling is that far from being a risky strategy in this image-conscious world, Royle argues that this "low road" strategy is sustainable from a business perspective even in the "medium" term (Royle 2005, 52). And it's getting even worse in the digital age with work models such as Amazon's Mechanical Turk (Scholz 2016, 8–10).

While McDonald's may seem an easy target, it is an important one for those who defend stakeholder theory because corporate social responsibility is supposed to be more appropriate for larger firms (Jamali 2008, 226–229).

This failure illustrates some dangerous tendencies or limitations of ST CSR. First is the tremendous power of management to interpret the needs and interests of stakeholders and then adjudicate conflicts in terms of the (low road) business model logic. Given the pressure that this logic puts on them, it is not surprising that managers pursue CSR initiatives that improve brand and reputations but are low cost. McDonald's utilization of the Ronald McDonald House is an excellent example. The Ronald McDonald House is a program that provides housing near hospitals for families who need a place to stay while their child receives medical treatment. It also has expanded in recent years to provide "essential medical, dental and educational services to more than 150,000 children annually."[28] Here McDonald's can argue that it is fulfilling its CSR responsibilities to the community. But as Lee points out, this is with respect to a social problem that has no direct relationship to its business sector where its actions could actually dramatically improve the situation of many of its stakeholders (Lee 2008, 65).

The second problem with ST CSR is that the research on it exacerbates the management-centricity problem because it gathers data about the vices and virtues of CSR *from the managers themselves.* Management tends to view and evaluate CSR not in terms of the value to stakeholders but from the strategic perspective of how CSR can contribute to the bottom line and the competitive performance of the firm (Lee 2008, 69).[29] For Lee, according to empirical evidence, the best way to get managers to respond to stakeholder interests that might conflict with profits or shareholder value is by linking to actors *outside* the firm, for example, social movements and protestors and in general by making ST CSR more "public" (Lee 2008, 62).[30]

Although Lee only gives a few glimpses of this model, Palazzo and Scherer develop a framework that takes a more public-oriented ST CSR approach. Palazzo and Scherer build on some of the analyses and criticisms of ST CSR just discussed, but they go further than views such as Lee's and argue that the corporation is undergoing a legitimation crisis and the way to improve its commitment to the social good is to shift the stakeholder network's deliberative process's center of gravity from within the firm—and under the auspices of management—to outside the firm, not within government and hard law but within the soft law of civil society.

The Civil Society Approach to Corporate Social Responsibility: Politicize the Corporation?!

> Anecdotal evidence shows that corporations already have started to assume enlarged responsibilities in their globally expanded business environments—responsibilities once regarded as genuine governmental responsibilities [. . .]. They engage in public health, education, social security, and protection of human rights in countries with repressive

> regimes [. . .]; address social ills such as AIDS, malnutrition, and illiteracy
> [. . .]; engage in self-regulation to fill global gaps in legal regulation and
> moral orientation [. . .]; and promote societal peace and stability [. . .].
> Those activities go beyond the common understanding of stakeholder
> responsibility and CSR as conceptualized in the positivist tradition.
>   —SCHERER AND PALAZZO, "TOWARDS A POLITICAL CONCEPTION," 1109

> In recent years, it has been maintained that the main threats to civic
> liberties no longer come from state authorities but from private economic
> actors.
>   —PALAZZO AND SCHERER, "CORPORATE LEGITIMACY AS DELIBERATION," 77

In medieval times citizens and merchants rightly complained about the arbitrary power wielded by kings and their bureaucracies, but, today, many consider corporations to be the major purveyors of such abuses. For this and other reasons, argue Palazzo and Scherer, firms must be "politicized" (Palazzo and Scherer 2006, 71). This means taking the corporation out of the confines of management theory and business ethics and placing it squarely within the terrain of political theory since "management theory has paid too little attention to the relationship between business and society [. . .] or interpreted that relationship in a purely economic way (Palazzo and Scherer 2006, 82). Such a view is problematic because, as the quote above notes, economic firms are more like governments than we like to admit especially since they provide services and engage in programs from education to health care and disease prevention (Scherer and Palazzo 2006, 1109).

According to Palazzo and Scherer, ST CSR views fail to appreciate the scope of corporate power and do not adequately comprehend the lack of public trust in MNCs (Palazzo and Scherer 2006, 72). The erosion of this legitimacy goes back at least to the 1960s when a series of corporate scandals and abuses prompted federal legislation that not only created new regulations but entire agencies such as the EPA and NLRB (Lee 2008, 57–59). Yet, as subsequent scandals and crises have shown, such changes were inadequate. Even before the Great Recession and the Fannie Mae and Freddie Mac mortgage debacles, there was an all too steady parade of corporate calamities ranging from Enron and Arthur Andersen to the BP Gulf oil disaster. The common view for this mistrust is similar to Lee's analysis discussed above: yes, many companies publicly state a commitment to CSR but they do so to improve their image or brand. Enron is the poster child for such egregious duplicity: it was regarded as an exemplar of CSR and its shares were widely held by "socially responsible" funds (Lee 2008, 66)! On this view, when they can, or when profits or power is at stake, corporations will violate any if not all of their CSR principles. When the violations occur, corporations often plead ignorance or claim that they are not the responsible party (it was a contractor, supplier, etc.). And when they cannot deny it, firms will plead necessity or fiduciary responsibility and argue that the core interests of the firm demanded the action (due to legal requirements, the pressures of shareholders, etc.) In other words, when push comes to shove, and periodically it does for any firm, CSR doesn't work.

For Palazzo and Scherer, the distrust expressed in the above points toward two kinds of legitimacy that corporations *fail* to obtain in the current milieu. The first is "pragmatic" legitimacy, the other, "cognitive" legitimacy. Pragmatic legitimacy means that persons regard a firm as legitimate if enough stakeholders believe they will *benefit* from the activities of the firm. The preceding paragraph rules that view out. Cognitive legitimacy obtains when a society believes that the organization is a *necessary and inevitable* part of the society's landscape and is consistent with the norms and expectations of the society (Palazzo and Scherer 2006, 72). This view is in disrepute as well since the idea that the free market apolitical corporate model is "natural and inevitable" has been weakened considerably (Healy and Graham 2008). Because of corruption (e.g., Enron, Fannie Mae and Freddie Mac), disasters (e.g., BP oil spill), and bailouts (GM, Citibank), the idea that the economic sphere can or should be "self-regulating" seems more and more far-fetched (Palazzo and Scherer 2006, 74).

For Palazzo and Scherer, confronting this legitimation crisis requires a politicization of the corporation. This shouldn't surprise those familiar with earlier phases of CSR. As Compa points out, a key phase in the development of CSR occurred in regard to acts that crossed from the terrain of the moral to the political in the 1970s with respect to the role of U.S. corporations in the coup against President Allende in Chile and other firms' support of apartheid South Africa (Compa 2008, 2). Although this led to new legislation regulating the transnational activities of U.S. firms,[31] Palazzo and Scherer are not calling for more regulation of corporations by government agencies. *Instead they call for a new arrangement of stakeholders in civil society.* This sets the stage for a different mode of communication, discourse, and debate among stakeholders. Unlike the output orientation of the pragmatic approach, this communicative process is more input-oriented and focused on "will formation." (Rousseau is back!) Unlike the cognitive approach, it does not presume shared ideological commitments but instead aims to connect differently situated stakeholders through the mechanisms of deliberative democracy. Yet, unlike any version of ST CSR, this conversation should happen not *within* the firm, but in the realm of civil society. Because the setting is within the terrain of civil society, the politicization of the corporation, ironically perhaps, calls for a *moral* view of legitimacy and in that sense is consistent with most formulations of ST CSR. It also taps the view we have called, following Keane, "monitory democracy."

Palazzo and Scherer, like watchdog democracy discussed in the Introduction and Chapter 1, believe that their view diverges from both ST CSR (see above) and liberal theory. Two problems with liberal theory is that it assumes or enforces a hard distinction between the public and private realms and treats individual preferences as fixed. Liberalism then aims to insulate "corporations from direct democratic will formation" by arguing that "the state is the only public and political actor who has to justify decisions, whereas corporations are private (and therefore) apolitical actors who do not have to expose their decisions to public scrutiny, as long as they comply with the law and moral customs" (Scherer and Palazzo 2007, 1106). As deliberative democrats, Palazzo and Scherer argue "corporate as well as governmental actors depend on processes of civic self-determination (Habermas, 1996) and [. . .] there is no reason to exclude some spheres of society from democratic scrutiny (Gutmann & Thompson, [1996])" (Scherer and Palazzo 2007, 1106).

The other problem is that the liberal model construes individual preferences as fixed and deems that the political process's role is to channel conflict, usually understood as bargaining over scarce resources. This model of liberal democracy was infamously articulated by Schumpeter (see my Chapter 1). Interests, again, are considered to be "competing and incompatible" (Scherer and Palazzo 2007, 1106). Also, "despite its suspicion regarding a strong state, liberal theory rests on the assumption that the state system is more or less capable of regulating the economic system so that its output contributes to the common good" (Scherer and Palazzo 2007, 1106–1107). At this point, Palazzo and Scherer argue against the separation of the economic and political spheres and call for the political appropriation of the firm within the framework of (late) Habermasian deliberative democracy.[32] It is through this process of "giving good reasons" in discussion and debate in a public setting that moral agreements are formed. Empowered participatory governance (see my Chapter 2) theorist Archon Fung channels Rawls and Habermas and writes, "The distinctive idea of deliberative democracy is that binding rules and practices should be determined through open and fair processes of public reason in which parties—be they citizens, political officials, or groups—offer arguments and evidence to persuade others (Fung 2003, 52).[33] This process is legitimate if and when it satisfactorily includes competing discourses and views and gives them a fair hearing in the process (Palazzo and Scherer 2006, 80).

The virtues of deliberative democracy are well articulated by Fung (whom Palazzo and Scherer cite) who draws upon other noted theorists in that tradition including Cohen and Rogers. Fung writes,

> First, individuals—as citizens, workers, or officials—*can become more knowledgeable and other-regarding* in the course of exchanging views and reasons. Arenas of deliberation can thus function as *"schools of democracy"* in which people learn the skills and dispositions necessary

to be good citizens (Cohen and Rogers; Levine; Mattson). Second, deliberation can increase the wisdom and efficacy of standards and rules by introducing additional information and diversifying the perspectives considered (Fearon; Robb). When participants are engaged in implementing resulting policies, public action also gains from their cooperation and contributions (Fung and Wright). Finally, deliberation can also enhance the *legitimacy and credibility* of standards and rules, and of the entities that set them as well as those that follow them, by subjecting them to the scrutiny of open public debate, review, and determination. (Fung 2003, 52, my emphasis)

This requires a public sphere that has institutions and procedures that are designed to facilitate such conversations with different and competing actors and discourses (Palazzo and Scherer 2006, 82).

Because their focus is not on corporate management, Palazzo and Scherer clearly break from the ST CSR model. Indeed, corporate managers, for better and/or worse, are strikingly absent from the picture. Instead, the emphasis is on the public venue and the setting up of a communicative network of stakeholders where "true dialogue" can occur without overwhelming the corporation with demands or demonizing it (Palazzo and Scherer 2006, 81–82). Corporate managers are no longer at the center of the stakeholder nexus, instead they are one among many stakeholders who are now positioned within a network in the terrain of civil society. Such a civil society network can also help to overcome the inefficacy and immorality of bureaucratic forms of coordination that are too formal and "command and control"–oriented and thus unfairly subordinate persons. They are also inefficient with respect to outcomes (Scherer and Palazzo 2007, 1114).

To be sure, Palazzo and Scherer believe that political institutions and representative mechanisms will still play important regulatory and legislative roles with respect to the economy. But they argue that deliberation in civil society should become the principle venue for addressing the crisis of corporate legitimacy and reintegrating the political and economic spheres. Also, as Lee argues, social movements have and should continue to play a role in both exposing and shaming corporations that violate CSR. What is curious is that Palazzo and Scherer hold this line even though they acknowledge that there is no guarantee that these communicative processes will result in an agreement among all the stakeholders (Palazzo and Scherer 2006, 82). Indeed, it could, like the current corporate pragmatic approach, provoke even more conflict. But they believe their deliberative, civil society approach is better than the output-oriented pragmatic approach that overly empowers management and fails to address the underlying issues of corporate power and the role of the firm on the economy.

Building upon the critiques of Lee above, Scherer and Palazzo also argue against ST CSR's management-centricity not just because of what it does to nonstockholding stakeholders but also because of its stance toward the rest (nonstakeholders) of society.

> What can be a justified social claim in the eyes of a social interest group may be different from the moral ideas of managers, suppliers, customers, or other interest groups. In the case of conflicting business morals, the CSP [corporate social performance] models state that a company's top managers simply consider those views that exert the greatest economic or legal pressure—via the capital market, procurement, employment, sales market, or legislative body. (Scherer and Palazzo 2007, 1099)

Thus, if one cannot exercise power or sanctions through the market (investments, purchasing power) or through the state (e.g., legislation, lobbying), then ST CSR is unlikely to value said group's interests when it is decision-making time (Scherer and Palazzo 2007, 1099). Indeed, for Scherer and Palazzo, strictly speaking, *managers do not morally deliberate*. Rather, they act in terms of the *"empirical dominance* of particular interests, structures of power, and sources of influence" rather than on *"ethical justification* [. . .]. Therefore, the CSP models cannot prescribe how management practice can reasonably move from 'what is' to 'what should be'" (Scherer and Palazzo 2007, 1100). If Palazzo and Scherer are right on this point, then, operationally speaking, *there is no such thing as stakeholder theory corporate social responsibility!* The ST component requires deliberation among stakeholders, but there is none, only managers aiming to fulfill the demands of CSR.

Not only is the internalist ST CSR model not adequate but neither is the externalist state regulatory model (a version of which, counterintuitively perhaps, was favored by Milton Friedman). The state can't adequately address these conflicts because of domestic ideological differences and interests, globalization, and the operational limits of bureaucracy in complex societies (Scherer and Palazzo 2007, 1101, 1108). Here Scherer and Palazzo build upon the views of all those who critique the state not so much because it is corrupt but because it is incompetent.[34] This includes anti-PD "governance" views (Hooghe and Marks 2003) and rights-based civil society views as well as pro-PD associationists (e.g., Hirst, see my Chapter 1). Scherer and Palazzo write:

> This model for the integration of business and society may work well in a world where the state is actually able to predict problems and conflicts in society, to formulate regulations *exante,* and to enforce these rules through the legal and administrative system. In *modern*

societies, however, because of the complexity and variability of conditions, law and the state apparatus are insufficient means for the
integration of business activities with societal concerns. (Scherer and
Palazzo 2007, 1100–1101)

Thus, not only can business not regulate itself; government cannot regulate
business! The answer to corporate corruption is not more government regulation, it is civil society–based deliberation. Civil society is the best venue for
moral, political, epistemic, and instrumental reasons. It allows for diverse
groups to come together and be heard, does so in a democratic manner, and
has the flexibility and organizational capacity to manage the complexity of
the global economy. Unlike the liberal model of fixed preferences and a
public-private split, this deliberative venue allows for "private" preferences
(of individuals, firms, and civil society groups) to be subject to discussion
and debate and the common good pursued (Scherer and Palazzo 2007, 1107–
1109). And the deliberative model does this in a way that is not utopian but
begins where people are with their everyday concerns.[35]

Applying the Civil Society CSR Model: The Forest Stewardship Council, Students Against Sweatshops

Palazzo and Scherer critique the internalism of ST CSR and don't believe
that the hard law of the state will solve the problem either. Instead, they reposition firms and redefine their role within a civil society (CS) framework
that attempts to carve out a space for the public in between the market and
the state. This is a view that goes back at least to Hegel but gains in popularity especially after the fall of the Soviet Union (Cohen and Arato 1992) and
with the incredible rise of NGOs at the end of the last century (Hooghe and
Marks 2003). However, Palazzo and Scherer's development and implementation of this watchdog democracy view in a business ethics context is novel. I
examine two cases for the articulations of their view: their own case of the
Forest Stewardship Council and Students against Sweatshops from the related perspective of PD proponent Fung.

The Forest Stewardship Council (FSC) is a nongovernmental organization that works to promote ethically sound and environmentally sustainable
forest management programs and activities. In their own words, the mission
is to "promote environmentally appropriate, socially beneficial, and economically viable management of the world's forests." Their vision is make
sure that the "world's forests meet the social, ecological, and economic rights
and needs of the present generation without compromising those of future
generations."[36] FSC does this by determining the *norms* and criteria for ethical forest management and then creating a *mechanism* so that the management programs can be regulated and the products emerging from them

certified as meeting the aforementioned norms (Diamond 2005, 473–474; Scherer and Palazzo 2007, 1110). Thus, "FSC *certification* provides a credible link between responsible production and consumption of forest products, enabling consumers and businesses to make purchasing decisions that benefit people and the environment as well as providing ongoing business value."[37]

The FSC emerged after the failure of the UN Conference on Environment and Development (also known as the 1992 Rio Conference) to develop shared standards and activities for forests worldwide even though the damages of such activity were well known. In other words, the FSC was created because states could not agree on how to regulate corporate activity in this sector and corporations were incapable of regulating themselves.

The FSC is funded by businesses, governments, foundations, and environmental organizations. Its membership includes corporations such as Home Depot and IKEA along with human rights activists, development aid agencies, indigenous peoples' groups, and environmental NGOs. In other words it includes those engaged in industrial forestry as well as those most affected by it and also those who possess the capacities and knowledges (both moral and scientific) to address the situation. In terms of its structure, the FSC resembles neither a corporation nor a state. Instead, it has a general assembly (hello PD!) of members with three different "chambers": social, economic, and environmental. To address global power imbalances between developed and developing countries, each chamber is divided into "north" and "south." There is also a board of directors and a director general based in Bonn that handles the everyday operations (Diamond 2005, 473; Scherer and Palazzo 2007, 1110).[38] *

Another case of a civil society approach to corporate social responsibility is Students against Sweatshops or SAS. Founded in 1998, SAS activists carry out public information campaigns to rally consumers and entice or shame corporations to come to the table and sign agreements to guarantee worker rights. These agreements have been monitored not by corporations but by independent third parties and involve recurrent mobilizations and deliberations in a civil society context. SAS created an independent organization to actually do the monitoring, the Worker Rights Consortium (WRC). The WRC sends representatives to facilities in the Global South where the apparel is being produced to monitor whether the code of conduct is being upheld. In classic watchdog fashion, the WRC then issues reports every year on the working conditions in the facilities. When a factory is found to not be upholding the code of conduct, SAS and its allies usually pressure those who are issuing the license (e.g., universities) to terminate their contract with the firm (Featherstone 2002).

This model has proved advantageous for all stakeholders because the power of multiple groups in the process and the deliberative venue's relative autonomy from the state and market makes it more flexible and responsive to differing contexts and the needs of those affected. For example, of particular concern for Students against Sweatshops is child labor. But, as Fung argues, "The outright prohibition of child labor in poor areas can make matters worse by driving families below subsistence levels or by pushing children into less regulated, more degrading and dangerous work. International conventions now recognize this reality and call for the elimination of the worst forms of child labor, rather than a more encompassing immediate ban" (Fung 2003, 59). A state enforced rights approach does not have such flexibility and receptivity to context. Also, because the economy and supply chains in particular are so globalized, this also brings diverse actors to the table from across a variety of nations and states that "may spur the development of a cosmopolitan public around labor standards by fortifying an inclusive global discourse and crystallizing cross-national solidarities among heterogeneous actors such as activists, consumers, workers, and managers" (Fung 2003, 58).

The cases of FSC and SAS are not (internalist) implementations of ST CSR but reterritorializations of CSR in civil society. Palazzo and Scherer write, "The FSC does not represent a form of stakeholder dialogue, in which corporations invite stakeholders into their internal decision-making processes. Rather, it represents a corporate move into the political processes of public policy-making through the creation of and collaboration with global institutions of political governance" (Scherer and Palazzo 2007, 1110). And the same can be said of SAS. As places for deliberation, SAS and FSC are separate from both governments and businesses. This can be seen in their norms and decision-making structures. The dynamic is located outside of the firm and is not controlled by corporate managers. This feature makes it both more democratic and moral, which is to say, more amenable to demands that are ethically justified rather than decided in accordance with the framework of corporate social performance. Corporate decision-making processes are then required to fit into civil society discourses in which ethical forestry is defined not by a "self-regulating" corporation but through a dialogue with environmentalists, residents of the forest, and those who work it. In other words, "ethically sound" forestry is not to be determined by corporate managers but in the general assembly.

There are numerous benefits of this model. First off, instead of requiring managers to be ethical, SAS and FSC *politicize* corporations. As was seen with McDonald's and many others, many times corporations aim to *show* how ethical they are by setting up or donating to charities that have nothing to do with their sector. They do this to enhance their brand. Although this may directly benefit some persons (as in the case of Ronald McDonald house), it does not address the moral concerns or the unique capabilities and responsibilities of the firm relative to its sector (Scherer and Palazzo 2007,

1115). Fung makes the same point about the powers of deliberation located in a civil society venue with respect to labor rights. By creating a dialogue between firms and their critics, which is not controlled by corporate managers, corporations are required to construct solutions for problems posed not by shareholders but by, in this case, workers and their communities.

There are both ethical and epistemic advantages to this kind of decentralized deliberation. In this context, "decentralized" means that there is not one stakeholder group that is dominating the process. Instead, as the structure of the FSC indicates, there are multiple stakeholders and multiple norms (social, economic, ethical) and the goal is to generate policies and programs that satisfy each of these norms. Because of the complexity of implementing this goal, the knowledge and capacities of multiple actors are required. Corporations by themselves lack many of these capacities as do "distant" regulators who focus too much on generating and applying uniform standards. This decentered civil society deliberative frame was also used by Students against Sweatshops. SAS used it to enable firms "to incorporate labor-standards monitoring into their internal supply-chain management and evaluation practices, thus redeploying organizational methods and capacities designed to improve quality, product diversity, and cost to the task of improving labor standards" (Fung 2003, 60).

By now the advantages of the civic society model over ST CSR should be apparent: in a nutshell, CS is more democratic, which means that more stakeholders have more power in the corporate policy-making process. But increased procedural democracy is not the main goal. In the case of the FSC, it is social, economic, and ecological health. In Fung's case of Students against Sweatshops, the goal is labor rights. More democracy means having input from key stakeholders not merely to hear their voices, but to tap their knowledge and capacities to generate solutions that realize the norms in question. ST CSR does not do this.

But how does one know if these norms are actually fulfilled? Who decides? And who punishes if they are violated? This is a big problem with ST CSR, but CS CSR seems to have more success on compliance. Palazzo and Scherer make this point with respect to ecological considerations and forestry: "Companies sometimes position themselves as sustainable and drown the readers of their CSR reports in technical data but do no more than comply with basic environmental laws [. . . and] 'without external, third party verification and monitoring,' it is impossible to differentiate between genuine efforts and CSR rhetoric" (Scherer and Palazzo, 2007, 1114). In the civil society model, corporate codes of conduct are signed by corporations and independent third parties (NGOs). States too play a role here because they help to fund and gather info for the NGOs. But NGOs are more flexible than states and better at monitoring than corporations.

So why should corporations enter such an agreement with a third party and an arrangement with civil society? Because social group pressure and discriminating consumers increasingly threaten the legitimacy of corporations. Scherer and Palazzo argue that once corporations are politicized and enter the terrain of civil society—which unlike the corporate boardroom they do not control—they can become "trapped." That is, if the civil society venue is perceived as adequately democratic and deliberative, it will be very difficult for a corporation to leave or ignore it (Scherer and Palazzo 2007, 1111). As Fung puts it, "In an environment where their claims can be checked, the demands of activists and responses of corporations become more reasonable, not because these actors are necessarily motivated by ethical considerations but because that is what public credibility demands" (Fung 2003, 56). Though firms appear to lose power in this model, there are benefits. Because the deliberations are happening outside the firm, the internal operations of the firm are not being overwhelmed with demands to make them more democratic (as can happen with ST CSR) (Scherer and Palazzo 2007, 1110–1111). Both sides win.

In sum, the strength of the CS CSR approach is that it takes CSR out of hands of corporations, since managers are too likely to violate it, do things that don't address real issues, and bury the public with rhetoric. Civil society provides a venue for third party regulation that is independent. It also creates a will formation process that is more democratic and organizationally flexible to deal with these issues than governmental regulatory bodies and hard law. Another difference between the two views is that ST CSR calls on corporations to become moral arbiters, but Scherer and Palazzo's civil society view does not. Rather, the civil society framework aims to make them subject to moral demands. But does a CS CSR type model actually deal with these problems and perform better from the standpoint of the norms invoked?

Too Civil? Problems in Enforcement for CS CSR

But does CS CSR actually work? Does it improve the lives of workers and the ecological health of forests? There are two issues: (1) are CS CSR watchdogs groups *effective* at getting corporations to comply with CS CSR norms? (2) Are CS CSR norms adequate from the perspective of PD and more general justice concerns?

The efforts of SAS are admirable, and I believe that the FSC design structure is innovative and enticing from a PD perspective. One strength of the FSC is the composition of its membership and structure. As sketched above, its assembly model is inclusive and attempts to deal with inequalities among groups and countries by having two chambers. FSC's membership is made up not just of firms but on-the-ground stakeholders who have serious criticisms of the firms including workers and communities, and environmental scientists. Thus, when compared with other forest certification programs such as the Sustainable Forestry Initiative (SFI), FSC seems much more legitimate since SFI is funded only by forestry companies and investment groups while FSC receives government and foundation support. And investigations into SFI forestry operations have shown their operations to have been so duplicitous that many companies that had been using the SFI label have opted out. And many of those have switched to FSC.[39]

While such an increase in membership would seem to lend more credibility to FSC, FSC too has faced considerable criticisms; so much so that the watchdog has its own watchdog, FSC-Watch! The main problem with FSC is that some forestry operations have been improperly certified. The case of Sweden is particularly troubling since it is a first-world country with lots of assets and goodwill among many parties but still has failed to protect much of its considerable forests.[40] A more difficult issue might be that the measures meant to implement the norms might not be working. And an additional problem is that in some markets, FSC certification has become a serious competitive advantage but the cost of certification puts undue pressure on small businesses. If said small business are violators of the norms, then such a disadvantage could of course be justified, but if FSC's programs are not protecting these norms then obviously they are not.[41]

Another major difficulty facing the civil society model is that in so many sectors corporations have not been willing participants nor have they been effectively "trapped." The case of McDonald's is illustrative here. Indeed, because of the considerable assets combined with incredible market pressures, many corporations actively undermine the CS CSR model by either funding and thereby attempting to control it (e.g., SFI, "greenwashing" in general) or actively working against regulators, NGOs, unions, and social movements (e.g., McDonald's). Put another way, despite their public impact and the formation of the Workers Rights Consortium, many clothing companies have not effectively changed their ways or changed for a while and then reverted back. The Dhaka fire of 2012 which killed 117 and injured more than 200 was a horrifying example of major players such as Walmart actually working against the enforcement of basic safety standards.[42] Even if such CS CSR watchdogs were effective on all of their norms, it's not clear that they would be meeting most PD goals or at all addressing the economic inequality crisis. For SAS and WRC, the code of conduct requires that companies not engage in forced overtime, child labor, bonded labor, or discrimination of any kind, including sex discrimination. The code of conduct also "affirms workers' rights to a living wage, a safe work environment, and freedom of association and collective bargaining."[43] But there is no demand that workers develop capacities or control the running of the firm as PD requires. This requires another moral-political framework and business model.

The Worker Cooperative Model and the Case of the Mondragon Corporation

Based in several towns in the Basque Autonomous Community in northern Spain, the Mondragon Corporation is a federation of worker-owned firms that employs nearly 80,000 people in 260 companies in several sectors including industry, retail, education, and finance. Hereafter called simply "Mondragon," MC, or the "Federation,"[44] it started small in 1956 with a single worker-owned firm making paraffin stoves in the town from which it obtains its name. And now its products and services are world renowned: its Orbea bicycles have won several Tour de France races and an MC firm provided construction services for one of the most lauded buildings on the planet—the Bilboa Guggenheim Museum designed by superstar architect Frank Gehry (which is located in Basque Country only forty miles from Mondragon itself). MC firms are known for producing a range of high-quality products from basic goods such as washing machines to high-tech MRI machines. As the seventh largest firm in Spain, its wares and services are well known especially with the spread of its retail cooperatives, the Eroski grocery and convenience store chain. And since the 1990s, MC products are sold across the globe (I recently bought an Orbea bike) and its supply chain extends well beyond Basque Country. MC has subsidiaries in several countries including China, Brazil, and the United States. And, last, it is not just involved in manufacturing and retail, crucial to MC's evolution has been its bank, insurance firm, university, and fifteen technology research centers (Tremlett 2013).

Mondragon is a private corporation that was formed to benefit the people of its region (Basque Country). But it differs from the great majority of corporations in its mission, norms, and structure, including those that are committed to ST or CS CSR. Its self-professed norms express this divergence from CSR: cooperation, participation, social responsibility, and innovation. But its structure is where the real difference can be seen: the firms in the Mondragon Corporation are owned and managed by their workers. The requirement that workers be owners is grounded in the notion of the "sovereignty of labor," which is the central feature of the ethical framework guiding the structure and operations of the firm. In the material below, these principles are explained in terms of the structure of the MC.

Ten Principles of Mondragon Corporation
1. Open admission: anyone who agrees with the principles may join.
2. Democratic organization: each worker-owner has one vote.
3. Sovereignty of labor: worker-owners are the central (but not the only) decision makers.
4. Capital is to be subordinate to people.

5. Self-management.
6. Pay solidarity.
7. Group cooperation among co-ops.
8. Social transformation.
9. Universality.
10. Education.
(Gibson-Graham 2003, 140–141)

Anyone who agrees with the principles is eligible to work at Mondragon regardless of race, religion, or ethnicity. There is a fee to join, though if one is unable to pay it but otherwise qualified, one cannot be rejected. One joins as a worker-owner (following Mondragon's terminology, hereafter "coopera-tor") within a specific firm. But because each firm is part of the federation of cooperatives, each co-operator has a vote at the level of the firm and the federation.

As we have seen in preceding sections, in a traditional corporation, power is concentrated at the top, away from the workers, and instead lodged among the CEO, top management, and the board of directors. In the firms of the Mondragon Corporation, power is held by the workers. Within each firm there is a *governing* or *directing* council whose members are elected and serve a four-year term. This council meets every day before work, carries out the decisions of the annual general assembly of all workers, and oversees the day-to-day governance. The governing council is the most powerful organization within the co-op: it appoints and supervises the co-op man-ager, supervises the membership, determines the job classifications, moni-tors the accounts, and takes note of profits or losses, financial commitments, and business plans (Whyte and Whyte 1991, 31–35; Gibson-Graham 2003, 148–149).

The other organization of significance within a cooperative is the social council. In this body, cooperators voice the concerns they have not as owners but as *workers*. The social council "focuses on monitoring personnel matters, salary grades and advances, health and safety issues, and administering the co-op social funds. It aims to evaluate and possibly counter decisions made by the governing council that might be more influenced by business consid-erations" (Gibson-Graham 2003, 150). As Gibson-Graham puts it, the social council is akin to a union and acts as a check on the power of the governing council (see also Whyte and Whyte 1991, 39–41).

As described above, one of the most striking differences between Mon-dragon and non-worker-owned firms concerns the relationship between workers and management. Managers are democratically accountable through two different mechanisms: elections and the deliberative forums that shape the decisions of the governing and social councils. Managers at Mondragon are also "co-operators," that is workers owners. Thus, not only are their goals different than corporate managers operating under ST CSR, so are their powers and status, and even pay.

In the United States, in 2013, the average CEO compensation of an S&P 500 company was $11,700,000. The average (nonmanager) worker made $35,000. That's a ratio of 330:1.[45] Within the MC co-ops, the pay range between the bottom and top worker is 8:1 (Tremlett 2013). That there is a range at all reflects that there are different valuations of skills and jobs due to pressures from the market and other factors (such as the need to attract and retain highly educated engineers). However, the narrowness of this range reflects a number of factors including the desire to avoid inequalities that would lead to class divisions within the firm (Whyte and Whyte 1991, 44–45). This same desire is at work with respect to the pay scale relative to the wages in the surrounding Basque region.[46]

The reason for this is that Mondragon was founded not just to advance the cause of workers; it was designed as a project to benefit the Basque people during the incredibly difficult time of post–civil war Spain, which was ruled by the dictator Franco. Amid this trauma and devastation combined with continuing civil conflict, fear, and distrust, the instigator and architect of the project, the local Catholic priest Father Arizmendi worked "to foster democratic economic and social arrangements that might benefit all in the community and find a strong footing for postwar society" (Gibson-Graham 2003, 127). The cooperatives were and are part of a larger struggle for the survival and benefit of the Basque community (Whyte and Whyte 1991, 12–21). For those familiar with the official guidelines of worker cooperatives, this should not be surprising. In the Rochdale principles (see next chapter), which greatly informed the ten MC principles listed above, worker interests are not to be pitted against those of the community. Insofar as the workers are the owners, and thus are not "absentee" as in the case of shareholders, it is not so difficult to combine the interests of these groups because these interests are more likely to converge in the same people. Still, difficulties arise.

Wages at the co-ops are to be in line with those of similar workers in the region. The consequence of this is to actually depress the wages of some in the MC. The reason for this reduction of wages is to ensure that "the Mondragon cooperators do not become a new wealthy 'social class' within the region" (Gibson-Graham 2003, 143). Here the value of solidarity is supplemented by what has come to be called the striving for balance or *equilibrio*. It also means that the wealth that is generated is not solely funneled to individuals for personal or household consumption (Whyte and Whyte 1991, 45). This reduction of wages means that those moneys can be used in other ways, most important for funds to create more cooperatives and the institutions that promote and support them. Thus, a significant portion is funneled

to the largest unit possible, the federation of cooperatives. This helps to ensure that the needs of the region itself can best be considered and that the
support structure necessary for individual cooperatives is being attended to
adequately. Specifically, 10 percent of annual profits must be donated to
charitable or "social" institutions such as educational programs (conducted
in the Basque language), community and public health programs, and "support for cultural maintenance" (Gibson-Graham 2003, 144). The rest of the
90 percent is controlled by the cooperators but these "individual accounts"
have to be deposited in the *Caja Laboral Popular* (the Working People's
Bank), which is a cooperative of cooperatives. As a bank, it serves co-ops and
their members by providing low-interest loans and financial assistance to
new co-ops. It also helps to coordinate and support organizations that provide a range of services to co-op members and their families including health
care, insurance, social security, day care, and educational programs from
pre-K to university. The Caja is then "both a bank and a business development agency" (Gibson-Graham 2003, 145).

Worker Cooperatives and Community Solidarity

The most obvious beneficiaries of the Mondragon model are its cooperators.
Most large corporations grow and increase profits by cutting labor costs.
This is a well-documented and accepted practice at this point, but a particular case helps to bring the point home. General Electric, the stalwart high-
tech U.S. firm known worldwide, tripled its revenues and profits between
1985 and 2000. GE also shrank its workforce from 435,000 to 220,000. During roughly the same period, Mondragon's revenues and profits also tripled
but the size of the workforce doubled. This helps to explain why only two
firms have ever left (Schweickart 2011, 68–70). Then there are the wages and
benefits to the workers discussed above.

But Mondragon has also contributed to the broader community and
nonmembers in many different ways (Schweickart 2011, 70–71). It has funded cultural programming as well as created quality affordable services in
health care and education, which are open to nonmembers. The education
programs do not just develop individual capabilities (maxD#2), they reproduce community solidarity because they are taught in the Basque language
(maxD#4). And the *Caja* also works to keep the capital local, which promotes more economic activity in the region (both within and outside of the
federation) and helps to fund social programs that positively impact on public health and meet the needs of the unemployed and elderly (Gibson-
Graham 2003, 144). In other words, because the co-operators manage the
surplus, MC is in a much better position to address the needs of all the stakeholders. The federation's commitment to the Basque region shows that not
only does it democratize the economy for its members; it also contributes to

the cultural maintenance or social reproduction of the community (Gibson-Graham 2003, 124–125).[47]

Conclusion: The MaxD Advantages of Mondragon

In this chapter, we considered three approaches to making corporations socially responsible. The first, stakeholder CSR, seeks to do this by requiring the agents of capital (corporate managers) to consider not just the interests of stockholders but all those directly affected by a business's operation including consumers, community, the environment, workers, and suppliers. The second, civil society CSR, argues that corporate managers are not up to this task, and that the scene of decision making should be located outside the firm in civil society, à la "watchdog democracy." The third, the Mondragon Corporation worker co-op model, calls for a restructuring of the firm itself in terms of both ownership and management. We have argued for the community solidary focused MC model.

In the end, then, perhaps Milton Friedman was right: corporate managers are ill equipped to actualize CSR (Lee 2008, 56), but he was wrong that the economy and society can be effectively separated. Although the CS CSR literature understands this point, Palazzo and Scherer rightly point out that ST CSR has not effectively addressed it. While their move to shift the center of decision making to civil society is understandable, the institutional mechanisms for the operation of such a framework face considerable difficulties as the FSC case in particular shows. A main reason for this is that it leaves the corporate form largely untouched. Indeed, Palazzo and Scherer consider this an advantage of CS CSR over ST CSR. However, CS CSR has not been able to adequately "trap" corporations and this shows the limits of the SAS model as well. And with so much financial and political power located in the corporate form, benefits to workers and their communities have not been much realized. When we shift to Mondragon, we see real benefits to workers and the community. The main reasons for this are: the democratization of the firm in terms of management and ownership, the principles that articulate the subordination of the economy to the social realm, and the recognition of the centrality of democratic control of the surplus. The collective determination (maxD#1) concerning the surplus delivers multiple real benefits, develops capabilities (maxD#2), reduces inequality, creates a more shared authority of resources (maxD#3), and fosters solidarity across groups (members and nonmembers) and sectors.

The worker co-op's internalist approach is akin to ST CSR, but it plays out quite differently because in the normative framework deployed, the economy, and firms themselves, are considered to be projects of the social realm. Thus, MC principle #4, "The instrumental and subordinate character of capital (people over capital)." Gibson-Graham writes, "In all instances people are valued over capital, which is seen as 'basically accumulated labor and a necessary factor in business development and savings' [. . .] This helps to further ground not just the principle of democratic self-management, but also to *expand* the size, number, and type of cooperatives which is itself seen as a mechanism for social transformation guided by the norms of cooperation and solidarity" (Gibson-Graham 2003, 140–141). Crucial to this notion of a federation of worker cooperatives as a community development project is the focus on the control of the surplus. While worker rights advocates never raise this demand, Mondragon made it central. The institutional expression of this centrality is the popular bank, the Caja Laboral. The Caja enables

> the community of cooperators to oversee the distribution of individual cooperatives' surpluses represents an exercise of communality that enables the sharing and proliferation of this different economy and society. All these decisions have brought into being distinctive spaces of collectivity in which we can see a communal class process being enacted. They privilege relations of social connection and interdependence between workers and workers and citizens, bringing the sociality of the economy to the fore. (Gibson Graham 2003, 156)

Evidence of this rather high-sounding proclamation can be seen in the creation of "pay solidarity" and the funding of cultural and education programs as well as many other of the institutional features of Mondragon. Such a mechanism is nowhere considered by ST CSR or by CS CSR. And as the evolution of the MC shows, this model was able to deliver the normative and the economic goods that CSR so often talks about, but rarely obtains.

From a PD perspective, even though MC model is decidedly preferable to ST and CSR, a number of questions remain and problems are posed. In the next chapter, we delve much more deeply into the justifications for worker co-ops from a PD/econD perspective in terms of the six PD frameworks, explore how other co-ops articulate these views and the challenges they face. And we raise a number of criticisms of co-ops, their limitations, and question their relationship to broader PD system change.

4

Democracy in the Workplace: Freedom, Equality, and the Sovereignty of Labor

In the previous chapter we discussed the failure of stakeholder theory and civil society approaches to make firms "socially responsible" much less bring about participatory economic democracy. As an alternative, we offered a worker co-op model and showed its real-world feasibility by delving into the details of the most famous example of economic democracy (econD) in the world, the Mondragon Corporation (MC), a federation of worker cooperatives in northern Spain. But even if we grant the superiority of MC to the other models, it's just one example. Can co-ops in other cultural contexts survive and flourish amid present political-economic systems? And even when they do succeed from an economic perspective, are co-ops truly democratic enough to help spread participatory democracy throughout the political, economic, and social spheres? The answer is an emphatic "yes!" but with lots of qualifications, twists and turns, and some honest unknowns. It's an econD adventure—so keep reading!

In this chapter, we will look at the motivations that drive econD, the norms that structure it, and the mechanisms and institutional forms that bring it to life. We pan out from Basque Country to look at cooperatives more generally but also dig deeper into the normative and economic justifications for econD and worker cooperatives. And we deal directly with the tensions and conflicts that arise in labor's pursuit of liberty, equality, solidarity, productivity, and property. Consistent with the pluralist spirit of this book, worker co-ops will be examined from a variety of philosophical perspectives: Robert Dahl's classic *political* work, which argues that businesses are not property but minigovernments, David Ellerman's contentious and technical *moral* take that argues that wage labor is a modern day form of slavery, and David Schweickart's system-level analysis that makes reference to a pluralistic mix of economic and political arguments but nevertheless considers itself (democratic) market socialist.

As one would expect, there are many conflicts and tensions among these views and we explore them while harking back to the six PD routes (Chapter 1) and my own view of maximal democracy (maxD). In the middle of the chapter, we look at an array of forms of business ownership: from private and state run to worker and community owned. Throughout, we address the problems that actually existing democratic workplaces face, their limitations and weaknesses, and even consider alternatives to worker co-ops (e.g., multistakeholder co-ops and nonprofits). We conclude with a consideration of the critiques from the six PD routes, and others both good and bad, and strategic considerations about how to use co-ops to create econD at a system-wide level. We begin with a short history about the principles that define and guide worker-owned democratically run firms.

"Fire the Boss!" Defining a Worker Cooperative

> The relationship between the worker and the firm is membership, an economic version of "citizenship," not employment—the employment relationship is abolished.
> —Gordon Nembhard, *Collective Courage*, 5

A democratically run business is one where workers run the show and they do so in a way such that they all have an equal say in its governance. This means that workers have the powers that are held by owners in a traditional capitalist firm. We saw this put into action by the federation of worker co-ops called the Mondragon Corporation (MC) in the previous chapter. In MC and other worker co-ops, the organization of the workplace, the production techniques used, what and how much to produce, what to charge, how the net proceeds are to be distributed, all of these issues are subject to the control of the workers (Schweickart 2011, 50). Such enterprises go by different names but we shall use the name most frequently used in English, which is "worker cooperatives." We refer to the constituents of said organizations as "worker-owners," "cooperators," or "members," depending on the context, but not "employees."

The formal organization of a worker co-op emerged in the mid-1800s as industrial capitalism began to take shape in England. The first "modern cooperative" is usually considered to be the Rochdale retail co-op founded in England in 1844 (Howard, Dubb, and McKinley 2014, 234). Out of this business model, a set of guiding codes called the "Rochdale principles" were created and they continue to guide the normative and operational structure of co-ops to this day.[1] But the current guiding framework for worker cooperatives is generally considered to be those of the International Cooperative Alliance (ICA). Formed in 1895, the ICA defines a cooperative as "an autonomous association of persons united voluntarily to meet their common economic, social, and cultural needs and aspirations through a jointly-owned and democratically-controlled enterprise."[2] And co-ops are to operate in accordance with the following principles:

Seven Principles of Worker Co-ops
(International Cooperative Alliance)[3]

1. **Voluntary and Open Membership:** Cooperatives are voluntary organizations, open to all persons able to use their services and willing to accept the responsibilities of membership, without gender, social, racial, political, or religious discrimination.

2. **Democratic Member Control:** Cooperatives are democratic organizations controlled by their members, who actively participate in setting their policies and making decisions. Men and women serving as elected representatives are accountable to the membership. In primary cooperatives members have equal voting rights (one member, one vote) and cooperatives at other levels are also organized in a democratic manner.

3. **Member Economic Participation:** Members contribute equitably to, and democratically control, the capital of their cooperative. At least part of that capital is usually the common property of the cooperative. Members usually receive limited compensation, if any, on capital subscribed as a condition of membership. Members allocate surpluses for any or all of the following purposes: developing their cooperative, possibly by setting up reserves, part of which at least would be indivisible; benefiting members in proportion to their transactions with the cooperative; and supporting other activities approved by the membership.

4. **Autonomy and Independence:** Cooperatives are autonomous self-help organizations controlled by their members. If they enter into agreements with other organizations, including governments, or raise capital from external sources, they do so on terms that ensure democratic control by their members and maintain their cooperative autonomy.

5. **Education, Training, and Information:** Cooperatives provide education and training for their members, elected representatives, managers, and employees so they can contribute effectively to the development of their cooperatives. They inform the general public—particularly young people and opinion leaders—about the nature and benefits of cooperation.

6. **Cooperation among Cooperatives:** Cooperatives serve their members most effectively and strengthen the cooperative movement by working together through local, national, regional, and international structures.

7. **Concern for Community:** Cooperatives work for the sustainable development of their communities through policies approved by their members.

These seven principles are exemplary instantiations of maxD in action and operationally express each of the four maxD tenets. All are expressions of the desire for freedom and collective determination (maxD#1) but especially two, three, and four. Three articulates the material benefits tenet (maxD#2) and five concerns capability development (maxD#2), one, two, and three seem to address the inequality concerns of maxD#3 (we will debate that below). Five, six, and seven show how co-ops aim to interconnect with other organizations outside themselves in order to spread maxD and better sustain their own efforts (maxD#4). In the previous chapter, we saw how the Mondragon Federation of Cooperatives did a fine job of embodying all of these, though with some compromises (more below). So how do worker co-ops and the PD conception of them fit into debates in political philosophy about democracy and the economy? In the next sections, we look at three views: the political frame of Dahl, the ethical frame of Ellerman, and the systems view of Schweickart.

The Political Justification of Workplace Democracy: Robert Dahl

Robert Dahl was one of the major figures in Anglo-American political science for decades. His political view was structured around a very particular conception of political equality. For Dahl, the right to self-government is fundamental. Liberals and even nonliberals agree on this. But for Dahl, like Pateman and Mill, we have not paid enough attention to the conditions required for democracy to flourish. For self-government to work, political equality must be present. Dahl defines political equality in terms of five criteria/conditions. When they are present, this means that a democratic process has taken place. Because of the nuanced articulation of the criteria, they are worth quoting verbatim and in their entirety; they are:

1. **Equal votes:** "The rule for determining outcomes at the *decision stage* must take into account, and take equally into account, the expressed preferences of each citizen as to the outcome; that is, votes must be allocated equally among citizens."

2. **Effective participation:** "Throughout the process of making *binding* collective decisions, each citizen must have an adequate and equal opportunity for expressing a preference as to the final outcome."

3. **Enlightened understanding:** "In order to express preferences accurately, each citizen must have adequate and equal opportunities, within the time permitted by the need for a decision, for discovering and validating his or her preferences on the matter to be decided."

4. **Final control of the agenda by the populace:** "The demos must have exclusive opportunity to make decisions that determine what matters are and are not to be decided by processes that satisfy the first three criteria."

5. **Inclusiveness:** "The demos must include all adult members except transients and persons proven to be mentally defective."[4] (Dahl 1985, 59–60, my emphasis)

These criteria specify the democratic process and "fully specify what we mean by political equality" (Dahl 1985, 60). The economy is within such bounds. As such, the economy should be framed by these five goals.

Five Goals of the Economy in a (Political) Democracy
1. To support, or at least not conflict with, the goals of political democracy
2. To obtain justice
3. To promote efficiency
4. To promote the virtue and excellence of the demos
5. To promote economic freedom
(Dahl 1985, 84–87)

Three of these goals (#1, #2, and #4) are related to Pateman and J. S. Mill's liberal PD justification. In Chapter 1, we noted how Pateman, building on Mill, argues that partaking in participatory democracy at the workplace—and in local politics—can prepare citizens for more important national political engagements. While Dahl is not convinced that such venues can create more politically engaged citizens much less produce a "democratic personality," as Gould and others argue (Gould 1988, 283–306; Dahl 1985, 95–97), he does argue that "the best *economic* order would help to generate a distribution of voting equality, effective participation, enlightened understanding, and final control of the political agenda by all adults subject to the laws" (Dahl 1985, 84–85, my emphasis). In other words, an economic democracy would provide elements necessary for political equality and effective democratic participation.

The next goals that help to justify worker cooperatives are that (#2) the economic order be just, (#3) efficient, and (#5) promote economic freedom (Dahl 1985, 87–88). These three are strongly interrelated for Dahl. First off, worker co-ops and other econD efforts are only worth doing if they can deliver the goods. If they cannot, then co-ops cannot promote economic freedom even if they are in some general sense "just." Equality doesn't require that we all be equally poor and starving. For Dahl, justice does not require *economic* equality; that kind of inequality is permitted so long as it doesn't undermine *political* equality. But it does require that each person possess *the means* to act freely. This entails not just negative freedom but positive freedom and that some resources be distributed to all. Indeed, for Dahl, "political equality is a form of distributive justice" (Dahl 1985, 85). Thus, though the current system is, however, highly productive,[5] the incredibly unequal distribution of resources (e.g., property, income) undermines political equality because it prevents too many people from exercising economic freedom, from developing their talents, and from having a range of job choices.

The question, then, is the following: can these conditions for political equality be obtained in the economic sphere without undermining businesses such that the whole system of production would be impaired? In other words, and now I'm addressing the particular political and historical context in which Dahl is writing: can we democratize the economy without ruining it like so many socialist states did when they attempted to make their economies "just" (e.g., the USSR)? *If we cannot, then we are not obligated to democratize the economy.* This is the case even if those norms governing the economy conflict with our basic political values such as political equality (Dahl 1985, 86–91).

But this is NOT the case, argues Dahl. There is enough empirical evidence that econD formations such as worker cooperatives can literally "deliver the (consumer) goods," enhance worker rights and power, and reduce economic and political inequality in the process (Dahl 1985, 86–91). Because U.S. capitalism intensifies inequality and thus undermines economic liberty, redistributing assets and/or creating forms that promote a more equal sharing of assets is required to obtain equality. But does this redistribution require the *democratizing* of firms? For Dahl the answer is "yes." And *democratization* involves a redistribution not just of goods but of power.

Businesses Are Economic Associations: Dahl on the Four Types of Business Ownership

For Dahl, business are associations, and "in any association for which the assumptions are valid, the adult members possess an inalienable right to govern themselves by means of the democratic process, whether or not they choose to exercise that right" (Dahl 1985, 61). Most businesses in their current governance structure violate this right. In other words, for Dahl, if U.S.

capitalism kept its current authoritarian structure but produced a much more equal distribution of wealth and assets, we would still have good reason to democratize its structure provided that our new system did not severely diminish our economic life based upon our current standards.[6]

There are two traditional capitalist reasons for refusing the democratization of the workplace in particular or the economy in general: (1) workers are not competent; (2) it would violate business owners' private property rights and diminish this (and probably other) freedom(s). Dahl rejects the first—what he calls the "guardian" critique—quickly and decisively. First off, he reminds us that in larger firms, workers need not be more competent than managers; they only need to be more competent than stockholders. This is highly likely, says Dahl, because stockholders have set the bar so low: most know very little about the workings of the firms in which they invest. Indeed many smaller stockholders don't even know in which firms they have investments (Dahl 1985, 117–119). Second, even in smaller firms, all workers need not possess all or even most of the skills that managers do. He writes, "The strong principle of equality does not require that citizens be equally competent in every respect. It is sufficient to believe that citizens are qualified enough to decide which matters do or do not require binding collective decisions (e.g., which matters require general rules)" (Dahl 1985, 118). In other words, the citizens debate and then determine what they can decide and what they need help with or should not decide and then delegate powers to others such as managers (Dahl 1985, 118).[7] What they are likely to decide—and this is largely based on the workings of actual worker co-ops—is how revenues are spent and the pay scale. And they should elect the managers and/or choose to whom to delegate authority (Dahl 1985, 92–93). The key here is that management is accountable to the workers. The workers are sovereign. And this brings us to the second critique.

For Dahl, we have the right to self-government in all associations that make binding decisions upon us. Most businesses are such associations and like all associations should be run as self-governing enterprises (Dahl 1985, 91–92). Dahl's principal argument for this is his theory of democratic associations, which builds upon his view of political equality.[8] Dahl also relies heavily on the analogy that a workplace is like a government and should be run as such. The question then is what form of ownership/governance is most appropriate for a business? Dahl states there are four possibilities: individual worker ownership, collective worker ownership, state, or social/civil society. First the state option.

As we have seen from even the best examples of state socialism, state ownership interferes with the autonomy of workers, and bureaucracies often impede effective management. The classic case here is that of Yugoslavia under Tito (see Pateman 1970, 87–102; Schweickart 2011, 62–63). State ownership also dangerously subjects business to the influence of political parties who wield considerable power in the state apparatus. If the state leased firms to workers and had real power over the firm, then the firm would not be autonomous and the workers have little power over their work (Dahl 1985, 143). But for Dahl there are less ideological dangers as well. Even in capitalist states with multiparty systems, well-meaning bureaucracies could interfere with workers' abilities not just to *efficiently* manage the firm but *meaningfully* manage the firm. With the growth of large-scale technological systems and immense bureaucracies, both in the public and private spheres, persons have less and less opportunity to have power in their everyday life, to learn about the consequences of their choices, and to cultivate individual and (small-scale) collective senses of responsibility. These are the moral dimensions of efficacy and capacity development, and the workplace needs to serve these ends, not undermine them. State ownership then violates the norms of political equality and is ruled out.

Individual worker ownership could avoid these problems so long as the firms are not too large. But, while such an ownership model would ensure decentralization and avoid bureaucratization, Dahl rejects this option for counterintuitive empirical reasons. There are too many cases where firms owned by their workers sell their shares when the firm does well! Such a cashing out ends the co-op since then nonworker members own the firm. This happened with successful plywood co ops in the Northwest United States (Dahl 1985, 140; see also Ellerman 1990, 69–70). Also, workers in such businesses were less likely to hire more workers because they did not want to dilute the value of their shares. This interfered with growth possibilities, which impacted the competiveness of the co-ops. It also in some cases led firms to hire nonmembers as workers, thus creating a class system within the firm that partially replicates the power and economic inequalities of traditional capitalist firms (Dahl 1985, 140–141). Individual ownership is not sustainable and is ruled out.

One could prevent these problems by making the firm a kind of trust so that the shares could not be sold at market rate. This is the "social" (but not state socialist) or civil society ownership option and it can work well for land (Lewis and Conaty 2012, 85–110). But Dahl rules out this option, too: it is too dependent on the state for regulation, and tips the scales away from worker autonomy. The best option is the one that's left: private but collective worker ownership.[9]

Is the Workplace Really a Polity? Debating Dahl

We noted that for Dahl a main justification for econD and worker co-ops is that we value democracy and worker co-ops bring democracy into the workplace. Indeed, Dahl says, workplaces themselves are minipolities and thus should be ruled by their members. Dahl writes, "If democracy is justified in governing the state, then it must also be justified in governing economic enterprises; and to say that it is not justified in governing economic enterprises is to imply that it is not justified in governing the state" (Dahl 1985, 111). But is this analogy legitimate? Besides problems arising as a consequence of having to explain away the major differences between these two type of organizations, deeper issues arise pertaining to the particular philosophical mode of argumentation Dahl utilizes, with respect to concepts central to my book, especially autonomy and justice. According to Mayer, for Dahl, "Labor is entitled to democratic voice in the firm as a matter of right, as a kind of compensation for subjection to the rules" (Mayer 2001, 222). And this is where Mayer objects to the analogy. Workers are not subjected to bosses the way citizens are subjected to governments. This is especially evident when looking at the difference between emigration and quitting one's job.

One of the more common points of debate that comes up when discussing freedom in the workplace concerns entry and exit. The work contract is voluntary in the United States and most other countries. That means workers are not forced to take a job, nor are they forced to stay at a job. Dahl disputes this, and we have already stated many good reasons for recognizing that there are high costs for leaving many jobs because of the tight job market.[10] Although for most it's much tougher to leave a country than to quit a job, Dahl claims that the difference is not as intense as it once was. Indeed, within the United States, people frequently move, sometimes explicitly in order to change political jurisdictions (for reasons of taxes and schools). And, second, with immigration and emigration, it is more common and doable for persons to leave the United States for another country. Yes, there are costs, but actually, given the difficulties of the job market and the increase in i/emigration, the differences between the two has shrunk. Indeed, sometimes people switch countries in order to keep their jobs with multinational firms! Dahl is not claiming that there are no high exit costs for moving, just that, again, the differences are not so great. This helps to further justify Dahl's "analogy" argument (Dahl 1985, 114–115).

Mayer does not buy it. Immigration and multinationals noted, the difference is this: workers are not conscripts, but citizens are (Mayer 2001, 242). The problem for Mayer is that workers as a class have so little bargaining power. If workers had more bargaining power, then they could exercise their economic freedom. Mayer agrees that the economic liberty of workers has diminished in ways that conflict with many notions of justice. And yes we need to do something about this. But, the "proper cure for exploitation, then, is not workplace democracy but a generous welfare state, or, more radically, redistribution of property" (Mayer 2001, 243). Many other countries do this, northern European ones are most famous for it. And in recent years some Latin American countries have done it and seen worker power and wealth increase and inequality decrease.

Mayer doesn't think equal voice is necessary to eliminate exploitation: "The aim should be to block tyranny (abuse), but full fledged democracy is not the only cure for tyranny at work" (Mayer 2001, 244). Part of his reason for this view is that he thinks most people don't want democracy at work. Mayer writes,

> Even in the tight labor conditions of the past few years [the late 1990s], when many employees were in a stronger position to negotiate, they did not press for recognition of the moral right which Professor Dahl claims they possess. Not even the Silicon Valley cyber-whiz kid did. I doubt this can be explained by false consciousness. I think it is more plausible to conclude that most people don't think such a right exists. My critique of his proof is an attempt to spell out the reasons that underlie what I believe is a widely shared intuition. (Mayer 2001, 256)

I quote this passage at length because I think this a common argument against co-ops in particular and PD in general, and it is wrong. First off, while Dahl supplies empirical evidence when appropriate for most of his key claims, Mayer supplies none here on what is a crucial point. As it happens, there are studies on worker desire for participation and they showed that worker demand for participation in management in the 1970s through the early 1980s was commonplace in the United States and other countries. And a variety of more participatory management frameworks emerged both in practice and in theory (including stakeholder theory; see my Chapter 3) because of, or in conjunction with, these demands. Indeed, new practices for worker participation were put into place, from codetermination in Germany to co-ops in England and "quality management" in the United States (Bachrach and Botwinick 1992, 102–104; Malleson 2014, 34–35, 48–49). Second, the remark about the "silicon valley cyber whiz kid" seems odd now. Indeed, the image is the opposite at least in small- to medium-size firms. In such situations, many share in ownership and in management; firms are much more collaborative and "horizontal." Indeed, so much so that entirely new forms of participatory workplaces are emerging.[11]

Third, even if no one is demanding it, one still has to ask "why not"? Workers may not be demanding it not because "the right does not exist" but because they can't imagine it being doable. Most of the U.S. public is unfamiliar with worker co-ops and econD. Given that, even if one did believe in a moral right to participation, it would be rather foolish to make such a demand in a job interview if one had no idea about how it would be implemented and other workers were not present. (Also, who uses the language of moral rights when trying to bargain for a compensation package?)

Although this last critique is weak, I think Mayer is right about two other points: workplaces are not analogous to governments, and not all associations need be democratic. First, one can argue for workplace democracy without relying on an analogy between business and government. I think this is a mistake by Dahl, but it's a minor one, because Dahl's argument does not really depend on the analogy. He could rely on Gould's notion of "common activity" for example (Menser 2008, 6–8). The point is that—and I think Dahl is right about this—the default should be that humans when uniting in any association should have the right to collective determination. The question, though, for Dahl, and for Gould too, is what associations need *not* be democratic? Mayer's specific example is that of a monastery where the monks have taken an oath of silence. Nice case. The members have literally chosen the association presumably in part to give up their (democratic) voice! Let's say, OK fine, they are permitted to do this. What does this example have to do with issues concerning workplace democracy? There are some monasteries that brew beer but my guess is that the members who brew must talk, at least to each other. My point is that, in this chapter, we are focused on the issue of whether or not all economic associations need to be democratic. I think a better case for Mayer's argument is public employees. Most (?) public agencies are meant to serve the public. And their mission is set by the public. This is very different from a worker cooperative. While there could be room for public employees to have input with respect to hours and workplace conditions, other aspects should not be under the control of the workers, such as what to do with the profits. Indeed, Mayer calls for more public control of the economy in general, and worker ownership is in a sense too local and dispersed a strategy to make the economy more fair. (More below.)

In sum, Dahl's view provides a powerful justification for worker ownership. His argument appeals to traditional arguments for political democracy—which he himself has extensively articulated in his considerable body of work!—and shows how democratizing the economy through worker ownership can increase equality and dramatically extend the terrain in which humans can practice the art of collective determination. It's also likely that econD can decrease economic inequality and increase political equality. But Dahl leaves us with many questions concerning the role of the state, the nature of labor, and the ownership structure of a worker co-op. For more detailed considerations of rights, property, and labor we turn to the work of David Ellerman.

An Ethical Labor Contract: Ellerman's Democratic Workplace

> The employment contract is the Archimedean point that moves the capitalist world. From the conceptual viewpoint, the *capitalist* corporation is a "wholly owned subsidiary" of the employment contract.
> —ELLERMAN, *THE DEMOCRATIC CORPORATION*, 43

Like Dahl, Richard Ellerman goes to great length to argue for democracy in the workplace. And like Dahl, roughly half of his argument focuses on the right to self-government, or what I've been calling collective determination (maxD#1). Unlike Dahl, *Ellerman's second pillar concerns not the consequences of subjection but the entitlements of production*. So what about the nature and value of human labor? A strange aspect of Dahl's theory of workplace democracy is that it has nothing to say about *work*. Indeed, he spends much of his theoretical energy arguing that business is just another (social) association and should be structured like a political association (e.g., a government). The more economics-oriented Ellerman takes a different route. First the democracy part.

For Dahl, the right to self-government is based upon a kind of Kantian rationality in which I (must) will the law that I obey combined with a dose of Habermas (1996): if I am subject to some governing body or law, I must have the right to participate in that governance process. Ellerman agrees with this kind of reasoning as well. He states,

> Who ought to have the ultimate direct control rights over the decisions of the enterprise? Democracy gives an unequivocal answer: *the governed.* THE DEMOCRATIC PRINCIPLE. The direct control rights over an organization should be assigned to the people who are governed by the organization so that they will then be self-governing. The shareholders, suppliers, customers, and local residents are not under the authority of the enterprise; they are not the governed. (Ellerman 1990, 32)

Here the scope of the polity is determined not by who is *affected* by the process, but by *who is subject to its authority*. Already we see a stark split with corporate social responsibility in both its stakeholder theory (ST CSR) and civil society (CS CSR) forms (see previous chapter). Workers are in; consumers and stockholders and all other stakeholders are out. This is why Ellerman (following Vanek and others) often calls worker co-ops "labor managed firms" or LMFs (Ellerman 2013). Consumers are certainly impacted by products, but they are not subject to the laws that govern the production of the product. Thus, they are not part of the democratic workplace's demos.[12]

What is striking, however, is that the traditional capitalist governors of the corporation, the owners, have been dethroned. For Ellerman, and this seems obvious, shareholders are not subject to the authority of the firm, thus, they are not proper members of demos. On this justification for workplace democracy, Ellerman and Dahl agree, only the workers are the proper subjects (rulers). Ellerman writes, "When the democratic principle is applied across the board, then workers would always be member-owners in the company where they work and never just employees. The employment relation would be replaced by the membership relation" (Ellerman 1990, 34). But unlike Dahl, Ellerman calls self-determination a "natural right." It's a right that I am due based on the kind of being that I am. And even if I wanted to, I cannot trade it away. It cannot be traded away in any kind of contract that I enter into, no matter what I get in return. It's inalienable.

Ellerman's usage of the phrase "natural and inalienable" (see below) signals a divergence in their approaches. While Dahl focuses on his own "democratic principle" to justify worker control, Ellerman's first principle carves out another space for justification: labor. What's unique, and what differentiates him from Dahl, is this other principle and the way in which it grounds the right to self-government: "(1) The property structure of the democratic firm is based on the principle that people have a natural and inalienable right to the fruits of their labor" (Ellerman 1990, 5).

How does the current system then get us to believe that shareholder control over the firm is legitimate? By "pretending" that a corporation is a piece of property. Ellerman claims this is the same type of ontological "error" perpetrated in the United States during slavery.

"Abolish Human Rentals!" Wage Labor as Slavery

> To analytically treat labor as being fundamentally different—when the capitalist system treats labor as a salable commodity like the services of capital and land—would be a perversity as abhorrent as preaching abolitionism in the middle of the Ante-bellum South.
>
> —ELLERMAN, THE DEMOCRATIC CORPORATION, 15

Aristotle, that great promoter of deliberation (see my Chapter 1), defended patriarchy and slavery both in the abstract philosophical realm and in the real world of Athenian life and politics. His justification was simple: ruling oneself required the ability to reason. *Most* humans lack this ability—all women and some men. It is then just for humans with reason to rule over or master those without it. We can regard those humans without reason as property because they are akin to tools, and it is reasonable to regard tools in this way. Furthermore, slavery is natural. That is, it is in the nature of some beings to be slaves; they actually require other beings to rule over them in order for them to flourish. For both sets of beings to flourish, masters require slaves and slaves require masters (Aristotle 1981, 56–57, 64–75; Schwarzenbach 2009, 8–9).

It's not just that Aristotle's arguments are offensive; they are poorly constructed and argued. It's embarrassing. This is one of the greats of so-called Western philosophy, and in my estimation he truly his—especially his writings on being, on existence and purpose, on life, on science and causation, much of the biology, some of the politics. But his views on slavery are both scary and scary bad. And, for Ellerman, these mistakes have major implications for how we think about work and wage labor. The issue of who possesses reason is particularly farfetched. Indeed, even Plato worried about this. It's easy to demonstrate that most if not all humans possess the capacity to rule themselves even noting drastic differences in intelligence, experience, and capability (Schwarzenbach 2009, 29–58).[13] But what is interesting for the debates of this chapter is the following tangle: as noted above, a common argument for regarding employees' labor as the property of owners is that owners and their managers have capabilities that employees don't and this justifies the power differential and ownership relation. Second (a different issue), it is the owners of the firm that enable the business to exist through the contribution of their wealth to purchase the equipment and so on. Thus, they are entitled to control the benefits of these operations, even though they are usually not doing any of the actual labor. Ellerman dismantles both arguments.

Aristotle's errors notwithstanding, over the past hundred years, in most countries, slavery has been banned for moral reasons: it violates the core of our conception of personhood, and, indeed, of what it means to be human. When human beings own other human beings, a number of moral violations arise. Property has no voice; it is *being* silenced. To own is to speak for. Persons have agency, a point of view, and the ability to choose. They make judgments about other persons and things. Properties are assessed; their value is determined by external beings. Also, the political and economic consequences of such ownership are bad. In sum, slavery is a degradation of the human.[14] Ellerman feels the same way about wage labor. He even calls himself an "abolitionist." His abolitionism leads him to call for econD in a form similar to Dahl but with two subtle twists. To follow his argument, we must revisit the conception of liberty.

Even if a person (supposedly) wants to be a slave, and claims to freely choose to be a slave, we have outlawed this choice. Why? The simplest objection is that such a choice eliminates all further choice. Thus, it is irrational on most views. This reasoning has a Kantian flavor to it; it's akin to when the categorical imperative is used to rule out suicide (Kant [1785] 1987, 21–27). And Mill makes a similar argument (Mill [1859] 2001, 101–102). To go from person to slave is a kind of death: even if the biological body of *Homo sapiens* continues, it's the demise of the person as an agent capable of making choices and planning one's life. Wage labor thus poses a deep moral problem since it requires that one choose to give up one's right to liberty; one alienates one's capacity for self-determination. Again, it's *being* silenced: you do not have the right to speak your mind at work! This not only goes against libertarian or atomistic versions of the self but against communitarian ones as well, since those too presuppose a self with moral agency. For a self to have moral agency one must be responsible for one's actions. If one is a slave, one is not responsible for (all of) one's actions; one is the property of another. This is where justifications for slavery break apart into a series of contradictions that sheds light on the incoherence of the doctrine of wage labor.

Treat Them Like Criminals!

> The second normative principle (here called the responsibility principle)
> is just the standard jurisprudential norm of assigning to people the legal
> responsibility for the results of their deliberate and intentional actions.
> —ELLERMAN, "THREE THEMES, 335

Let's imagine the case of a slaveholder, Thomas J. And he's riding in his horse-drawn wagon down the road to visit his slaveholding friend—Jimmy M.—to talk about a constitution they recently wrote. One of his slaves, let's call her Sally H., is traveling with Thomas, who holds the reins. As Jimmy M.'s wagon approaches Thomas's, at one point, Thomas's horse, American Pharoah, charges Jimmy M.'s wagon and causes it to run off the road. It turns out that Thomas J. mistreated American Pharoah earlier in the day and she was still angry. Jimmy M.'s wagon is broken in the encounter. Who is responsible for the damage?

Now let's imagine the same situation but this time the wagon's axle breaks. It was old, and this causes the accident. To keep matters simple let's say Thomas J. bought and installed the axle. Who is responsible?

Now let's imagine the same collision, but this time, Sally H. takes the reins from Thomas and leads the horse into Jimmy M.'s wagon. Same result, the wagon is busted. Who is responsible?

While American Pharoah is certainly much respected for winning horse racing's Triple Crown (she is a time traveling horse), she lacks the cognitive capacity required to render her legally or morally culpable. This is even more true for the axle. Now what about Sally H.? In our case, she possesses all the usual cognitive capacities, is an adult, and displayed intent. And she even confessed. But she is also the property of Thomas J. As Ellerman points out, in the U.S. South before the Civil War, when slavery was legal, a number of contradictions arose around this issue of a slave's agency and responsibility. He writes,

> The legal system faced the same internal contradiction when it treat-
> ed slaves as legal chattel in the Ante-bellum South. The legally non-
> responsible instrument in work suddenly became a responsible
> person when committing a crime. "The slave, who is but 'a *chattel*'
> on all *other* occasions, with not one solitary attribute of personal-
> ity accorded to him, becomes 'a *person*' whenever he is to be *pun-*
> *ished*." [. . .] As an Ante-bellum Alabama judge put it, the slaves in
> fact "are rational beings, they are capable of committing crimes; and
> in reference to acts which are crimes, are regarded as persons. Be-
> cause they are slaves, they are . . . incapable of performing civil acts,
> and, in reference to all such, they are things, not persons. (Ellerman
> 1990, 26)

If slaves are rational beings, with the ability to plan, act, and contemplate consequences, then obviously they are moral agents. And if they are moral agents, they should not be regarded as property. But is wage labor really the same sort of subjection?

One counter is that with wage labor there is consent; it is temporally and spatially restricted and one can leave. One is a slave for life and in all aspects of one's life, from worship and work to family and play. From birth until death. And there is no exit. Consent, temporariness, and the right to exit: none of these arguments holds for Ellerman (Ellerman 1990, 44–45). Aristotle, oddly, has returned, but with a twist. Part of his argument for slavery is that some don't possess the ability to reason and deliberate. But what Ellerman argues is that wage labor requires a transfer of precisely that capacity from the worker to the employer/manager. This is ontologically impossible, says Ellerman. The right to decide, to be an agent, is not transferrable. Imagine a case where I rent my foot to a colleague named Robert. Then Robert orders me to sneak up behind my department chairperson and kick him in the tush. I do so. Who is responsible? The foot, and my decision-making capacity, are not alienable, even for one kick. Again, Ellerman, "Decision-making capacity is *de facto* inalienable. A person cannot in fact alienate his or her decision-making capacity just as he or she cannot alienate *de facto* responsibility" (Ellerman 1990, 5). This rule can be seen at work in the case of kids, parents, and peer pressure. "But dad, Jimmy M. Jr told me to steal the horse." Dad replies, "If Jimmy M. Jr. told you to jump off a barn would you do it?" So why doesn't this form of reasoning apply to workers?

Maybe the preceding does not properly understanding the nature of wage labor. One might object: what about cases where a person delegates power of attorney for situations in which one is incapacitated? I draw up a contract to specify who controls my fate if I go into a coma. Maybe wage labor is like that? First off, as Ellerman wonderfully notes, when one signs an employment contract, one is not delegating authority to the boss. The boss is not looking after your best interest! That is not the responsibility of the boss under capitalism. The boss's job is to maximize profits by getting as much out of you and the other inputs as possible. Employees, just like Aristotle's tools, are inputs. You are free to sign the contract or not, the boss has no control over that. And in that regard, the wage laborer is free.[15] But note here that the freedom of the wage laborer is not as a wage laborer. The freedom occurs at the level of a person choosing which situation in which to become unfree. If slaves were free to choose among masters, would that make slavery moral? No. The same holds for wage labor. Again, one might object, "but wage earners also get to bargain for their salary and benefits" and so on. What about those situations when those needs are met? Again, for Ellerman, it still does not correct for the violation. Slaves, too, could be well cared for, some lived in the master's house, received education, and chose their mates.

The reception of these benefits does not remove their unfreedom (Ellerman 1990, 30). He writes,

> The archaic [Aristotelian!] name for the employer–employee relation is the "master–servant relation" (language still used in Agency Law). That authority relation is not now and never was a democratic relationship. The employer is not the representative of the employees; the employer does not act in the name of the employees. The right to govern the employees is transferred or alienated to the employer who then acts in his own name; it is not a delegation of authority. (Ellerman 1990, 41)

Wage labor may be legal (for now), but it is deeply undemocratic and is a violation of individual liberty. Indeed, Ellerman following Hobbes calls it a *pactum subjectionis*, where the members of the polity transfer the rights of governance to the ruler. (And now we are on the terrain of the concerns of Dahl.) This is very different from a democratic (e.g., Lockean) constitution of a social contract where the members of the polity *delegate* powers to the ruler. Since those members do not transfer their agency, they remain sovereign. For Hobbes, of course, the ruled are not Sovereign, the ruler is sovereign.[16]

As was noted in our discussion of Charles Mills' reading of Rousseau (see my Chapter 1), the *pactum subjectionis* resembles a "domination contract." Because I am convinced that another has more power than me, and that my situation could get worse, I agree to a contract that grants me equal rights with others but actually formalizes a relationship of inequality and subjection. Specifically, I agree that all property should be protected, but I have very little, you have a lot, and property as it turns out is convertible into political power, thus you end up having more economic and political power over me, though "on paper"—that is, constitutionally—we both have the same set of formal rights. Or, more specifically, we both have freedom of speech but if money can be converted into speech and you have more money, then, in a crucial sense, you have more speech than I do. The same with equal protection under the law, we both have the right to an attorney and trial by jury, but if the quality and extent of legal protection is in large part determined by money, then our status before the law is not effectively equal.

The Revenge of Ellerman's "Residual Claimant"; or, Abolishing the Employment Contract

So let's say we adopt Ellerman's view, how would the employment contract work? He doesn't argue that the workers should own the firm as a piece of property; the firm is not a piece of property, it's a social association (as in

Dahl). What workers should own, and control, are the fruits of their labor (i.e., the profits). To understand this move, we have to take a step back, and look at how actually existing capitalism works. For Ellerman, and I think this is the case for all those working in econD, "'capitalism' is not a precisely defined technical term; it is a molecular cluster concept which ties together such institutions and activities as private property, free markets, and entrepreneurship as well as the employer–employee relationship" (Ellerman 1990, 2).[17] If we change the employer-employee relation (from master-slave or boss-worker) to worker-owner, that changes the meaning and scope of the other concepts (Ellerman 1990, 2). Ownership in capitalism has two roles: (1) ownership of the means of production *and* (2) entitlement to any profits (and responsibility for debt). In the above, Ellerman isn't objecting to shareholders or whomever owning the means of production, he objects to nonworkers ("outsiders") controlling the profits resulting from the labor of workers. This second function of ownership is what Ellerman calls the "residual claimant." He writes, "It is the myth that the residual claimant's role is part of the property rights owned in the capital-owner's role, i.e. part of the 'ownership of the means of production.' The great debate over the public or private ownership of the residual claimant's role is quite beside the point since there is no 'ownership' of that role in the first place" (Ellerman 1990, 6). The shift here is game changing. If workers are not entitled to trade their labor for a wage, then they control their labor. Their labor is their property, and the products of those activities belong to them. Workers should always be the owners of their products.

If this is the case, why do we so willingly accept the idea that the profits should go to the owner of the business and not the workers? For Ellerman, there are a number of delusions at play, but a key one is that workers are just another "input" along with capital and land/materials. That is, the production process requires investors to purchase or "rent" what's needed—a space, materials, equipment, etc.—and labor to make the product. There are two versions of this, the "animist poetic" view and the economistic "passive engineering" view. The "poetic view animistically [*sic*] pictures land and capital as 'agents of productions' that (who?) cooperate together with workers to produce the product. Land is the mother and labor is the father of the harvest" (Ellerman 1990, 11). On this view, labor is (properly) recognized as an agent, but (improperly) regarded as the same type of agent as land and capital. Ellerman rules out this view because this "personification of land and capital is an example of the *pathetic fallacy*" (Ellerman 1990, 11). As in our horse and wagon example above, only a person has the requisite capabilities to obtain the standing of a moral agent.

The second, more common, view "favored in capitalist economics (particularly in technical contexts) is the *passive engineering view*. Human actions are treated simply as causally efficacious services of workers alongside the services of land and capital" (Ellerman 1990, 12). In this view, labor is functionally understood as just another input. Indeed, it is purchased on the market just like wood and machines are. The idea that labor is an input is especially evident in talk of businesses cutting costs by reducing labor expenses. "Cutting costs" means reducing the wages or hours of workers and/ or laying persons off. But as we have seen in the discussion above, workers are not just another input. They are moral agents.

To be clear, Ellerman does think that it is permissible to own a corporation. He is not opposed to corporations as such. Nor is he opposed to the idea that many things can be owned, even privately. But humans should not be owned, even temporarily. Ellerman writes,

> Yet people's right to the fruits of their labor has always been the natural basis for private property appropriation. Thus capitalist production, far from being founded on private property, in fact denies the natural basis for private property appropriation. In contrast, the system of economic democracy based on democratic worker-owned firms restores people's right to the fruits of their labor. Thus democratic firms, far from violating private property, restore the just basis for private property appropriation. (Ellerman 1990, 40)

Ellerman's Labor-Managed Firm

Now that we have abolished the employment contract and restored the rights of workers to their labor and its products, what does a business look like? Ellerman explains: "Without the employment contract, the corporation as an asset-holding shell is comparable to a condominium. The tenants in a condominium unit (whether a unit-owner or a renter) are not under the authority of the condominium association" (Ellerman 1990, 43). Like Dahl, a business for Ellerman is a community or association, a minipolity. And just like any other minipolity, the members should be sovereign. And like Dahl, "In a democratic firm, work in the firm qualifies one for membership in the firm. The employment relation is replaced by the membership relation" (Ellerman 1990, 2). As we discussed above, the structuring principles are also similar: "(1) The property structure of the democratic firm is based on the principle that people have a natural and inalienable right to the fruits of their labor." This takes the form of the "internal capital account." [And] (2), "The governance structure of the democratic firm is based on the principle that people have a natural and inalienable right to democratic self-determination." This takes the form of voting rights (Ellerman 1990, 5). The difference with Dahl is that there are two different rights. Dahl focuses on (2), and this justifies the personal rights of the member which grounds his or her voting rights in the firm as a democratic polity. (1) has to do with the rights of the person as a *laborer*. This is what is called the "residual claimant's" rights (Ellerman 1990, 47). To understand how this works, and how it relates to Dahl's view, let's tell the story from the perspective of a new worker.

A person, let's call her Emma G., is hired by an Ellermanian democratic firm. A contract is signed. After a probationary period of some specified time that makes sense for both (a kind of tryout for the worker and the firm, probably a few months or so), both sides agree the worker should stay. At this point Emma G. becomes a member of the firm. This means that she gets a vote. Voting is a "functional right" that comes with membership (Ellerman 1990, 53). This means Emma gets to deliberate and vote with respect to a range of policy decisions, from choosing her boss to deciding what to do with the profits. The second thing Emma G. receives is an "internal capital account." This is a piece of property. It's a bank account in which the firm makes deposits based on the net asset value of the firm. Since she became a member, Emma has been making a contribution to this account in the form of a membership fee. This could come from her "salary" or out of pocket (Ellerman 1990, 54–56). The size of a member's internal capital account is based primarily on tenure (how long a worker has been employed at the firm). Thus, a newbie's account is smaller than a veteran's. Again, "The balance in a worker's internal capital account is a property right, not a personal right" (Ellerman 1990, 60). It is based on annual revenue and distributed to members based upon their labor. This is because members have rights to control over the profits because they are residual claimants due to their *functional* role as members (Ellerman 1990, 56–57). Ellerman favors a Mondragon type model where upon retirement, a member takes the balance of the internal capital account. Or, if a worker dies, that property is transferred (to his or her heir, etc.). The right to make decisions in the workplace or access (future) profits, however, is not transferrable, which is why it is deemed a "personal right."

The innovation of the internal capital account helped Mondragon avoid the problems faced by co-ops in other circumstances, such as the plywood firms in the United States and the state-owned firms in Yugoslavia. In both locales, especially in Yugoslavia, problems arose from the requirement that retained earnings be regarded as the common property of all the members. Frustrations arose because workers wanted access to those funds. So what they did was distribute them annually as pay and bonuses. This left less money for long-term investments and hindered the businesses. The Mondragon model solved this problem by dividing up earnings: one portion is held in common by the firm for investments, another portion goes into individual worker's internal accounts. A third portion goes to a general fund (Ellerman 1990, 91).

The other problem that some co-ops faced is that if each member has an *equal* share of the firm, then those who are there longer are in the same financial position as those who just finished their probationary period. This is how it was in Yugoslavia. This led to a situation where members didn't want to hire new workers because they would lose a sizable portion of their share to the one who just started. Some co-ops structure themselves this way in the name of equality, but, for Ellerman, this violates the labor theory of property: "The labor theory of property implies that Labor should have the residual claimant's role. It does not imply that the current workers in any enterprise should own the capital assets of that enterprise which have been accumulated from the past" (Ellerman 1990, 20).

This model also avoids problems experienced in the United States where workers owned *individual* shares of the firm. (Note this option was considered by Dahl above.) This was common among the aforementioned plywood co-ops in the Pacific Northwest. The successful ones saw their share values go up. This tempted workers to cash out and many sold their shares to outsiders, thereby leading to the end of the worker ownership of the firm! The demise of co-ops in such circumstances was sometimes deemed to be due to the moral failure of the members: they were being selfish. But Ellerman argues that the problem was not a moral one, but a technical one arising because of the structure of the co-op (Ellerman 2013, 332–333).

In sum, the firm for Ellerman is a social institution and should be democratically run by its members. This requires that managers be elected by the members and the profits of the firm be made the property of the members. Additional assets also could be the property of the firm (Ellerman 1990, 53). This is what it means to say, as they do in Mondragon, that "labor is sovereign." This model differs from traditional capitalist business because labor is not an input like capital and machines. For Ellerman, capital, machines, and nonhuman inputs are not agents. Labor is an intentional activity carried out by humans. Workers cannot alienate this activity from themselves even if they wanted to. As such, nonworkers shouldn't own or control the profits of the laborers.

Another difference with Dahl occurs in terms of how Ellerman defines private, public, and social. Because of his different understanding of private rights, he views the opposition between capitalism and socialism as a misguided one riddled by much conceptual confusion. He writes,

> This "great debate" is ill-posed. It is based on a pair of false identifications: (1) that the sphere of government ("the public sphere") is the sole arena for personal rights, and (2) that the sphere of social life outside the government ("the private sphere") is solely based on private property rights. That is the traditional public/private distinction. Capitalism has used it to quarantine the democratic germ in the public sphere of government, and thus to keep the democratic germ out of industry. Instead of redefining those public/private identifications,

democratic state-socialism compounds the error by holding that industry can only be democratized by being nationalized. (Ellerman
1990, 36–37)

Socialists aim to make the workplace democratic by having the state seize it,
hence all those nationalization of industry policies. Ellerman's econD comes
at it from a different angle. He democratizes the firm by arguing that the
individuals who work there have a right to govern it in part because of a
private right to control the fruits of their labor. But the main right to govern
comes as a *social* right because the firm is not a thing; it's a group of humans,
that is, a polity (Ellerman 1990, 51). Social rights are based on personal rights
fulfilled by this functional role (Ellerman 1990, 37–38). Taken together, this
entails the *collectivization* of self-determination and the decentralized *indi-
vidualization* of ownership.

Ellerman is opposed to the state ownership and management of firms,
what he calls "nationalization." Even if there was a truly democratic socialism where the citizenry ruled—and were not pawns of the party—this still
would not achieve econD or workplace democracy. Workplace democracy
requires that those subject to the laws of the workplace rule. In both state
socialism and actually existing capitalism, the firm is governed by the wrong
group: in the case of the traditional corporation, the shareholders, in the case
of state socialism, the party or the citizenry (Ellerman 1990, 34).

One could argue that such state socialism is "better" than traditional
capitalism. Maybe. But it is still not democratic. This also means that Ellerman stands with Dahl against democratic socialists such as Mayer. A robust
welfare state may improve the bargaining position of workers, but it does not
bring about democracy, nor does it restore the rights of workers to control
the fruits of their labor (the surplus) as "residual claimants." But what about
state ownership and the workplace? Is there really no role for the state to play
in econD? For this debate, we turn to the most systematic of economic democracy theorists, David Schweickart, and his much more state-centered
market socialist theory of econD.

Schweickart's Democratic Market Socialism

We have brought together Dahl, Ellerman, and Schweickart in order to create the basis for a theoretical understanding and justification of econD. We
used Dahl primarily to lay out the conception of workplace democracy as
self-governance. Ellerman was brought in for his understanding of labor and
property. We will now employ the work of Schweickart to put workplace
democracy in the broader context of remaking the economic system. This
requires extensive reworking of both major economic institutions (e.g.,
banks) and the political ones that empower, support, and regulate them

especially with respect to banking, investment, and taxation. We need a structural alternative and a theory that can show us how succession can happen (Schweickart 2011, 13–15).

Like Dahl and Ellerman, Schweickart also believes that workplace democracy is essential for econD. For Schweickart, econD is desirable because it taps our dearest values—equality, liberty, and democracy—and uses them to reshape our economic life in a manner that is doable; that is, econD can deliver the goods. Our focus on Schweickart, however, is not on his justifications for worker co-ops. He doesn't dwell too much in the philosophical debates around equality, liberty, and property that we saw above with Ellerman, Mayer, and Dahl. Instead we will use Schweickart's corpus to shift our focus back to system-level econD. He also presents the strongest case for its feasibility from an *economic* and political perspective, mostly from a consequentialist perspective, but also in terms of rights and duties to a lesser extent. He assembles the arguments and evidence to show that econD can be as good if not better in regard to productivity and efficiency. And—this distinguishes him from Dahl and Ellerman—he shows that econD is doable from a legal and institutional perspective even in a country as committed to so-called free market capitalism as is the United States. And the consequences of it are highly desirable too: it would decrease income and wealth inequality, lessen social antagonisms, and make ecological sustainability much easier to obtain (Schweickart 2011, 87–126). In this he greatly expands on the range and deepens the content and evidence for econD justifications noted in the discussion of Dahl and Ellerman. He is also much less moralistic and dogmatic than Ellerman, which will spawn an important debate about whether or not to permit traditional privately owned firms at all.

For Schweickart, the problem with capitalism is capitalists. Despite all the positive press, that category of being just isn't that productive (Schweickart 2011, 37–40). We could see this reasoning at work in Ellerman: owners of traditional firms claim the profits and maintain control over the workplace even though they aren't the ones doing the actual work, or even much of the management. But it's even worse than that, says Schweickart: "capitalists qua capitalists make no contribution to production. The stock market and other 'investment games' are unfair. Private savings is not only not necessary for economic growth, but is often positively harmful—hence interest income is undeserved" (Schweickart 2002, 17).[18] However, Schweickart charts a different path to econD than Ellerman. For Schweickart, the goal is to "transcend" capitalism by eliminating the private ownership of the means of production. Individuals, corporations, and/or shareholders should not own the factories and shops, nor restaurants and hospitals. Such enterprises should be democratically managed and "socially owned." If this sounds "socialist," that's because it is. Says Schweickart, "I use the term socialist to refer to any attempt to transcend capitalism by abolishing most private ownership of the means of production" (Schweickart 2011, 48). Unlike Dahl and Ellerman, Schweickart explicitly comes out of a Marxist socialist tradition. But like Dahl and Ellerman—and unlike the former Soviet Union and many other socialists—he utilizes markets.[19]

While the phrase "market socialist" may sound contradictory to some, Schweickart points out that the basic premise of the pairing is actually well established and there is a whole theoretical tradition behind this view. Since the rise of capitalism, even nonsocialist societies have used *both* states and markets to create jobs, expand production, and coordinate investment. Major economists such as John Maynard Keynes called for the state to act to promote employment and increase the purchasing power of the masses of workers, and recommended high tax rates and governmental job programs to do this (Schweickart 2011, 100–101). And in developing countries in that same period, such as Korea and Japan, there was strong government "interference" in the economy, which led those countries from wartime economic collapse to becoming contemporary global superpowers (Schweickart 2011, 65–66). Consistent with my earlier discussion of the "diverse economy" (Chapter 3), Schweickart points out that countries with successful (capitalist) economies often violated the dictates of neoliberal capitalism. Indeed, in South Korea, Japan, and the United States of the 1950s–1960s, high economic growth occurred with high tax rates, high tariffs on imports, and state intervention into the economy (Schweickart 2011, 65, 169–171). And we haven't even mentioned the successes of avowedly socialist states such as Cuba, Vietnam, and China. Schweickart points out that

> Proponents of globalized capitalism like to point out that the percentage of desperately poor people has declined in recent years. They fail to note that this is largely due to the success of well-protected, market socialist China in lifting hundreds of millions out of poverty. On the other hand, the most precipitous drop in living standards ever witnessed in peace time occurred in the ex Soviet Union, following its renunciation of socialism. (Schweickart 2011, 114)

But again, Schweickart is not calling for centrally planned economies. He is a critic of such models. But we do need to study these examples, understand their successes and failures, and contemplate them given the current economic crisis.[20] The dogmatic programs of neo-liberalism such as privatization and deregulation have failed us, spectacularly. And contradictions abound as big banks are bailed out by governments who are simultaneously cutting both social services and taxes. The state has not "withdrawn" nor should it; it is quite active right now! The question is, for whom and toward what end?

Schweickart isn't calling for the state to own all of the means of production. Not only are (some) small businesses permitted; so are (a few) corporations. What Schweickart does call for is *the social control of the majority of the means of production*, as well as the social control of the means of investment and finance (e.g., the banks) (Schweickart 2011, 51–58). Democratized workplaces are crucial, but econD will only work if these other larger components are part of the program. And much nationalization is appropriate and justified.

Should Labor Really Be Sovereign? Messy Multistakeholder Hybridity in the Democratic Workplace

Like Dahl and Ellerman, Schweickart believes that democratic workplaces are central for both the project of econD and for promoting a broader democratic transformation of the economy. Schweickart's conception of the firm is that it is not a thing but a community. He writes, "In essence, a firm under EconD is regarded not as a thing to be bought or sold (as it is under capitalism) but as a community. When you join a firm, you receive the rights of citizenship, that is, full voting rights. When you leave one firm and join another, these rights transfer" (Schweickart 2011, 50). Here he is similar to Dahl and Ellerman. He also agrees with Ellerman that labor is not a "factor of production" but is a "residual claimant" (Schweickart 2011, 51). But where he differs with Ellerman is in regard to who (or what) should own what (or who). There are six basic options for the ownership of firms and for each I've stated the position of our three figures:

Types of Business Ownership
1. **Privately owned:** a for-profit business owned by private individuals; for example, privately or publicly held corporations, single individual owned firms, family-owned firms (Schweickart permits some; Ellerman opposes; Dahl may permit small ones)
2. **State owned:** government-owned businesses or utilities that are worker-managed but sometimes in conjunction with nonworkers; for example, public utilities for water and energy (Schweickart favors this; Ellerman opposes?; Dahl generally against)
3. **Worker owned:** ownership and management by members who are workers; for example, worker co-ops; (all are for them)
4. **Consumer owned:** ownership and management by members of the organization who are consumers: consumer cooperatives, credit unions (not much discussed by any of the three)
5. **Nonprofits:** organizations dedicated to benefit some part of the public, no private ownership or profit taking; (not much favored or discussed by any of the three)

6. **Multi-stakeholder-owned cooperatives (MSCs):** owned by workers and other stakeholders; for example, community land trusts, (Schweickart permits some; Ellerman opposes; seems that Dahl would permit)

1. Private Ownership of Firms. Most econD views permit some, but Ellerman does not. Ellerman opposes all based on moral grounds. Put another way, just as no slave "contracts" are permitted, no business may utilize the employment contract. Thus, there are no private firms permitted. Schweickart disagrees for economic and/or consequentialist reasons and also, I think, because he takes a more system-level approach to econD. For Schweickart, the point seems to be this. EconD will happen in a piecemeal fashion. We will create some co-ops, change some regulatory laws, put in a new tax, take over a bank, get rid of some corporate tax breaks, etc. So the economy will be mixed. To make econD work, the majority of firms need to be co-ops, or more accurately, the majority of the workforce needs to work in co-ops. We can permit a few privately held firms for political and/or economic reasons. Interestingly, Schweickart is quite permissive here. He does not even put the requirement that they be "high road" firms. We may keep them because they deliver an exceptional product, or for some other economic reason: they are superefficient, have a great supply chain, employ many workers, have significant expertise, etc. (Schweickart 2011, 79). Ellerman would reject this. What if there was a superefficient well-run slave plantation that was delivering a product of great value? This is nearly the case with respect to some large agribusiness farms. While Ellerman would morally rule out such an option, Schweickart would build a system of institutional support that would presumably resolve the exploitation problem from another angle. In Schweickart's econD, there is a job market that has plenty of democratic options for workers, but if workers can't find one that meets their needs—or desires—then a robust safety net, one with a basic income guarantee, will ensure that they don't need to take such jobs (Schweickart 2011, 183).

2. State Ownership. Ellerman's argument is that whomever did the labor should own it. Persons labor, not governments. So, in general, as he notes, external ownership (state based or private based) of private property created by workers is immoral and not the solution. But presumably workers could transfer property to the state (say upon death). And the state can lease property to workers, but the profits of the firm would also have to be the property of the workers.

A different set of moral and political concerns arises not just because of size, but because of the sector and the purpose of the business. Worker ownership, and even worker management, might not be appropriate because of what is being produced or the constituency being served. For example,

Malleson argues that worker co-ops may not be appropriate for public sector services since workers then would have too much power in the dissemination of a public good.[21]

For example, the workers at hospitals and schools should not be "sovereign." Both workplaces are designed to serve the "public," and, in a democratic process, the delivery of those services should be determined by the diverse members of that public: the recipients of the service, taxpayers, and other relevant stakeholders (including the workers). It's also possible for workers to get too rich. Thus, co-op's might not be appropriate in industries that are extremely capital intensive such as pharmaceuticals, automobile, oil, and steel (Malleson 2014, 44). For Malleson, the better model in these cases is nationalization with comanagement between workers and community (not the state). Like Schweickart, Malleson takes a pluralist and pragmatic approach to these cases: let's see how it goes. These kinds of problems have been issues within the co-op movement for years, and figures such as Hirst (and his precursor G.D.H. Cole for that matter) have theorized different schemes to balance the needs of various stakeholders. For example, in service delivery, associations could be formed that are co-ops, but the government funding of these services could be determined in a market situation where service providers compete with each other, thus giving recipients power through the market to influence the content of service delivery.[22] Co-management between the state and private ownership is another model, but it does not seem to be democratic enough because of the power of the state in such models. (See Malleson 2014, 85, 120, and the Dahl critique above.)

3. **Worker Ownership.** All are for it. See above.

4. **Consumer Owned.** None discuss it. See next chapter.

5. **Nonprofits: The Cases of Beyond Care and Cooperative Home Care Associates.** There are many organizational forms that allow for some control by an association of stakeholders that are not part of the state, nor strictly operating as private individuals. Often lumped together into the category of "civil society," such organizations include everything from nongovernmental organizations such as Amnesty International and the National Rifle Association (NRA) to churches, mosques, and recreation leagues. While there are many forms of nonprofits, most are structured in a way that distinguishes them from privately owned businesses *and* cooperatives. The first reason most nonprofits are clearly not either is that the mission of a nonprofit is not to benefit its owners or workers, but some external constituency or section of the public (e.g., public housing residents, gun owners, doctors). Second, the source of revenue for nonprofits is not the sale of a product or some market-based revenue but charitable donations and grants. Third, any surplus from services delivered is not paid out to individual owners but put back into the organization. Indeed, there are not any individual owners. There is a requirement that there be an executive director

who oversees the operations and is paid more than others in the organization, but the fiscal health of a nonprofit is the charge of the board of directors (Lund 2011, 16).

While nonprofits are usually not considered traditional businesses, they are economic organizations and are "part of the economy" insofar as they have budgets, pay workers, deliver services, and own and manage property. While a subset of these organizations is often included in econD frames,[23] its inclusion is trickier from our PD perspective. This is because, though some may certainly contribute to the public good and/or benefit marginalized groups, many of them are not *participatory* democratic in any real sense. On the contrary, nonprofits are *legally* required to be hierarchical in their management structure and do not require members or employees to participate in their governance. Again, organizations that benefit a disadvantaged group may be laudable from a variety of normative frameworks, but that does not mean that they are PD. For this reason, in this chapter, we will focus on a subset of these organizations: those that promote participatory social ownership or management and are more "business" oriented and participatory in their operations. Indeed, sometimes what many think is a "worker co-op" is actually a democratically structured nonprofit.

Some democratic workplaces are not owned by private individuals, on site workers, or by the state but by some other organizational form that is based in civil society (e.g., nonprofits). For example, a group of well-known "worker co-ops" in NYC based in Sunset Park are well regarded by the co-op community but workers do not own these firms. They are instead operated as nonprofits and are owned by a sponsoring organization, the Center for Family Life, which is also a nonprofit (Estey 2011, 360). We shall focus on one, a child care provider called Beyond Care (BC). BC is a powerful and comprehensive expression of the depth of the fight for econD, and the different routes that groups can take to form PD workplaces. Its members describe it as follows: "'Beyond Care' is a socially responsible cooperative business whose members provide child care services. Founded on the basis of democracy, equality and justice, Beyond Care promotes living wage jobs in a safe and healthy working environment, while promoting personal growth and educational opportunities for its members. Our core values are solidarity, respect and professionalism."[24] Formed in 2008 at the onset of the great financial crisis, Beyond Care started when twenty-six women—none of whom spoke English as a native speaker—came together to form a business that could increase their pay, develop their leadership skills, and promote mutual support among them (Estey 2011, 356, 369). Beyond Care now has thirty-five members (Estey 2011, 362) who deliver child care services throughout Brooklyn. BC's pay rate is above average for the sector and members have benefits, paid sick days, and vacation. And crucially from the PD perspective, they routinely meet to share knowledge, discuss and deliberate about hiring and firing, clients, and working conditions, and socialize to cultivate solidarity and trust (Estey 2011, 356–358).

Beyond Care was formed at the behest and under the guidance of the Center for Family Life (CFL), a social service provider based in Brooklyn and Long Island. For years it operated an Adult Employment Services program in Sunset Park, Brooklyn. But in the 2000s, staff realized that the program was problematic on two counts: much of the training was for jobs no longer available to their members, and many of the available jobs "contradicted" the mission and values of their organization: that is, the jobs were not only disempowering, they were exploitative, even abusive. CFL was inspired by an Oakland nonprofit called WAGES to try a democratic workplace (Estey 2011, 356). As a business model, such a form could not just protect workers from abuse but empower them individually and collectively, and in a way that promoted multiple community benefits.

In Beyond Care, true to the worker co-op spirit, democracy means "one person, one vote" and the members elect a president, vice president, two secretaries, and two treasurers. Each of these positions has a one-year term and can be reelected once. Leadership rotation helps to prevent the concentration of power among a few members (maxD#1 and maxD#3). Also, rotation not only encourages the sharing of *power*, but the sharing of the *skills* needed for the various positions (maxD#1 and maxD#2). This also helps to foster a horizontal decision-making style. Indeed, workers receive training in consensus decision making as part of their co-op education (maxD#2 and maxD#3). In addition, there are two members who run the education component (they have six-month terms) as well as two others who handle publicity (Estey 2011, 358–359).

Although Beyond Care is managed democratically, it differs from other worker co-ops on a few counts. First, although each member pays a fee upon entry ($150), members do not pool together the money they receive from their clients. Beyond Care has opted for a "referral marketing" business model. Thus, each member keeps what she makes from her clients. At first this sounds like an "agency" where each worker is a kind of independent contractor. But, Beyond Care is not an employment agency: the owners do not take a cut from the clients' payments; there are no individual owners. BC is owned by CFL and that's why it is both a marketing co-op and a nonprofit. But the staff and board of CFL do not run BC. The workers control the surplus and manage the firm collectively. For example, unlike in a referral agency, the wage range is set by the members (not the private owner), and the negotiating with clients is done by the co-op as a unit (not by individual service providers).

The contract that Beyond Care uses for its workers and clients embodies not just the values of the organization, but links BC to other movement forms (maxD#4). The sector in which BC operates is one that (until recently) was unprotected by labor and civil rights law and rampant with underpayment, wage theft, and even physical abuse (Estey 2011, 354–355). For years, child care workers—and here we include various categories and self-identifications from nannies to paid babysitters—were not guaranteed sick days, vacation, overtime, or even (unpaid) days off! Also, "mission creep" was common—the adding of unpaid tasks to workers' duties after hiring (e.g., cooking, cleaning, additional children). To combat this range of exploitation, theft, and abuse, an organization of Caribbean, Latina, and African nannies called Domestic Workers United waged a two-year campaign to get a Domestic Workers' Bill of Rights law passed in the NY state legislature.[25] They were successful. This legislation sets a standard for contracts in terms of both payment and working conditions. It mandates paid overtime, a guaranteed (unpaid) day off a week, and three paid days of vacation after one year of service. And part-time babysitters and "live in companions" now have minimum wage protection. Estey writes, "Beyond Care has demonstrated that the cooperative model is a viable structural alternative for the most-privatized sector of the workforce with the most purposefully marginalized workers in America's working class" (Estey 2011, 361). What this legislation does is give workers in this sector bargaining power with employers. That is, they have integrated the social democrat critique of Mayer (see Chapter 3) and worked with another organization to change the legal structure of the sector (more below). BC has benefited from this enormously since the legislation sets a standard for the industry that reduces "race to the bottom"-type employment practices that cut wages and forgo benefits not to mention promote abuse.

But BC's co-op framework goes beyond the domestic worker bill of rights standard. What BC has sought to do is "professionalize" child care in a maxD manner. Not only is child care underpaid but the work itself is undervalued. It is often treated as an unskilled "biological" activity rather than the intentional act of a thinking person. What is the goal of child care? For BC, it is "growth": the health and development of the child. To do this well requires the engagement of the cognitive faculties of reflection, reasoning and deliberation, emotional intelligence and empathy, as well as particular pedagogical abilities and specialized knowledges (e.g., nutrition) (Schwarzenbach 2009, 155–157). As Schwarzenbach puts it, drawing upon the work of Aristotle: "Care is that intelligent and emotionally competent activity which not only aims at the concrete and general good of a person (or object or thing), but actively seeks to bring that good about" (Schwarzenbach 2009, 138). BC seeks not only to better equip those doing it, but to "professionalize" it in a worker-empowering manner.[26] This point is powerfully put by BC member Amezquita. She says,

> I like to say that we're child care providers because we take care of children, we help them grow; personally, I don't care for the word nanny. I've never cared for it. I'm not taking anything away from it.

I just like the idea that I'm a professional and that I offer services that give me that title of child care provider. I'm providing a service for your family to take care of your children to help them grow, to give them whatever it is that they need, whatever it is that that family needs to help them do what they need to do and in turn, I'm receiving payment so that I can help my family survive and grow. (Amezquita quoted in Estey 2011, 363)

The contract specifies what the co-op member will and will not provide. And the training enables BC's members to deliver what helps the child grow within in the context of the needs of the contracting family.

In the quote above, we see the importance of individual and collective determination with respect to language and capabilities (maxD#1 and maxD#2). This is why there was so much time spent in the preplanning phase of the co-op with respect to the logo and branding. Estey writes, "The hierarchical class relations that are central to capitalism, and a constitutive feature of daily work life cannot be unlearned abstractly. The experience of learning to create and share power is historical and embodied. Cooperatives are places where this occurs" (Estey 2011, 362).

In a democratic workplace, the brand reflects the norms that the members choose. In the case of BC, members' identities are tied up in the mission that frames the brand: "beyond care" connotes a higher level of caregiving. This is why there is a robust array of training and education programs within BC. There is an intensive two-month apprenticeship for each new member (Estey 2011, 362). Members receive training in CPR from the FDNY, take child development courses from Sunset Park Head Start, and Domestic Workers United helps them to understand all the legal aspects of the contract. They also have to take an eight-hour course on consensus decision making and receive English-language courses (Estey 2011, 357). Center for Family Life also provides a range of supports.

The reason I mention the organizations that provide the services to the members harks back to maxD#4 and is twofold: as we will discuss more below, one of the impediments to co-op formation and growth is lack of access to the relevant business services. The individual members of BC, even acting together, could not have negotiated with the range of agencies that CFL was able to bring to the table with their clout and experience (Estey 2011, 360–361). This required strategic solidarity. Second, one will note that other NGOs and federal, state, and local government all played significant roles in the support for BC, sometimes directly (state legislation for the bill of rights for domestic workers) or indirectly (the assistance of the federal Head Start program). These are again examples of the implementation of maxD#4, which assists in the cultivation of maxD#1, maxD#2, and maxD#3.

Cooperative Home Care Associates (Bronx, NY)

Another example of a co-op taking a sectoral approach is the largest worker co-op in the United States, the Cooperative Home Care Associates (CHCA). Founded in 1985 in the Bronx in NYC with a dozen women most of whom were on public assistance, the goal of CHCA is, like Beyond Care, to provide quality jobs in an industry that is infamous for low-wage exploitation. Indeed, home care is the fastest growing area of employment in the United States and it is one of the most profitable with gross margins between 30 percent and 40 percent (S. Bouchard 2012b; Paraprofessional Health Institute 2013).

Not surprisingly, one of the reasons for the high profits are the low wages. Indeed, as regulations in the industry change, business associations in the sector are nervous. Finance journalist Stephanie Bouchard writes, "Like many small businesses, home care franchise owners are concerned about regulations resulting from the Affordable Care Act, but the most pressing concern is the current attempt by the U.S. Department of Labor to extend minimum wage and overtime protections to in-home workers who currently fall under the companion exemption in the Fair Labor Standards Act" (S. Bouchard 2012a). In other words, among the reasons that home care franchises are so profitable is that employers don't have to pay minimum wage or provide benefits to workers who are being paid by taxpayers to take care of seniors and disabled people (Paraprofessional Health Institute 2014)!

CHCA provides an alternative business model to the privately owned "low road" low-wage franchise. In this sector, the median wage for home care workers is less than $10 an hour, at CHCA it's $16. The average home care worker has no guaranteed hours and works about 25–30 hours with no benefits. CHCA members average 36 hours a week, and they have power in setting their schedules, which is a big issue for workers in general but especially in this sector. And CHCA members have health and dental care. All these are factors as to why CHCA has grown tremendously over 30 years and now has around 2,300 members, most of whom are worker-owners. CHCA had $64 million in revenue in 2013 (Flanders 2014).

What also distinguishes CHCA are its training and professional development programs, which improve care for their patients so much so that they are recognized as an industry leader. They have also set up an institute to disseminate these best practices throughout the sector (more below). These training programs may also be combined with professional development programs thus enabling self-development and economic mobility for its members.[27] This means that even though the pay ratio within the firm is higher than that of Mondragon (CHCA's is 11:1), workers within CHCA are able to ascend the professional ladder to raise their income and share of the profits (Flanders 2014). Because of its success it has even helped to start another worker co-op, Home Care Associates in Philadelphia.

The reason to discuss CHCA in a section on nonprofits is twofold. While Beyond Care was formed by a nonprofit to help a social service delivery organization better serve its clients, CHCA formed two nonprofits in order to better serve its workers and their clients. In this regard, CHCA is similar to Mondragon; as it grew, it created other organizations to help it survive and scale up. MC formed a bank (the Caja Laboral) and a university. CHCA formed a multi-billion-dollar managed care agency (which is how it obtains part of its funding), the Independence Care System, and Paraprofessional Healthcare Institute (PHI). PHI is a nonprofit that spreads best practices not just to other worker co-ops but throughout the home care industry via workforce development programs, job training, and policy advocacy. With this set of integrated organizations, CHCA has switched its perspective from that of an anomalous outsider fighting against an industry to that of an insider working to change standards and practices through its own actions, partnerships, and lobbying. This also explains why CHCA sought to unionize its workforce with Service Employees International Union (SEIU) local 1199. Not only does this help CHCA's workers get access to supports for training and benefits, SEIU is also a player in the legislative and policy arenas in NY State and nationally (Flanders 2014).

In a further twist, in 2012 CHCA became a B corporation in order to better communicate to the public its values and mission (S. Bouchard 2012b). A B corp is a business whose mission is to serve not just its owners or shareholders but the triple bottom line of "people, profits and environment." In a sense, it's a fusion of the stakeholder and civil society models of Corporate Social Responsibility (CSR) discussed in Chapter 3. When a business becomes a B corp, it commits as an organization to serving a range of stakeholders including employees, suppliers, community, and environment. In some states there is a legal option for becoming a B corp, in others, a business can still become one but they are not incorporated as one. This is possible because the evaluation of a business's practices is not done by the government but by B lab, a nonprofit.[28]

Multistakeholder Cooperatives

Although CHCA is partnered with nonprofits, it is still owned and run by its workers. But there are other democratically run workplaces that are run not only by their by workers but by other stakeholders. They are called multistakeholder cooperatives (MSCs). An MSC is a firm that is managed and owned by more than one class of stakeholders. MSCs are owned and run by a combination of workers, investors, customers, and/or community members. Generally speaking, MSCs are worker co-ops that have determined that other groups should be present and have standing in their ownership and/or governance process. They are then, strictly speaking, not labor-managed firms in Ellerman's sense.

A frequent reason for opting for the MSC model rather than a worker co-op model is to raise funds to start the business. Lack of access to financing and credit is a frequent barrier to co-op formation in the United States. Some groups looking to form co-ops have individuals willing to financially contribute but are not interested in or able to work at the firm. Unlike worker co-ops, MSCs enable a supporter to make an investment and to sit on the governance board. An agreement is drawn up for returns to the investor member and the rules for exit. All parties agree to this at the start (Lund 2011, 8–10).

Another reason for forming an MSC rather than a worker co-op is the need for expertise. This can take two forms. There may be a person in the initial planning group who is an expert in the field or in finance and management, but he or she does not want to work at the firm. Yet, this person is willing to assist and be a voting member. As in the first case, an agreement is drawn up for the person to be a member and on the board.

The third reason goes back to concerns raised by Malleson with respect to the service delivered. Some businesses have more intimate relationships with customers. This is particularly true in health care delivery. In such cases, customers are asked to be part of the governance unit not just because they are *affected* by the service but because of their *expertise*: they know their needs best and whether they are being met, and this feedback should be present in the management of the firm. Of course, they are also greatly impacted by the operations of the firm, sometimes more so than the workers! This is often the case in social services delivery co-ops in eldercare and with the disabled. In Italy's Emilia-Romagna region, many such co-ops have operated along these lines (Lund 2011, 24–25; Malleson 2014, 65–69; Restakis 2010, 73–116).

A different version of reason three is to include a customer because of their size or clout. For example, in the food sector, some MSCs have placed institutional buyers on their board because of their expertise, purchasing power, and/or connections to the community. Relatedly, adding nonworker members can increase the legitimacy and/or attractiveness of the firm. Some community members bring critical social networks with them. Adding them to a co-op board can greatly expand the profile of the co-op and hopefully help to build trust with the community. (This is why the MSC model is sometimes also called the "solidarity" co-op model.) This is crucial particularly because most people are unfamiliar with co-ops and for some their strangeness can be off-putting or make them seem like they are not a "real business." New nonprofits often employ a related strategy by seeking out "big names" that are well known and respected by potential funders and clients (Lund 2011, 7–8).

So how would our theorists respond to this mixed model? Two issues jump out. The first is that all our theorists consider a co-op to be an association or polity, not a piece of property. Given the reasons for workers to expand the board to offsite nonworkers, one could also argue that it is not just the self-interest of workers that justifies the inclusion; it is that all these groups make meaningful contributions to the firm. That is, they are all contributing members to the business as *polity*. Note that this differs from the stakeholder theory claim that such groups should be included because each is *affected* by the firm. For example, in the MSC model, customers are included not just because they are affected by the firm but because of their expertise as users and social capital to make a contribution to the management of the firm. In some ways this is a more Gould-ian "common activity" justification than a Freeman "stakeholder" consideration. But, Gould follows Dahl and others and favors a distinction between "inside" and outside the firm stakeholders (e.g., consumers, community) and privileges the inside (e.g., workers, and, to some extent, investors) (Gould 2004, 228–234). But the case of MSCs and the idea that consumers should be included not just because they are "affected" but because they have expertise scrambles some of the distinctions made by Gould.[29]

Because MSCs bring nonworkers into management and control of the surplus, labor is not the sole governing agent. Instead the governing agent is a diverse composite in which power is distributed in an ad hoc arrangement. Flexibility is crucial because local conditions vary and businesses must adapt quickly; there is no "one size fits all" model for MSCs. Some MSCs allow for nonworker board members from any class and don't just limit it to customers or investors (Lund 2011, 12). (This is also how nonprofit boards often work.) In addition, a "successful multistakeholder cooperative has inherent in its board structure the 'checks and balances' that characterize any successful democracy" (Lund 2011, 11). I like this quote because it highlights the idea that a co-op structure can handle a diverse community of heterogeneous interests without relying upon or assuming an underlying homogeneity. But even though MSCs integrate nonworker groups, they still generally ensure that workers have majority power in the managerial mix, and not just theoretically but in practice.[30] But if workers do not have majority voting power, then MSCs not only differ from but *conflict* with worker co-ops insofar as they violate the "sovereignty of labor."

Another issue of concern for our theorists is not who controls the co-op (the board does), but who is permitted to materially benefit from it. The MSC model allows for investors to receive dividends. Indeed, they may even receive a preferred dividend: that is, they get a share of the surplus before anyone else (Lund 2011, 13). Gould would be the most at ease with a pluralistic arrangement, but Ellerman would be concerned. A related issue concerns the rules for the dissolution of the co-op. Lund basically favors the model in which a portion of the surplus is in indivisible reserves, and another part in the internal pay accounts of workers. But the question is, should other classes receive a dividend? Why only investors or workers? Why not community members or customers? If customers are providing expertise, then isn't that a form of "immaterial labor" for which they should be compensated (though at a rate less than workers)? (Indeed, in the next chapter's analysis of the Seikatsu *consumer* cooperative, it is clear that some consumer-members labor extensively.) Ellerman would be opposed to investors being compensated as such. If they want to provide assets in the fashion of a lease, that is permissible because it is labor renting capital, but to grant investors a portion of the *surplus* smacks of the theft that is part and parcel of the employment contract and such a transfer is immoral. However, if consumers could be shown to be "producing" (hence the awkward term "prosumers"), they could deserve compensation for Ellerman, but as laborers not consumers.[31]

Building an EconD System: Ownership and the Role of the State

So which form of ownership is the most econD? Schweickart favors state ownership, but it's not totally clear why. It's not that he's ambiguous about the fact that the state should own businesses—or a business's property assets, to use more Ellermanian language. Schweickart repeatedly stipulates that businesses should be democratically managed by the workers and that the capital assets of the firm should be leased by the workers from the state. He writes, "Although workers control the workplace, they do not 'own' the means of production. These are regarded as the collective property of society" (Schweickart 2011, 50). But again, for Schweickart, unlike A-PD, for example, when he says "controlled by society," he means, "controlled by society through the machinery of the state." But he doesn't give any specific moral or political argument for this. My sympathetic reading is that he sees it as a coordination and power problem: capital assets are too important for the workers themselves to own. They might have too big of an impact on society, positively or negatively. It's been pointed out, for example, that if Apple was a worker co-op, each member would make at least $400,000 a year (Keng 2014)! As Malleson notes above, there may be some firms that are so valuable that they should be owned by the state. Intriguingly, Schweickart permits the existence of such wealthy firms, even if they are privately owned, if they seem exceptional with respect to the product they make or the service they deliver or even some other reason.

So why, then, have the state own most of the firms? Because that's what it takes to get rid of (bad) capitalism and bring about democratic market socialism. The reason that most business assets should be managed by the state is because if such assets were distributed by the market, they may not be used in ways that maximize the satisfaction of social need. Even worse, they may contribute to the concentration of wealth and/or prevent assets from being used by vulnerable parts of the population, or the most talented constituents. As we saw in Chapter 3 , market failure along these lines is not uncommon. Schweickart writes,

> Worker self-management extends democracy to the workplace. Apart from being good in itself, this extension of democracy aims at enhancing a firm's internal efficiency. The market also aims at efficiency, and acts to counter the bureaucratic overcentralization that plagued earlier forms of socialism. Social control of new investment is the counterfoil to the market, counteracting the instability and other irrational consequences of an overextended market—what Marx calls the "anarchy" of capitalist production. (Schweickart 2011, 58–59)

Against the "anarchy of production" is the "wise use" of production. For example, the social control of assets through state ownership would enable a transition to a more ecologically sustainable economy to happen more quickly and efficiently. Phasing out wasteful or damaging technologies would be much easier, as would promoting the adoption of better ones. One can think of all sorts of environmental sustainability and worker health items here, from the gradual elimination of carbon-based fuels to the adopting of renewables. Rather than the government using its regulatory power to encourage or dissuade, it could simply not lease out land for coal production and/or only do so for wind and solar.

The general point here is that Schweickart calls for an economy that meets the needs of society. For him, the state ownership of (most) of the means of production is necessary for that. But the state should not manage the firms, the workers should. And the state should not distribute the *goods*; (mostly) the market should do that. In Schweickart's model, there are three features: worker self-management, the market, and the social control of investment. Workers control the firm in a manner congruent with Dahl and Ellerman: each has one vote, they deliberate together, they elect the managers, etc. Management is not appointed by the state (Schweickart 2002, 50). Workplaces interact with one another generally without government interference: "Raw materials, instruments of production, and consumer goods are all bought and sold at prices largely determined by the forces of supply and demand" (Schweickart 2002, 49). And all firms must pay a tax on their capital assets. The money from this payment goes into a publicly run investment fund. And, firms must set up a "depreciation fund" from their profits so that they can properly maintain the assets of the firm (Schweickart 2011, 50).

But here we see a divergence from Ellerman. Ellerman argued at great length that private individuals who do not work at a firm have no right to own the labor of the workers or the fruits of those labors. But off-site nonlaborers could own the equipment. Schweickart takes a much more state-centric approach to ownership. Even when he states that raw materials would be bought and sold on the market, government run banks and investment programs are sponsoring much of the buying and selling. My sense here, again trying to read Schweickart sympathetically, is that he is trying to counterbalance the market by recognizing the latter's virtues but also its limits and failures. Here he resonates with Dahl, when push comes to shove, the economy is fundamentally a political matter. The difference is that Schweickart tends to see the state as a central vehicle for managing the economy; that is, both setting priorities and owning the key assets.

The reasons for this state-centricity are twofold: the most obvious is that the well-being of the great majority of humans and the Earth depends on who controls capital and toward what end. If only a minority controls investment and the end is profit, inequality and ecological degradation are not surprising. The other reason for states being the vehicle for investment is that they are pretty good at it. Examples discussed above, from Korea and Singapore to Japan and the United States, have shown that when there is state coordination of development, there is less regional inequality and a relatively more harmonious national polity with less divisiveness. There is more local stability because people don't have to move for economic reasons nearly as often (e.g., to follow jobs). Community life is richer. People have more control over their everyday life because more investment moneys are dedicated to them for their needs *as defined by them*. This also encourages participation, which further increases community capability and cohesion. And, finally, regions are not subordinate to global capitalism because they do not have to worry about capital flight (Schweickart 2002, 66).[32]

However, Schweickart does not call for the state to actually manage the economy; state bureaucrats would not decide where to invest funds. Individual banks with independent management would. Indeed, individual banks would compete with each other to best serve the regions in which they operated. Whichever did the best would receive the most funding from the state. Any that failed to properly serve their constituencies and communities would have their funds cut off (Schweickart 2011, 53).

Criticisms of Workplace Democracy/EconD

In the previous chapter and half of this one we have justified worker co-ops from a variety of moral and political perspectives and have argued and brought evidence to show that they can dramatically improve the lives of persons and communities both economically and politically. So why would intelligent people still oppose them?

First let's get rid of the really weak critiques; for instance, those that are poorly argued and/or not supported by the evidence.

The Weak Critiques

1. Co-ops are not economically viable. **False.** Worker co-ops have succeeded in many different sectors and in a variety of different types of economies. Furthermore, where there is evidence about them, it often shows that co-ops have a lower failure rate than noncooperative businesses. (See, for example, Lund 2011, 21; Malleson 2014, 55, 72–80.) In addition, what studies there are show that co-ops—when compared with traditional firms—are more productive according to traditional economic criteria: "The evidence is thus robust that being your own boss does seem to improve productivity. This likely comes from two main sources: the *increased motivation* that comes from profit-sharing and the *smoother coordination* that comes from increased trust and reduced alienation" (Malleson 2014, 73). Because there are more individual and collective incentives to work hard, there is less turnover and absenteeism. Also, supervision is more efficacious thus there is less need for middle management (Schweickart 2011, 63; Malleson 2014, 72–80).

2. Co-ops might work in some (sub)cultures, but in most (i.e., the US?!) they have not, do not, and/or will not. **False.** Read Curl 2012, Restakis 2010, and Gordon Nembhard 2014. Co-ops are not just a white hippie thing, nor are they just an anarchist or socialist thing. They are a northern Italian and French Canadian thing, a Japanese housewives and Indian weavers thing. Some of the most vibrant efforts are happening in these places and in Latin America (hurray Argentinian recuperated factories!), but they are happening in many different cultural contexts (hurray U.S. mechanical engineers!). Japan has the largest number of democratically run businesses, Germany has just seen a new wave of energy co-ops, and South Africa and India have impressive well-studied efforts. Also, the United States has a very underappreciated history of worker cooperative and other econD efforts: examples from colonial times to present are addressed in detail by Curl (2012), and one of the most myth-busting and inspiring co-op traditions has been reconstructed by Gordon Nembhard and concerns African American efforts at economic democracy, including such figures as W.E.B. Dubois, A. Philip Randolph, Marcus Garvey, Nannie Helen Boroughs, Ella Jo Baker, and many many others (Gordon Nembhard 2014, 2).

3. OK, so for some people in some contexts, co-ops could (and have) worked, but for the majority of people, it's not their thing. **False.** This critique combines 1 and 2. It's the idea that worker co-ops fail because there are "so many meetings" that members don't have enough time to actually carry out core business activities. Relatedly, some worry that because they are "too democratic," there is no effective leadership but instead a chaos of competing voices that interferes with the smooth running of the firm.[33]

This is a sort of "intuitive," incoherent, half-true, half-insane critique. First off, the insane part. Could you imagine in the current U.S. downturn with the proliferation of precarious part-time jobs that someone would turn down a good, well-paying job, where he or she would become a part owner of the firm, because of the number of meetings? "Sure, this sounds like a good job and all and sure I would love to have job security and build equity so that I could afford a house but I prefer a low wage gig with no benefits and dangerous working conditions where the boss yells at me but at least I don't have to talk regularly at meetings. So yeah, thanks, but no thanks."[34]

The Strong Critiques

Strong Criticism #1. "Co-ops still need capitalists." **True.** *Revisiting Mondragon.* For defenders of worker co-ops and econD in general, Mondragon is not just a frequent citation, it is a kind of trump card one lays down when critics claim that co-ops cannot deliver long-term benefits for members, survive in a high-tech landscape, scale-up, and/or compete on the global market. MC does all of these, plus, as we saw last chapter, it genuinely and extensively benefits its local community. Even from a *traditional* business perspective, Mondragon is incredibly successful. And furthermore, the success is not as a mom and pop store selling baked goods, but as a multinational firm making sophisticated medical imaging machines and providing construction services for big name buildings including the world-famous Guggenheim Museum in Bilbao. After enduring several economic downturns, it has increased employment, revenues, and profits. And it has expanded the number of firms, branching out into overseas markets. But it has done so while delivering benefits to workers and others that traditional large firms do not generate.

But when advocates of econD or worker co-ops cite Mondragon as an exemplar, to what exactly are they referring? There are at least two Mondragons: phase 1 lasted from its founding in 1956 until 1989 or so when it underwent a series of changes. Mondragon's phase 2 form takes shape in the 1990s and by the 2000s departs from the phase 1 form in a few crucial ways.[35]

The date of the transition should not surprise. The 1990s were a time of marked economic shifts with the collapse of the Soviet Union, the formation of the World Trade Organization, and the entry of China into the global market. For example, in the 1990s, the Basque-based Mondragon firm Irizar produced a bus for about $180,000. In China, a comparable vehicle could be made for $12,000 (Malleson 2014, 59). To compete, Mondragon began to add firms abroad for the first time, and these firms were not co-ops. It also undertook an internal reorganization and shifted from a regional model to a sector model of four business groups to allow for "greater inter-firm coop-eration and synergy as well as economies of scale" (Malleson 2014, 59). The four groups are financial, retail (mainly Eroski, more below), industrial, and research and knowledge.

Besides the overseas non-co-op firms, the most obvious transformation happened in terms of the workforce. In 1990, about 80 percent of the busi-ness federation's workforce were full-time worker-owners. By 2006 that number dropped to 38 percent. In other words, full-time worker-owners became a *minority* of the workforce. On the face of it, this is a change in *es-sence*: should we even call Mondragon a co-op? Malleson says "no," it's a "capitalist partnership" (Malleson 2014, 60).

So what was the reason for taking on so many nonmember workers? To save the (full-time) members' jobs (Malleson 2014, 58–61). To compete with MNCs, Mondragon had to grow, cut labor costs, and enter new markets. Is it moral for members to hire nonmembers in order to save their jobs? (Let's note how bizarre this question is from a traditional economic perspective: is it moral for my firm to *hire more workers* to do all the work necessary for the firm to survive?) To answer this question, we must look at who was hired and to do what, and then look at the answers relative to the mission of Mon-dragon and the econD project more generally.

Most of MC's nonmembers are part-time.[36] And most of these jobs are not in China but are in the (Spanish-based) grocery chain Eroski. The rea-sons that so many are nonmembers is largely due to the sector. Eroski was founded in 1969 when ten consumer co-ops combined to form one large co-op supermarket. But it's not a secondary "co-op of co-ops," it's a multistake-holder co-op. As of 2001, Eroski had 1,400 supermarkets, 55 convenience stores, as well as gas stations, perfume shops, travel agencies, and "cash and carry" shops and it now operates across Spain and in France. Indeed it is the second largest retail chain in Spain and rivals the scope and size of the French food firm Carrefour (Lund 2011, 35). Intriguingly from a stakehold-er theory and civil society CSR perspective (see my Chapter 3), Eroski is a market leader in the sale of fair trade, organic, and locally grown products. As for the (consumer) membership, it costs $75 to join and that gets you a 5 percent discount on purchases. There are 500,000 members and it is proba-bly the largest MSC in the world. Indeed, because of its multisector selling and regional scope, Lund calls Eroski "the distribution division" of the Mon-dragon Corporation (Lund 2011, 35).

As it grew, Eroski formed worker co-ops within itself. Worker members are required to provide a much more substantial equity stake of approxi-mately $6,500, which can be financed through payroll deduction over a three-year period. Workers receive a regular distribution of the surplus through their internal pay accounts. But even if most workers are owners, what can be done to balance the needs, and, more critically, formally represent the interests of the workers amid so many *consumer* members? (Remember, Eroski started out not as a worker co-op but as a consumer co-op.) To address this governance puzzle, Eroski struck upon the following MSC style arrangement: the president of the board of the co-op is always a consumer member, thereby remaining true to its consumer co-op heritage, and guaranteeing the primacy of its much larger class of consumer members. But the board itself is composed of an equal number of consumer and worker members. Each group elects 250 delegates to the general assembly, which in turn selects six workers and six consumers to the board (Lund 2011, 35). While Ellerman might be nervous that such an arrangement violates the sovereignty of labor, Malleson and Lund regard the MSC format as econD. But, the problem for Malleson is that within the federation of *worker* co-ops, the worker-owners are a minority. Part-timers who are not members are the majority.[37] To correct this, Malleson argues we need to "redemocratize" Eroski and bring up full-time membership to about 75 percent (Malleson 2014, 64).

The other class of nonmembers are the employees working at the Mondragon subsidiaries in a variety of (mostly) low-wage countries including China, Brazil, Mexico, Poland, Czech Republic, and, yes, even the United States (Malleson 2014, 59). Why aren't these businesses co-ops? Three "official" reasons have been given: (1) legal barriers, (2) some are joint ventures with conventional capitalist investors, and (3) lack of worker interest (Malleson 2014, 59). Are these good reasons? MC member Irizar pays its foreign subsidiaries' workers 20 percent more than its local competitors (Malleson 2014, 63). This might suggest that its workers are being treated well. But for Ellerman, the matter is moot: the employment contract is invalid no matter the compensation involved, so the expansion of workers as "employees" is, in itself, worrisome. Put another way, Mondragon has explicitly hired nonmembers to protect the jobs of members, thereby creating a "privileged class" within the firm and/or federation.

The Schweickart perspective, however, seems less fazed by these developments and states that we can draw two powerful conclusions from Mondragon's success and persistence: (1) that even faced with the pressures of "globalization," large-scale industrial enterprises can be structured *democratically*, and (2) such a large-scale technological dynamic and globally competitive business shows that "we don't need capitalists anymore" (Schweickart 2011, 73). In other words, the workers not only are the owners; they are the "capitalists" (Malleson 2014, 57). But that depends on the reasons given above. If this is mainly because of the need for capital, and Mondragon has also been investing more in *traditional* capitalist businesses, then Mondragon has come to *need more* access to capitalist finance and is undermining maxD#4 by partnering with organizations explicitly against its norms. Schweickart, then, is either naive or misleading us (Schweickart 2011, 72).

Even worse, Mondragon is not a "worker's paradise" even for those who are full members. Intriguingly, according to at least one study, most of them do *not* feel that the firm is "theirs," which seems to indicate they are still "alienated" (Schweickart 2011, 72). Huet brings this back to the problem of scale:

> For many a primary benefit of working in a cooperative is being a respected, vital part of a democratic community. As a cooperative grows from 20 to 200 members, it may lose some of its sense of community and democratic involvement. No longer can everyone sit together every month and make all the major business decisions. As work functions become more specialized and the business complex, it is increasingly difficult to communicate and make decisions with anything approximating equal participation. If you work at multiple sites (e.g., bakeries) the lines of communication and bonds of trust/friendship will be even further stretched. (Huet 1997)

In smaller co-ops, it is common for workers to report a tight bond to the business. This is especially the case when workers are on the board (Lund 2011, 29–30) or are in the "egalitarian co-ops" (see below). So it doesn't seem that "alienation" is an inevitable feature of co-ops. Should co-ops remain small and only be composed of full members to address the alienation problem? If yes, how can they compete with traditional firms? Huet writes, "Unlike capitalist cancers which grow for their own sake and destroy their host environment, cooperatives aim for homeostasis, a healthy balance. Unfortunately this pro-social characteristic of cooperatives can be a fatal weakness in economic competition with capitalist businesses" (Huet 1997). At this point econD defenders of co-ops might be stymied by this seeming paradox. But again, recalling Schweickart, we must be careful not to ask too much of co-ops. For co-ops to do what they do well, the *system* must change.

Strong Criticism #2: Co-ops cannot bring about econD by themselves. **True.** *For individual co-ops to become more stable and for the movement to proliferate, institutional changes need to occur.* The most frequent problems faced by co-ops are financial, legal, and cultural. There is a kind of cultural blockage that can cause co-ops to seem strange and distant, and inaccessible to "regular" people. Although the evidence shows that they *actually* work, for many, it's hard to *imagine* themselves doing that work. As Huet says, "Acculturation is always a challenge for democratic workplaces as they must reshape the behavioral/thought patterns incoming workers have acquired from autocratic employers and schools" (Huet 1997). Besides the cultural gaps, there are the economic realities. Sometimes there is a group of actually existing humans with the vision and the courage to take the plunge and start a co-op, but they lack adequate financial resources to purchase all the equipment, secure an adequate space, or have enough to support themselves while the business struggles to get off the ground in its first months or years. Indeed, one seeming positive for workers in the traditional business model is that only the owners put up the capital and/assets, not the workers. The employee in a new restaurant may lose out on a few paychecks if it fails, but the owner could lose his life savings as well.

Then there are those situations where the business makes it through those difficult first years but later has some new expense arises and can't get a line of credit or loan because of legal hurdles or general ignorance among banks about co-ops. In each of these situations, we would say that the co-op has a "capitalization" problem: it can't get the capital it needs to function and grow; it is "undercapitalized." Again, this can occur for a variety of reasons: legal constraints, lending institutions lack of familiarity with their model, and/or actual opposition because they are democratic and this perceived as a threat to dominant hierarchical models (more below).

When co-ops do fail, it is sometimes because of vulnerabilities that all businesses share—an economic downturn—and/or the failure to adapt to new technologies. This happened in the late 1800s when co-ops became attached to a business model that depended on a technology that was no longer cost effective (e.g., barrel making; see Curl 2012, 96–100). But in other circumstances co-ops were attacked precisely *because* they were democratic or part of political movements that were opposed to some form of injustice supported by other sectors of the society. For example, white supremacists recognized that econD was a potent part of black efforts for collective determination and sometimes grouped together in plantation blocs or in local government corporatist coalitions to undermine co-ops and their members. As Gordon Nembhard tells us, they used all kinds of tactics from legal to extralegal, from misinformation to murder to undermine econD efforts including "slander, violence, murder, physical destruction, and economic sabotage" (Gordon Nembhard 2014, 300). The details are dreadful:

> They burned down the offices, farms, and houses owned by these organizations [e.g., co-ops] or their members. They shot and lynched leaders, members, and their families. They accused Black leaders of mail fraud and treason, jailed them, and initiated federal indictments. They denied loans to fledgling businesses. They established their own businesses to undercut and outcompete Black products and services. They even passed laws to outlaw the activities in which Black organizations and collective economic activities often engaged. (Gordon Nembhard 2014, 30)[38]

When considering the past limits and failures of co-ops in the United States, extralegal actions including violence need to be noted. However, in the present, probably the biggest impediment to the co-op movement is the lack of access to capital and credit. This makes it difficult to start a co-op, and it also makes it difficult for them to grow.

The undercapitalization problem illustrates the importance of Schweickart's system level view. If private individuals, and organizations controlled by private individuals, are the main source of capital, then co-ops will have serious difficulties raising capital because individual investors are not permitted! While the banks that they control could lend to them or invest in them, why would they if they offer private investors fewer opportunities to participate? This is what leads Schweickart to favor a system in which the public controls much, but not all, of investment. If that doesn't happen, an alternative is for existing co-ops and workers to pool together their assets and form their own bank. This is what the exemplary Mondragon did, but it still had to make compromises as well (see above).

For co-op's to proliferate, a major reorientation would have to take place in the investment and finance sectors. There are elements of this already in place with credit unions and other community development institutions but they are inadequate. More changes to banking are required as well as more mundane changes in business law. For example, in the United States, the ability to incorporate as a co-op varies from state to state. And for existing co-ops, access to business supports and services is oftentimes more difficult because existing departments and programs are not familiar with co-ops, or have requirements that make it more difficult for co-ops to receive supports or services. A seemingly trivial example is that in NYC, to receive support from small business services, each owner must fill out a range of paperwork. CHCA, which is based in the Bronx, has more than 2,000 owners! Relatedly, there is a lack of familiarity and understanding about how worker co-ops depend on multiple constituencies, especially investors, lawyers, government agencies and regulators, and the public (who is after all the source of future employees and customers). All these factors—from the legal and formal to outright bias or ignorance—can either impede or support the co-op movement.

Whatever one thinks of the specific institutional proposals of Schweickart, the more general point is indisputable: for co-ops to flourish, and for the economy to be democratized, an entire ecosystem of actors supporting and defending each other is necessary. Glimpses of this were seen with Beyond Care and CHCA in home and health care. The sectoral, national, and global proliferation of neoliberal industrial corporate capitalism is not a result of limited liability corporations defeating worker cooperatives in a Darwinian survival of the fittest competition. When Orkli (from the Mondragon Federation of Cooperatives) competes with General Electric to sell goods in Brazil or China, each acts not as a solo gladiator fighting mano a mano upon the "level playing field" in the capitalist version of the Roman Coliseum. MNCs and privately held businesses have an incredibly intricate system of supports from states, banks, international associations, and even militaries. A major multinational firm's success requires a competent regulatory apparatus, advantageous taxes and subsidies, marketing and media, not to mention an educated workforce and extensive water, energy, and transportation infrastructure. Then there is the nitty-gritty training by business schools, the organizing and lobbying of chambers of commerce, research and proselytizing by universities and think tanks, and the funding of foundations. The question is what does an econD version of this system look like?

Support Networks and System Change: Learning from Italy and Quebec

In Basque Country, the growth of Mondragon was made possible in large part by the banking services provided by the Caja Laboral and the training and research of its university and schools as well as extensive legal changes all occurring in a cultural framework that promoted community solidarity (Malleson 2014, 56–65 and my Chapter 3). In this section, we look at two other examples of well-developed econD systems that also have cultural frames similar to Mondragon but received more formal state support and were driven by different social movements. They are Italy (especially the Emilia-Romagna region) and the province of Quebec in Canada.

In Italy, large worker co-ops are major players across sectors: they employ 18 percent of workers in the food processing sector, 23 percent in construction, 19 percent in hotels and restaurants, and 17 percent in facilities' management. And there are field-leading co-ops in ceramics, agriculture, housing, catering, transport, health, furniture, and high-tech machinery (Malleson 2014, 67). These large co-ops have been part of a 100-year movement coordinated by the federation known as La Lega, which has played a role similar to that of the Caja Laboral and the broader federation of Mondragon but in a more state allied way: "La Lega lobbies the state for support, it provides legal, business, and accounting services, it provides research and development information, it helps coordinate business evolution, and helps finance the development of new cooperatives" (Malleson 2014, 66).

And there is a new growth sector among co-ops since key legal changes in 1991 allowed both funding and service delivery contracts to businesses and other organizations who organized as "social co-ops." Lund writes, "In all social cooperatives, membership can consist of classes of workers, users, investors, supporters such as public institutions, and volunteers. All cooperatives abide by the one member, one vote rule" (Lund 2011, 24). Social co-ops are similar to MSCs with their heterogeneous member classes, but they adhere to one member, one vote rule, which MSCs often do not. Social co-ops receive tax breaks from the state in regard to payroll, land, and mortgages. Now most social co-ops are state funded, which marks a departure for the Italian co-op movement that had been more focused on "member benefit" rather than the good of the community (Lund 2011, 24–25). This also shows a major sectoral difference with Mondragon, although there are other co-ops in Italy that are engaged more in manufacturing for both domestic consumption and export.

But Italian social co-ops are similar to Mondragon in terms of support networks that "provide everything from technical assistance and training to the sharing of resources" (Lund 2011, 24). These second-tier "apex" organizations operate at the local, provincial, and national level. One way in which they offer a different model than Mondragon is that these co-ops are smaller, less than 50 workers each. But how can such small firms handle the scale problem? Many contracts require capacities well beyond any single firm. What the Italian co-ops do is combine on a contract-by-contract basis as needed through "joint bidding" (Lund 2011, 24). Interestingly, this kind of strategy is not particular to co-ops, but to areas that require lots of labor flexibility and are not dominated by large firms. Indeed, NYC for much of its history operated this way with respect to manufacturing (Fitch 1993).

In Quebec, like in Italy, there was a kind of partnership between the regional government (province of Quebec) with social movements, especially the women's movement, as well as unions. As in Basque Country, banks were key, especially the Desjardin Credit Union and the Coopérative fédérée de Québec. But the financing component also involved key legislation at the provincial level, which enabled tax breaks for co-op members and investors in co-ops (e.g., hence the proliferation of multistakeholder co-ops). Indeed in 2009–2010, $31.5 million (in Canadian dollars) in new financing came in because of changes that allowed co-op members to defer tax on their patronage dividends so long as they were reinvested in the cooperative. Not only have the Desjardin Credit Union and the Coopérative fédérée de Québec been crucial to addressing the major problem of financing and credit for co-ops but they are also, respectively, the first and fifth largest employers in the province. Overall, there are more than 3,300 cooperatives in Quebec. They employ 90,000 people and have a total of 8.8 million members.[39] The largest sectors in which there are co-ops are in leisure and services (social and business), but they operate in many other areas as well from food and housing to manufacturing and utilities (Lund 2011, 21; Lewis and Conaty 2012, 223–230).

In sum, in order for co-ops to proliferate and for the present economy to move toward an economic democracy, five components seem crucial: a strong social or cultural movement that is multi-issue, a university to provide both training and research, a bank and/or government agency to provide financing, legal supports that often favor co-ops relative to traditional businesses, and a nongovernmental association that can coordinate the aforementioned actors.

Strong Criticism #3: Worker ownership does not guarantee a good life. **True.** *Meaningful work, job rotation, and the cultivation of whole humans.* Yet, even if co-ops did succeed and spread, and the economy becomes more participatory, equitable, inclusive, and empowering, what kind of *labor* model are we spreading? In the preceding justifications for worker co-ops and econD, we have focused on ownership and management of workplaces but not much about the *kinds of work* performed nor the *division of labor* within and across firms. Is "who does what" a moral issue? Is it a democracy issue? If individuals are stuck or trapped in particular kinds of work, would it be right to say that their freedom has is diminished even if they "own" that work? In this section, we will look at a range of critics who argue that the worker co-op frame elucidated above is not democratic enough. Who does what work is important not just as a freedom issue (e.g., freedom of choice, equality of opportunity), but as a self-development issue because the kind of work one does shapes one's character, social standing, relationship with the natural world, and even the meaningfulness of one's life.

Worker co-ops go to great lengths to make sure that workers own their work but they don't do enough to make sure that workers have *meaningful* work. This is the argument of Michael Albert, Robert Hahnel, and the Parecon view (Albert and Schweickart 2008).[40] It was also the argument of a former student of mine who worked in a furniture co-op in North Carolina. He said it was nice to own part of the shop and to have a say about the surplus, but the work wasn't gratifying, indeed, it was deafening and dangerous. Certainly, we could imagine a scenario where workers across sectors come to own and manage their work, but they are still stuck doing particular kinds of jobs. This can be seen in examples from NYC above. Although CHCA does enable some meaningful career advancement from a position with little status and respect (home health care aide) to one with more clout (e.g., registered nurse), many other co-ops in NYC (e.g., Beyond Care) are in low status professions such as child care, food preparation, cleaning, and dog walking. The Parecon problem here is that even if all of these businesses were co-ops, there could still be a hierarchy among jobs that goes against the norms of econD. This is the inequality not of "who owns what" but "who gets to do what."

Michael Albert characterizes the contemporary job market as one composed of three classes: capitalists, "coordinators," and workers. Capitalists own the means of production and most other productive assets (Albert 1997, 100–119; Panayotakis 2011, 121). The coordinator class performs work that "conveys information, skills, confidence, even personal initiative and energy," *and* exercises significant influence on what happens in the economy. In other words, the coordinator faction is a privileged class for two distinct reasons: its work is personally fulfilling *and* has a great impact on society. The problem is that this class is only about 20 percent of the working population. The remaining super-majority usually is paid less, and more often than not, their work is less gratifying. Indeed it often squashes all those good qualities that make work something to take pride in—self-direction, creativity, social impact—and instead is constituted by tasks that are repetitive, debilitating, and exhausting and/or don't seem to have much of a positive impact. Like, for example, receiving an "un-living" wage to sell unhealthy food to poor people. (See Chapter 3.) In an economy where there is a scarcity of meaningful jobs, those who possess them will want to monopolize them, and that causes a class war not just over wealth and income but over the "empowering work that gives them greater status, their greater influence, their great power, their greater income" (Albert and Schweickart 2008, 58).

One could argue with Albert's characterization of the job market. Maybe there is some overlap among these categories. Many jobs that are meaningful—in the sense that the individuals performing the labor derive meaning or pride from them—are poorly paid and/or low status. Teachers, caregivers, and persons working in nonprofits and charities often see their work in such terms and are sometimes seen positively by others even if they are not "high status." These positions are different from those well paid and influential ones that one finds in law and medicine, the tech sector, entertainment, and so on, where persons not only enjoy high wages and benefits but also influence politics and dominate the media. There are also well-paid persons who have outsized influence in their communities because of the prestige associated with their positions in government or business or even civil society associations (e.g., Chamber of Commerce). If we are true to the econD framework, all of these dimensions must be addressed.

Perhaps Albert is wrong and there are more jobs that are meaningful and impactful, and/or maybe there are some very well paid jobs that are mind-numbing. Even if this is true, I think Albert's overall point is right: there is a scarcity of meaningful and impactful jobs. And because there are privileges and status that come with said work, this becomes a democracy issue. (One hears these sentiments echoed when those from wealthy families and/or with wealthy spouses take on more socially meaningful (but less well paid) work and/or are able to refuse work perceived as demeaning.) Thus, even if the majority of firms in the U.S. economy were worker co-ops, the hierarchy among jobs would still threaten core tenets of econD with respect to the very basis of freedom and self-development that is part and parcel of collective determination.

Albert's remedy is multidimensional. We need to break our obsession with specialization and pursue "balanced jobs complexes" in which workers rotate tasks and develop multiple skills (Albert 1997, 104–119). This can happen in different ways and situations: sometimes workers learn different specialized skills or trades: cooks also work the cash register and take orders. In Argentina's famous co-op Hotel Bauen similar sorts of rotations are seen: from hostess to cook, cleaning person to security, manager to bell-boy (Rossi 2015; see also Sitrin 2012, 134, 156–161). But there is also the need for rotation among key categories of work. While management and finance are sometimes regarded as specialized skills that few possess the talent for, at many smaller firms, both are doable (Albert and Schweickart 2008, 67). Even in firms that require highly specialized skills: say medical or engineering— there are still a range of tasks that are often delegated to a few staff that could easily be rotated: for example, engineers could rotate through a cleaning or security position. While some co-ops do pursue such rotations, many do not. And indeed, none of our previously discussed econD theorists name it is a moral or political issue.

We might frame the issue as follows. Some jobs suck because they are boring and repetitive, etc. But there is another class of jobs that *really* suck. These take a debilitating toll on the human body. Construction work in the deserts of Dubai comes to mind, or cleanup after a nuclear accident in Japan. Others aren't as painful but are strikingly unpleasant: hospital orderlies, for example. Even if these jobs are well paid, with great benefits, and even if the workplaces were democratically owned and managed, there is still an issue of fairness. This kind of work is deeply disagreeable to most humans and does not engage the capabilities of said beings in a self-development type of way. It does just the opposite, it punishes the senses and the body. So what to do? Isn't it unfair that some people *only* get these kinds of jobs?[41]

Even if we do rotate them, for Albert, we should pay those doing the less desirable jobs more. When comparing wages of cooks and security guards and professors at Harvard University—there was a strike by the former over low pay and working conditions—Albert argues that guards and cooks should be paid *more* than professors because the former work longer in worse conditions. Professors are paid more because of a "monopoly over information, skills, and circumstances, that has nothing to do with an economic need of society per say [sic] and that has nothing to do with anything moral" (Albert and Schweickart 2008, 66; Albert 1997, 118–119).

Instead, compensation should not be based on market value for skills but on how long you work, how hard you work, and the onerousness of the conditions in which you work (Albert and Schweickart 2008, 62–63).[42] Changing the compensation system would also change the incentive structure. The present economy rewards nastiness and selfishness, "nice guys finish last" (Albert and Schweickart 2008, 58). Albert calls for an economic system that rewards trust, skill-sharing, cooperation, and solidarity. While this may sound moralistic and practically demanding, Parecon's econD frame actually converges with others across the social spectrum including many religious traditions, the "sharing economy" and various facets of the creative class and cyberculture as well as S-PD and A-PD (more below and in Chapter 6).

In others words, the reasons for job rotation are economic, political, and moral. In many businesses, a specialization of *function* makes sense, but specialization of the *laborer* does not. In other words, maybe it makes sense for one job only to be answering the phone or driving the truck, but there is no reason that a person should *only* do that function for the duration of their tenure. Doing the same task over and over for years limits worker competency and experience. Even more basic, variety is useful for overcoming boredom. Specialization also inhibits a member's understanding of all the different aspects of the firm. This might not be a drawback in a traditional firm, but in a co-op, even if most workers never occupy managerial positions (as in Mondragon), those same workers make crucial decisions in the general assembly regarding a range of issues that go beyond one's job description.

Relatedly, the disposition toward job rotation also makes retraining easier when technical or economic conditions change and warrant the phasing out of certain positions and the adoption of new ones. It also gives good reason to keep a narrow compensation range among co-op members especially if managerial positions are rotated (Wolff 2012, 135–136). There is also a personal benefit: having a range of experiences increases one's freedom: by switching spots or tasks, individual members get a better sense about what he or she is best at or not, and what is most enjoyable or not. It can also give one a better understanding of the different tasks involved in the business from a psychological frame, not just an economic one. Anticipating more economistic worries that job rotation could decrease efficiency, Wolff writes, "If a fully rounded personality and a diversely engaged body and mind are connected to personal happiness, genuine democracy, and work productivity, then a WSDE-based [worker self-directed enterprise] economic system with rotation of jobs will be far more fulfilling—and quite possibly more productive—than work has been under private or state capitalism" (Wolff 2012, 137). On my view, even if most co-ops are hierarchical because of economic demands, there should be a commitment to job rotation when possible for all the moral and political reasons noted above. Job rotation should be the default; that is, any firm that does not have job rotation must give good reasons not to do so and these should be agreed to by the members.

But what about those jobs that suck and are not necessary? Aren't there some jobs that should be eliminated altogether even if there is a market for them? This issue is underaddressed in the econD literature. There are some jobs that are so bad, either for the worker or the society, that they should not exist. One example that comes to mind is microwave popcorn manufacturing. The item is not particularly healthy and the flavoring causes severe respiratory malfunction in workers. It's one thing for fire fighters to risk damage to their lungs to save lives. But is it worth it to individuals and societies for workers to do it for butter-flavored popcorn? Indeed, the food additives industry is notorious for all sorts of worker safety violations and many times in the production of foods that are themselves unhealthy![43] In other words, *we have an economic system that employs workers in dangerous conditions to manufacture things that people don't need and are actually bad for them.* And some of it is even subsidized by taxpayers. Then there are the psychologists who are paid to figure out how to attract people (including children!) to these products (Patel 2007, 270–281). Should econD ban such jobs and businesses? Should there at least be a PD debate?

The Perfect Co-op and Its Limitations: The Culture of the Economy

Given the criticisms above, from an econD and maxD perspective, the ideal work situation would seem to be a collectively managed worker-owned firm where each member is able to switch jobs and develop a range of skills. Malleson discusses a community newspaper with about fifteen members that rotated tasks from photographer to writer to layout artist. This firm not only provided variety and encouraged skill development, it prevented expertise from being lodged in one person, which could lead to hierarchies of status and power within the firm. The PD ideal—especially for the horizontalist A-PD—is when management positions are not rotated; they are eliminated. This is sometimes done in smaller firms that are willing to make the time commitment to have decisions made collectively. In this newspaper example, this took about four hours a week (Malleson 2014, 70).

In Latin America, there are several examples of similarly radically egalitarian worker co-ops. For example, in Venezuela, the CECOSESOLA (Cooperatives of Social Services of Lara State) founded in 1967 is a food co-op consisting of 538 worker members who sell to 60,000 shoppers each week from three locations in the city of Barquisimeto. This business operation has no bosses or managers: the workers rotate jobs and all workers receive the same pay. And they are successful at scale and in sales. Though their prices average 30 percent less than those of commercial supermarkets, their annual sales top US$20 million. The network also has many different types of small producer cooperatives, credit unions, a health clinic with both conventional medicine and alternative therapies, and a network of cooperative funeral homes (Fox 2006).[44]

While such egalitarian horizontally managed firms do exist, Malleson argues that it is not the right model for most firms. For egalitarian collectives to work well they must be small, not require much capital, and have members who are culturally connected enough to have an almost intimate degree of familiarity with one another.[45] In this case the ideal co-op is also the stereotypical co-op discussed above and suffers from similar limitations. This model is just not doable for most firms and not desirable for many workers.

Relatedly, egalitarian co-ops will be subject to the same kinds of problems that befall all radical egalitarian organizations: the trade-offs among motivation, merit, and equality. In a business, if everyone is making the same amount of money, and there is no hope for making more than anyone else, why work harder than anyone else? Indeed, why not *try* to do less? This is the classic "free rider" problem. A reason to not do less is because of duties to one's fellow co-op members or other moral reasons. But this also concerns Malleson, "Pure reliance on moral incentives also brings with it a culture of moral expectation and conformism—why aren't you sacrificing as much for the collective as I am?—which can be oppressive in its own way" (Malleson 2014, 71). Malleson sees it as a balance issue. Too much workplace inequality raises justice issues, but too much equality decreases incentives. But maybe Malleson is too pessimistic.

Yes, in the current economy, nonegalitarian co-ops might be more doable. But for co-ops to proliferate, the current economy must be transformed anyway and there must be more institutional supports from finance to education and small business services. Once these supports are in place, egalitarian co-ops will likely become more *doable* from a business perspective. But there is another issue that lurks: would they be *desirable* from a cultural perspective. This raises the issue of the relationship between the economy and society.

Businesses Don't Just Make Stuff; They Make Us

Panayotakis makes this point in his Albert-inspired critique of Schweickart's view. He states, "Schweickart acknowledges the importance of people's consciousness, values, and priorities, but views these cultural traits as largely external to the economic structure his model proposes" (Panayotakis 2011, 127, 131).[46] For Panayotakis, econD depends not just on economic institutional transformation but on "people's democratic skills, values, and needs" (Panayotakis 2011, 132). In other words, for democracy to work in the firm, there must be a *cultural* change that encourages and cultivates worker agency and the skills required to exercise it. Just because workplaces have assemblies doesn't mean they are effectively democratic workplaces. Attendance might be poor, and/or there might be a small clique or group that dominates. Even in radically egalitarian collectives informal hierarchies arise (see Mansbridge 1980, 139–183).

Economics and politics are both sociocultural operations. We encountered elements of this view with Mill who argued that a robust workplace democracy is necessary for the cultivation of a democratic political sphere.

For Panayotakis, all the spheres are interconnected. Thus, if one wants to counter political apathy and cynicism one must activate the agency of persons in the workplace and stoke their individual and collective desires for cooperation. If one wants to combat the passivity of leisure and the mindlessness of consumerism, again, *workplace* culture must be changed. While Schweickart warns of the limitations of democracy and the importance of legal and institutional changes, Panayotakis calls for a cultural reconstruction (Panayotakis 2011, 132–133), more akin to the A-PD and S-PD views discussed in my Chapter 1.

Thus, even if egalitarian collectives only work in a limited array of cases or sectors, they are still important because they are committed to this deep level of PD. Panayotakis writes, "Hahnel and Albert's insistence on the need for balanced job complexes reflects their conviction that economic activity has a constitutive effect on human beings. In other words, the nature of the work people spend much of their lives on has a big impact on who people are, and what skills and preferences they have" (Panayotakis 2011, 122). This leads us into a set of arguments for job rotation that go beyond the normative frameworks employed so far. The first concerns labor and self-development. The cultural PD view of A-PD and S-PD holds that the split between intellectual and manual labor needs to be overcome for reasons of personal self-development. That is, all humans should engage in intellectual and manual labor to fully develop their own set of capabilities, to become a more "rounded" person. One should utilize one's brain and one's hands, the contemplative and the physical: time at the computer, and time in the ditch or the field. Note that this is different from the demand that management tasks within a workplace be shared (that would only involve "intellectual" labor). And it is different from demanding job rotation in general since all those rotations could be confined to either the intellectual *or* manual realms. At many workplaces from machine shops to kitchens, from construction sites to physical therapy clinics, there is the potential to work with one's hands and work with one's head. Imagine academics out on the quad weeding flower beds and members of the grounds crew coteaching classes in environmental science and business management!

But isn't this too ambitious? Isn't this asking too much of organizations already so embattled, so in need of support? Co-ops offer much potential from a more limited PD framework, why subject them to additional normative demands? When we do so, don't we risk losing the benefits that they are well suited to deliver? The reason for subjecting co-ops to these sorts of demands is that if we don't they could end up reinforcing a conception of *labor* that violates some tenets of econD even as it fulfills others. In other words, why create a democratic version of body-crushing, mind-numbing, senses-degrading labor? Why not remake labor itself so that it promotes self-development, creative collaboration, social solidarity, and the physical and emotional development of all humans in all their multidimensionality? This (utopian?) demand can be seen in the work of anarchist Murray Bookchin who expresses it with much metaphysical and political gusto in his definition of anarchism. He writes,

> Anarchism is not only a stateless society but also a harmonized society that exposes man to the stimuli provided by both agrarian and urban life, to physical activity and mental activity, to unrepressed sensuality and self-directed spirituality, to communal solidarity and individual development, to regional uniqueness and worldwide brotherhood, to spontaneity and self-discipline, to the elimination of toil and the promotion of craftsmanship. (Bookchin 1964, 14)

Here we see a concern not just for meaningful work, but for a meaningful life, and one that connects not only to the (human) social realm but to the ecology of the Earth and the breadth of the cosmos. This requires *a rotation that would integrate the social, economic, political, and spiritual*: "The rotation of civic, vocational, and professional responsibilities would stimulate all the senses in the being of the individual, rounding out new dimensions in self-development" (Bookchin 1964, 15).[47] But again, isn't this requiring too much on co-ops and econD? Doesn't this seem too far-fetched; utopian in the negative sense of a disempowering fantasy?

If we had PD in the political and economic spheres, these kinds of changes would be both desirable and doable. Think of the incredible waves of technological innovation that have swept across the globe in the past decades. There are incredible opportunities and powers that come with them, but they have also eliminated millions of jobs, devoured natural resources and dispersed waste and pollution into fields, farms, forests, the oceans, and the atmosphere, throughout the entire web of life. Now imagine technological innovation that doesn't treat labor as a cost and persons as blips on the screen but instead empowers workers and communities, that promotes health and collective determination. Technologies that conserve resources and replenish ecosystems, that promote friendship and solidarity.[48] From material, technical, and engineering standpoints, nearly all of these devices exist or are possible. What stands in our way are not the laws of nature but the politics of our institutions. But this kind of transformation requires a more ecological-cultural (S-PD) approach to econD, one that we will take up in the next chapter.

Conclusion

Worker co-ops are critical to the PD transformation of the economy, and can be justified from several different normative perspectives. We focused on three: the egalitarian political framework of Dahl, the labor-based moral view of Ellerman and the democratic socialist system perspective of Sch-weickart. We looked at criticisms of co-ops and showed how many are not backed by the evidence: co-ops can function with diverse populations, across many cultures, and at different scales. But co-ops are limited in two impor-tant ways: just like traditional businesses, they need a system of supports to flourish. And, even when they do flourish at scale in places such as Quebec, Spain, Japan, and Italy, there are issues they don't address well and problems they cannot solve. But they also continue to evolve as forms, as in the case of multistakeholder co-ops shows, and when paired with other PD institutions and programs (basic income, regional planning, state support) they could be potent sites in the PD transformation of the economy.

5

From the Culture of Consumption to Democratic Social Reproduction

One of the most popular (and tasty!) sites for participatory and economic democracy is the food system. From informal neighborhood gardening collectives to group purchasing through community-sponsored agriculture to national and international farmer and consumer associations, the food sector has seen an incredible amount of econD and PD innovation among a truly remarkable range of people in terms of culture, race, class, and geographic location.[1] In this chapter, we will look more closely at this sector through one of the largest and most robust *consumer* food cooperatives in the world, the Seikatsu Club Consumer Cooperative Union or SCCCU.[2] Founded as a buying club of Japanese housewives in the 1960s, it now has more than 300,000 members and operates dozens of co-ops across several districts in and around Tokyo.[3]

Like Mondragon, the Seikatsu club contains a multiplicity of organizational types linked together in a federation. But unlike Mondragon and worker co-ops, its central focus is not production but social reproduction. In this chapter, we shall examine how a *moral and political* focus on PD consumption and social reproduction—in and beyond the food sector—can forward the mission of econD and PD and offer a set of strategies that have different potentials, and limits, than workplace and labor-oriented ones. Whereas feminist and environmentalist concerns are often underdiscussed in the worker co-op literature, they are central in this chapter.[4] Also, there is an antagonism that drives SCCCU—and many other consumer food co-ops—that is not present in MC and worker co-ops: the opposition to consumer culture. Like many other food collectives and co-ops including the transnational association of peasant farmers La Via Campesina (Menser 2008), SCCCU seeks to decommodify food and create a kind of econD "moral economy" that is ecologically sustainable. Whereas the Mondragon Corporation avoids the (anti)capitalism debate, food movements such as SCCCU embrace it. Indeed, their best-known slogan is "Stop Shopping!"[5]

The chapter proceeds to discuss social reproduction, consumption, and consumer co-ops before entering into a detailed account of the history and practices of SCCCU before critically juxtaposing SCCCU's approach with that of Mondragon. Of particular importance are the innovations SCCCU made in creating an antistate PD form of regulatory bureaucracy and its construction of a large-scale ecologically sustainable PD supply chain oriented around human health, which serves hundreds of thousands of customers. Key philosophical issues include tensions between individual and collective freedom (the section on the "consumption committee"), feminist concerns about wage and unpaid care work (see the section on critiques of SCCCU), and the reconstruction of the distinction between production and consumption (which harks toward Chapter 6 as well). Debates among A-PD, S-PD, and EJ-PD also come to the fore as do strategic questions about how best to pursue the PD transformation of the economy.

Consumer Cooperatives

In a worker co-op, the firm is owned by a group of people who come together to produce some good or deliver a service. In a consumer co-op, the firm is owned by people who come together to collectively purchase some good or service. Consumer co-ops are econD because members pool resources and make key decisions about policy and who is in charge. And just like worker co-ops, the rule that governs them all is one member one vote.[6]

Consumer cooperatives are the most familiar way for people to encounter econD (Lund 2011, 6). In the United States, about 7,000 people are members of about 300 worker cooperatives[7] but 100 million people belong to consumer co-ops.[8] For example, the Weaver Street Market—a cooperative enterprise including three grocery stores and a restaurant that had sales of nearly $30 million in 2012—has 185 worker members and 18,000 consumer members. REI—a firm that sells outdoor and recreation equipment and clothing—is the largest consumer co-op in the United States and has 3.5 million members and 100 stores.[9] There are consumer co-ops in a variety of sectors including health care, insurance, housing, banking (e.g., credit unions), and in service delivery especially water and power. Among the most notable in the United States is the Park Slope Food Co-op, the largest single site co-op grocery store in the United States.[10] Globally, there are major consumer co-op traditions and presences in the United Kingdom, Scandinavia,

Australia, Italy, and Japan. And across sectors, from wineries and bookstores to marketing firms and health care providers.[11]

For many in the econD movement, consumer co-ops are not nearly as econD as worker co-ops. Consumer co-ops aren't about making money, they're about saving money.[12] They're a different way of purchasing, not a source of livelihood. To economically survive, consumer co-op members have to derive income from somewhere else. In addition, worker co-ops are more PD because people have to collaborate on a daily level about something important to all of them: their source of income and workplace. Members of consumer co-ops donate some money and maybe some time, but fellow purchasers don't bond the way coworkers do because the contact is less regular and less is at stake. If your consumer co-op fails you can always shop somewhere else. But consumer co-ops deserve serious participatory democratic attention not just because of the numbers of people involved, but because of the particular way they implement the principles of econD and the impact this has on people's self-understanding and subjectivity and social reproduction.[13]

Seeking Safe Milk and a Living Economy

It began with housewives sitting around kitchen tables talking about tainted milk, corporate corruption, and government complicity (Evanoff 1998, 1; Restakis 2010, 123). Because of the urgency of their needs, they couldn't settle for protest and critique. The health of their families and communities was in jeopardy. Kids were getting sick. Animals around them were dying. All they wanted was an economy that supported life: the life of their children, the life of the community, and local ecology. Was this too much to ask? The food companies were too powerful and unaccountable and the government was supporting them. How could they remake the whole economy?

At the crux of their concerns was the most basic of staples: milk. If they could make sure that it was not contaminated by radiation or toxins, that it was not just "untainted" but healthy, that it was produced in a way that treated the animals and the environment with respect, and the farmers too, that would be a meaningful and tangible start. So in 1965, 200 families came together to buy 300 bottles of milk from farmers that utilized such practices. Fifteen years later they launched their own milk factory and now run it as a worker co-op.[14] Today they have over 340,000 members in their consumer co-op federation ("union") and have launched dozens of worker-run sustainable businesses providing everything from soy sauce and biodegradable soaps to eldercare. Their name is the Seikatsu Club Consumer Cooperative Union (SCCCU). There are now thirty-two Seikatsu Club Consumers' Co-ops in twenty-three prefectures (similar to U.S. states) across Japan.[15] This is the kind of success story that every student of democracy (and environmentalism) should know.

These women wanted an economy that supported life, a "living economy" (see the discussion of S-PD in Chapter 1), so they named their movement, *Seikatsu*, "living people." Yet this was not a movement that cared only for humans. Public health requires environmental health. This understanding was especially prevalent in postwar Japan due to the destruction and subsequent contamination caused by the nuclear attacks on Hiroshima and Nagasaki. But all industrial nations were learning this painful lesson as pollution and contamination reached intensities and scales not from war and destruction but for production. In the United States, efforts to track the movement of toxins such as DDT through the food supply brought this to public consciousness thanks to the courageous and comprehensive work of Rachel Carson (P. Thompson 1995, 27–31). And this had a big impact on the emerging environmental (Gottlieb 1993, 81–86) and food movements (Carlsson 2008, 85). In Japan, a devastating episode that caught public attention was the release of methyl mercury into Minamata Bay. This led to more than 2,000 human deaths and thousands more poisonings and malformations, which impacted a range of beings, from fish to birds. A particularly brutal image of this catastrophe was of cats that were poisoned such that their nervous systems were degraded and they moved uncontrollably in a horrific series of motions that came to be called "dancing cat fever."[16]

These episodes showed the deadly impacts of industrial processes on human and environmental health. But they also revealed the contamination of the political system. Where were the public regulatory bodies in all of this? Unfortunately, they were less concerned with monitoring the environment and informing the public than with enabling the responsible parties to elude blame. The body of the democracy, too, was degraded. The devastation caused by DDT and Minamata disease demonstrated the interlinking of environmental and personal and public health in the industrial era, as well as the rising power of corporations as they shaped state policy and constrained agencies, violating the public trust and foreshadowing of level of secrecy that has become all too common across sectors, including but not limited to the food system[17] (Restakis 2010, 123).

The post–World War II "boom" is often praised by progressives for its creation of the modern welfare state with its social safety net, public services, and large-scale publicly funded infrastructure not to mention the emergence of the middle class.[18] But others *never* regarded this "public" and its middle class as so innocent, nor considered the era a "golden age." Even the rise of the family wage—which seems so desirable in the "precarious" low-wage no-benefits present—often meant a new form of domestic servitude for women (Mies [1986] 1999, 106–110). And many of these scholars and activists as well as numerous others regarded the rise of the state—both in its corporate dominated welfare capitalist form or communist party state socialist guise—as a bureaucratic "big science" driven "megamachine" and a threat to the very fabric of life.[19] But the rise of this megamachine was not due solely to the actions of some elite that imposed itself upon the rest of humanity; regular people were (and are!) complicit in this degradation, especially as consumers. And if "we fail to take commodity consumption seriously as a political fact, we ignore a crucial aspect of our everyday exercise of power" (Orlie 2001, 139). It was this type of insight that led the women of the Seikatsu Club to tap their power as consumers and utilize it to formulate a bold and comprehensive maxD program.

"Stop Shopping!" Decommodification and Household-Driven maxD; Retaking Time and Place

The initial motivation was to feed their families healthy food: "Safe food at a good price." But this meant the supermarket was no longer an option. This local instantiation of the corporate-state food complex seemed to offer incredible "liberty and the pursuit of happiness" with its fantastic variety but the scope of choice actually undermined *freedom as collective determination* because persons did not have effective power to determine the content of the options. Indeed, oftentimes it was difficult or impossible to ascertain the origin and/or quality of the items sold. How these goods were produced and presented was not only outside the influence of shoppers, marketing seemed to mask the production process and packaging aimed to deceive. The supermarket as a site was in some ways tantalizing and convenient but also unaccountable, manipulative, and contaminated (AsiaDHRRA 2006, 12; Patel 2007, 215–252).

SCCCU women thus bypassed the supermarket to purchase directly from farmers (Lewis and Conaty 2012, 134; Evanoff 1998, 1). But they didn't go to the farmer as individual consumers, they went as members of a mobilizing association. One didn't join the SCCCU as an isolated individual or an independent family, one joined as one household among 7–10 others. In Japan, this form of associationism is called the *han*. Evanoff explains that this notion of group collaboration goes back to the practice of *yui*, "the feudal custom of exchanging labor on a day-by-day basis during planting and harvesting seasons (and for other services such as assisting with funerals and rethatching [sic] roofs). *Yui* associations were often formed in which neighboring households agreed to help each other in times of need—a clear antecedent to the han system of the modern Seikatsu movement" (Evanoff 1998, 11). There are 11 million han in Japan, mostly in consumer cooperatives. The aim of the *han* mode of association is to facilitate face-to-face interaction to build trust, develop capabilities (maxD#2), and cultivate solidarity (maxD#1 and maxD#4). In this regard, it is motivated by reasons similar to associationism, communitarianism, and/or anarchist mutual aid. Such associations are not so much the worker-oriented ones of the job site, but more affect-oriented and affinity-based ones of the domestic realm. Indeed, *han* meetings were held in homes and attended overwhelmingly by mothers and children (Evanoff 1998, 11).

At *han* meetings women met to buy in bulk, exchange recipes, and discuss child care and community issues. Marshall explains,

> Early in its history SCCC [*sic*] developed the three fundamental and interrelated practices that continue to distinguish this organization as a consumer co-operative: small group ordering and distribution (*han seido*) by co-operative procurement (*kyōdō kōnyū*) directly from the producer (*sanchoku*). Together, these three systems take the place of stores and shopping. But they also require carefully coordinated activity among members, especially at the level of the small group, the han, whose 8–15 members stay in frequent contact. Seikatsu Club activism extends outward from han solidarity. (Marshall 2006, 16)[20]

Intriguingly, not only is the han a distinct spatial setup (in the house rather than the store), it produces a unique temporal frame. Lewis and Conaty write, "underpinning the Han concept within Seikatsu is a countercultural perspective on human time and how it can be used creatively to strengthen human connection with each other and the environment" (Lewis and Conaty 2012, 135). Time spent conversing with the members of the han and helping out with each other's children may seem unproductive from the commodity production standpoint, but it is undoubtedly crucial for creating trust and is the basis for reciprocity, care, and stewardship. The motivations are important. SCCCU members are not foodies obsessed with the hot new "superfood" or culinary trend. They are parents focused on family, kids, neighborhoods, kitchens, friends, food, plants, and places. They take the time to learn about a farmer's practices and soil health, and what biodiversity entails in the regions surrounding Tokyo. SCCCU (re)takes place and (re)takes time. Such considerations inspired the co-op's members to call SCCCU an actual "living instrument" (Lewis and Conaty 2012, 135). Could one imagine the stove makers of MC member Fagor referring to their co-op as a "living instrument"? One doesn't find this language used by the members of the Mondragon cooperatives nor among the theorists that describe them. It's more akin to the terminologies invoked in the phenomenological renderings of the conceptual framework of S-PD or Slow Food.[21]

But what does sound more Mondragon-like is the management function of the *han*. From a more business perspective, the *han* cultivates a kind of antibureaucratic (and anti-middle management) grassroots administration that empowers the members since they are in charge of selecting the goods and arranging for their acquisition. Conversely, "shopping," which takes up

so much time of housewives' time, is seen as a "waste" of physical and psy-
chic energy since it so often involves the pursuit of unnecessary wants and
encourages an obsession with placeless things with prices divorced from
use-value. Furthermore, "shoppers" are not empowered to shape the production process, they must choose from the options presented to them. Not so
with the SCCCU model of the consumer co-op.

This notion of the co-op as a "living instrument" is demonstrated in
SCCCU's internal organization as well as in its partnerships. SCCCU choos-
es farmers who utilize methods that promote animal and environmental
health, and both biological diversity and ecological integrity (Evanoff 1998,
7).[22] And their practices also embody the democratized "living economy" of
Mies and Shiva. (See Chapter 1.) This comes through in the structure and
language of the contract drawn up between the *han* and the farmers. The
price is negotiated and both sides weigh-in in terms of their needs. But there
is even more to it than that. The contract is one of both trust and solidarity.
The notion of *tekei,* which literally means "partnership," also is taken to
mean "food with the farmer's face on it" (Lewis and Conaty 2012, 134). This
expression encapsulates a conception of democracy that emphasizes the importance of the recognition of the other not just as a producer but as a person
with individual needs and aspirations and myriad social ties to a community. It also means that the consumers are seen as persons by the farmers,
and not just as passive recipients of goods (with cartoon "dollar signs" lighting up their eyes). As Evanoff explains, "In the traditional market system the
flow is from producers to consumers: producers produce goods which they
must then advertise and persuade people to buy. The cooperative system
provides an alternative to the market system by reversing this flow: consumers take the initiative by telling producers exactly what they want" (Evanoff
1998, 1). SCCCU members place their orders one month before expected
delivery (AsiaDHRRA 2006, 11). This more extended temporal frame is consistent with their conception of time elucidated above, which also helps to
battle the short-term temporality of temptation and instant gratification.
This might at first sound like a small-scale version of a "command economy." But the SCCCU doesn't have the coercive power of a socialist state. The
relationship is democratically interactive and driven by dialogue and interdependence. Participatory democracy goes beyond simple representative
"recognition" and instead constructs a means of interaction that positions
each as an equal in the negotiation. This requires dialogue: a two-way conversation about practices and values, needs and hopes: "The principle of
sanchoku—'direct from the producer'—creates a relationship of interdependence between producers and consumers" (Evanoff 1998, 1).

Democratizing the relationship between producer (farmer) and consumer (housewife/household) is crucial, but SCCCU's very S-PD moral econD
vision does not stop there.[23] To make the food system a *living* system requires

changing practices at all stages: not just growing but storage, transportation, distribution, and waste disposal. As in all consumer co-ops, the products sold there must meet the *moral* criteria set by the organization, which in the case of SCCCU means respecting consumer rights (transparency, safety, health) and ecological integrity (organic/nontoxic, sustainable use of soil, energy and other resources). But they also create mechanisms for empowered participation and autonomy in management.

Collective Determination and Consumer Freedom: The SCCCU Consumption Committee

> The heart and root of the Seikatsu movement is a collective purchasing model that seeks to make the co-op itself a "living instrument" for social and ecological change.
> —LEWIS AND CONATY, *THE RESILIENCE IMPERATIVE*, 135

All these norms can be seen at work in what might be one of the two most innovative structures of the SCCCU: its consumption committee. In this group setting, a subset of members meet to figure out what items to purchase. They do this not based upon their own views but by having the broader membership fill out questionnaires regarding their preferences.[24] They then test products for taste, assess the packaging and price, evaluate the production process, and even calculate the unit cost for both price and amount of waste generated. (Yes, the members even have a role in setting the price!) One particularly unusual rule that SCCCU has settled upon is that only one brand of each product is sold (thus only one brand of ketchup or soy sauce, soup, rice, etc.).

There are numerous benefits that result from the elimination of product competition. For one, it makes it easier for farmers and producers since they don't have to compete with other brands (Evanoff 1998, 6). And it saves them money on advertising and marketing, reduces food miles, and encourages consumers and farmers to interact more. This reduction in options enables more standardization in terms of the packaging, which makes reuse and recycling easier and more cost-effective, and lowers costs for consumers and for waste disposal. (SCCCU devised different packaging to decrease household waste, over 60 percent of which comes from packaging.) In 1994, the SCCCU also created a "multiple reuse returnable jar/bottle," in conjunction with the producers and the bottle industry called the "Green" System (Garbage Reduction for Ecology and Earth's Necessity). They also reuse milk bottles, recycle milk bottle caps, and reuse bags for different household's orders (AsiaDHRRA 2006, 12–14).

Since the mainstream food system is filled with a seemingly endless number of options (some of which are overtly unsustainable and/or unhealthy and some which, well, who knows!), this means that there are far fewer choices for SCCCU members than for shoppers at a supermarket. But "far fewer" is a relative term. Indeed, "While the major supermarkets stock 300,000 kinds of merchandise [!], the Seikatsu Club deals only with about 3,000 general consumer goods of which 60% are basic foodstuffs, such as rice, milk, eggs, frozen fish and vegetables" (AsiaDHRRA 2006, 12). Is this a decrease in freedom? In some ways, yes, there are fewer brands and sizes and there are fewer choices. However, "freedom of choice" is not only a matter of the number of options, it also requires the capacity to choose. This requires time, information, and the ability to discriminate and evaluate. An increase in the number of choices can impair the ability to choose by taking up too much time, and/or overwhelming one's capacity to discern. (Anyone who has shopped for a gift online is quite familiar with this feeling!)

Then there is the crucial, and oft discussed, issue of *informed* choice. Freedom entails not only that I am choosing without restraint, but that I am not being manipulated or deceived. This is eloquently and comprehensively articulated by J. S. Mill in his classic *On Liberty* (Mill [1859] 2001). If I am choosing in a scenario where others are supplying me with information that is intended to sway my choice but is not accurate, or false, then I am being deceived. And if someone is trying to sway my decision by invoking emotions that are irrelevant then I am being manipulated.[25] In the food sector, deception and manipulation are commonplace. Indeed, the food industry employs child psychologists to help them design labels and ads to appeal to kids! Even the placement of items in a supermarket influences shopper choice in manipulative ways (Patel 2007, 214–252).

The SCCCU dispenses with such forms of deception and manipulation through a range of practices. As described above, members choose what products they want to be offered. And they do so deliberatively in groups, not isolated in the checkout aisle. Beyond the benefits of cost and waste reduction is a psychological transformation around the understanding of food now that it is not a commodity but a socioecological product of a real farmer in a real environment where consumers set the price. The rejection of labeling visually and psychologically splits with the advertising frame of the mainstream food commodity economy. Indeed, "members see themselves as employing their collective purchasing power to secure goods for their 'use value' not as 'commercial goods'" (Lewis and Conaty 2012, 135–136).[26] Again, for SCCCU, shopping is a kind of work that is itself a waste of time (Lewis and Conaty 2012, 135).

SCCCU's goal is not just transparency and informed choice, it is collective determination (maxD#1) and member empowerment in terms of both capabilities (maxD#2) and solidarity (maxD#1 and maxD#4). This involves setting up a democratic process that actually decommodifies consumption and where consumption becomes more like labor. A further illustration of this is that the SCCCU supplies foods that are to be cooked and require care, thought, and skill to prepare (Evanoff 1998, 6–7) and thus calls these products "consumer materials" to emphasize that the consumer is a laboring agent who shapes the good through cooking and preparation. These are not the precooked organic microwavable foods that have become so popular among U.S. families pursuing sustainable healthy meals. In this aspect, SCCCU resembles the Slow Food movement, which is not just about animal rights and ecological sustainability but culture and time and human social agency (Patel 2007, 281–284).

Popular PD Regulation: The SCCCU Independent Control Committee

The second structural innovation of SCCCU is its Independent Control Committee in which members inspect each stage of the process—from farm to storage, transportation and distribution to waste disposal—to make sure it is operating in accordance with SCCCU norms. 6,500 members have participated in 790 unannounced spot inspections (Lewis and Conaty 2012, 136–137)! SCCCU calls this "mass auditing" (AsiaDHRRA 2006, 13). SCCCU doesn't trust the government to do this. This is an extremely unique example of maxD#1 since it gets at an aspect of collective determination that is often overlooked: regulation and the monitoring and *assessment* of the implemented practice.

Most discussions of collective determination focus on the norm construction and policy formation phase. This is especially true of deliberative democracy views as discussed in my Chapters 1, 2, and 3. More robust versions of collective determination focus on administration. At this level issues and details about ownership or management arise. (In the literature, associationist-PD advocates tend to be attentive to this phase.) But another level is often overlooked: regulation, assessment, critical reflection, and adaptive learning. After PD processes or programs are implemented, even assuming all the right intentions, how do we know they are fulfilling their goals and values? This level of oversight is built into the robust versions of participatory budgeting discussed in Chapter 2. We also see this in the best worker co-ops—Mondragon's social council would seem to help facilitate this by ensuring the "co-operators" have a voice as workers. But this can be very difficult in many other econD efforts, as noted in Chapter 3 with the civil society model of Fung and the Forest Stewardship Council. It is also a sticky issue in the food movement, with respect to both safety and quality. For example, even if foods are accurately labeled USDA organic, verifying the *sustainability* and *safety* of organic practices is not so easy. That requires a much more developed relationship among producers, distributors, and customers. "Mass auditing" is a wonderful example of an effort to make sure producers and consumers are on the same page when it comes to standards (Busch 2013, 104–106). And how a consumer co-op, which is often not considered as robust a form of econD as a worker co-op, can show maxD efficacy.

Consistent with the mutual aid logic of the *han* grouping discussed above and the importance of capacity development in PD, "In place of the government-centered, bureaucratic approach to welfare common in capitalistic societies, Seikatsu emphasizes self-help and local mutual assistance" (Evanoff 1998, 2). But SCCCU does not opt for the neoliberal route and contract it out. Instead, "In keeping with the fifth Rochdale principle which calls for member education, many cooperatives feel that knowledge should be widely diffused within the organization rather than remain in the hands of specialists" (Evanoff 2011, 9). Evanoff comments on a tension of concern to Albert and that came up with Mondragon re: the relationship between cooperators who are "workers" and those who are managers (see my Chapter 4). He writes of the SCCCU members, "They are able to know its inner workings through direct experience and do not need to rely on the leadership of 'experts' who often tend to form managerial elites within organizations. Member participation is thus the key principle on which the entire democratic structure of cooperatives is based" (Evanoff 1998, 9). SCCCU seems to have solved the "managerial elite" problem; there are no paid managers! Not only does this save customers (i.e., members) money, but it also makes SCCCU mobilize its members to take on these roles, thereby increasing avenues for participation, power-sharing, and collective learning. And because farmers are producing with respect to expressed *han* member demand, there is little time needed to spend on market analyses and those traditional types of mainstream manager functions (Evanoff 1998, 1). Instead, "new consumer materials are developed with mass participation of members. Recruited members complete a questionnaire for taste, packaging, price etc., together with market research, to decide the specifications. They then discuss with producers the area of production and the production process, experiment over packaging materials and content volumes, and decide the price."[27] *This is what democratic management without bureaucracy looks like.* It's grassroots administration, decentralized and horizontal, distributed yet collective. And it's effective. A food system analyst makes the point bluntly: "The cooperative system thus eliminates overproduction and waste, improves efficiency, reduces the stress caused by discrepancies in supply and demand, and helps to stabilize prices. Ultimately, it provides more security for both producers and consumers. The consumers are assured that their demand for goods will be met while the producers are confident that the goods they produce will be sold" (AsiaDHR-RA 2006, 11–12). Consumer (participatory) democracy works.

Scaling Up: Neighborhood, Region, State, World

While many co-ops, whether worker or consumer, are intimate affairs involving just a few people and thus seem like tiny row boats in an economic sea dominated by corporate supertankers, SCCCU is neither demure nor diminutive. SCCCU has "scaled up" in quantity, function and quality and along three different dimensions. Most obvious is size (number of members and participating organizations) and geographic reach. But also they have "scaled up" in terms of organizational capacity, moral aims, and avenues for maxD participation.

The first two are the easiest to explain. The Seikatsu Club began with 200 women purchasing 300 bottles of organic milk in a small section of Tokyo. They started out as a buying club, then became a consumer co-op. Now there are twenty-nine consumer co-ops, as well as a union of consumer co-ops.[28] As of 2009, they had 320,000 plus members in nineteen prefectures across Japan. They started with one product; now they distribute 1,600.[29] By 2008, the total annual retail sales had reached about 87 billion yen (US$870 million), while the accumulated funds from all the investments of members is approximately 30 billion yen. By 2007 they employed 17,000 staff in *worker* co-ops they themselves created.[30] And SCCCU, as discussed above, formed committees for product selection, innovation, and regulation.

There also has been an expansion of the range of *functions* taken on by SCCCU and its associated co-ops that takes it beyond the food system as such to the terrain of community-driven economic development. For example, the Tokyo club has partnerships with two dairy firms, a delivery company, a cattle ranch, and a publishing house. Also, congruent with the need for collective assessment and reflection discussed above, it has established a Social Movement Research Center that "promotes research, organizes study exchanges, and publishes the monthly magazine, Social Movement" (Evanoff 1998, 1).[31] As solidarity economy advocate Yves Poirer relates,

> The Seikatsu Club believes that, a cooperative society, a society that works together, is a prerequisite for global social change. To this end, Seikatsu Club is working to create local Community Cooperative Councils, especially in Tokyo, composed of all organizations in a given territory: cooperatives, local producers, citizens' movements, unions, workers collectives, associations, educational institutions, etc. The objective is for the community to take charge of itself. The principles are quite similar to sustainable local development or community economic development as it is known in Canada. (Poirier 2008)

With all these functions and responsibilities noted, Seikatsu members are not merely ethical consumers. In their own words, "It is not our ultimate purpose in life, as individuals, to buy safe reliable consumer goods at reasonable prices" (Marshall 2006, 3). Rather, they call themselves *Seiskatsu-sha*, "Seikatsu citizens." All members pay a fee of about US$10 a month (1,000 yen) and are responsible for financing, purchasing goods, and management. And there are many mechanisms to create empowered participation in a manner that aims to optimize the equality of its members (maxD#1 and maxD#3). There is a general assembly that meets every year and at it each member has one vote. (The general assembly elects the board of directors that handles much of the association's operations, but the local han carry out most of the activities as discussed above.) Indeed, SCCCU has evolved from a buying club focused on one product to a multitiered and multisector organization carrying out an array of services and functions by a variety of organizational forms.

Although the Seikatsu movement was born of a distrust of corporations and the government, it does not reactively ignore and/or oppose "the state." Rather, it has developed a transformative electoral and political strategy. In this it is much more S-PD than A-PD. A turning point on this issue was the controversy over the use of synthetic detergents. Many Seikatsu members joined this struggle against this key source of water pollution. SCCCU not only lobbied for changes in its regulation and processing as wastewater; they also assisted in efforts to come up with sustainable alternatives. Indeed, SCCCU members ended up developing practices to use old cooking oil—another damaging source of water pollution—to make a soap that is biodegradable and not harmful (Marshall 2006, 162). But to stop the environmental damage, system-wide regulation was needed. When elected officials in Kanagawa Prefecture failed to change the regulation, the SCCCU ran its own candidates and eventually won (Marshall 2006, 163). They then ran candidates in other local elections and successfully lobbied city councils to pass resolutions on this and other environmental health issues, such as banning GMOs. In 2008, there were more than 141 Seikatsu Club members serving as local councillors. They chose the name "Seikatsusha Network," which means "people who live" in the sense of "inhabitants." Through lobbying, protest, and coalition work, the Seikatsu Club also changed aspects of national agricultural policy and joined with regional partners in Korea and Taiwan and the global antinuclear movement (Poirier 2008; Mies and Shiva 1993, 259–262; Evanoff 1998, 1).[32]

The SCCCU and its worker co-ops and other affiliates show that a scaled up complex econD effort can start as a buying club and yet be driven by holistic yet pragmatic ethical framework anchored in the public health and environmental movements. It also is an example of a successful econD movement that is driven by a constituency that doesn't get much political attention much less respect in either mainstream political discourse or in the econD literature: first-world housewives.[33] Despite obvious privileges, the economic and social position of this group is particularly constrained in Japan due to both social custom and tax law (see Marshall 2006). But does SCCCU help women overcome these inequalities or does it (inadvertently) reproduce them?

Criticisms

First Critique: SCCCU empowers women in some ways, but it reproduces gender inequality. **True.** Unlike worker co-ops, you can't make a living being a member of a consumer co-op. To be in SCCCU requires "outside" financial support and it also requires "free" time. These are major reasons why it is composed of mostly middle-aged housewives: married men and young single men and women generally don't have the time. On the one hand, as noted above, this is a strength of SCCCU: it activates a group facing a set of exclusions. But even if we grant that the *consequences* of SCCCU's activities do much good on the environmental and public health fronts, does it empower the women performing the work in a manner that maxD requires? Or is the SCCCU another group of laborers who benefit society but are not justly compensated for their efforts?

To answer these questions, we must look at women's participation in the two different organizational forms separately. We also have to note changes that took place in Japan's economy since SCCCU's inception. Like many other industrialized nations, by the 1980s, Japanese women entered the workforce in large numbers because of a labor shortage and desire for more household income. But they did so as *part-time* workers for a mix of reasons: tax law, social custom, and women's own preferences. First we talk about part-time worker co-ops, and then the consumer co-op membership.

Marshall argues that the *worker* cooperatives formed by the SCCCU largely fulfill the conditions of the maxD version of collective determination even though they only provide part-time employment. He states, "Worker co-operatives offer an opportunity for housewives in Japan's new middle class to work part-time and, by controlling the conditions of their own labor, still care for their families to their own exacting standards" (Marshall 2006, 155). As he notes though, "Its critics assert that the WWC [worker co-ops] alternative to the economic status quo can only continue as long as these women remain dependent on their husbands' substantial incomes" (Marshall 2006, 156). But then consider another view: "The independence most women working in WWCs want, however, is from waged employment and the constraints of current tax law, not from their families or communities. Independence from families or communities has not been a reason Japanese women mention for taking employment" (Marshall 2006, 158). These SCCCU women don't want more paid employment, they want part-time co-op work and the fact that it's part-time allows them to protect their nonwaged work time for family and social activism (Marshall 2006, 165). (Again recall that *time* is an ethical-political issue for SCCCU.) Marshall puts it as follows: "Many women will continue to prefer to work part-time in order to be better caregivers and better human beings, rather than 'shopping robots' or 'worker bees'" (Marshall 2006, 170). And their view on men and work? *They want men to work less* (Marshall 2006, 159). This stands in stark contrast to the conception of work at play in Mondragon. There, the rise of part-time work is seen as an affront to workers who, of course, want the dignity of full-time work, as well as its economic benefits. The possibility that part-time work could be empowering is never discussed.

For SCCCU, similar to S-PD, there are three kinds of labor: employed work, work for the environment, and work for others and/or the public good. The last two are often unpaid, but the more important issue here is that each is part of a different economy: the formal economy, nature's economy, and the caring (for humans) economy. The work of the *han* is largely of the second and third types, also understood as care work (Lewis and Conaty 2012, 135). And even though most don't receive wages, their work is meaningful and productive in the sense of bringing about benefits from the standpoint of social reproduction and human and environmental health as well as individual capability development. And the members receive some direct economic benefits: they can buy products at reduced prices. They also get access to products that satisfy other than financial considerations (sustainability, environmental health) and are healthier for their family members. They also exercise *agency* (maxD#1) in the collective deliberations that are part of the *han,* in the general assembly, and, if they belong to one, on a committee. That is, SCCCU affords them opportunities to develop their individual and collective agency in a democratic space. It also enables individual women and households to link with others and develop relationships and enjoy the benefits that come with those: from social capital enhancement to friendship. Last, and most obviously I hope, members benefit insofar as SCCCU has a political impact: it enables individuals to act with *effective* agency as political activists. As we have seen from the discussion above, SCCCU's accomplishments are myriad and extensive, but also complicated and even compromised. Evanoff notes, "One interesting feature of the citizens' movement in Japan is the fact that it involves many female householders who, precisely because they are more or less excluded from obtaining significant employment in male-dominated capitalistic corporations, have the time and energy to engage in social activism" (Evanoff 1998, 2).

With respect to the question: "does SCCCU empower its women from a maxD perspective?," members seem to reply in the affirmative on many counts above, including individual agency, collective determination, economic and political benefits, capability development, shared authority, and the ability to interconnect with others who share values but operate in different organizational forms, movements, or sectors (e.g., antinuke, anti-GMO). But there is one obvious major limit: women don't gain much *economic* power. They don't gain the kind of equity that they would in a worker co-op like Mondragon much less the kind of economic power that women possess in Iroquoia (see Chapter 1). I think that this critique is consistent with the subsistence perspective approach of Mies and others in S-PD. This type of critique can be made while acknowledging the achievements of Seikatsu, which are considerable. Indeed, Mies herself praises them, but when it comes to financing and landownership, obviously SCCCU is quite limited. And limited in ways that developed worker cooperative complexes in Quebec, Basque Country, and Emilia-Romagna have in part overcome.

The Evanoff quote above, then, contains *two* paradoxes: if women enter the mainstream workforce, they cannot join SCCCU because they do not have the time. If they do join SCCCU their donated labor gets them goods at a reduced price, but they don't collect a wage, build (much) equity, or obtain land. One could reply, "So what?!" SCCCU is not about traditional economic success, it's about transforming the economy into one that is no longer dominated by wage-labor and commodity consumption. That is true. But the problem is the inequality issue. Most women in SCCCU do not improve their relative economic power either in the household or socially by being in the Seikatsu Club. SCCCU is thus very limited in addressing the wealth gap between men and women that is profound in Japan as in many other locales.[34] And this is a concern for all six PD frameworks (e.g., that economic inequality undermines political equality).

Second Critique: SCCCU (and consumer co-ops generally) only work for privileged populations and these groups are shrinking in size, therefore they are not only politically fraught but strategically limited for econD. **Seemingly True but Potentially False.** As noted above, SCCCU is dominated by first-world housewives. Yes, they are exploited and subordinate in real ways, but, comparatively, they are in a much better position globally than most women and some men (Mies [1986] 1999, 100–144). Also, given the most recent global financial crisis, the middle class and "stay at home" housewives in particular, are a shrinking group, so why hold up SCCCU since this kind of consumer co-op model seems to be doable only for a population that is decreasing? These weaknesses are especially pronounced insofar as more people are in need of economic security and assets. Whether or not consumer cooperatives could play such a role remains to be seen but they would have to be developed for low-income persons who often are also time constrained.

But there is another population that is tapped by SCCCU that is expanding: retirees and the elderly. It's true of course that many of these members are limited in what they can do and require support services. Others are home bound or disabled. But many are not, and even those that are can still perform a variety of tasks that would be valuable for consumer co-ops such as accounting, outreach/marketing, and online communications. This is a point on which SCCCU and Iroquoia converge. Mann writes that there was no such category of "surplus labor" in Iroquoia; rather, each member of society was obligated to contribute to society. This was their way of dealing with the "free rider" problem, but also a challenge to society in general, and economic organizations in particular, to include the differently abled—from those limited since birth or injured to the "too" young or "too" old (Mann 2000, 211). This brings up an incredibly underappreciated constituency to be tapped: those that are un- or underemployed and *not* extensively time constrained—some of which are in the increasingly large "precariat." Again, noting that there certainly are persons such as caregivers who might not perform wage work but still lack free time, there are many others that do have such amounts of time but lack venues in which to be productive and develop their social and democratic agency. In the United States, the formerly incarcerated are another such population, as are differently abled or persons on disability. Persons on fixed income and/or social services in general with free time could be excellent candidates for Seikatsu-styled consumer cooperatives that offer a range of benefits to members that are economic (discounted goods), social (participation in associations), and political (lobbying, organizing, etc.).

Third Critique: Organizing around consumer co-ops cannot produce econD system change as well as worker co-ops. **False.** Within the econD perspective, consumption is not the main site of contention. The "real action" is around property and labor; that is where real power lies. Efforts around ethical purchasing and consumer cooperatives are not "bad" but they are limited and problematic for a number of reasons: they are too individualist, antipolitical, or depoliticizing, and can be condescendingly moralistic (Mies and Shiva 1993, 259). Also, in many consumer co-ops, individuals join to buy things more cheaply, which almost reinforces an antilabor mind-set because labor may be a seen as a "cost." And the collective component is weak. Even SCCCU had to drop the *han* requirement (Marshall 2006, 163). Unlike in worker cooperatives where members must regularly interact, members of consumer co-ops usually don't spend more than a couple hours together every couple weeks or so at best. For example, Thompson notes this difference within the Mondragon Federation with respect to the MSC worker-consumer hybrid co-op Eroski. Even though the latter is more PD than the average consumer co-op, he writes, "Most of the Mondragon Industrial Group member co-ops are generally one-location enterprises where the worker members see the board members everyday at work, at meetings or in the local community. The Eroski Board members and Councils are spread at close to a thousand locations throughout Spain—there is a different sense of direct governance with few workers knowing board members" (D. Thompson

2001). And the kind of labor that consumer co-op members perform is much less collaborative than regular employees. And the turnover is much higher (D. Thompson 2001). To make it worse, consumer co-ops are sometimes condemned for cultivating a mind-set that is elitist and/or not much focused on broader social transformation.

SCCCU is a consumer co-op that successfully responds to almost all of these criticisms. It challenges the consumerist mind-set and replaces it with the notions of stewardship and simplicity. Because of its utilization of the multiple forms of association—not just the *han* but the general assembly and numerous committees—it promotes cooperative and collective determination at every turn. And, it was political from the start and continues to be (Mies and Shiva 1993, 259, 261–262). Also, crucially, as it expanded it evolved, it did not limit itself to the consumer co-op form; it produced worker co-ops, programs for self-education, and media. And it figured out how to effectively federate these diverse bodies as they grew both in number and in type. It also developed its political advocacy in a very advanced way by not just lobbying but running candidates for office. Furthermore, and this is the real trump card: SCCCU constructed a supply chain, which includes social service delivery. Lewis and Conaty sum it up:

> The evolution of the Seikatsu Club has secured a federated, multifunctional, democratic, profoundly local, but strategically linked, national movement for transformative change that operates through horizontal networks and vertical production chains as appropriate. Every stage of the food value chain is subject to member reviews, principled evaluation, constant scrutiny, and regular adjustment. In this way members leverage their purchasing power to transform the food system and the production and distribution of other essential goods and services, supported by a multi-tiered capacity to aggregate functions where effective. (Lewis and Conaty 2012, 138–139)

As for the weaknesses and limits of SCCCU, the one noted by Evanoff is a frequent problem of voluntary associations anarchist or otherwise: "The difficulty is that these price discounts apply equally to everyone who purchases goods and does not take into account the fact that some people do a considerable amount of work in the cooperative while others do little or nothing. To be fair, work and leadership responsibilities should be shared equally among the members of each han, but equal participation rates are difficult to enforce" (Evanoff 1998, 10). This is an advantage that worker co-ops have over consumer ones because such forms have more developed mechanisms to distribute tasks and enforce them, and the costs of exit are higher so there is more incentive for members to perform their duties.

As SCCCU evolved, they have also created more ways for their members to participate. At first one was required to be part of a *han* to be in the buying club, but now there are also direct deliveries to households—as in the US CSA model—and there are depots were people can purchase goods.[35] The depot emerged in the 1980s as more housewives for the first time were working (part time) than not. The depot solved two problems: it enabled busy women to pick up their food independent of a han, but it also employed SCCCU women looking for work (Marshall 2006, 163).

In some ways, this is similar to the evolution of the Mondragon Corporation, which created a university and a large consumer co-op grocery store chain. But what distinguishes SCCCU from Mondragon is the evolution of its moral norms. SCCCU became more comprehensive and ambitious in its *moral* framework. Originally it was focused on safe affordable milk for middle-class Japanese households. It now covers many sectors of production and overtly confronts poverty and inequality through the provision of food and affordable social services such as day care and elder care. Also, on the international front, SCCCU pushes for domestic and international food policies that help to empower poor countries not able to meet their food needs because of the way the global market serves wealthier nations. Indeed, "the Seikatsu Club supports the notion that all countries should be moving towards forms of self-sufficiency which are both ecologically sustainable and in accordance with local cultural traditions" (AsiaDHRRA 2006, 8). For example, SCCCU pushes for Japan to increase its domestic rice production not just for the benefit of its local ecology and Japanese consumer preferences, but so Japan does not buy rice stocks from countries who need it to meet domestic demand. SCCCU is also engaged in Gould-ian cross-border solidarity alliances with similar groups working on food, environmental and economic democracy issues in Korea, Taiwan (anti- GMOs) and for preservation of local biodiversities.[36] I am not aware of Mondragon overtly participating in any kind of larger international political movement.

Like all *existing* econD efforts, SCCCU has of course hit a wall, and it is a familiar one, the state. As an SCCCU organizer states,

> In each town and city and village where there are co-op members we have worked with the City Council, the town council, to adopt resolutions demanding that the national government consider the compulsory labeling program on genetically-engineered food. These kind of resolutions have already reached over 1,000 city [sic] and towns. But the national government has not responded to the petitions or resolutions. This is the norm in Japan. Unfortunately there is a kind of democracy failure. When we are working under this kind of failure of democracy the consumers' groups have to find out how to protect themselves. (Paget-Clarke 1998)

This inability to more deeply influence state legislation or even the actions of an agency is something that separates SCCCU from econD movements in

Latin America that have had much more developed political PD components (Menser 2009). But even those state-supported movements also seem to have regressed. Among current efforts, the state that is most supportive of the co-op economy is probably Italy. (Although the largest worker co-op effort of all time—in terms of the percentage of the sector of the nation's economy—is the former Yugoslavia under Tito [Pateman 1970, 85–102]). And a vibrant worker co-op and econD economy will require strong state financial support and coordination (see Chapter 4). But before we go to the prospects for econD at those larger scales, let's first draw out some of the similarities and differences of SCCCU with the more attention-grabbing Mondragon Federation of worker cooperatives.

Strategically Juxtaposing Seikatsu and Mondragon

Juxtaposing MC and SCCCU shows how two very successful econD efforts are similar and different in terms of their norms, cultural and historical frames, organizational forms and relationship with the state and the political realm. First the similarities. Both originated at the most intimate of scales, five young men in a study group led by a priest, dozens of women talking at kitchen tables. Both were organized initially around quintessential household objects (e.g., producing stoves, obtaining milk). Both arise after World War II in a postwar period amid much physical, cultural, and political devastation, and yet without government help. Each is loosely connected to a larger ideological framework (Basque nationalism/Japanese environmentalism). Both are suspicious of dominant economic models and firms, and the actually existing state in which they resided. Both have expanded over time to create or include myriad PD organizational forms not present at inception.

As for the differences: SCCCU was all women at the start and is still overwhelmingly female. Mondragon was all male at the start, but is now mixed though still male dominated. Mondragon emerged as an economic effort within a larger cultural project within a nationalist frame with a Catholic priest as its founding figure. The SCCCU is neither religious nor nationalist but does link with a cultural tradition that goes deep into Japanese history re: the *han* mode of association.

Back to the similarities. Curiously, some commentators give anarchist readings of each. Neither characterized itself as anarchist at the start, though both locales had anarchist presences in the late nineteenth and early twentieth centuries, especially Spain.[37] Although SCCCU does not have an explicitly anarchist forerunner, the SCCCU has much in common with the social anarchism of Kropotkin and more overtly, the recent work of Murray Bookchin's municipal libertarianism (see Chapter 1). Evanoff writes,

There are also parallels with anarchist theory, particularly with Kropotkin's principle of mutual aid and Proudhon's ideas on mutualism. Han are similar in some respects to anarchist affinity groups, although their purpose and function are different. Seikatsu's decentralized, grassroots approach has much in common with the American Green movement (perhaps more so in fact than Japan's now-defunct Green parties did), and the system of local face-to-face groups confederated at the city and prefectural levels has interesting parallels with Murray Bookchin's concept of libertarian municipalism. (Evanoff 1998, 11)

I have no stake in such ideological debates (at least not in this book!), but two issues are worth noting. First, econD in general is almost always characterized as diverging from if not totally opposing both state socialism and free market capitalism. As discussed in Chapter 3, it is portrayed as a kind of "third way" and in this sense is similar to other "third ways" such as anarchism and associationism. Also, econD is a pluralist frame—unlike more sectarian forms of anarchism—and certainly does not dispense with capitalism or socialism entirely. Thus, for example, the market plays a key role in many econD projects and programs though some call for its elimination. (See Chapter 4.) EconD attempts to integrate (not eliminate) such differences. At the other extreme, the state almost always plays some sort of role, but as was discussed in Chapter 1, some are much more antagonistic to it than others. But back to the here and now of actually existing econD.

There are three major strategic differences between the two that are crucial for those pursuing the economic transformation of the economy: their relation to the market, the surplus, and the political and the moral. What I want to show is that these two exemplars of econD have not only different strategic paths but they actually are opposed to one another at specific points, yet both are PD and econD!

Juxtaposition 1: (anti-)Capitalism?

> Additionally, it was concluded that if MCC [Mondragon Corporation] is to compete against large industrial multinationals, it must develop its own multinational supply and distribution network. MCC has now established traditional capitalist plants in such low-wage countries as Egypt, Morocco, Mexico, Argentina, Thailand, and China.
> —HUET, "CAN CO-OPS GO GLOBAL?"

Mondragon aims to beat capitalists at their own game: to sell a quality product at a price that is competitive with traditional firms. It is praised (by some) for doing capitalism better than traditional capitalists: better wages and benefits for more workers, more stable employment, and a high-quality product. It is proudly high-tech and industrial. Of course its reasons for doing this are different from traditional firms: to secure employment, and use the surplus to benefit workers and their communities. But the production processes and the commodities sold, the stoves and MRI machines, the bicycles and refrigerators, they aren't meant to be ontologically different from their competitors, only a better quality and price. And MC *advertises* this!

While MC's slogan is "humanity at work," SCCCU's is "stop shopping." Indeed, one of their goals is "to reveal [the] absurdity and mechanism[s] of society from the viewpoint of ordinary citizens."[38] Although inspired in part by Mondragon (Evanoff 2011, 11), the SCCCU's goal is not just "safe food at an affordable price"; it is to change the food system (and social service delivery). Its goal is not a better mass-produced milk; it's a just and sustainable and democratic food system that cares about animals, plants, soil, and the watershed. This requires a reconstruction of investment, ordering, production, packaging, distribution, and waste disposal. SCCCU itself is to be a "living instrument" and the goal is the health of the living system. This requires a holistic approach both logistically and morally. And SCCCU does not to aim to outcompete corporations, it seeks to *undermine* them and reduce their power and scope in the food system.

Impressively, both SCCCU and Mondragon have reconstructed supply chains. Mondragon has grown largely by forming new co-ops that provide services or supplies to existing co-ops. SCCCU engaged in a version of this as well, except that it was a consumer co-op that started the process, and then worker co-ops were created to serve it. But SCCCU also works to transform the system by remaking the commodity, and Mondragon does not. SCCCU refuses the global and national markets, and instead tried to build local-regional supply chains. Not only do they oppose the corporate supply chain and related markets but they aim to undermine them through consumer exodus, alternate supply chain construction, and changes to government regulation, subsidies, tariffs and domestic and foreign agricultural policy. Seikatsu is not naive about the opponent, but instead actively works against it. This is unlike many other consumer co-ops who do not oppose corporate food outlets but instead portray themselves an as alternative in a range of options that can coexist. However, what is underappreciated in the literature about Mondragon's most recent stage of evolution is that it has, with controversy, further integrated and developed consumer cooperatives, most notably the Eroski supermarket chain, but without the radical decommodifying subjectivity of SCCCU. Instead the growth of Eroski with its part-time workforce and focus on distribution and consumption is considered by some to tarnish the integrity of the worker co-op project. And to "survive and compete," MC has joined the globalization supply chain. Such a move would be inconceivable for Seikatsu.

Juxtaposition 2: A Moral Economy? Converging on Social Reproduction

SCCCU is explicitly countercultural, "to seek another (an alternative) lifestyle based on the idea of a conscientious consumer's autonomy, not just a rebellion against or assimilation of the industrial society" (Evanoff 1998, 1). This is true of many consumer co-ops (Curl 2012, 204–211). Indeed, this is especially obvious insofar as what inspires members to donate their "free" time to its operations is its moral norms alongside the access to the affordable healthy goods. This is clear in SCCCU's attack on commodification and its aim to remake consumption. "In place of passive consumers who are heavily influenced by advertising and think they have to buy more and more simply to keep up with what 'everybody else has,' cooperatives encourage their members to make active decisions about what their real needs are and how they can best be satisfied" (Evanoff 1998, 1). Talk about "real needs" goes both against and outside of economistic reasoning and cost effective efficiencies now take on a much more moral framework.

Again, diverging from the Mondragon and worker co-op justification, here we encounter norms more associated with the environmental (ethics) movement, including stewardship and simplicity.[39] And the freedoms enjoyed by the worker-owners of Mondragon are seen more as obligations to environmental and public health, "While cooperatives offer freedoms, however, they also involve responsibilities" (Evanoff 1998, 1). This is a different moral framework than the freedom-based one I developed for maxD that drew upon Gould (Menser 2008). SCCCU's moral view is more congruent with virtue ethics and the communitarian subsistence view as laid out by Mies and S-PD. The SCCCU then is more like the Indian andolan described by Shiva than the worker-oriented associations theorized by Gibson-Graham.[40]

But I don't want to overplay the differences between MC and SCCCU. Even if MC is not interested in decommodification nor ecosocial reproduction, it is interested in social reproduction beyond production. From the start MC has sought to democratize the workplace and to take control of the surplus for the benefit of workers and their communities, for place-based community development in accordance with the values of *equilibrio* and solidarity: moneys for community-based cultural programming, schools, and the arts. Here there is a similarity to the community development components of SCCCU, but Mondragon achieves this not through the decommodification of consumption, but through the democratic management of the surplus for its Basque homeland.[41]

SCCCU is also about the home, but it is more about the household. It operates not in the spirit of a nation but as a network of housewives anchored in a Japanese tradition (the han) that is nevertheless urban and transnational. However, both have universalist aims, and value autonomy whether as "humanity at work" or "living people." But SCCCU's goal is to seek health, eco-social collective determination, to be "living people." The framework is consistent with the S-PD approaches of Mies, Bennholdt-Thomsen, and Shiva. Although there are elements of this approach in Gibson-Graham's take on MC, it is much more intensely articulated in SCCCU.

Although inspiration for (some) anticapitalists across the world, don't ask the members of Mondragon if they are capitalist or anticapitalist. Indeed, besides their support for Basque causes, MC is famously not political. Why? Like most large workplaces, their membership is ideologically diverse. So, if they are truly democratic, then, not taking a political stance on many questions may be the correct move from a maxD standpoint. This is not to say that MC is not committed to certain values. We noted that it is, just as do all ICA worker co-ops. However, MC does not identify with a specific ideological frame or political or social movement beyond the worker co-op frame.

In contrast, SCCCU has a politics and an ethics and is ideological. They join campaigns in protest of GMOs and in solidarity with peoples in countries who are food insecure. They run candidates for political office. And their ethics are holistic and antagonistic. MC is part of the international co-op movement to be sure, but it does not engage in much moral or political proselytizing. But what it does do is create a much more egalitarian distribution of wealth and poverty and invite everyone to visit to see how it is done.[42]

Conclusion: So Who Is More EconD, Mondragon or Seikatsu?

That is the wrong question. In this chapter we dug deep into the example of the women initiated and led Seikatsu Club Consumer Cooperative Union of Japan to show that consumer co-ops can also be econD and PD, but they are driven by different norms than worker co-ops. This chapter showed that there are multiple econD approaches and that they are robust in a maxD style that empowers communities by developing their capabilities and delivering real material benefits. Each approach is limited and faces contradictions, but neither is stopped by them.

The right question is: can the approaches be combined or work together? Could MC's Eroski retail chain take on a more SCCCU framework? Is there some way to bring the decommodifying and social reproduction aspects of SCCCU into Eroski to make "part-time" work into something more liberatory

and pragmatically anti(corporate) capitalist? And how might SCCCU evolve
to empower more workers in the food system and democratize the enormous
profits accrued by food multinationals? Yet, channeling Schweickart's system-level perspective from the last chapter, it is difficult to imagine either
development occurring without the transformation of state politics and the
actual machinery of regulation and administration. This is the focus of the
next chapter.

6

We Administer! From the Public-Private to the Social-Public

> As the twenty-first century begins unpromisingly—with a financial crisis, economic recession and reheated neoliberal regime of fiscal austerity—there is an urgent need for a more democratic, egalitarian and participatory politics that reclaims public services and assets from their appropriation by elite interests. Yet, while private ownership is largely discredited, so too are older models of public ownership. Although there is a popular uprising, taking different forms, but nonetheless a genuinely international set of movements against corporate-driven globalisation and its supervision by political elites [. . .], there remains a paucity of alternative thinking about how a progressive reclaiming of public assets might take place.
> —CUMBERS, "MAKING SPACE FOR PUBLIC OWNERSHIP," 547

Introduction: From Difference to Disarticulation

Can the state assist in bringing about a PD transformation of politics, economics, and society? Can movements disarticulate the state (Menser 2009)? For many, such a hope seems far-fetched. After all, over the past thirty years, many states have been actively working with private sector entities and elitist associations to create policies and programs that increased the power of investors, enlarged corporate subsidies, and doled out upper income tax breaks while decreasing worker protections and social programs for the poor and middle class. The consummate instance of such inequality in action was the U.S. Supreme Court's "Citizens United" decision, which treated money as speech so that now the size of one's bank account determines the volume of one's voice. What could be more anti-PD than that! Yet even as states have participated in antidemocratic, inequality-enhancing "neoliberalism," some *parts* of the same states have played a supportive role in the initiation or cultivation of PD projects, from co-ops in Italy and Quebec to participatory budgeting processes across South America and beyond. And there are many other programs that not only reduced inequality but increased citizen power, from elements of the United States' New Deal to Sweden's Meidner plan, co-determination for workers in Germany, and Bolivia's recent constitutional convention.[1] The state then seems a mix of contradictions, perhaps with more bad then good of late for sure, but how should we understand its internal heterogeneity? Is it naive to hope that the state could be fractured and the PD parts magnified thereby reterritorizing the government apparatus so that it's captured by PD pushing communities? Could this disarticulation propel a (r)evolution?

In this chapter we join with many others in the call against privatization. But we do not call for a return to the welfare state, or the social democratic state, or even the socialist state. Instead, against the "public-private," we call for the social-public evolution of the state. Building upon earlier discussions of the internal heterogeneity of the state (in Chapter 1) and "disarticulation" (in Chapter 2), we distinguish among three different logics of state governance: state-public, public-private, and my conception of the social-public. Throughout the chapter I discuss each logic in terms of its ownership and management models and relations to investors, workers, customers, and the community. Our first case study is 1970s neoliberal restructuring of NYC. After critically evaluating arguments for and against public-private and state-public modes of governance, I argue for the superiority of the concept of the commons but bolstered by the social-public framework. My case studies here are (following Ostrom and others) water utilities and Internet and web-based models of "platform cooperativism" building on the work of Bauwens and Restakis and their "P2P" perspective. Key philosophical concerns include clarifying confusions in the critiques of privatization, reconstructing the distinction between producer and user (this time in the context of service delivery), how to better operationalize the concept of the commons and redefine the relations among public, community, and infrastructure.

The State Is Not a Monolith; Three Logics of Governance: State-Public, Public-Private, and Social-Public

At first glance, the claim seems either obvious or wrong. Sure, the US government is "heterogeneous" insofar as it attempts to carry out a quite staggering array of functions—it taxes and subsidizes, imprisons and protects, regulates, owns land, and employs millions. And it is involved in so many sectors: from telecommunications (FCC) to farming and food (USDA, FDA), education and science (Dept. of Education, NSF) and the largest branches, providing for retirement and the military (Social Security Administration, DOD, Veterans Affairs). And yes these agencies don't always cooperate, sometimes they even fight with one another, over funding or jurisdiction (Homeland Security, the CIA and FBI come to mind here), but they are all part of the state. Which is to say, that they are part of the state bureaucracy; they have to report to the executive or legislative branches but are structured by the same (bureaucratic) logic, right?

Wrong. When one looks at the United States and other industrialized nations and their myriad levels of government, much diversity can be seen. Agencies within the same state often follow different sets of norms and/or have different organizational logics. Some are much more inclusive in their conception of the "public good" and more accountable to the public. Indeed, we could assign taxonomists this task: look at the agencies and departments of each city or state and ask the following questions: what norms guide its actual operations? What constituencies set its agenda, shape policy formulation, and guide implementation? What constituencies benefit most or are excluded most from its services (Abers and Keck 2013)?

I argue that there are three normatively dissimilar organizational logics that differentially structure state agencies and departments: the public-state, the public-private, and the social-public. Organizations shaped by the **public-state** logic are dominated by publicly accountable officials (elected or otherwise), are transparent in their decision-making processes and aim to serve some notion of the public good. Such a model tends toward an egalitarian distribution of goods and treats persons/users as citizens with rights. It tends to treat labor as a constituency (part of the voting public, with rights).

The **public-private** model aims to govern or deliver a service in a way that is efficient from a market perspective; it is dominated by those who bring private assets to the financing of the process and tends to privatize gains and socialize costs (Eckersley 2004, 95) and treats persons as consumers with differential amounts of disposable income (Sachs 2008, 32–33). It treats labor as a cost (Ellerman 1990, 11–12). Both of these logics are well studied and their merits infamously debated over the past couple decades. The third option, however, while present in various forms, has remained elusive theoretically, and underutilized politically.

Defining the Social-Public

The social-public is a governance or service delivery configuration which is dominated by the community members[2] impacted by the governance process and/or the recipients of the services. The social public framework is a mode of managing as well as a node of governance lodged within the bureaucratic hierarchy operating within the state. It aims to serve some notion of the common good as defined by the community in conjunction with government. It tends to treat constituents or service recipients as agents in the process such that the distinction between producer and user and/or governor/governed is blurred. It tends to regard labor (the public employees of the operation) as comanagers in the process.

In this context, a social-public organization is "public" because it directly involves a function or asset under the authority of the state. In others words, we are using the term public in its narrow state-centric sense. For example, an NGO could make part of its budget available to its clients or members and even create an exemplary participatory process for spending the funds, but this would not be social-public in the sense discussed in this chapter (and book). Thus, if Greenpeace set up a participatory democratic participatory budgeting process for some of its budget and let its members decide how to spend it, it would be a PD PB, but it would not be social-public because it is not dealing with a state asset or function. In contrast, if the EPA turned over part of its budget to such a process, it would be social-public.

A social-public process is "social" because it is dominated by residents of the jurisdiction: that is, persons or groups that are members of some community and not elected officials or representatives of businesses or other economic organizations. By "dominated" I mean that these community members set the agenda and have relatively more power in the decision-making process than other groups.[3]

A social-public modality of governance must be PD: that is the agenda must be community driven and the community must possess decisive power in the process. While there is a large gray area, or flexibility, in terms of how this can occur, it is easy to contrast this social-public modality with what it is not. For example, in my Chapter 3, we discussed stakeholder theory and civil society ("watchdog democracy") approaches to corporate social responsibility. While the latter may be "public" because affected parties meet outside the private sphere of the firm, civil society approaches are explicitly not part of the state. Also, even if we took the stakeholder model and applied it within the state, it would still not be a social-public process. Stakeholder boards are advisory; a manager has the power not the stakeholders.[4] To best understand the landscape of options, we proceed with a discussion of the more familiar public-private and state-public models before undertaking a more detailed explication of the social-public model.

The Rise of the Neoliberal State and the Public-Private Partnership

In the period following World War II, states—which is to say, political leaders (elected or not), political parties, and government agencies—were the primary agents in both governance and economic development. During this period, most states aimed to utilize their natural resources and organize their labor pools to increase economic activity to meet domestic need but also, if possible, to increase their standing in the emerging interstate system. Economic development was a way of both honoring the social contract and increasing state power (Litfin 1998, 121–122; 129–138; Kamieniecki and Granzeier 1998, 257; Eckersley 2004, 72–73, 206). In a subset of states, there were broad gains and a middle class was the result: the United States and

Canada, many states in Western Europe, Japan and the "Asian tigers." And, however poorly they may have been viewed by the West, many states in the Soviet Union and Eastern Block achieved economic gains from the 1930s to the 1960s for broad swaths of their population (Sachs 2008, 7–8, 24–25).

The state-driven model of governance and economic development, however, faced an array of challenges in the 1960 and 1970s, from domestic unrest from groups seeking more political and economic power to global challenges arising from economic and energy crises to ecological degradation and wars in Africa, the Middle East, and Southeast Asia. Furthermore, state-led development was not as noble economically or politically as it was portrayed in the above. In many locales, corruption and patronage not only pitted groups against one another, programs were often incredibly wasteful (Cumbers 2012, 23–37; McDonald and Ruiters 2012c). Amid all this conflict and chaos, a new political-economic model emerged. Its name was confusing, "neoliberalism" (or the "Washington Consensus"), and its call for "privatization" turned the previous state-dominated political-economic strategy on its head. Privatization was not just a management scheme to be employed within states; it was a condition that powerful states used to structure their relationships with weaker states (McDonald and Ruiters 2012c, 169–170; Stiglitz 2008, ix). At this worldwide level, the process of neoliberal globalization came to be defined by the rise of the power of international and transnational financial institutions. Global bodies such as the refigured World Bank and International Monetary Fund (IMF) along with the new World Trade Organization (WTO) came to play a prominent role in the domestic policies of specific states. This happened as foreign investors gained more access to domestic markets and national economies became more engaged in production for export to the "global market" (Sassen 2006, 247–264).

But (neoliberal) "globalization" was made possible by the concomitant rise in power of *domestic* investors and the relative decline of the power of workers and the broader "public" in both economic and political life. *And it was the state that made this happen* (Sassen 2006, 222–227). Part of the neoliberal package was government legislation diminishing the funding or scope of programs designed to benefit workers and broad sections of the populace—so-called "welfare state" policies in basic goods provision from housing and health care to unemployment insurance. And, governments redeployed assets and resources to initiate an array of programs designed to attract private capital to areas that needed economic development—especially urban zones that had been deindustrialized. Politically, this meant bringing investors and representatives from the institutions of finance capital into the *governance* process through the appointment of such figures to political agencies and departments. And more importantly for this chapter, the creation of new models of public management and even governance forms (e.g., urban development corporations) to insert the logic of privatization *within* political institutions and *upon* communities. An exemplary illustration of both the crisis and the shift was what happened in, and *to*, NYC in the 1970s.

"From Welfare State to [Racialized] Real Estate"

In the 1960s and early 1970s, NYC lost many well-paying jobs—mostly tied to manufacturing—and both people and tax dollars fled to the suburbs (Moody 2007, 56–58). As the tax base shrunk, the city government engaged in budgetary practices that were not only nontransparent, but fiscally unsound and even illegal. As a fiscal crisis ensued, the federal government famously told the city to "drop dead"; it would not bail it out with new loans. Where could the city find the money to avoid default? NYC government looked for assistance to a "community" just a few blocks from its offices in city hall, Wall Street. But the financing came with strings attached. Private sector investors wanted not just a seat at the table, they wanted a new table, that is, a new decision-making logic. Call it what you will—"revolution in governance," "regime change," "the politics of creditor intervention," bailout, coup d'état—with this shift in power, NYC was an early site for the creation a new political-economic regime that came to be called "disaster capitalism," or the "shock doctrine" of neoliberalism (Klein 2007, 6–9; Moody 2007, 31–38; J. Freeman 2000, 256–287).

The new power bloc's name was an acronym, "FIRE." This business elite was anchored by three interconnected constituencies: Finance, Insurance, and Real Estate. Although federal cuts combined with a shrinking tax base were obvious factors that caused the crisis, FIRE claimed the cause was a bloated city workforce and a too generous array of city services. NYC was a fairly distinctive American megalopolis with its strong unions, extensive city hospital system, and free education at its public universities (J. Freeman 2000, 66–71, 334–337). But it wasn't the services in and of themselves that offended—many "well off" New Yorkers had been beneficiaries of public housing, generous pensions, and quality free public education. The issue was *who* was receiving them had changed. Thanks to new waves of immigration, NYC underwent a demographic shift in the 1950s and 1960s, and the city workforce as well as the public school system became populated with many more African Americans, West Indians, and Puerto Ricans. From the FIRE perspective, these groups didn't deserve these services. Indeed, the real estate developer contingent blamed the fiscal crisis on expanding welfare roles and a mismatched job market with too many blue-collar blacks and Puerto Ricans not able to take on new white-collar jobs (Fitch 1993, vii–viii).

But many other cities had similar problems, and they were not on the edge of default. Why not? A major reason NYC didn't have enough money to make payments to its bond holders was that it had to make payments on *short-term* loans. Governor Rockefeller and Mayor Lindsay had created a program where the city was borrowing billions in the short-term money market to enable local developers to get long-term mortgages (Fitch 1993, viii–ix). No other U.S. city did this! This was beyond negligence, but who took the blame for the fiscal crisis? As Fitch puts it "welfare moms, municipal workers and incoming freshman at CUNY" (Fitch 1993, x, 214–215; see also J. Freeman 2000, 228–233, 275–277).

What's even worse is that unionized city workers put up their pensions to help stabilize the finances of the city, but they were excluded from the new ruling block (there is no "U" in FIRE!) and the new logic sought to disempower them (Moody 2007, 46). They also took the hit financially: it was city workers and their families who covered the increase in the subway fare and newly imposed tuition at the CUNY system. And it was city workers and their neighbors who suffered as welfare, police and sanitation services were cut. Even worse, the coup was not only supported by its victims, it was in part *administered by them* (Moody 2007, 31–38).[5]

Neoliberal Governance

Critics of neoliberalism often accuse it of promoting privatization and the "corporate state," but what does that mean? As the NYC case shows, what it means is that the priorities of investors structure city policies. In order for this public-private model to work, elements of the financial elite of the private sector (e.g., FIRE in NYC) had to participate directly in governance: that is, they sat beside members of the government at some specific governance "table" and set priorities and created policies. This often happens through the staffing of agencies and leaders from the finance industry are employed by the mayor's office. But, of course, it's not just about the identity of office holders, it's about the logic they employ. The "rules of the game" are just as important as the people at the table. For example, why didn't the city unions demand that their pensions be used for policies and programs that would benefit them such as more affordable housing rather than luxury condos and worker-owned businesses rather than high-end retail (Kelly 2001, 182; Malleson 2014, 140–142)?

Neoliberal governance often takes root in times of crises (Klein 2007, 6–9). As we saw, in the case of the NYC fiscal crisis, it wasn't just getting the right people on the fiscal boards or in the comptroller's office. There was a realignment of the governance apparatus that not only created a new body but changed the formal power relationships between the city and the state. Because of the instability of our contemporary capitalist system, these kinds of emergencies are not just one time events but (ir)regular occurrences that happen in different places at different times and for different reasons: Chile after the coup, Russia and Poland after the collapse of the Soviet Union in the 1990s, New Orleans after Hurricane Katrina.[6]

A related form of privatization of governance occurs when policy making or administration is shifted to quasigovernmental bodies that are dominated by such groups and/or are run according to the management logic of neoliberalism (more below). Examples of this would be decreasing the prominence of city agencies in forwarding and administrating development plans and shifting such duties to quasigovernmental entities such as the city's Economic Development Corporation which is not as accountable to the public. In NYC, this especially happened during the tenure of Mayor Bloomberg and his priorities for economic development reflected that as did the inequality crisis that galvanized support for his successor (Angotti 2008, 2013).

This shift in governance logic is part of a larger reorganization of powers within the state that started to happen across the globe in the 1980s. As a general trend, legislatures lose power, and executive branches gain power and there is a subsequent privatizing of authority within the executive.[7] This was especially the case after the September 11 attacks and the launching of the "war on terror." Indeed, the national security state is the most private (nontransparent) and least accountable part of government and *is the largest growth sector* (Sassen 2006, 176–184). And it is the largest growth area for *privatization* through the contracting out of services to privately owned contractors (Priest and Arkin 2010).[8]

Neoliberal Service Delivery

A more visible feature of the neoliberal state is the privatization of services. As in the governance model, privatization can take two different forms: first, as a transfer of *ownership* of what were state assets or operations to privately held firms. (Examples include natural resources (e.g., mines, forests) to physical assets and actual services (railways, an electrical grid, homeless shelter). Or privatization may occur as a change in the *management* of some asset or delivery of some service (without a change in ownership). This is often called "corporatization" (McDonald and Ruiters 2012b, 4). For example, when a state builds a new bridge but there is a toll or families must pay for after school programs. In the state-public model, a service is allocated based upon the needs of some segment of the citizenry and the amount of revenue available from the state collection through taxes, etc. In the public-private model, it's not just that private entities own or manage the asset or service, the goals and logic of management are different. For example, from a public-state perspective, workers are a constituency; they are members of the local body politic and deserve treatment in accordance with such a conception. For private firms, labor tends to be regarded as a cost rather than a community stakeholder (Sassen 2006, 197).[9]

One of the best ways to understand this reconfiguration of public and private is by looking at the public-private partnership (PPP). A PPP is a government service that is funded and operated through a contract between some state office or agency and a private firm under which a private business finances, builds, and operates some element of a public service. Said business is paid over a number of years, either through charges paid by users and/or by payments from the public authority (Hall 2015, 7). The motivation for PPPs was largely driven by states' need for capital. Many were heavily in debt after the economic turmoil and changes of the 1970s (e.g., NYC above).

While there are different models of PPPs, the same general features are in play. First, the management model is quite different from state-based service delivery or asset management. Capital comes from the private sector, recipients of the service are viewed not as citizens but as customers, and control of the profits is transferred from the state to a private firm. Why would states do this? Again, besides the need for capital, another layer of legitimation comes from the notion that the private sector has more expertise, more technical capacity, or managerial acumen. Also, private sector firms are viewed as being less constrained than local government: they can act quicker to deliver the service, and make changes more easily and nimbly.

One of the more visible expressions of the PPP in urban areas is the business improvement district (BID). Deindustrialization in the 1960s and 1970s left vast stretches of cities abandoned or drastically underserved. Giant factories sat closed in towns such as Detroit and Pittsburgh, and throughout the Northeast, crumbling buildings and abandoned lots became part of the identity of places such as Newark, New Jersey, and the South Bronx. After much contestation, BIDs emerged as a framework for bringing in the capital to transform such areas. A BID is a geographically bounded area where a group of businesses are given jurisdiction by a city to collect a fee from other businesses in order to attract economic activity to the area (Becker 2010, 420). BIDs often do this by providing services that the city is unable or unwilling to provide: security, street maintenance, and cleaning services are frequent examples. BIDs are known for using a low-end wage model (rather than unionized city workers). Times Square is perhaps the most famous, but from Baltimore to Boston, nearly every "economically revitalized" city has them. And not just in the United States, the United Kingdom was an early forerunner of the model, and it can now be found across the globe (Becker 2010).

In BIDs the costs and benefits of the service are distributed differently than in the state-public model. PPP advocates argue that the private sector takes on much of the risk and taxpayers do not. But while users' views of the service may figure more prominently in management, in some cases of privatization, taxpayers are required to cover unexpected costs and comparatively more benefits go to investors. Also, PPP critics claim that because the goal is profit, community rights and well-being are more likely to be ignored (CEOs can't be voted out of office), private investors view workers not as members of the body politic but as a cost, and, users are viewed not as citizens with equal rights but as customers with differing amounts of disposable income. This often ends up reorienting service delivery to those who have more disposable income and cuts or downgrades to those with less income (McDonald and Ruiters 2012c).

Another problem with privatization is that the resources themselves are managed differently. Private management is oftentimes more subject to short-term economic calculation. This can lead to asset use that is not sustainable. For example, a rise in paper prices may lead to a profit-seeking firm cutting forests faster, engaging in practices such as clear cutting that radically damage the environment (Newton 1989).[10]

From a PD perspective, there are two types of privatization failure: the first is when privatization succeeds on its own terms, but fails with respect to PD norms. For example, there are cases where conversion of publicly run schools into privately operated schools improves the performance of some students, but this is in part because such charter schools can more easily reject or expel students whose chances of success are less. Public schools are less able to do this because as a public we believe there are obligations to educate those children as well; not to mention the social benefits from educating all students. But in these cases, PPP critics must admit that some students did fare better in this model than in the public model. The problem is the norms of equality and inclusion were violated.

The other way that privatization fails is in those cases where it is unsuccessful with respect to its own self-professed goals: to cut costs and improve services. Examples of such failures abound: privatized water and energy utilities that failed to make the investments necessary to upgrade infrastructure but still increased rates. Privatized mass transit operations that cut costs and changed working conditions in ways that decreased safety and even lead to deaths. In fact, in some of these cases, de-privatization occurred and after the state reclaimed it, service did improve and/or fees were reduced. The case of a commuter rail in the United Kingdom and the water utility of Paris stand out in this regard (Wainwright 2014, 26; Petitjean 2015, 66–74).

Was the Public-State Any Better?

> So, it is clear that bringing in private companies leads to water, trains and other public utilities that quite simply do not serve the public. Do we therefore work to return services to the state as it was, turning a blind eye to all its inefficiencies, unresponsiveness and in some cases endemic corruption, simply because they are formally "public"? This is not a rhetorical question."
>
> —WAINWRIGHT, "PARTICIPATORY ALTERNATIVES," 3

> In the mid-1980s, however, most state enterprises ran aground: the state
> could no longer fund nationalised firms, service quality was poor, and
> corruption and persistent strikes by public sector workers led to large-
> scale public resentment.
> —McDonald and Ruiters, "Careful What You Ask For," 157

As state capacity expanded in the postwar period, state agencies did not
necessarily improve in their protection of the public good. As industrialization and urbanization spatially proliferated and energetically intensified,
ecological and public health took a hit, hence the rise of the environmental
movement broadly construed. Indeed, from the 1950s to the 1980s, some
public utilities and regulatory bodies were so incompetent if not corrupt that
citizen action groups emerged to not only to pressure the government but
conduct their own investigations (Gottlieb 1993; McDonald and Ruiters
2012c, 157). Sometimes the government agencies were complicit with business, but other times it was public bodies themselves that were to blame.
Indeed, in cases involving Con Edison in NYC and the U.S. Army Corps of
Engineers, the so-called "public-state" logic had run amok from a public
good standpoint (Morgan 1971)!

But from the PD perspective, conversions to the public-private model
often made things worse: especially since the state as a whole became less
accountable. This was not the fault of individual agencies as such but often
because the power of legislatures was reduced, and there was less efficacious
deliberation with local publics (Sassen 2006, 175). What further confounded
is that as agencies became more under the sway of the executive, the regulatory apparatus actually grew: new private authorities and the courts wielded
more power, further empowering actors with more assets. And as courts
conducted more oversight they shifted their logic of justification from a
Keynesian public good frame to a more market-based notion of efficiency
(Sassen 2006, 174–176).

Public-private partnerships often fail on PD terms and sometimes fail on
their own terms, but is state management consistently better? Plenty of state
agencies ignored public needs, degraded ecosystems, and frustrated citizens/
users well before the onset of neoliberalism (McDonald and Ruiters 2012b;
O'Connor 1998, 255–279). For example, "The negative attitudes toward public sector water are partly explicable by the disappointing experiences of the
1980s. During the International Decade for Clean Drinking Water (1981–
1990) when development banks made loans available, public operators failed
to deliver sufficient extensions to water services" (Kishimoto 2006).

The list of failing state-owned and managed public services and utilities
(hereafter state-owned enterprises or SOEs) is long and diverse, but what
were the causes of these failures? One of the most in-depth studies argues
that it was "primarily a lack of democratic process, rather than an inherent

problem with the public sector" (Kishimoto 2006). One argument that supports this view is the number of cases where a public service that was privatized was de-privatized because of revolts by users and others. Even in the United States, "a fifth of all previously outsourced services have been brought back in-house. The research found that primary reasons for 'insourcing' were a failure to maintain service quality by the outsourced contractor (73%) and a failure to achieve cost savings (51%)" (Wainwright 2014, 5). (Though one might reply, "but 4/5ths worked?" See below.)

One of the most common problems with SOEs concerned labor. The costs were too high and the incentives to deliver a quality service not present. Stiglitz notes, "Even advocates of state ownership, like Greece's socialist prime minister, Andrea Papandreou, talked of the challenges of 'socializing' the SOEs, making them act in ways that were consistent with social objectives, not just the interests of their managers and workers" (Stiglitz 2008, x). Some even castigated public sector unions for acting like monopolies.[11] A version of this criticism of SOEs is also present among PD advocates, but in a different form and with a different understanding of the situation.

One of the major motivations for privatization was and is to reduce corruption (Becker 2010). Part of that corruption equation concerns workers, another part managers, state bureaucrats, and elected officials. First, let's focus on the workers. Critics of SOE often criticized workers for a mix of reasons: compensation packages cost the public too much, job security made them lazy or unaccountable to the public, and a general lack of competition made them unwilling or unable to meet user demands much less upgrade their operations in the way that the private sector does. The answer for public-private advocates is to remake the department and run it like a private sector firm. This often involved the restructuring of contracts and benefit packages to increase accountability through merit pay, and the ability to fire workers. The attempt to impose such changes put workers and their unions on the defensive and they often fought simply to defend their own interests, and/or the status quo. This defensiveness is a problem not only for PD advocates but for users and the public since all consider the status quo to be less than desirable if for different reasons: service delivery was too costly, the quality low, ecological degradation, management was not transparent, and/or users' needs weren't really being met (Wainwright 2013).

The best response to this situation, however, is not to transfer ownership to investors and subject the organization to market competition. For too many goods this would reduce the likelihood that the service in question would increase in quality and affordability for the broad public, especially those least economically advantaged, that is, the people who often need the service the most. And such a workplace model would also likely reduce most workers' wages and benefits—though upper management often stands to benefit. The better response is to connect the interests of the workers to the interests of the users, and to empower all groups in the process. How might this work? Through an alliance between workers and users, supported by the state. Consider the case of BT (formerly British Telecom).

In the early 2000s, British officials aimed to privatize part of BT. The service was poor, costs were high, and workers were not adapting to the technological changes in the industry. So how did workers respond? Understandably, they wanted to save their jobs, but they also realized that service had to be improved and their operations restructured. This was tough because many of them lacked the skills necessary to make the upgrades and reconfigure the department to meet the new service demands. So when they negotiated with management, they decided not just to fight for their jobs; they also demanded retraining programs (maxD#2) and a right to participate in the restructuring process (maxD#1 and maxD#3). They won on all counts. And how did customers fare? They won, too (maxD#4). After the transition, not only did service improve but significant savings were made. If the department had been privatized, those funds would have gone to investors. But it had not. Instead, those funds went into expanding services for those who needed it, in this case the elderly and for adult education (Wainwright 2013, 5) (maxD#2). With costs contained, workers retrained, services improved, and surpluses generated for the state, everybody won. Similar fights and social public victories occurred in Capetown with the South African Municipal Workers' Union, and with other public sector unions and agencies in Norway, Germany, Uruguay, Brazil, and Italy (Wainwright 2014, 6). Wainwright writes, "In all these struggles against privatisation of public services, the trade unions moved beyond the defence of their own jobs and working conditions, to taking responsibility for both defending a public service and democratizing the way it is managed" (2014, 34). But this isn't just about unions and workers and users. The government too is at fault, and in the debates about privatization and the role and even the meaning of the public, the weaknesses of the welfare state and electoral democracy are on full display (Wainwright 2014, 4).

Indeed, across the political spectrum, there is much dissatisfaction with both the classic liberal state model, actually existing socialist states, democratic socialism, and the more recent neoliberal public-private hybrid. The first two models were oftentimes too centralized and hierarchical, not accountable enough to respond to the diverse public nor nimble enough to keep up with technological advances much less economic and ecological challenges.[12] The PPP model is more flexible and decentralized, but if and when it is participatory, it too often favors investors and already well-positioned members of the public thereby exacerbating economic inequality.

So what is the alternative? As the BT story shows, new forms have emerged in a variety of terrains. They include not just reconfigurations of the relationships among unions, public utilities, and consumers but extend to all sorts of constituencies and goods from the virtual realms of cyberspace to most basic material goods: land and water. They have names such as "open source," the "sharing economy," and "copyleft," and invoke concepts such as peer-to-peer (P2P), public-public partnership, and civil public partnership (Wainwright 2014, 9). They even inspire slogans such as "reclaim the state" (Wainwright 2003) and "disarticulate the state" (Menser 2009). All go beyond the hard and fast distinctions between state/market, public/private, subject/object and producer/user. All empower the "social." All aim to share resources in a way that is more collective. And all are linked to the concept of the commons.

Managing the Commons: "We Are the Common Good"

> Commons and commoning place the emphasis on sharing over possessing, presuppose equal access and power, and promote a sense of responsibility towards future generations.
> —Council of Europe, *Living in Dignity*, 177

> Unlike private or public goods, commons cannot be transformed into merchandise. They express a qualitative relationship. It would be too simplistic to say we have a common good; rather we should be saying we are the common good, just as we are an element of our environment, of an urban or rural ecosystem. Here the subject is part of the object. This is why commons are inseparable from associated individuals, communities and ecosystems."
> —Council of Europe, *Living in Dignity*, 177

The most notable precedent for this social public-frame is a notion almost as old as human societies themselves, the commons. Traditionally, commons are "natural resources" or artifacts collectively managed by their users. In each case, what makes a "commons" is not simply the "object" managed—e.g., lake, pasture—but the conception of the "object" and the mechanisms by which the resource in question is managed. The goal of such management schemes is to meet the needs of all the users, however differently positioned, in a way that preserves or reproduces the resource over an indefinite period of time. Thus, a well is a commons if it is managed to meet the differing needs of the households (e.g., for irrigation, bathing), a pasture is a commons if it is managed by all the different shepherds whose animals graze upon it in a manner that is sustainable for many generations, and so on. It's not just about the grass, *or* the animals, *or* the shepherds, it's about the animals *and* the grass *and* shepherds together. Hence "we are the common good."

Because of its inclusive and needs-oriented character, it is tempting to regard the commons as a space that is available to anyone, a free space where anything goes, but this is a dangerous mischaracterization: "We are not free to use the concept 'common property resources' or 'Commons' under conditions where no institutional arrangements exist. Common property is not 'everybody's property' . . . To describe unowned resources *(res nullius)* as common property *(res communes),* as many economists have done for years . . . is a self-contradiction" (Council of Europe 2013, 174). A commons may seem that way because it is not private property. In that model of ownership, an individual has rights over some space such that he (it's often a he!) can exclude others from using it regardless of need. This point is driven home quite unforgivingly by J. S. Mill in his discussion of the businessman who is hoarding corn while others are starving (Mill [1859] 2001, 52–53). But even though a resource is managed in terms of profit rather than need (as in the case of the corn dealer), it is a regulated space with rules for use. However, the logic of regulation which defines a commons is very different than that identified with private property (e.g., the maximization of profit or personal interest) or with public property (e.g., national interest) because control over the resource is tied to use rather than ownership. Even though this conception could overlap with public property in those cases where the state decided that national interest coincided with social need, traditional commons are managed not by government agencies but by associations of users with rules that are often anchored in cultural traditions.

Although there are a diverse array of theorists and activists employing the commons perspective (especially in A-PD and S-PD), the most relevant for this chapter is found in Ostrom's *Governing the Commons.*[13] In this classic work, the successful management of a commons—what economists call a "common pool resource" (CPRs)—requires that the following conditions be satisfied:

Conditions for Commons Management
1. The jurisdiction must be well defined; that is, those who have rights to use the resource must be well defined. (Ostrom calls individuals with use rights "coappropriators.") (Ostrom 1990, 38)
2. The rules for appropriation must be well suited to local conditions. These rules will dictate the appropriate technologies to be used, time constraints (when or for how long) as well as the labor conditions, materials to be used, and financing.
3. Coappropriators set the rules and can modify the rules.
4. The monitors of the resource extraction and use are either the coappropriators or they are accountable to the coappropriators. In general, the penalties for offense are graduated, easy to enforce, and low cost in terms of implementation.

5. The external (governmental) authorities respect the decisions of the coappropriators so long as they are abiding upon their community-determined norms. (Ostrom 1990, 94)

Ostrom's CPR model meshes with what Wainwright calls the "potential of the public," which "starts from exactly that awareness of mutual dependence, and an ethics of stewardship, mutual care and collaboration that arises from it" (Wainwright 2014, 4). Ostrom writes, "The key fact of life for coappropriators is that they are tied together in a lattice of interdependence so long as they continue to share a single CPR" (Ostrom 1990, 38). In addition, these rules are an excellent articulation of our general understanding of PD and three of the four maximal democracy tenets. #3 and #5 are crucial for collective determination as autonomy (maxD#1). If the community goes through all the effort to set rules and manage the resource, but then the local government overrides it, then it is not a commons. The only time an external authority is justified to override or intervene is when the CPR group has violated its own rules or degraded the resource in a negligent manner or there is a conflict within it which it cannot manage. (Ostrom 1990, 208–213)[14]

PD Consumption

A difference between Ostrom's model and our previous articulations of PD and maxD is that in a commons the *users* are the rulers (e.g., governors). This breaks from the usual privileging of citizens or workers. This is crucial for several interrelated reasons. In industrialized nations, consumption is a mode of being that has come not only to dominate the self-image of individuals; it has been appropriated as a model for political life and even citizenship.[15] While there are numerous critiques of the dangers and drawbacks of this phenomenon from the standpoint of democracy, the notion of consumer as user sets the stage for a politicized remaking of this role from passive atomized customer to empowered collectivized "coappropriator." The language of "coappropriator" also has an impact on the conception of labor independent of political democracy considerations. This is because users become agents from the standpoint of the operations and utility of the service; this is why they are justified in being involved in management of the resource. Users are then coproducers and cogovernors and the line between producer and user and governor and governed are blurred. (This is even more so in cyberspace examples below.)[16]

Another virtue of Ostrom's framework from the general PD standpoint is that it allows for the expression of the sociocultural dimensions of collective determination. The guidelines above are not commandments. They allow for much operational flexibility. CPRs have had and will have very different rules. The reason is that the "differences in the particular rules take into account specific attributes of the related physical systems, cultural views of the world, and economic and political relationships that exist in the setting" (Ostrom 1990, 89). Relatedly, although there is a normative core anchored to the notions of access based on need and the requirement to use the resource sustainably, the commons can be justified, and theoretically defended, in different ways. For some, the commons is communitarian. But it is also justifiable in terms of human rights, equal positive freedom, and the right to subsistence. It may even be an essential part of the very idea of social contract (Council of Europe 2013, 179). I will not debate the merits of the different positions here, but instead point out that the notion of the commons is consistent with my notion of collective determination and, indeed, further articulates it as the power and right to set rules for oneself with others (maxD#1).

From Common Resource Pool Management to Social-Public

> Certain natural, social and digital goods and services could be managed as commons with a non-marketable status and democratic management, under the responsibility of communities. But we cannot consider a literal translation of the traditional management of commons in our complex urban reality.
>
> —COUNCIL OF EUROPE, *LIVING WITH DIGNITY*, 174

Anthropologists have shown that the commons functioned quite well before the rise of the state (Patel 2010, 91–110). But, is it desirable and doable in the current milieu with its challenges demographic, technological, and otherwise?[17] The rise in population density alone poses incredible challenges for thinking about how to arrange the social component in commons management. And the state would seem to have to be involved given its institutional powers and jurisdictional scope. But, where, exactly, is the state in Ostrom's account?

In many, but not all, of her cases, the CPR group not only has a relationship to some level of government; some part of the government participates in its management. The best understood positive way in which the state participates is through legislation that honors the authority of the CPR and assists in the meeting of the conditions named above—that is, getting the jurisdiction right, supporting the appropriate technologies, banning the wrong ones, and information provision. In other words, in the best cases, as in the case of PB, the state is a not a sovereign commanding from above but a "partner" standing-with, supporting and protecting.

Building on my discussion in Chapter 2 on PB, I call this configuration of the state and community "social-public." The social-public partnership does not aim to eliminate the state or the private. Instead, it aims to obtain the support of specific elements of the state and reposition or displace the private. Some will say that the goal is to make these social groupings "autonomous." But in our PD reading, and the concept of the social-public in particular, this does not mean that the social separates itself entirely from any relationship with the state. It means that relations are set up that subordinate the state to the social. This is the notion of autonomy we have been using it throughout this book. It is worth citing Santos again in this context: "Autonomy cannot therefore be conceived as popular spontaneity, as a native capacity to organize poor people in degraded communities without the support or influence of external, organized political forces. Autonomy must rather be conceived as the popular capacity to channel external support and put it at the service of objectives, demands, and agendas generated in the communities" (Santos 2005b, 349). The social-public version of the commons also involves another key PD move from Santos (and Avritzer) maxD#3: replacing relations of inequality with shared authority. As we saw in my Chapter 2, an example of this is PD participatory budgeting: if a community sets up a process by which they make the rules and set the agenda with respect to their needs then they are autonomous. But again this community is still dependent on the state: the money comes from the state, and the proposals generated and approved by the PB process are then submitted to the state.[18] In other words, the autonomy of the community is not just a matter of its will and capacity to formulate its own agenda; it is in part determined by how external bodies relate to the community.

The other factors at work here are the composition of the community and the management logic employed. In order for the community or social formation to be autonomous from the state, its membership must be distinct. In the case of PB, this meant that the various committees are dominated by the residents; elected officials and government employees are usually not permitted to be members. (See Chapter 2.) The same sort of concerns play out in Ostrom's CPR examples. What Ostrom's account adds are details on the rules generated by the community for the process, including the punishment of offenders.[19] But, in the case of the commons, who enforces the rules? It would seem that the state would have to be involved with enforcement. (This is ironically analogous to the practice of the private BID. There, private security is often hired, but they do not prosecute.)

If such a setup sounds both complex and demanding, it's because it is: participatory democratic processes, and community vigilance, are required at every stage. But if the state is acting as a "partner" this can be done with much greater efficacy. One might ask, why would a government ever agree to do this? Well, the government is already doing this. There is a partner state, it just oftentimes (but not always!) is partnered with the corporate private. Yes, pharmaceuticals dominate the FDA and big agriculture the USDA, but look at the recent battle over the FCC and the question of "net neutrality" and Internet regulation. The major corporations—(e.g., Time Warner)—lost. After much debate and contestation, the FCC decided to regulate the web as a public utility, which means that all traffic on the Internet will be treated equally. Thus, there are no fast lanes for which mega firms like Google would pay more; and slow lanes, for which little firms like Vimeo would pay less, but receive less quality service (i.e., Youtube videos would load and play faster than Vimeo ones). Net neutrality means the web would be treated like water. The rich don't get to pay more for higher quality water. No matter your level of income or assets, everybody gets the same quality stuff (FCC 2014; Fung 2014).

The point is that the present governmental landscape of departments and agencies is more heterogeneous than pro- or antistate partisans care to admit. This is in part evident because so many so-called antigovernment critics often have agencies or programs that they do support. Is this hypocrisy? From the "pluralist" institutional standpoint, it's not. It's a coherent approach because of the heterogeneity of the state: there are meaningful normative and operational differences among agencies and departments. In other words, it is not hypocritical or contradictory to be pro-state on the FCC net neutrality ruling and antistate on the USDA Farm Bill subsidies to agribusiness. The former enables fair distribution of and access to a public good, whereas the latter impairs public control over the contents of the food supply as well as funding for community-driven agriculture, which fosters public health. Then there are more mixed operations like HUD and DOI. Within the former there are rules for spending funds that favor low-income residents, local hiring, and community participation and promote transit-oriented development that combines sustainability and social justice norms (Alliance for a Just Rebuilding et al. 2013, 20). The DOI used to be dominated by the DOD but after rounds of military base closings and the challenges of climate change, it is now becoming more responsive to communities in its ecological restoration projects (Hourdequin and Havlick 2011).[20] But these agencies are not fully social-public. So what, exactly, would a fully social-public agency look like?

Two Cases of the Social-Public: Water Utilities in Brazil and Bolivia

> We can learn from experiences across the world how the popular struggle against privatisation can go further and become a force to make public services and companies genuinely public: transparent to the public, valuing the knowledge of the public, sharing power with the public, and genuinely serving the public rather than private interests.
> —Wainwright, "Participatory Alternatives," 1

The sector with the most robust articulations of the social-public framework are water utilities. This is not surprising since water has been managed as a commons throughout human history, and, relatedly, was one of the last basic goods to be commodified. One exemplary case is from a city that is often cited for its PD innovations and was discussed at length in Chapter 2, Porto Alegre, Brazil. Not only is Porto Alegre famous for originating PB, its water utility—though facing numerous challenges—is known for its participatory processes, ability to serve those most in need, and comparative technical proficiency and financial stability. "In what ways could we intervene and participate collectively in order to construct an inclusive notion of the common good? How could we sow the seeds of full autonomy in relation to the state through our proposals to regulate water?" (Gutierrez-Aguilar 2004, 55). In my Chapter 2, when we discussed examples of Porto Alegre PB's demonstrably positive impact, one of the most frequently cited cases was its expansion and improvement of sewage system coverage. Indeed, Porto Alegre's water utility, the Departamento Municipal de Agua e Esgotos or DMAE, is praised not only by other municipal water engineers but by the business community who cite it as a key element in the high level of quality of life in the city (Maltz 2005, 35). But this was not always the case.

Up until 1989, DMAE primarily served the downtown area and wealthy neighborhoods. Water-borne illnesses were not uncommon among the underserved. But after the implementation of PB, over a ten-year period (1994–2004), the number of household water connections increased by 22 percent and the number of households served by sanitary sewage collection went up 40 percent. And, equally important, the quality of the system improved so that even when other parts of Brazil endured a cholera outbreak, there were no deaths (Maltz 2005, 31). And, from a PD perspective, there is even more to admire about the city's water utility, which to this day is publicly owned, despite attempts to privatize it (Maltz 2005, 32).

Since the 1960s, DMAE has been "autonomous." That is, it is administratively and financially independent from city hall. It has its own budget and sets its own internal operational processes but reports to the city council. But as we have seen throughout this volume, "autonomy" does not equal participatory democracy. Indeed, with respect to government agencies, autonomy often leads into a lack of accountability if not outright neoliberal corporate capture. So how does DMAE operate? The mayor appoints the director. The community sets policy and priorities directly through the Deliberative Council, which reports to the City Council. The workers implement projects through the Technical Council, but are able to express their own concerns and interests through the *ouvidoria*. And the community gets to propose its own projects, with technical assistance provided by DMAE staff, through the citywide PB process (Viero and Cordeiro 2003, 29).

The budget of DMAE does not come from city tax revenue but from user fees. And the price structure of those fees is determined by DMAE but through the *community*-dominated Deliberative Council. Because of the independence of the Deliberative Council, some even call it a "non-state-public sphere" (Viero and Cordeiro 2003, 23). Because is it led by social associations in terms of its governance, priorities and agenda, others call its mode of governance "social control" (Balanyá et al. 2005, 249). But DMAE is clearly part of the state, so it's a genuinely public agency. But it's a hybrid. Hence my preference for the phrase "social-public."

DMAE is PD because of its twofold managerial structure. The first is the Deliberative Council, which is composed of delegates from civil associations representing a diverse range of relevant constituencies (thirteen in all) including the medical community, businesses, residents, and households, "from experts to organizations of ordinary citizens" (Viero and Cordeiro 2003, 16). The other is the Technical Management Council. It administers the installation and delivery of services. The head of DMAE ("the director general") is in charge of the council, but its structure is "horizontal" and collectivist and "its meetings provide a forum for the exchange of information, deliberation and evaluation of projects and infrastructure work" (Viero and Cordeiro 2003, 15) (maxD#1).

One of the most distinctive features of DMAE is its fee structure, which shows its commitment not just to efficiency and public health, but to the econD framework discussed in Chapters 3, 4, and 5. The rate one pays for a unit of water is lower for low-use customers. In Porto Alegre, such households also tend to be the poorest. This then enables the poor to pay less but it also encourages others to use less in order to pay much less. So how does DMAE collect enough fees to cover the costs? It charges the rich more. The rates increase dramatically for use that goes beyond basic needs, such as water for swimming pools. The rate structure allows not only for subsidies for low-income users but the creation of a sizable reserve for upgrades and investment (Maltz 2005, 32–33). Here we see a robust example of a program that intersects economic justice with sustainability and has broad public benefit (maxD#4).

DMAE also empowers its workers through on-the-job training and well-supported capability development programs (maxD#2). These services have enabled the agency to face "technical difficulties such as the large-scale proliferation of the golden mussel (Limnoperna fortunei), which obstructed important pipes and other facilities. Research done to combat this challenge has made DMAE one of the most important references in the country on this subject" (Maltz 2005, 30). Workers also have their own venue within DMAE, the ouvidoria, to "vindicate their rights, make claims, make criticisms and suggestions as well as denunciations and demands" (Viero and Cordeiro 2003, 16). This internal organizational feature is to make sure that the worker demands are heard and takes some of the pressure off the more multistake-holder meetings in the council but also makes sure worker rights are not lost in the shuffle.[21]

In addition to the econD and PD benefits, there are epistemic and efficiency advantages from this model; users benefit because their particular needs are better understood because of the participatory governance structures. DMAE workers and managers benefit from user participation because such community-generated place-based knowledge enables engineers and workers within DMAE to develop projects that are more technically appropriate and cost effective: "For the utility, getting active input based on the unique knowledge of the citizens is an asset in itself. The increased sense of ownership contributes to the willingness to pay and thus make new investments and improved maintenance possible" (Balanyá et al. 2005, 248). That is, DMAE is seen not as some detached government agency impenetrable to the public, but as a competent and fair partner that is not only socially responsive but democratically collaborative.

The social-public DMAE then is a true alternative to privatization. It even shows that in some cases the social-public model can beat the public-private model at its own game: DMAE improved service while cutting costs. But it was only able to do this by utilizing a PD management framework within a social-public frame. As Maltz states, "Among the important features that made DMAE become an international alternative model to water privatisation, are its sustainability, both in financing and technological terms, and its accountability with regard to safe water and environmental protection. A very important and distinguishing characteristic, however, is the democratic decision-making process of its participatory budget" (Maltz 2005, 30). The trick was that it was able to improve service for everyone by increasing costs only for those who could afford it. The importance of the rate structure cannot be overstated: not only does it favor those most economically disadvantaged; it sets a differential price structure not because some users have more money but because those wealthy users use water far beyond basic needs. In a time when water preservation is so crucial, such a program not only increases sustainability—by pricing water to discourage excessive nonbasic needs use—it also enhances resilience: it creates a reserve fund for upgrades plus it reduces costs to an already vulnerable population. One only need look to the north and contrast Porto Alegre with the political, social, and economic emergencies in Sao Paolo and California due to disastrous water shortages caused by mismanagement, negligence, and extravagance. Indeed, the DMAE price and management structure is a best practice that would be appropriate for relatively wealthy cities with severe inequality.

DMAE is not the only public utility pursuing such a model. There is an incredible array of models of water management that articulate the social-public model throughout the world. 1,300 miles west/NW from Porto Alegre, on the drier side of the continent, stands the city that made the fight over water globally famous. The story of the "water war" of Cochabamba, Bolivia, has been told in books and movies, and inspired citizens both urban and rural across the globe to fight against both privatization and state corruption (Olivera 2004). In 1999 the city council voted to sell the municipal-owned water utility SEMAPA to an international conglomerate called Aguas del Tunari with promises of cutting costs and improving services. Instead rates went up, service did not improve, and the new firm even charged city residents for collecting rainwater (Olivera 2004, 10; Spronk and Webber 2007, 39–41)! Residents literally revolted, shutting down the city for days. The government agreed to "de-privatize" the utility, but residents, obviously, were not satisfied—how could they trust the city to run it well after so many years of bad service? A new SEMAPA was re-created along social-public lines, with community organizations more empowered and represented on SEMAPA's board. However, the challenges are enormous especially because of climate change and the utility has struggled to provide an adequate level of service to its users although improvements in governance and costs have been made (Gómez and Terhorst 2004, 125–130).

The victory in Cochabamba initiated a wave of de-privatizations from South Africa and Spain to Tanzania and India, from Berlin to Maputo (Mozambique). Since the uprising in Bolivia, 180 successful de-privatizations have occurred. Ironically, most remunicipalizations have occurred in the home countries of the conglomerate that privatized Cochabamba: the United States and France (Atlanta and Paris de-privatized!). And many have integrated elements of PD and the social-public framework in their governance and operations (Lobina et al. 2014, 2–6).

Water and the Social-Public

As with the case of the commons, the social-public model is defined by activities in two dimensions: the internal structure of the organization that does the management and the on (or in)-the ground dynamics of the resource (water, education, defense, oil and gas, Internet, land, etc.) The fight over *water* utilities in particular is crucial for the promulgation of a participatory democratic politics for at least three reasons. First, and most obviously, water is essential for life. Water is a kind of resource or "good" that seems especially ill-suited for privatization or commodification because all humans need it. And, while there has been tremendous ingenuity involved in creating the infrastructure for water collection, storage, distribution, and purification, humans are in no sense authors or producers of water. It is, truly, a gift (Shiva 2002, 101–102). Since the rise of agriculture and cattle-raising, the management of water has been a key political issue, it's even cited a major reason for war in Book II of Plato's Republic. And water management did and continues to play a key part in the rise and fall of empires and states as a form of governance (Chew 2001, 1–40). Water also plays an essential role in myriad cultural rituals from baptism and bathing to rain dances and recreation (Shiva 2002, 131–140). And it plays a critical economic role from transport to large-scale energy production (hydroelectric) and microchip manufacture; even the Internet is a water intensive operation (Shiva 2002, 33–34). For all these reasons, water is a well suited for the social-public framework.

Second, this seemingly inexhaustible "given" (for some) is becoming all too scarce for far too many. Pollution, mismanagement, and climate change are all factors. And climate change intensifying flooding and drought are playing even more major roles in migration and war (Parenti 2011). The private-public frame has failed to deliver effective and fair management of water. Building upon and working alongside the commons and CPR frames, the social-public offers a time-tested alternative model that is better equipped to adapt to these even more dire circumstances. The effective management of water provides lessons for how to manage a good sustainably and enhance social and ecological resilience.

The third reason for stressing the importance of water management for the proliferation of PD and the social-public framework is strategic. Not only is water quality impacted by local and global forces, water management bodies (if not formal utilities) are almost everywhere.

Communities differ in all sorts of political, economic, and cultural ways, and some PD practices are not so universalizable: not every region wants a federation of large manufacturing co-ops like Mondragon, participatory budgeting might not be suited for sparsely populated regions, and public banks may not be appropriate for urban areas in states with low capacity and large informal economies. But all these peoples and places need water. A water department was the first public utility in the United States (McDonald and Ruiters 2012b, 165). If each locale had a *social*-public water utility, and again—the arguments for this are multiple and very strong—then each government would have at least one agency that is social-public. The water utility could then be used as a staging ground on a variety of levels: it would be a place to both see participatory democracy in action and to learn about PD by doing it. Persons and groups could get hands on training and experience in how to implement PD processes and develop PD skills and then put them to use in other arenas such as schools, businesses (e.g., co-ops), or neighborhood-based housing collectives.

In many locales, the implementation of a needs-based, sustainable water utility could also lead to positive changes in the local economy. In California, which just experienced a mega-drought, 10 percent of potable water goes to almond farming and lawn watering is another major use. Both jeopardize the integrity of the water supply and both seem unlikely to have been approved from a needs-based perspective. Indeed, across the globe, some of the most water-intensive industries produce products that we could do without (or at least use much less frequently) such as soda, hamburgers, sugar, and jeans. If subsidies were cut and a price structure was in place that charged more for nonbasic or luxury use of water, many incredibly wasteful operations could be drastically reduced and others that are more sustainable would be at an advantage. In other words, a social-public water utility could be used to remake the economy to make it more sustainable, more democratic, and environmentally just (EJ-PD).

Another reason why water utilities are such strategic opportunities for advocates of participatory democracy is that they own, manage, and control infrastructure, which literally goes down every street and into every home. Imagine if all those pipes and drains, all those holding ponds, gutters, and water towers were not the exclusive space of state employees but a commons that belonged to the public?

But the skeptic asks, why would a water utility want the ignorant public climbing up water towers? They would not, hence the fences. But what they do want is the public to stop flushing handy wipes down the toilet.[22] And they do want the public to clear debris from sewers after heavy rainfalls—which are becoming more frequent. And they do want the public to purchase rain barrels, stop using impermeable surfaces for driveways, and, oh yeah, take better care of your cars while you are at it, because oil leaks cause major problems for the watershed and aquifers as well. The problem is that information campaigns that treat residents as isolated households paying for a service don't lead to effective stewardship. People need to feel a sense of ownership (Keck and Sakdapolrak 2013, 9). Guess what, if your jurisdiction has a public water utility, you already do own it! But, you reply, "I don't feel like an owner." Why? Because there is too often no real chance to meaningfully participate either in management at the policy level or in everyday life, even though all those pipes which *you* own come right into *your* house! In the case of DMAE—and many others that utilize such a model—we saw a model where segments of the public can meaningfully participate in a truly significant way especially in terms of priority setting.

But let's face it, that's not going to involve very many people, only a few organizations and their representatives. However, if the locale also has a PB, that enables a much wider range of people and groups to participate, because then the broader public has the ability to make proposals. And we have seen such proposals in places with PB so if those budgets were expanded even further, there is good reason to expect even more public participation. And with this same public making proposals and working with agencies, the sense of ownership is likely to increase.

PB is well suited for water infrastructure because it often operates on a much larger scale and gets into key issues highlighted by S-PD and EJ-PD.

Reservoirs, holding ponds, marshes, and drainage areas can easily be made into public spaces that encourage appropriate interaction with the public such that accessible green space is provided while water integrity is maintained. Even waste treatment plants can be made into public spaces.[23] For example, on the upper west side of Manhattan, EJ-PD community groups fought the city to ensure that a waste treatment facility would be both well run and safe for the community living nearby. But they also demanded a design such that the same space could be safely used as a recreational area and provide much needed public space to an especially underserved community. Here a water utility becomes a (social) public space that rectifies an environmental injustice and promotes EJ-PD.[24]

The Cyber Social-Public: Platform Cooperativism and the P2P Partner State

> All the beloved Apple devices cannot be considered without first reminding ourselves of the labor conditions at what Andrew Ross called the "Foxconn's suicide mills" in Shenzhen, China. Or take the rare earth minerals in the Democratic Republic of the Congo; it is essential to follow the supply chains that facilitate all those seemingly clean and glamorous digital life styles.
> —SCHOLZ, "PLATFORM COOPERATIVISM," 3

Another piece of infrastructure that comes into many households is the landline.[25] While this use to be domain of the phone company, now it is better known as the link to cable and the Internet. Though not as ubiquitous as the water pipe, it's being called as basic, and some even argue that in the information age access to data is as necessary as water. For those who are connected, the Internet is part of all parts of our lives: from work to school, communicating with family and friends, shopping and learning, loving and exploring. The web has also led to the blurring or confusing of all these sectors: we check work e-mail at home, send personal e-mails at work, communicate with family while on dates with friends, and check in on social media everywhere at any time. But the blur that matters most for this chapter is that between labor and consumption, between producer and user.

A great example of this is Facebook. There I post my thoughts, share pictures, comment on news stories, and make plans to attend events with others. It's a medium that interconnects so much and so many, and with the greatest of ease. It fosters so much collaboration and exchange, a place where we make connections and learn. And it's free! So then how is it that Facebook makes money? Facebook makes money by granting advertisers access to the space and our content. You see, we users are not mere consumers, we are laborers. Facebook provides the platform, we provide the content. Without us engaging in all those activities on the site, FB goes bankrupt. But with us, it is one of the most highly valued and powerful companies on the face of the planet. But we are not paid for our work, instead we are subject to commercial surveillance and our data is not our own.

In this "cognitive capitalism," most of the "products" of all that wonderful creative collaboration are owned by large firms who "monetize it" (Scholz 2016, 2). The creative collaborators ("users") of social media don't get paid, but Facebook employees are paid wages and Facebook shareholders reap the profits. But what about Linux and other open source systems and platforms where people willingly donate their labor? While the benefits to average users are high because the costs to them are so low, corporate others (e.g., IBM) take advantage of all that free (collaborative) labor to make even larger profits (Bauwens and Restakis 2014, 17). P2P theorists Bauwens and Restakis[26] write, "Under the dominance of neoliberal, cognitive and netarchical capitalist forms, commoners are not able to create livelyhoods in the production of open knowledge commons, and under most open licenses, private companies are free to use and exploit the common knowledge without secure return. This obliges many and most commoners to work for private capital" (Bauwens and Restakis 2014, 6). And the role of the state? In this "neoliberal vision, value is created in the private sector by workers mobilized by capital; the state becomes a market state protecting the privileged interests of property owners; and civil society is a derivative rest category, as is evidenced in the use of our language (*non*-profits, *non*-governmental)" (Bauwens and Restakis 2014, 2, my emphasis). Indeed, throughout the immaterial labor landscapes of social media, companies have users in the millions but have paid employees by the dozens (if that!) yet some are valued in the *billions*. P2P views call this neoliberal public-private model "cognitive capitalism" or "netarchy" (Bauwens and Restakis 2014, 3).[27]

But a PD platform is possible. All these sites where we share and collaborate, where we create and connect offer an incredibly powerful mode of sociality that reconstructs the producer/user distinction. This form of collaborative immaterial labor is sometimes called peer-to-peer production or P2P. One of the leading theorists of how to democratize this corporatized "sharing economy" is Michael Bauwens. The challenge is this:

> In order to turn peer production from a transitional mode within capitalism to a potential new dominant mode of production, we have to bring together the commonist [*sic*] aspects of immaterial cooperation with manufacturing companies that do not reward shareholders and owners of capital but rather the value creators themselves. By interconnecting these emerging players we will create a powerful seed form for the future. (Bauwens 2012)

For Bauwens, this social mode of production or "commonification" can out compete capitalism because it is more innovative and more cooperative. Why? Traditional patents and copyrights are replaced with licenses that permit and even encourage sharing while *prohibiting exclusive use* (e.g., copy left, creative commons). In other words, because there is no privatization of innovation, commonification is actually more productive. Commonification is also more innovative and efficient because it replaces the formal hierarchies of bureaucracies with all their hardened divisions of function and labor with malleable modules of distributed parallel development. But what is the right model of ownership and management for this fluid socioeconomic morphology?

The sentiment—reward the creators, not the "owners"!—could easily be supported by the arguments of Ellerman's "residual claimant argument" (see my Chapter 4). But how should these players be interconnected? What kind of organizational form is best equipped to not only foster collaboration but also enable the creators to take back the product (and profits!)? While co-ops have a role to play (Scholz 2016), Bauwens and Restakis criticize worker co-ops for being too caught up in the proprietary economy of intellectual property and global market competition and not involved enough in the production of the commons (Bauwens and Restakis 2014, 20). Sometimes they favor B corps: firms that abide by a corporate charter that legally requires them to not just maximize return for stockholders but benefit multiple stakeholders including consumers, labor, and the community (Bauwens and Restakis 2014, 12).[28]

I suppose B corps could be (theoretically) better than worker co-ops because the latter values workers *alongside* community, but why not combine them with co-ops as in the case of CHCA? (See my Chapter 4.) But even discounting this issue, another one runs deeper: what about all those aforementioned immaterial laborers who are not and do not want to be part of any firm? If I make creative contributions to some software or social media platform, can't I be compensated without joining the firm? For Bauwens, and for PD, there are two issues here: compensation and governance. A range of compensation schemes and investment mechanisms already exist from freelancing contracts and the "click" economy to kickstarter, but none of those models reliably covers the costs of one's basic needs (from housing to health care) much less can reverse inequality trends (Scholz 2016).

Here Bauwens opts for a common econD solution: a basic income guarantee.[29] But even if there were one to cover basic needs, that would still not solve the governance issue. P2P and the social-public frame require that some mechanism be in place to enable "social control" over the enterprise—noting that "social" could be a community of producers and users (or produsers). For P2P, democratically run for-benefit nonprofit associations (e.g., FLOSS) could fill this role.[30] Some also cite the multistakeholder cooperative model (Bauwens and Restakis 2014, 3) that we discussed at length in my Chapter 4. They write, "The aim is to create a level playing field, in which hyper-exploitation of social value becomes a gradual impossibility, and in which extractive rent-taking becomes equally impossible and counter-productive through the existence of well-protected open commons" (Bauwens and Restakis 2014, 5).

What is clear in Bauwens and Restakis's version of P2P is that any hope to transition from cognitive capitalism to a commons political-economy will require more than radical coders and PD platform developers (as important as they are). Nor will it be solved by nonprofits and businesses. It's going to take the state to distribute wealth/income (paid or "guaranteed") and regulate the economy. Here they converge with Wainwright and her "reclaim the state" model, and my own social-public "disarticulate the state" framework. Like some of the advocates of PD PB discussed in my Chapter 2, they call their model the "partner state" and it's worth quoting at length:

> The Partner State is the institution of the collectivity which creates and sustains the **civic infrastructures and educational** levels, and whose governance is based on participation and **co-production of public services** and collective decision-making. The Partner State retains the solidarity functions of the welfare state, but **de-bureaucratizes** the delivery of its services to the citizen. **It abandons its paternalistic vision of citizens that are passive recipients of its services.** The Partner State is therefore based on wide-spread participation in decision-making, but also in the delivery of its services. Public services are co-created and co-produced with the full participation of the citizens. (Bauwens and Restakis 2014, 6)

A number of critical points are housed in this passage. Students of the history of participatory democracy theory will recognize the older, pre–"immaterial labor" version of this view in the work of Paul Hirst and earlier associationists such as G.D.H. Cole: that is, the social transformation of the bureaucracy. Like P2P advocates, associationists were critics of bureaucracy and fans of decentralization, and they also called for the delegation of operational authority to self-organizing associations outside the state. But they also realized that the state had a role to play: in taxation, regulation, allocating funds, and being a watchdog. That is, as a partner state! Associationist PD also emphasized the importance of PD not just in policy formation but in administration and service delivery. And associationists recognized that this view of the role of the state challenged those who considered it sovereign and believed that hierarchy and coercion were central for effective governance (Hirst 1994, 26–34).

More specifically, as Bauwens and Restakis note, hopes for commonify-ing the present system hinge on our ability to transform the education and civic infrastructure systems. They are all obviously crucial for an economy tied more and more to knowledge production and for the administration of public goods in ways that promote and protect the commons. Bauwens and Restakis also believe that "digital natives" social movements must transform politics as has been seen in the cases of the Occupy! Movements and with the Spanish Indignados and "Pirate" political parties throughout Europe. How-ever, they warn, "there is a stage in the evolution of a new social movement and culture when political power is crucial to ensure its survival and devel-opment. It is not enough to create new institutions on the margins of society; effective defence mechanisms against the constant attacks of the dominant powers become a necessity. This means building a political coalition" (Bau-wens 2012). Drawing upon Wainwright and my own view the coalition re-quired is clear: immaterial laborers and public sector workers should unite![31] But this isn't just about workers, immaterial or factory. Nor is it about privi-leging some vague notion of "community." One of the real innovative con-tributions of the social-public model is that it recognizes that the producer and user are no longer so distinct, and this changes notions of ownership and management, and makes possible a new understanding of governor and governed. And with a reinvigorated and more operationalized and state friendly understanding of the commons, wealth could be reappropriated in ways that address economic and political need in a resource-sustaining manner.

Conclusion

Traditional welfare and socialist state governance and service delivery suffer from myriad drawbacks in terms of both democracy and efficiency, but the public-private "cure" for these ills has mostly made too many political bodies worse off. In particular the public-private model has intensified both the ecological and inequality crises. We developed the social-public model to articulate an alternative to both the state-public and public-private models and argued that it is better disposed to fulfill the PD framework as well as the demands of sustainability. Established cases of water utilities were cru-cial for our argument, but emerging examples from the digital commons of cyberspace also offer much promise. The social-public model offers a doable alternative because it enables communities to define the public good while empowering public agencies and workers in the process. Such comanage-ment processes enable efficiency gains that privilege the needs of users in a manner that reduces both political and economic inequality. The social-public model is conceptually innovative from a political and economic the-ory standpoint because it reconstructs the hard and fast distinction between governor and governed, producer and user, and even subject and object; hence the terms *produser* and *commoner*. It also shows how the tradition of the commons can be updated for the present urbanized global scene. Last, the social-public model allows us to avoid the stifling debates about whether or not to work with the state: instead it instructs us to fracture and reclaim. This process of "disarticulation" shows that the state can act as a partner, and that states, like so many other beings, are capable of evolving. While I think the social-public model has much to offer all of the six PD Routes, I think S-PD has concerns re: social reproduction but these can be addressed (see the discussion of the water utilities and households). I also think the model has much to offer EJ-PD, but A-PD, with its intense antistate stance, is likely to remain skeptical.

Conclusion

Opportunities for Research and
Scenarios for Action

P articipatory democracy works. It is justifiable from a broad swath of political and philosophical perspectives, desirable for reasons personal and collective, economic and social. And it is doable in multiple sectors across diverse cultural locations. Though critics deem it too "demanding," more and more communities are calling for it. Others say it can only work at small scale in homogeneous communities, yet it continues to grow and proliferate from the hills of Chiapas and Basque Country to the cosmopolitan megalopolises of Tokyo and New York.

Part of the reason PD is so underappreciated and/or misunderstood is that there has not been a systematic theoretical account defining and justifying it relative to political and moral categories and traditions since Pateman (1970). *We Decide!* does that in great detail through the articulation of the four principles of maximal democracy and their relationship to the norms of self-determination, equality, freedom, capability development, resource distribution, authority, and solidarity. Another distinctive contribution of *We Decide!* is that it shows how six different normative traditions/perspectives have and should utilize PD to further achieve their ends. Just as PD should not be confined to a sole sector, nor is it owned by a single ideology. Instead, **participatory democracy is a cross-platform[1] convergence space, enabling constituencies with diverse and even conflicting values to engage with each other in ways that reduce inequality, enhance individual and group capabilities, share authority, and foster solidarity.**

But we were also honest, and critiqued each model and effort from both PD and anti-PD perspectives and showed the limitations of participatory budgeting, worker, consumer, and multistakeholder cooperatives and social-public utilities. But showing the limits should not end the inquiry. Instead, in the last sections of each chapter, we showed how many of these problems could be addressed and PD could even scale up and transform public budgets (Chapter 2), production (Chapters 3 and 4), consumption and social reproduction (Chapter 5), and the state bureaucracy (Chapter 6). And we argued that if PD is able to fracture and reclaim the state, it could proliferate in ways that could promote system-wide change that is democratic, equity enhancing, and ecologically sustainable. In the rest of this brief conclusion, I want to name some best practices that have emerged from our studies and point toward challenges and opportunities for both researchers and practitioners.

Research, Theory, and Social Innovation

We do not know our own strength. It's maddening. Too much political theory is obsessed with critique. Too much of it aims *only* to tear apart, and if it does end on a positive note, it is with a vague and faint cry of hope. Also, it's incredible how many successful efforts and organizations are out there that too many don't know anything about and the interested few don't know enough about. For example, it's well understood that assemblies are crucial for PD. But we have no history of assemblies! Nor philosophical analyses of how different assemblies in different periods have functioned (Athens is the exception). Imagine a history of assemblies, from Keane's ancient middle east to Kropotkin's medieval cities with their guilds to indigenous nations' councils to the Paris and Oaxaca Communes,[2] syndicalist workplaces, from the Soviets to worker co-ops to the Zapatistas to PB, the Argentinian assemblies movement and Occupy! to Mondragon and Seikatsu's cooperatives!

But we need even more research on the other PD forms. For example, Mondragon's governing and social councils and the relationship between the two (Chapters 4 and 5). SCCCU's "consumption committee" and "independent control committee" offer insights into what a nonbureaucratic form of regulation could look like (Chapter 5). What would it take to spread this throughout the food system given the failures of state agencies such as the USDA and FDA? How many would welcome such a project! Book length studies should be done of all of these. Marie Bouchard's 2013 book on Quebec's movement is one to emulate as are the works of Gordon Nembhard, Curl, and Restakis, but we need more detailed histories and many, many more philosophical investigations of those practices.[3] (The historians are far ahead of us.)

And when we are successful, new questions arise: for example, now that there are PB's running for multiple years in several cities, how do we support those who do so much work to make the process happen? As we saw in

Chapter 2, budget delegates are crucial: they develop the rough ideas into real proposals. They put in weeks of work. Should they be compensated? By whom and how? Perhaps with gift cards or coupons to dine and shop at local co-ops to strengthen a local solidarity economy? Or should being part of a process count as "government service" like jury duty? Maybe participating in a PB should be *required* like jury duty to foster a more participatory state? How can we justify such an expanded sense of political obligation when the world is dominated by rights talk? And what about the women of SCCCU, should they be paid as governmental regulators or as a counter-government body? Which political theorists and ethicists will take up these questions?!

Best Practices

In Chapter 4, I argued that in order for co-ops to proliferate and the present economy to move toward an economic democracy, four components seem crucial. After consideration of the cases discussed, it's fairly clear that for any PD effort to emerge, evolve, and proliferate from both a normative and logistical perspective the following is required; (1) a bank; (2) a university or research center; (3) a nongovernmental association to coordinate the various actors and garner state support; and (4) a strong social or cultural movement that is multi-issue.

A Bank

Having a bank means that the fruits of one's labor can further the cause of PD rather than be used against it (see Chapter 4). It means that the producers of the surplus control the management of the surplus. This is the power that the city unions lacked during the NYC fiscal crisis and their own money was used against them (see Chapter 6). But this is what the co-ops of Quebec continue to have with the Desjardin Credit Union and the Coopérative fédérée de Québec. The Italians have it as well with La Lega (see Chapter 4). Mondragon has a private (nongovernmental) version of this with its *Caja Laboral Popular* (the Working People's Bank), which enabled co-ops to retain their profits which then led to the creation of services and support systems for co-op members, investment capital and credit lines for new co-ops, funds for the education and retraining of members, and programs for the benefits of nonmembers in the surrounding Basque Community (Chapters 3 and 4). And SCCCU has a (much reduced) version, but one that still enabled them to obtain financing for the formation of worker co-ops such as their organic dairy (Chapter 5). Interestingly, PB's do not have this. They are funded largely through governmental allocations, and don't have specific funds or banks, and that does make them more vulnerable and limited in what sorts of projects that they can undertake (e.g., game-changing infrastructure projects like mass transit, large-scale affordable housing, and sustainable energy need to be on the table).

A University or Research Center to Promote, Critically Reflect, Educate, and Cultivate Adaptive Learning

In our data-driven information age and knowledge economy, it is not surprising that the most successful PD organizations and processes have independent high-quality research centers. SCCCU has the Social Movement Research Center, Quebec the Social Innovation Research Center (M. Bouchard 2013), the Mondragon Corporation has a university and *fifteen* research centers, and Italy has La Lega.[4] Such epistemological-pedagogical operations are crucial for at least three reasons: (1) to reflect upon and develop the capabilities of practitioners; (2) to spread (PD) knowledge, skills, and culture to others; (3) to make the case to figures in power (elected officials, media, funders) to convince them to undertake or support PD projects.

Part of the genius of PB was that the first group to do it in Porto Alegre put together a research team to study it from the start (e.g., CIDADE) and others have followed suit, including NYC and North America. (See Chapter 2.) Having info on who does and does not participate helps PB practitioners make adjustments to attract excluded groups or provide additional support for different phases of the process to make them more effective. Also, CIDADE and other research institutes promote what we would now call adaptive learning or learning for adaptive management. The idea here is that creating a reflective feedback loop is also helpful not just to address past failures but to innovate to address changing conditions. (This is particularly important for addressing climate change [Ramasubramanian et al. 2016].) Co-ops and other econD organizations need research on economic trends as well as on populations that are to be served as well as particular technical knowledges (mechanical engineering, agroecology, etc.) to train their members. Mondragon's units have been particularly effective in this regard. PD requires not just research, but educational institutions that are part of the movement.

A Nongovernmental Coordinating Body

It's counterintuitive, perhaps, but in this time of networks, there is a striking lack of regularized coordination among movements and organizations. Financial support, legal representation, outreach, media, web design, conflict resolution are all knowledges and skills that organizations need. In the United States they are often available but because organizations are already overwhelmed with demands and constraints, they miss out on opportunities for assistance and collaboration. But in our PD success stories, this kind of coordination happens: in Mondragon, the Caja largely fulfills the role. In Italy

La Lega does this and more, "La Lega lobbies the state for support, it provides legal, business, and accounting services, it provides research and development information, it helps coordinate business evolution, and helps finance the development of new cooperatives" (Malleson 2014, 66). In Quebec, this role is also shared among financing and research organizations. Another support that an effective coordinating body can secure is legislation that favors co-ops in social service delivery or government contracts. (Italy has such laws, and NYC is exploring them [Foster and Iaione 2016].)

A Multisector Movement or Party Aiming for System Change

This was definitely the case in Quebec with the women's movement and unions (Neamtan 2008; M. Bouchard 2013, 36, 53–54), with PB and econD in Brazil (e.g., the Worker's Party and other movements) and to a lesser extent with SCCCU and the environmental movement in Japan but much less so with Mondragon. (As remarkable as he was, Father Arizmendi was not a movement.) In general, though, for the evolution and support of a PD ecosystem, multisector movements have proven crucial and to reach the next level, they are necessary (Santos 2006b; Alperovitz 2012).

This brings us to our next challenge: who will fight for such changes? Many argue that public sector unions are critical to the mix (Wainwright 2014) but obviously things have not played out as positively as earlier manifestos had hoped (Santos 2005b, 2006b). One of the inspiring facets of PD is that so many different groups have fought for it and won and innovated new forms, including groups addressed in this volume but also others including peasants farmers such as La Via Campesina (Menser 2008). If the social-public has any chance of happening, elected officials and government workers will have to be involved and local governments in particular will have to take on a much bigger role in the service delivery game. A particularly potent convergence could happen if local governments ally themselves with the new precariat in opposition to the corporate takeover of the "sharing economy." As platform cooperatives advocate Scholz argues, "Silicon Valley loves a good disruption, so let's give them one. What follows is a call to place the people at the center of virtual hiring halls and turn profits into social benefit. It's a call to city councils to consider running businesses like Airbnb themselves. Historically, American cities used to own and operate hotels and hospitals and some still do. It's time to revisit that history" (Scholz 2016, 10).

Scenario 1: The "Checkerboard" Strategy; Horizontal Proliferation as Exodus or a New Federalism

What if instead of trying to spread every model to any city, we focused on bringing several models to several cities and coordinated resources for residents and government to develop every PD practice that made sense for that population given its problems and potentials, from a local multistake-holder co-op version of Uber (Konczal and Covert 2014) to PB? NYC has two major PD efforts going on right now with the city council in its second year of supporting co-op development and its sixth year of doing PB (now over half of the fifty-one members of the city council participate). Also, a new community land trust is taking root in East Harlem. The problem is that so much elite-oriented development and gentrification is taking place at the same time that the PD efforts are a proverbial small drop (OK, three drops) in the very big (OK, ginormous) ocean. But then again, if we can make it here, we can make it anywhere, right!?

Maybe not. NYC could influence other global cities (see Barber 2013) but taking on the high-priced enclaves of global capital is a tough slog.[5] What about the less sought after locations or places of capital flight? For the U.S. situation, it could be more potent to "make it" in deindustrialized towns like Buffalo, Rochester (NY), Detroit, Richmond (CA and VA), and Cleveland. As it turns out, there are attempts under way in all these places, the most notable of which may be Cleveland (Kelly and McKinley 2015).

Like many Midwest "rust belt" cities, Cleveland has suffered from years of deindustrialization and white flight. Despite many mainstream capital intensive attempts to promote development that would attract tourists, the Rock and Roll Hall of Fame alone can't reverse the jobs crisis or prevent rounds of foreclosures. This history of failures helped to open up possibilities for an alternate model of economic development. So the Democracy Collaborative (a nonprofit) acted as the coordinating body and connected a foundation (the Cleveland Foundation) with two anchor institutions[6] to purchase services (laundry, vegetables, solar power arrays) delivered by worker co-ops. Not only do the co-ops supply jobs but they enabled the workers to develop equity (as owners) to buy homes, and address the local foreclosure crisis.[7] This is what Alperovitz calls the "checkerboard strategy": take advantage of openings on the board and fill them with our model (Alperovitz 2012, 65–71). Once we occupy a few spaces, leverage is created, more people are attracted and different kinds of moves open up as the imagination envisions a new possibility. Imagine if in Cleveland a SCCCU inspired food co-op opened and then a PB sponsored by the Mayor's office took root, and then the co-ops begat or partnered with a credit union and opened an investment fund controlled by their members who were local residents and then invested in a green infrastructure job training facility and then residents of Toledo saw this and they got their mayor to visit and he became jealous and then funded a solar array worker co-op and . . .

This brings up a favorable feature of Cleveland: its size (population 390,000). It's the kind of place where people still can have influence on their elected officials, were genuine home grown grassroots types can dominate the city council, or even win the mayoralty if the right kind of coalition can take place between whites, blacks, and immigrants.[8] If one can make this happen there, there are many other jurisdictions with similar budgets and institutional dynamics. Also, once it works at one level—and there is research to show how it happened and demonstrate its success—then it could spread to other cities of the same size. Cities like to copy things that work from each other, just look at bike lanes (Barber 2013, 7–8) and PB (Chapter 2)!

The other aspect of this model to highlight is that it's neither bottom up nor top down but diagonal (see Chapter 2). It involves elected representatives, agency officials, community members, and a nonprofit or two. It's inside-outside but with an edge (again, diagonal). And the great thing about that sort of packaging of actors is that it can travel. We have seen this happen with PB (Lerner 2014b) and the Democracy Collaborative hopes to do it with co-ops and anchor institutions. The goal is to spread it to as many locales as possible to create a dispersed set of PD territories. OK, sounds great, then what?

Take over the state and federal governments? Associationist and EJ–PD would say build the base to *remake* the different levels of government, to devolve powers and rebalance U.S. federalism in ways that would please at least some of the Founding Fathers (Franklin, Jefferson, see Chapter 1). But for A-PD the endgame is exodus: delegitimate the state, shift power away from the governmental institutions, and build a new social horizontal frame in its stead. What would this look like? A neo-Hanseatic federation of PD cities (see Kropotkin and Bookchin in chapter 1)? Would that entail secession or just a radical rearrangement of borders that would promote more PD amenable jurisdictions? One of these would have to happen because otherwise, a single PD city would be too isolated and dependent without such a national/international restructuring.[9]

Scenario 2: Economic Meltdown and State-Based Scaling Up

Another scenario could have happened during the financial crisis of 2008. In his book *After Capitalism* David Schweickart imagines how system change might occur in a way that could realize the transition to economic democracy. He describes three situations. The first is a situation that resembles what happened during the financial collapse of 2008. He argues that if the government made a few of its decisions differently, a totally different postcrisis situation would have emerged. A key moment in the 2008 crisis was when the auto companies were on the verge of collapse and the government stepped in to purchase sizable amounts of shares of GM and Ford. Once it did this, the government should have exerted its majority shareholder authority to restructure the firms as worker co-ops and require them to serve the public good and make not more gas guzzling cars but green vehicles and motors for mass transit, etc. This in conjunction with a number of other measures that could have "bailed out mainstreet" rather than Wall Street were well within the government's powers but not acted upon (Schweickart 2011, 181–185). Again, associationist PD would be totally supportive of such a move, though A-PD might recommend letting them all fail.

Scenario 3: Civil Clash

From Occupy! and the Movement for Black Lives to Standing Rock and other episodes of "blockadia," disruptive direct action is intensifying and proliferating (Klein 2014, 293–336). The publicity and response to the police killings of several black men and women in recent years led to a contentious form of politics across the United States that had not been seen at this scale since the 1960s. In terms of the PD frameworks we have discussed, Movement for Blacks Lives has the antagonism of A-PD and the multidimensional depth of S-PD, but the focus is less on the patriarchy of S-PD (though it's there) and more on white supremacy à la EJ-PD. M4BL explicitly adopted econD and PD in its 2016 platform (including PB at the local, state, and federal levels).[10] As it evolves the politics of M4BL may become more "checkerboard" and is less like Occupy! and more akin to the Climate Justice movement which is grassroots but nevertheless aims to influence state policy. Here we see a mix of S-PD with EJ PD and it is spreading globally.

Scenario 4: Climate Justice

Is Klein 2014 right? **Will *climate change change everything* and enable PD to proliferate?** As many have argued for years, this calamity requires massive system change in terms of our economy, our political institutions, and our culture. There are many aspects of this challenge that PD is well equipped to address: the need to get way from the culture of consumption and focus on ecologically sustainable social reproduction (SCCCU, S-PD); adaptive learning (PB); climate justice (EJ-PD); the proliferation of local sustainability and resilience practices (A-PD and S-PD); ecological communities or transition towns (communitarian PD); and bioregional economics (S-PD). As impossible as this sounds, climate change may make it necessary.

In conclusion, over these past six chapters, I have attempted to shift the focus of political theory from justification to illustration, from critique to strategy. From "why should we do it?" to "how can we do it?"; from why it won't work to what can we do to make it work. And with the further interconnecting of researchers and organizers, of thinkers and doers, there is no reason to think that participatory democracy won't continue to attract, evolve, and surprise.

Notes

INTRODUCTION

1. The event was the 2003 NYC Social Forum. The two speakers were Latin American social movement scholar Jack Hammond and Bonnie Brower from a budget watchdog nongovernmental organization (NGO) called the City Project.

2. My first direct interaction with organizers and participants in PB processes was in 2005 in Porto Alegre, Brazil, at the World Social Forum. It was there that I met fellow PB researcher Josh Lerner. We went on to cofound and run the Participatory Budgeting Project, a nonprofit that sets up PB processes in the United States and Canada. Available at www.participatorybudgeting.org (Baez and Hernandez 2012, 320; Lerner 2014b).

3. We first met Joe Moore, the first elected official in the United States to do PB (in Chicago in 2009), at the U.S. Social Forum in Atlanta (Lerner 2014b). It was there that our PB session was asked to join the PD-oriented US Solidarity Economy Network, where we were put into contact with all these other organizations and movements. See Allard et al. 2008.

4. Menser 2005, 2008, 2009, 2014.

5. I do this throughout the book but especially in the last third of Chapters 2, 4, and 5 and in much of Chapter 6 and the Conclusion.

CHAPTER 1

1. I sometimes call each PD view a "route" because although all views within any given framework do not endorse PD (e.g., not all liberals endorse PD), there is a pathway from each view to PD. That is, PD can be justified by each of these frameworks, and PD can be utilized by each of these frameworks in its own problem-solving pursuits.

2. "Watchdog" or "monitory" democracy refers to the civil society–based approach of NGOs that do not have formal power but use persuasion, shaming, and protest to

protect the rights of workers, the environment, women, immigrants, and other groups and change the policy of organizations, whether government or businesses (Young 2000, 154–180; Keane 2009, 721–727). For Keane, such a politics is extraparliamentary, but as a supplement not as a replacement. However, for Keane, monitory democracy is a replacement for assembly democracy because such a PD modality of governance is too tied to the spoken word and face-to-face relations (Keane 2009, 737–739). "Watchdog" and "monitory" are both apt terms to express the spectator aspect of this kind of politics, since it aims at "scrutinizing" power rather than taking or remaking it as PD does (Keane 2009, 688–690). I delve much more into debates about such "civil society" approaches and their differences with PD in Chapter 3 and on deliberative approaches specifically in Chapter 2.

3. On the problems posed by families and tribes for democratic politics and the Greek transtribal polity, see Bookchin [1992] 1995, 38–40, 66–67.

4. Athens was a sizable urban area, even by today's standards: the region around Athens, called Attica, had about 200,000 people (Held 2006, 16–18).

5. Such gatherings took place about forty times a year. The agenda was set by a council of 500 (Keane 2009, 33). See also Van Reybrouck 2017, chapter 4, for more details, especially regarding the Greek version of PD as sortition.

6. Majority voting was rarely employed; instead, a consensus process was used. Consensus is often very superficially understood. For example, Mansbridge defines it as "a form of decision-making in which, after discussion, one or more members on the assembly sum up prevailing sentiment, and if no objections are voiced, this becomes agreed-upon policy" (1980, 32). But what happens if there are objections? There are many different models of consensus, but a general form that is quite common now goes as follows. If someone does object, then someone else tries to clarify the proposal to deal with the objection. If that does not work, attempts are made to modify the proposal to deal with the concerns in the objection. If the objection cannot be resolved by modification (a "friendly amendment" in the lingo of Robert's Rules), there are three possibilities. After hearing more about the reasons for the proposal and how many people support it, the objector may withdraw the objection. If this does not happen, and no modification solved the problem, then the objector has two options: he or she can "block" the proposal, thereby rendering it dead. Or, if the objector does not feel strongly about it, and can live with the proposal being accepted, he or she can "stand aside" and not consent. In such a situation, the objector does not prevent others from carrying out the proposal, but he or she does not abide by it. For a lengthy discussion of many of these issues, see Graeber 2013, 210–232.

7. On the importance of friendship in the Greek polis, see Mansbridge 1980, 9–10, and Schwarzenbach 2013. Schwarzenbach builds upon Aristotle's account to develop a modern view of civic friendship equipped for the contemporary nation-state that is very open to PD in governance (2013, 139, 237–241).

8. However, equality of status does not mean equal influence on decisions (Mansbridge 1980, 11). The underlying premise here is "that of equal worth or equal status which, for the Greeks, is derived from the notion of the *demoi*'s common birth" (Mansbridge 1980, 14). It is not that all were of the same competence, nor that each should have the same amount of power or influence. Even radical democrats like Democritus didn't argue for equality of influence. Mansbridge writes, "Democritus took it for granted that those who could make the greatest contribution to the common good should have the greatest power" (1980, 14).

9. For a detailed account of this process of sortition, see Van Reybrouck 2017, chapter 4.

10. The contemporary version (after the rise of the state and industrialization) of popular democratic administration is articulated with considerable detail by associationism.

11. As one might expect, slavery violates every tenet of PD (more below and in Chapter 4), and is thus not an option. However, one intriguing possibility that emerges in the present economic situation for "freeing up" citizens to do the work of government is that with the massive elimination of jobs due to recent rounds of technological innovation and automation, citizens might use that free time to do governance and/or administration. (See Chapter 5 and the Conclusion.)

12. See Dahl 1971; 1989, 13–23. This is not to say, of course, that PD can work at the level of a large megalopolis or even a small nation-state. We deal with the issue of scale and PD in politics and the economy throughout the subsequent chapters.

13. Indeed, one of the most influential A-PD efforts of the past twenty-five years—the EZLN, or Zapatistas, of Chiapas, Mexico—derives much of its PD practices of assemblies and councils from Indigenous traditions from the Americas (Mentinis 2006, 151–176).

14. Quoted in Held 2006, 12. See Keane 2009, 24–27, for a different view on slavery and Athens.

15. A different, and more relevant, criticism of Athenian democracy is that even if we set aside the fact that only the ruling class participated, Athenian PD worked because of cultural homogeneity and extensive support for regularized face-to-face interaction. Indeed, Athenian democracy required one-mindedness and for citizens to consider each other as friends. All these factors would seem to limit this "unitary" form of PD in much of the present world (see Mansbridge 1980). See Polletta 2002, 171–175, for different problems that arise when "friendship" is the basis of such a unitary model and Warren 1996, 267n3.

16. Following Grinde and Johansen 1991, *Exemplar of Liberty: Native America and the Evolution of Democracy.*

17. Just as my account of Athenian democracy, like all accounts of Athenian democracy, focuses on a particular historical period (506–338 B.C.E.), so does my account of the Haudenosaunee. Here the period in question is more loosely defined but is before the growth and consolidation of the British colonies. Like Athens, Iroquois governance changes throughout its history, especially during the time of the American Revolution, but continues as one of the oldest democracies to this day. I am not discussing the system after 1700. Although some scholars call the system before European contact the "League" and afterward the "Six Nations" or "Confederacy," I will use the term "Iroquoia" (following Mann) or "Iroquois Federation." I prefer "federation" to "confederacy" because of the resonance of the latter with the slaveholding U.S. South, and the convergence of the former with many other PD theorists, including Kropotkin and Bookchin. Also, following numerous Haudenosaunee leaders and scholars, I believe that the Haudenosaunee conception of federation not only influenced the U.S. founders; it has much to offer us in the present moment when deliberating about how to create a governance system that can adequately and innovatively address so much economic inequality, political turmoil, and ecological degradation in a democratic, sustainable, inclusive, and peace-enhancing manner. See Manno (2013) and later in this chapter.

18. The specific "influence story" shows that the Iroquois shaped the Albany Plan, which informed the Articles of Confederation. And, more broadly, that the Iroquois federal structure influenced the eventual U.S. federal structure. For a brief summary, see Young 2007, 21–22; for the book version, see Grinde and Johansen 1982. And for a philosophical treatment of the "influence thesis," see Pratt 2002. Pratt argues that many of the different indigenous nations influenced Europeans during the colonial period, from women's rights to science. And he makes the even more intriguing claim that the first homegrown U.S. philosophical school (pragmatism) was deeply indebted to a variety of views of and encounters with indigenous nations, from the Mohawks and Onondaga to the Huron.

19. Mann explicitly calls the Iroquois governance system a "participatory democracy" (2000, 38–39) and the PD economy "grassroots economics" (212–213).

20. Available at http://www.oswego.edu/library2/archives/digitized_collections/granger/ir.html.

21. Keane mentions the Iroquois twice noting their ability to play "whites" off of one another (Keane 2009, 363) but never discusses their PD practices, nor their influence on the U.S. Constitution. This is odd because he does so much to show the multicultural and multireligious origins of democracy, particularly the importance of Islamic traditions and societies (see also Isakhan and Stockwell 2012). However, he rarely notes the innovations of indigenous peoples. Even more strangely, although Isakhan and Stockwell have four chapters on indigenous democracy, they never mentioned the Iroquois. An exception to all this ignorance is Iris Young. But this too is strange because Young is well known for her critiques of PD! Indeed, she criticizes Bookchin's A-PD decentralized federalism for permitting the racially and/or economically advantaged to seclude themselves (1990, 249–250). And she questions civil society and associationist forms for not having enough faith in the state's abilities for coordination and protecting minority rights (Young 2000, 180–195). I think that Young raises many appropriate questions concerning PD, and we deal with them throughout the next chapters. But she remained quite state-centric until a later collection of essays, where she was more overtly searching for new models for our global cosmopolitan ripped-with-strife era. Here she identified Iroquois ideas and practices as an innovative source for postcolonial thinking and recognizing the agency of non-European peoples (Young 2007, 15–16). Young also notes, as have many others, how European enlightenment figures—who of course have profoundly shaped so many with their work on freedom and equality—were themselves significantly impacted by indigenous peoples in the United States (Young 2007, 20–24). A detailed work that shows how other indigenous peoples have impacted those same thinkers, including Diderot, Rousseau, and Kant, is Munthu 2003.

22. As with most (all?!) empires, ecological sustainability was not an espoused goal in Athens and, instead, expansion and intensive resource use were (Dahl 1971, 89).

23. There is some debate about the date. But 1142 seems the time, though others claim a later time (Mann 2000, 39, 95, 126). For more on the peace aspect, see Graeber 2001, 124–129.

24. The Tuscarora joined later as the federation expanded culturally, politically, and economically (Mann 2000, 41).

25. "Popular sovereignty" referred to the power of the people in each of these nations and combined in the federation. "Health" included both physical and mental health and domestic peace. And "righteousness" referred to the norms that guide those holding positions of political power (Mann 2000, 163).

26. We will explore more contemporary and nonindigenous views of this in the discussion of "social reproduction participatory democracy," or S-PD, later in the chapter.

27. Marx popularized this slogan in his "Critique of the Gotha Program," but it dates back to Louis Blanc and others (Graeber 2013, 293–294).

28. Available at http://www.tolatsga.org/iro.html.

29. For example, calling the Six Nations a matriarchy is misleading since it was not hierarchical in the usual sense (Mann 2000, 161).

30. This "postsovereign" model of governance holds important lessons for foreign policy and global cooperation in general (Young 2007, 26–38) but particularly with respect to the ecological crisis (Manno 2013). We return to this issue in my Conclusion.

31. While historians have written about New England Town Hall meetings, philosophers, even democratic theorists, have paid little to no attention to them. Curiously, even John Dewey, that great advocate of face-to-face democracy, did not draw much on the town hall meeting tradition even though he was from Vermont (Zimmerman 1999, 29). Such meetings continue to this day, though in somewhat reduced form, and are discussed in my next chapter in the context of participatory budgeting and other forms of political PD. For an in-depth sociological, political science account, see Bryan 2004.

32. For Green and Cornell (2005), the United States is *not* a republic but a "representative oligarchy." The lack of "respect for the law" and the Constitution is a key reason. See also Brennan and Ganguly 2009 and Lessig 2011 on the deformation of elections and Gilens and Page 2014 on the lack of power of nonelites on policy formation.

33. For more on them and other economic PD efforts, see Curl 2012 and my Chapters 3, 4, and 5.

34. For more on Dubois and the African American tradition of economic and social PD, see Gordon Nembhard 2014.

35. See Mattson 1998, 129–130, and Keane 2009, 351–358, on the Progressive Era. Zimmerman's detailing of the decline of PD from the early 1900s to the 1960s is fascinating, especially in political science and political philosophy where it is so disparaged (Zimmerman 1986, 30–54). For a PD take on what's happening in Europe during this same period, see Medearis 2004 on the council movements.

36. Pateman argues that Schumpeter's critique of what he calls "classical democracy" is a straw man argument (Pateman 1970, 5–8) and Held agrees (Held 2006, 152–156).

37. Schumpeter did not require universal suffrage; states could have racial and religious restrictions (Pateman 1970, 4–5).

38. Of course the history of elections shows that they have frequently played this kind of antidemocratic and elitist role (Van Reybrouck 2017, chapter 1).

39. Hilmer (2010) cites Kaufman but the great majority cite Pateman 1970 as the originary work including Held's influential 2006. Many classics of democratic theory, however, do not discuss participatory democracy or Pateman at all (e.g., Gutmann and Thompson 1996) and many reviews of the field do not even treat it as an actually existing view (Shapiro 2003).

40. For a very detailed PD analysis of social contract theory and the illegitimacy of this transfer, see Ellerman 2015, who has constructed a position based on a tradition from Martin Luther through Spinoza and Frances Hutcheson. For more on Ellerman's overall view and how it pertains to labor and property, see my Chapter 4.

41. See also Cunningham 2001, 123–126, for Rousseau's importance to PD accounts.

42. Although Pateman never cites Native Americans much less Iroquoia, Rousseau was influenced by reports coming from the colonies about the indigenous nations of America. See Munthu 2003, 32–33.

43. Interestingly, economic PD is then a nonelitist way to make the masses less prone to the fascists and demagogues that Schumpeter feared and used to justify his adversarial elitist model of democracy. (See above.)

44. We will pursue this topic with David Schweickart's account of such a transformation and debates thereof in my Chapter 4.

45. This is what Pateman calls "the philosophy of groups" (Pateman 1970, 37). I will refer to this view as associationist PD (see the six routes taxonomy later in this chapter).

46. But he does not go as far as Kropotkin's anarchist antistatism. More in the section below.

47. The associationism of Cohen and Rogers (1995) and Warren (1996, 2000) is less robust than Hirst's since it eschews the economic and focuses on political and social associations in civil society.

48. We are not here talking about stateless peoples as refugees but as those peoples who chose to rule themselves without the state form. See Barclay [1982] 1990 and Scott 2009.

49. Kropotkin is more frequently acknowledged in the histories of geography and evolutionary biology than he is in philosophy, despite several works that were well received in his day and influential at that time.

50. For more on federalism and its history from the anarchist perspective, see May 1994, 57–64, and Lynd 1971.

51. A version of this confederal model is in play in Japan with respect to the Seikatsu Cooperative Union. See my Chapter 5.

52. If one were to update Pateman's perspective of 1970, the most obvious trajectory would be to look at the literature on worker cooperatives and see how her questions played out. The case of the Mondragon Corporation—the largest economic democracy program in the world—would be most obvious to consider, and I do this in my Chapter 4.

53. Cunningham (2001) and Held (2006) give PD a chapter or so, but most devote very little consideration, or even nothing, as Hilmer notes (2010). Shapiro's 2003 book is typical of those that ignore PD.

54. For PD takes on other key movements of the time, see Bookchin 1995, 111–116, on the Paris Commune and Bookchin 1994 on the Spanish Civil War. On the worker movements of that period and into the present, see Ness and Azzellini 2011.

55. In between those dates are a range of exemplary efforts in both theory and practice across the Americas and Europe. See Katsiaficas 1983, [1997] 2006. Asia gets in the game a little later (Katsiaficas 2012).

56. See May 2010, Muñoz Ramirez 2008, and Grubacic and Lynd 2008.

57. Two major recent contributions have sought to further explore the diverse range of traditions of democratic expression, especially historically and culturally; they are John Keane's massive monograph (2009) and Isakhan and Stockwell's anthology (2012). However, each is a theory of democracy broadly construed and neither focuses systematically on PD nor explicates an actual theory of it. Interestingly, though, Keane does discuss PD as a view but then rejects it in favor of what he calls "monitory democracy" (see my Chapter 3). Confusingly, he wrongly classifies participatory budgeting as monitory democracy. (See my Chapter 2.)

58. For more on the tradition of economic democracy, see the beginning of my Chapter 4. For the solidarity economy framework, see my Chapter 3.

59. For an extremely detailed history of the 1960s New Left, which is very insightful on how PD was formulated, understood, justified, practiced, and critiqued in the nitty-gritty of contentious cultural politics, see Miller 1987.

60. Another important intimate history and ethnography of PD movements is Polletta 2002, but it does not develop a normative account of participatory democracy.

61. Contra Mansbridge 1980 and Dahl 1989, 18–19.

62. See also Cunningham's account (2001, 123–141). Katsiaficas puts forward a different periodization because he sees more global interconnections emerging from "1968" onward (Katsiaficas 1983, [1997] 2006, 2004). Yuen, Burton-Rose and Katsiaficas (2004) also further document such continuities. My periodization is less about the movements, however, and more about the theories.

63. The "basic income guarantee" (BIG) is a government program that ensures that "no one's income will fall below the level necessary to meet their basic needs for any reason." Well-known philosopher Bertrand Russell held such a view in the early 1900s and BIG has been argued for ever since in many different contexts. The most oft-cited best example of such a program is the Alaska Permanent Fund. Available at http://www.usbig.net/whatisbig.php.

64. Santos's work (2005a) and (2006a) is pivotal in PD studies but his focus as he states is more on the "reinvention of the social sciences," and less on political philosophy, and he does not present a normative account of PD systematically (Santos 2005b xxii–xxv, xxx–xxxi).

65. See also the excellent interview with EJ pioneer Carl Anthony by Yuen, Bunin, and Stroshane 1997.

66. On precarious labor and the precariat, see Hardt and Negri 2009, 146–147, 245–246.

67. The "A" should also invoke the circle A of anarchism, which comes from Proudhon who understood anarchism as a kind of order that is voluntary and is generated without the threat of violence from rulers (Graeber 2013, 187–192).

68. On dignity, see Holloway [2002] 2005, 212–215.

69. The phrase is the title of Holloway's 2010 book.

70. One may still take the money or assistance, says Holloway, just as we can fight to take over the state as we try to get past it. These contradictions are part of the nature of the moment. But we should never put our faith in the state, nor aim to be institutionalized within it. That form of "participatory democracy" is dangerous since it covers over the contradictions, or, worse, leads to an institutionalization that diminishes our power "to do" together (Holloway [2002] 2005, 235–236).

71. Here A-PD is in line with Macpherson's take on liberal democracy and modifies a claim we made earlier about political philosophy from an anarchist perspective: democratic theory is really "democracy-in-the-capitalist-state theory" (MacPherson 1997, 21). That is, it treats the capitalist system as given. That's the condition for it being doable, or "realist(ic)." As Dallmayr puts it, channeling MacPherson "'liberal democracy' signifies the fusion of political equality with capitalist market relations and the ensuing class structure, that is, the liaison of universal franchise with economic inequality and heterogeneity" (Dallmayr 1986, 147).

72. We shall deal with the consumer end of this equation in Chapter 5, and much more on government bureaucracy in Chapter 6.

73. See footnote 40.

74. An anarchist slogan seen on banners at various protests and events. For a more historical perspective, see Barclay [1982] 1990 and Scott 2009.

75. The "disobedienti" or disobedients were a famous direct action antagonist group in the Global Justice Movement (Notes from Nowhere, 2003, 202–204).

76. The key figures of S-PD in my view are Mies, Bennholdt-Thomsen, Shiva, Maathai, and Federici. As I repeatedly note, there are overlaps between A-PD and S-PD. Two figures

who are in both are Vandana Shiva and Sylvia Federici. Federici criticizes dominant views of A-PD for their lack of a feminist analysis of social reproduction (Federici 2004, 13). For an incisive analysis of tensions around social reproduction, participatory democracy, and the gendered division of labor, see Peller's 2016 essay about the understudied Oaxaca (Mexico) Commune of 2006.

77. Mutuality and reciprocity are values in all the key figures (Shiva 2005, 17) and the concept figures prominently in Gould, which is unusual for purveyors of liberal PD. She devotes a whole chapter to it in her 1988, 133–159, work. Also see Gould 2014, 111–113.

78. For reports on Bangladesh, see Akhter 2001, on Kenya, globalization from below, antagonism, and PD, as well as works on the Greenbelt movement, see Turner and Brownhill 2001, and on Polynesia see Dé Ishtar 1994. Interestingly, A-PD made many international links too in the 1970s and 1980s, but primarily within first-world countries. This changed though in the 1990s with the rise of many innovative and robust Latin American movements. See essays in Yuen, Burton-Rose, and Katsiaficas 2004.

79. Maathai and the Greenbelt Movement are named as S-PD in many of the view's central texts including Turner and Brownhill in Bennholdt-Thomsen, Faraclas, von Werlhof 2001, 115 and Mies and Shiva 1993, 3, 83.

80. On the Mau Mau anticolonial uprising and its links to S-PD, see Turner and Brownhill 2001.

81. The scenes of popular protest, conflict, and radical democracy recall those of the Arab Spring, especially Gezi Park in Istanbul with Turkey's Erdogan as a Moi type figure (Hammond and Angell 2013).

82. One element in the literature on GBM that is missing are details on the particular mechanisms and processes that they employed. We know that they were participatory, decentralized, and empowered women as individuals and groups (Maathai [1985] 2006; Michaelson 1994), but we don't have info on the size of the assemblies, whether they used affinity groups or other kinds of associations, how powers were distributed and so on.

83. Environmental justice (EJ) is now morphing into climate justice, but for this section, I will stick to the EJ label because most of the writings and research on these movements are on EJ, and climate justice is too new, not to mention understudied. But do see Dawson 2010.

84. This is the EPA definition as cited in Lawson 2008, 1.

85. The list of principles is available at http://www.ejnet.org/ej/principles.html.

86. Insofar as environmental racism causes degradation of health and even premature death, the medical notion of informed consent becomes a powerful tool to defend the community as a kind of body. See Shrader-Frechette 2002, 28–29.

87. Interestingly, EJ has sought to apply these principles not just when dealing with the government but also when lobbying the government and doing public outreach. That is, EJ groups have sought to have PD *within* the environmental movement (Schlosberg 1999, 17–24; Lawson 2008).

88. For a range of case studies touching upon these issues, see Bullard 2007, Hunold and Young 1998, and Walker 2012. Also, Dawson charts how these EJ movements have adapted to the new politics of climate change (Dawson 2010, 321–328).

89. Schlosberg and Carruthers also see the Indigenous framework as less about rights and distribution and more about community capabilities. This PD "community capacity" approach is also taking root in socioecological resilience frameworks. See Ramasubramanian et al. 2016.

90. A key political configuration here has been the International Environmental Network (Schlosberg and Carruthers 2010, 12; Whyte 2016).

91. While my use of the phrase "collective determination" is nearly equivalent to what most call self-determination, I use the term "collective" rather than "self" to emphasize two interrelated phenomena: PD always involves a group, and that group often does not have the kind of integration or integrity that merits the term "self." Second, even in what might seem to be a quite homogeneous and stable long-term group, there are always differences that undermine the notion that there is a strongly shared subjectivity present (Young 1990, 228–232). The term "collective" is more inclusive and better able to avoid the pitfalls of such a unitary understanding of "self."

92. My view of maximal democracy was first laid out in Menser 2005 and then more fully articulated in my 2008 work. It was modified slightly with respect to principle #4 in Menser 2009. The difference between all of those and the account in this present work is that I have combined what were principles #2 and #3 into principle #2, and principle #3 has been added to more explicitly state the inequality reduction dimension. And, principle #4 is now understood more explicitly as a view on solidarity.

93. For example, deliberation, facilitation, and public speaking skills are useful if not necessary in such settings. Some groups may also use consensus or particular modes of conflict resolution that require specific training. More in the sections below and in Chapter 2.

94. I do not specify a full list of capabilities but do require that deliberation be on any list. On my account capabilities can be individual or group (social). Indeed, for PD, group capability development is essential. While this is not a favored view in political liberalism (Young 1990, 228), one does see this view in indigenous philosophy and my work is definitely influenced by those accounts, in particular, Corntassel 2008. For an overview of this approach, see Schlosberg and Carruthers 2010.

95. Material benefits could be goods, money, assets, etc. This condition is meant to be general (hence the inclusion of "social"), but what it tends to eliminate are discussion groups, manifestos, and many a charette. Even if discussion groups, or say book clubs, allow members to make their own rules, learn a few capabilities, and interconnect with other groups, if there were no material or social benefits, then they might be good in many ways, but they would not count as PD.

96. For an excellent analysis of Unitarianism and PD in historical context, see Heller-Wagner 1995.

97. Constructed in part with Alexandra Sullivan.

98. For the case of the siting of a waste facility, there should be a regional framework in play so that alternative sites can be considered (Hunold and Young 1998, 91).

99. EJ often talks about procedural equity and meaningful participation, but the actual processes often look like consultation (Schlosberg 1999, 163).

100. This seemingly outdated essay is a gem. Arnstein worked for city and federal governments amid the tumult of the 1960s and tried to create processes in which groups excluded by government policy could get adequate services. And, she is upfront about what PD should be about: power. Available at http://www.aacom.org/news-and-events/publications/iome/2015/july-august-2015/Arnstein-bio.

101. Another category she uses is "therapy" (Arnstein 1969, 218–219). Participation as "therapy" is more often called "co-option" now and occurs when community members are added to some council or board to secure their consent for some policy or decision. This happens on governmental and university committees or councils. At my own university of CUNY, the administration recently changed the general education

requirements even though the great majority of the faculty were opposed. The administration was able to do this in part because they handpicked or pressured faculty and students who were on key committees that oversaw the process. When faculty cried foul, the administration replied that faculty were involved in the formulation of the policy and had approved it. One can see this kind of politics play out on boards, committees, and councils of many kinds (Hogness 2012).

102. For an alternate scheme, see Cunningham 2001, 128, and for participation processes as they play out in environmental management, see Reed's very comprehensive and illuminating literature review (2008). For best practices, see Nobachi and Leighninger 2015.

103. This happened with NYC's PlaNYC (Dawson 2010, 326–327).

104. There is still a role for public hearings and meetings and in those cases they can be done in better or worse ways. For ways of doing them well from a PD normative perspective, see Center for Advances in Public Engagement 2008. For more on a PD alternative to public hearings and town hall meetings, see my Chapter 2 on PB and Chapter 6 on social-public partnerships.

105. To be fair, we also need to get the perspective of elected representatives or governmental officials who do seek public input. They often see the public as "ill informed and too busy" (Immerwahr et al. 2013, 2). Options to this problem are discussed in my Chapter 6.

106. For an excellent argument against universalist solutions and for a PD defense of models that seem weak because they are only "partially" successful, see Santos 2004.

CHAPTER 2

1. In this chapter, we will examine PB as it operates in governmental jurisdictions: primarily cities and districts within cities, but also states within nation-states. But PB also has been used in public housing, in schools, and within NGOs. See www.participatorybudgeting.org.

2. As we shall see, "directly decide" is not the clearest of concepts when it comes to PB. While PB is always more than consultation, it is often less than full decision-making authority.

3. Analysts vary widely in their estimates of the number of existing PBs. Sintomer et al. identify "between 1,269 and 2,778 traceable experiments" but note there are many for which they have no info (Sintomer et al. 2014, 11). Cabannes (2014) puts the number at 1,700. That is near the low end for Sintomer et al. and out of caution I will use that number.

4. Much of the PB literature looks at the process and the politics; much less looks at the *products* of the process (Cabannes 2014, 8); and very little of it systematically analyzes the norms that justify and structure it and whether or not actual PBs fulfill these norms. For example, Cabannes (2004) is unusual because it explicitly uses the PD framework to characterize PB's operations, but it focuses on the mechanisms employed, not the norms embodied in these mechanisms (Cabannes 2004). Baiocchi, Heller, and Silva (2011) do excellent work on the process, but they do not look at the impact of the projects. Wampler (2007) does both to some extent, as does Cabannes, but neither systematically presents, much less evaluates or justifies, the normative frameworks. Sintomer et al. do get into the different political frameworks that drive and structure PB (Sintomer, Herzberg, and Allegretti 2013; Sintomer et al. 2014), but the approach

is not normative and their taxonomy, while insightful in parts (e.g., on the different role of associations, see below), is unwieldy. I believe the tripartite division I employ— neoliberal efficiency, good governance, and participatory democracy—is more clearly defined and easier to apply.

5. In this chapter, I use the terms maximal democracy and participatory democracy interchangeably unless otherwise noted. Put another way, maxD is my view of PD. (See my Chapter 1.)

6. See Chapter 1.

7. "Participatory budgeting" is a translation of this (Brazilian) Portuguese phrase.

8. This account is drawn from Santos 2005c, 321–322, Wampler 2007, Baiocchi 2003, and Pateman 2012.

9. They are: transportation and circulation; education and leisure; culture; health and social welfare; economic development; and city organization, urban and environmental development (Santos 2005c, 316).

10. Baiocchi 2003, 65. The power and autonomy of PB took a major hit in 2004, when the PT lost the mayoralty. I do not cover the controversies surrounding Porto Alegre's PB in this chapter. For more on this, see Baiocchi, Braathen, and Teixeira 2012.

11. Although there are precedents for PB in the United States, they did not play a role in the launching or even the motivation to do PB from the standpoint of PBP. After launching PBs in the United States, we would hear about occasional other PD efforts to allocate funds. But they were ad hoc processes or one-shot deals. The only repeating PD effort is a famous one, of course, the New England town hall meetings. (See my Chapter 1.) But for a variety of reasons, that practice did not figure in our justification for doing PB nor in our formulation of the process. The most obvious reason is that that radicalism was of small towns, and rather homogeneous populations, and trying to use that model to convince urban populations, not to mention urban elected officials, to turn over millions of dollars of capital funds didn't make much sense. U.S. PB then is a product of counterhegemonic globalization, not U.S. PD radicalism. (See Menser 2005, Baez and Hernandez 2012.)

12. Available at www.pbnyc.org.

13. All projects must cost at least $35,000, have a "useful life" of at least five years, and "involve the construction, reconstruction, acquisition or installation of a physical public improvement" (Kasdan, Markman, and Convey 2014, 7).

14. For more on youth participation, see Su (2012, 6–9). The voting age in some districts is now fourteen (Hagelskamp et al. 2016, 6).

15. PB was initiated in the United States by a couple of academic types (including yours truly) working with a few community-based organizations who then formed a nonprofit. (See the Introduction, footnote 2.) In the United States, the political parties have not jumped on board, though there have been some formal endorsements. At the federal level, the White House Office of Science and Technology Policy endorsed PB in their "open government" report (Lerner 2014b, 33–36).

16. For more on the considerable evolution in 2014–2016 of PB in NYC and across the United States and Canada, see Hagelskampf, Silliman, and Schleifer 2016.

17. For his 2014 report, Cabannes uses the definition from "Uribatam de Souza, one of the initiators of PB, as it conceptually embraces most of those that followed" (Cabannes 2014, 8 fn2).

18. Indeed, Celso Daniel, the mayor of Santo Andre, was likely to work on this PB model at the national level but was murdered by "drug mafias threatened by the new open method of government" (Wainwright 2003, 47).

19. Given intensifying inequality in terms of both assets and income, which are largely combined with, if not a direct product of, tax cuts, this might be the most important consequence of a PB given the current economic crisis.

20. Many PBs in Dominican Republic and Peru tend to be PB lite, though, and are dominated by their national governments (Sintomer, Herzberg, and Allegretti 2013, 35; see also Cabannes 2014, 21–23).

21. They also note the resemblance of these PBs to the "constituent assemblies in Bolivia and Venezuela" (Sintomer et al. 2012, 20).

22. Josh Lerner makes this point tangible in his in-depth analysis contrasting a citywide PB in the culturally homogeneous Rosario (Argentina) with a PB in a huge public housing authority in the cosmopolitan metropolis of Toronto (Canada) (Lerner 2014b, 49–51).

23. That these benefits are measurable is crucial, but also it is crucial that they are actually measured! The unusual persistence, evolution, and spread of PB is due in part to the fact that practitioners early on in Porto Alegre set up a research center to study it (CIDADE) (Cabannes 2004, 27). For a sense of the research team in North America, see Hagelskamp, Silliman, and Schleifer 2016, 3.

24. In the case of sewage and water infrastructure, it is fairly easy to understand if new proposals are working work, but for many other forms of service provision (e.g., education) it takes years of PB, and then years of study after the projects are completed to effectively analyze whether a project was efficacious and/or benefited wide sectors of the public (Touchton and Wampler 2014, 1451).

25. For more on the differences between deliberative democracy and PD, see Hilmer 2010. He also goes into the histories of both views.

26. The availability of research limits what can be said here. For example, "Most of the existing literature and research focuses on the political and social contributions that PB is bringing to social justice and participatory democracy. Much less work quantifies and qualifies the tangible benefits that PB brings (or not) to common citizens in their day-to-day life" (Cabannes 2014, 8).

27. Hence the "*" after each principle's number.

28. For purposes of this operationalized reconstruction, I have split maxD#2: the capabilities part goes with maxD#1* because it's about capabilities that increase collective determination. But the governance system's response to the processes of maxD#1 is construed as a "political benefit" and the actual projects as "material benefits" so they are in maxD#2*.

29. In year three, there were 333 delegates in NYC PB out of 18,000 total participants (1,600 attended assemblies, 16,000 plus voted) (Kasdan, Markman, and Convey 2014, 16).

30. What they call "multistakeholder participation," number four in their taxonomy (Sintomer et al. 2012, 23–24).

31. This large-scale intersection of planning, participation, power, the government, and the economy is the focus of work by Alperovitz, Schweickart, and Malleson. For more, see my Chapters 5 and 6 and the Conclusion.

32. The funding of a mural and dog park in the forty-ninth ward of Chicago caused controversy because in part more pressing needs for programs for youths and violence reduction were not eligible for funding (Clark 2014).

33. For more on Baiocchi's earlier take on this, see Baiocchi 2003, 57–64, and 2005, 49–70.

34. And here we are not even addressing those CSOs who might be participatory but are committed to an unjust goal (e.g., hate groups).

35. There is a history of this kind of problematic that is specific to Latin America. See Keane's discussion of the rise of representative democracy and *pactismo* (Keane 2009, 407).

36. For an excellent accounting of this conversation, which builds upon the perspectives of Zibechi and Holloway with respect to movements in Argentina, Greece, and Venezuela, see Sitrin 2015.

37. For a comprehensive analysis of the "multidirectionality" of governance processes by decentralizing states, see Hooghe and Marks 2003.

38. In an intriguing comparison, Baiocchi, Heller, and Silva note that PD movements fared much better in Brazil than in South Africa postapartheid in part because the African National Congress (South Africa's dominant post-apartheid political party), however radical, inherited a hierarchical and well-developed state apparatus from the apartheid state. In between was India where a political party was able to create a more participatory social-public milieu at the (sub)state level of Kerala (Baiocchi, Heller, and Silva 2011, 151).

39. "In between the radical autonomy of Diadema and Joao Monlevade and the more dependent Gravataí was Camaragibe. Here there was a 'long chain of sovereignty' that included many actors in the process from both the state and civil society. In this case, some groups were co-opted by the state, while others took on state level functions" (Baiocchi, Heller, and Silva 2011, 115).

40. And the economy! See my next three chapters.

41. Note that in the United States, PD activists are much more concerned with the private sector's dominance of CSOs; that is, the sway that corporations and wealthy individuals and foundations have in setting the agenda of nonprofits through their funding mechanisms (grants, etc.). Hence the emergence of the noncomplimentary phrase, the "non-profit industrial complex" (INCITE! 2009).

42. This is also the view of social reproduction PD. See my Chapter 1 and more examples in Chapters 4 and 5.

43. In Chapter 6, I argue that such disarticulation can lead to the formation of a community-driven relationship with (part of) the state. I call such a formation "social-public."

44. As noted above, Cabannes 2014 is an exception.

45. For a survey of views on the state and antistatism, and governance, see Smith 2009. For more on the scrambling of the categories of PD and representative models of government in related contexts, including but not limited to PB, see Selee and Peruzzotti 2009. Elements of the claim that PD PB's can produce a novel model of governance can be found in Wampler 2007, Stortone 2010, Touchton and Wampler 2014, Baiocchi, Heller, and Silva 2011, Cabannes 2014, and Sintomer et al. 2013. But none gives a detailed account of the full dynamics of this new form of governance and how it functions in relation to the state, civil society, and the economic spheres. Also, none fully spells out this dynamic with respect to the PD norms that I have been discussing. On the norms, Baiocchi, Heller, and Silva's 2011 work is comprehensive and insightful but they don't focus on the impact of projects on economic development. Cabannes 2012 treats the latter but does not give a detailed account or justification of the norms. Stortone 2010 gives a more political philosophical treatment, but at a much more general level—without attention to the specific mechanisms and relationships that are so wonderfully discussed in Baiocchi, Heller, and Silva 2011.

46. Of course autonomists such as Holloway and Zibechi favor "horizontal" as a description of this kind of intensely egalitarian PD notion of power. See Sitrin 2006 and 2012. But, because the state is involved, and it is still in part, to say the least, hierarchical, then the up/down dimension must be incorporated.

47. In reference to PB, the "nonstate space" phrase comes from Dutra, the mayor of Porto Alegre who developed PB. Dutra feared the domination of society by the socialist state, and instead wanted to "civilize" the state. Wampler himself takes a critical stance on the concept (Wampler 2007, 113).

CHAPTER 3

1. In practice, while I think it is true that econD favors more social-public and participatory schemes, exceptions are granted. In practice, there are privately owned large firms that realize many of the values of econD (sometimes called "high road" firms) (Lewis and Swinney 2008, 36–37). And, there are some central government operations that are econD because they allow for meaningful community participation in management. See Chapter 6.

2. This literature review, though, is not meant to be comprehensive, and it is biased toward those that have explicit links to a participatory democracy view. I do not explore market socialist views for example outside of Schweickart.

3. EconD's rollercoaster trajectory is similar to that of the rise and fall and rise again of PD movements in general, as discussed in my Chapter 1.

4. I discussed the "empowered participatory governance" view, which is generated by members of the Real Utopias crew, in the context of democratic theory and PB in Chapter 2. It should be noted that Wright and the Real Utopias conferences and anthologies were crucial for developing a theoretical model for PD across sectors and models—including PB and basic income (Ackerman, Alstott, and van Parijs 2006)—and with case studies from across continents (particularly Brazil, India, and the United States). See also Bowles and Gintis 1999, Cohen and Rogers 1995, and Roemer and Wright 1996. This group also put together research teams across movements and countries, which was crucial for both critically comparing views and learning from failures and developing better models. For example, Boa Santos who was part of the Real Utopias group also collaborated with others across four continents in his *Another Production Is Possible* and *Democratizing Democracy* research projects and PD PB researcher Baiocchi's early work appeared in Wright 2010.

5. In this characterization, I largely follow Howard, Dubb, and McKinley (2014), but my scheme is more expansive. For example, I include what many would regard as more communitarian projects such as indigenous nations and bioregionalism, which they do not. And they focus more on institutional forms associated with advanced capitalist states such as the United States including Community Development Corporations. I generally include everything they do, but I am less inclined to consider nonprofits as such because, even though I would agree they fall under econD because of their redistributive-empowerment and capability building efforts re: inequality and discrimination especially in the context of "market failure," they are *often* NOT PD in any meaningful way as I note in Chapter 2.

6. By socialism here I mean "actually existing socialism" or state capitalism (Wolff 2012, 79–84).

7. For a comparative analysis of the diverse approaches (and successes and failures) of nationalization programs in socialist and capitalist states after World War II, see Cumbers 2012, 11–37.

8. For theoretical takes on the contradictions and outright incoherence of the notion of a capitalist totality, see Gibson-Graham, 1996, especially Chapters 2, 3, and 10. For empirical arguments backing the idea that even the present capitalist system is made up of many different economies, capitalist and noncapitalist, see Gibson-Graham 1996, 174–223. For the related, but distinct, discussion about the role of the state (and the public) in supposedly capitalist states, see Cumbers 2012.

9. My approach converges in many ways with that of McDonald and Ruiters analyses of "actually existing states" in their work of 2012c, 161–175.

10. This was a favorite case of PD and econD advocates including Pateman (1970) and Cook and Morgan (1971).

11. Available at http://en.wikipedia.org/wiki/List_of_socialist_states.

12. He also claims "But all is not well with the neoliberal state, and it is for this reason that it appears to be either a transitional or an unstable political form" (Harvey 2005, 78–79). We explore this theme in my Chapter 6.

13. Available at http://en.wikipedia.org/wiki/Denmark#Economy.

14. Available at http://en.wikipedia.org/wiki/United_Arab_Emirates#Economy.

15. Available at http://www.doingbusiness.org/rankings.

16. For differences with respect to environmental regulation and state approaches to domestic and global economy, see Eckersley 2004, 65–70.

17. See Gibson-Graham 1996 for much more on the notion of economic diversity and the failure of the binary discussed above.

18. Because of these and other problems, some within econD reject markets altogether (e.g., Albert 2004) or in large measure (Fotopoulos 1998), but most do not. (See discussion of Schweickart in particular below.) See also Panayotakis 2011, 113–128.

19. A related reason for the public provision of these goods is that it is hard to charge for many of them because of what is called the "free rider" problem (Malleson 2014, 96).

20. For more on the privatization of water systems and its limits, see my Chapter 6.

21. See my Chapter 6 for much more on public service provision, the state, and PD.

22. There are positive externalities as well. Someone who plants a front yard flower garden may benefit neighbors because those persons value the beauty of it and if it feeds pollinators then other neighbors may benefit from the ecological services of those pollinators. See also my Chapter 6.

23. The "commons" so crucial for S-PD has largely been enclosed; but we'll reopen it in Chapter 6!

24. What about unions? If one is a member of a union that might increase one's bargaining power, but unions by themselves are not econD nor, of course, PD, especially since the management clause "reserves essential powers and decision-making ability to management alone" (Malleson 2014, 31–32).

25. Indeed, it's fascinating how many *businesses* do not heed Friedman's advice since they lobby politicians and appeal to the moral inclinations of their consumers. As we see in the sections below, CSR is for many part of a branding strategy, but Friedman overtly opposed this (M. Friedman [1970] 1997)!

26. The Obama administration has supported such initiatives for these kinds of reasons. See http://www.whitehouse.gov/blog/2011/03/25/building-partnerships-between -community-colleges-and-businesses.

27. However, Lee does note that the causal relationship between corporate financial performance and corporate social responsibility "has not yet been unequivocally verified through empirical studies" (Lee 2008, 64).

28. http://www.mcdonalds.com/us/en/our_story/our_communities/rmhc.html.

29. Note Jamali 2008 here.

30. Lee argues that some powerful purchasers can also do this. Here he cites the U.S. government as an example of a purchaser that has promoted worker rights because it is more subject to public scrutiny (Lee 2008, 62). But this is an odd case insofar as this entity is both a stakeholder (as purchaser) and a publicly accountable entity (government).

31. This led to the passing of the Sullivan principles. Intriguingly, both Lee and Compa (2008) note that even though CSR is not hard law it often relies on hard law and legislation or is greatly strengthened or weakened by various sorts of legislation.

32. Their concept is derived from Bohman: "The concept of deliberative democracy covers 'any one of a family of views according to which the public deliberation of free and equal citizens is the core of legitimate political decision-making and self-government' (Bohman, 1998, p. 401)" (Palazzo and Scherer 2006, 80).

33. For more on the EPG view and its relationship to PD, see my Chapters 1, 2, and 6.

34. We return to the "competence" critique of the state in Chapter 6.

35. "However, we believe that deliberative democracy delivers a better starting point for a communicative interpretation of CSR than Habermas because it lessens the problem of utopianism and, furthermore, takes the *direct practice of life* [. . .] as the starting and reference point of theoretical efforts, thus advocating the *primacy of democracy to philosophy* (Habermas, 1996)" (Scherer and Palazzo 2007, 1109).

36. Available at http://www.fsc.org/vision_mission.html.

37. Available at http://www.fsc.org/about-fsc.html?&L=8.

38. Available at http://www.fsc.org/governance.html.

39. "US Airways, Shutterfly Drop Sustainable Forestry Initiative," available at http://www.environmentalleader.com/2012/05/16/us-airways-pitney-bowes-drop-sustainable-forestry-initiative/; "7 Major Corporations Dump Shady Sustainable Forestry Initiative," available at http://www.care2.com/causes/7-major-corporations-dump-shady-sustainable-forestry-initiative.html#ixzz1v9DsG6qX.

40. "Sweden's Green Veneer Hides Unsustainable Logging Practices," Erik Hoffner, Yale Environment 360, December 1, 2011.

41. Available at http://www.fsc-watch.org/.

42. Available at https://en.wikipedia.org/wiki/2012_Dhaka_fire.

43. Available at http://www.workersrights.org/university/coc.asp.

44. Statistics are from 2015. See http://www.mondragon-corporation.com/eng/mondragon-in-2015-growth-in-jobs-turnover-and-earnings/.

45. See the reports by AFL-CIO Pay Watch, available at: http://edit.aflcio.org/Corporate-Watch/Paywatch-2014.

46. Within MC, pay ranges are set not by individual co-ops but by the Cooperative Congress, which is the democratically elected governing body of the entire federation of co-ops.

47. Though this facet will earn the praise of S-PD advocates, we examine an S-PD critique of MC in Chapter 4 and especially Chapter 5.

CHAPTER 4

1. The original version of the Rochdale principles (1937) are 1. Open membership; 2. Democratic control (one person, one vote); 3. Distribution of surplus in proportion to trade; 4. Payment of limited interest on capital; 5. Political and religious neutrality;

6. Cash trading (no credit extended); and 7. Promotion of education. Available at http://en.wikipedia.org/wiki/Rochdale_Principles.

2. Available at http://ica.coop/en/whats-co-op/co-operative-identity-values-principles.

3. Mondragon's principles (discussed in Chapter 3) are very close to these.

4. It is worth noting here that Dahl might take issue with participatory budgeting since it includes minors (ages 14 and over) and "transients" (one need only show that one is a resident at the time of the vote in the PB process), and there is no "mental health" test. See my Chapter 2.

5. Or "overproductive," since it creates all sorts of surpluses, good and bad (e.g., waste, pollution).

6. This distinguishes Dahl and econD views from traditional social democratic positions (including Rawls) (Malleson 2014, 122–124, 204–210).

7. Note, for Dahl, "In giant firms, where an assembly would suffer all the infirmities of direct democracy on an excessively large scale, a representative government would have to be created" (Dahl 1985, 119).

8. For Dahl, private property is an important right, but it should not override other freedoms or undermine democracy. Mayer notes that Dahl seems to favor a view similar to McMahon who argues that even if we think property is a moral right, it doesn't follow that ownership by itself has a "sufficient moral license to confer authority on managers" (Mayer 2001, 231). For Mayer, what Dahl wants to "take from capital is not the right to control property but the power to command labor" (Mayer 2001, 232).

9. Dahl's critique here is too quick and shallow, and we will return to social ownership below in the context of "multistakeholder cooperatives."

10. One might also argue that because workers do not have access to the means of subsistence they are coerced to perform wage labor. See discussion of Gould in Chapter 3.

11. One such model is "holocracy" (see http://www.holacracy.org/how-it-works/), which online retailer Zappos has adopted. See http://www.forbes.com/sites/drewhansen/2016/06/22/despite-its-flaws-holacracy-is-saving-the-future-of-business/#5de46743beb1.

12. However, it's not that other stakeholders have no moral standing, the *demos* (i.e., workers) are obligated to take into consideration the impacts on the rights of consumers and other stakeholders.

13. Schwarzenbach's view on Aristotle and agency and the political importance of friendship is extremely relevant to these issues re: economic democracy (Schwarzenbach 2009, 166–175).

14. Indeed, early econD theorist and advocate G.D.H. Cole is famous for his view that the major problem of our society is not poverty but slavery (Pateman 1970, 38).

15. But note my discussion of the "right to exit" above and in my Chapter 3.

16. For more on these historical issues in terms of the intellectual history of arguments for inalienability of agency and labor, see Ellerman 1992, 70–109. Also, Ellerman justifies worker control over profits based on the labor theory of property, which harks back to Locke and is more akin to guild socialists and the libertarian left than to any Marxist tradition (Ellerman 2010, 697).

17. See also Gibson-Graham 1996, 1–45, on this point.

18. For other views on the nonproductive role of stock markets and finance capital more broadly, see Kelly 2001 and Stiglitz 2015, 27–35.

19. Neither Dahl nor Ellerman favored the phrase "market socialist." Both prefer "economic democracy," and so does Schweickart. But the fact that Schweickart embraces the phrase more so illustrates two differences between his view and theirs.

First off, Schweickart is coming out of a different intellectual tradition and political framework than either Dahl or Ellerman. Though all three cite key economic figures such as Jaroslav Vanek, Schweickart is deeply influenced by Karl Marx, though he is also a serious critic of various Marxist lineages and models from Leninist politics to centrally planned economies (Schweickart 2011, xiv–xv).

20. This is especially the case with state or public ownership in service delivery. See Cumbers 2012, 1–8, and McDonald and Ruiters 2012a, 2012b.

21. Schweickart doesn't discuss public sector institutions and services (Schweickart 2011, 73).

22. This model is in play in Emilia-Romagna to some extent (Restakis 2010, 55-86; Malleson 2014, 44). Also, see discussion below.

23. Especially in social economy or solidarity economy frames. See M. Bouchard 2013 and Allard and Matthaei 2008.

24. Available at http://www.beyondcare.coop/.

25. For more on the exploitative working conditions among well-off and well-meaning families, see Estey 2011, 354–355.

26. This is different from top-down cookie-cutter professionalization that reduces worker power or autonomy. But there is another tension here regarding care as paid work and its commodification. For example, Schwarzenbach actually argues that care work comes with its own conception of labor and ownership (Schwarzenbach 2009, 152). I will address this in the next two chapters.

27. Available at http://community-wealth.org/content/cooperative-home-care-associates.

28. One can read how CHCA fared in its evaluation online, available at http://www.bcorporation.net/community/cooperative-home-care-associates/impact-report/2014-10-03-000000.

29. We will return to the issue of the distinction between producer and consumer in Chapter 5 with respect to consumer cooperatives and in Chapter 6 with regard to public service delivery.

30. The sovereignty of labor could be preserved even when nonworkers are the numerical majority of the board but there is proportional voting, which favors workers. For example, in Quebec, many new MSCs have community stakeholder members. This group is often larger than the worker member group. But community members are limited to a maximum of one third of the board seats. The reasoning is that their "stake" is much less than the workers' (i.e., workers' livelihoods are more directly affected by the business than other stakeholders) (Lund 2011, 11). "Stake" here could be read in "stakeholder theory" fashion, that is, in how much the group is affected. This would differ from Ellerman's logic, which Dahl also utilizes, that regards workers as the sole member of the polity because only they are subjects of the decisions of the firm. It could be argued, however, that customers of social service delivery are also "subjects" of the firm because of their dependence on the service (e.g., at home care for the elderly or disabled) and the difficulty in switching providers. Nevertheless, even in such a situation, workers could still hold majority power. Thus, there are two options: one could arrange the board such that the power of each voting member is determined by the numerical size of the class represented. In such a case, customers usually drastically outnumber workers, so this would favor customers. Or number of votes could be assigned by "stake," which would favor workers and give less weight to investors and still less to (most types of) customers (Lund 2011, 11).

31. We shall explore ontological issues concerning the distinction between producer and consumer in the next two chapters.

32. For more on how to pursue regional equity from an environmental justice (EJ-PD) planning perspective, see essays in Pavel 2009. My view on this is that the state in its current form should NOT own most of the means of production. It would be permissible for it to own some, but most should be owned by social-public configurations (see Chapter 6).

33. All these criticisms are stated by Sensat (1983, 623–624) in his review of Schweickart.

34. "In an interview with a team from the Prout Research Institute of Venezuela, Lisset Reyes admitted, and her colleagues agreed, that the only real challenge they face as a cooperative is that it takes a bit longer to come to a decision. But none of them would trade their weekly meetings for an autocratic workplace." Available at http://venezuelanalysis.com/analysis/11034.

35. I follow Malleson in this periodization (2014, 59–60).

36. Nonmembers have "standard employment contracts with the co-ops and do not have the rights and responsibilities associated with membership nor voting rights with respect to choosing members of elected bodies, no employment guarantee, and no obligation to be employee-owners. On the other hand, non-member workers do receive an annual profit share, at a minimum, this is 25% of the share a worker-member at the same pay grade would receive" (Arando et al. 2010, 18).

37. In 2013, of the 38,420 workers, only 12,260 were worker-owners (Navarro 2014).

38. For accounts of white violence against black participatory democracy efforts in the 1960s, see also Polletta 2002, 97.

39. The number of members is slightly higher than the total population because many belong to more than one co-op. This total number also includes what are called "mutuals" (Lund 2011, 20).

40. Key works here include Albert 1997 and 2004.

41. For Rawls's view on this and why he does not favor Albert's balanced job complexes, see Hasan 2015, especially 482–483, 493–501.

42. For a traditional business ethics perspective on pay and compensation, see Audi 2009, 74–85, 101–110.

43. Information available at http://www.ewg.org/research/ewg-s-dirty-dozen-guide-food-additives/flavoring-industry-and-worker-health and http://www.cdc.gov/mmwr/preview/mmwrhtml/mm5116a2.htm.

44. For more on Venezuelan co-ops during the Chavez administration, see Azzellini 2009.

45. For a more contemporary A-PD perspective on these features, see Sitrin 2006, 2012.

46. For different business ethics perspectives on the relationship between one's identity and one's work, see Desjardins 2011, 99–120. But for Panayotakis and those in the broader Marxist tradition, this is a structural issue, not a matter of how individual workers relate to their work.

47. This is exactly what our Athenians did not do. They expanded who got to participate in government only to those who did not work! (See my Chapter 1.)

48. This is precisely Bookchin's project in his writing on what he called "social ecology." For his view on technology's role, see especially "Ecology and Revolutionary Thought" (1964) and The Ecology of Freedom (1982).

CHAPTER 5

1. See Patel 2007, Menser 2008, Andrée et al. 2014.

2. Confusingly, in the literature, the incorporated Seikatsu Club Consumer Cooperative Union is referred to with different acronyms such as SC, SCCC, and SCCCU. I shall use SCCCU, which captures its full name. I shall also refer to it as the Seikatsu Club. The Seikatsu website has the basics on its history and current form; available at http://www.seikatsuclub.coop/about/english.html.

3. Japan has the largest organized consumer co-op movement in the world both in terms of raw numbers and proportion of the population. Indeed, one-third of Japan's citizens belong to a consumer co-op (Restakis 2010, 118).

4. And recur throughout the book, especially re: the S-PD framework.

5. "Stop shopping" is a SCCCU slogan (Marshall 2006, 157).

6. Available at http://cultivate.coop/wiki/Consumer_cooperative.

7. Available at http://institute.coop/worker-cooperative-faq#Q4.

8. Most (86 million) are members of (over 9,000) credit unions. Available at http://consumerfed.org/consumer-cooperatives/. A credit union is a bank that is owned by its members. The board is elected by the members and each member has one vote, regardless of the size of one's account. For more on the role of credit unions in econD, see Malleson 2014, 181–183, Alperovitz 2012, 36–37, and Lewis and Conaty 2012, 192–194.

9. Although it is routinely ranked as one of the best companies to work for, it is not worker owned. Available at http://community-wealth.org/strategies/panel/coops/models.html.

10. Available at http://cultivate.coop/wiki/Consumer_cooperative. For the Park Slope food co-op, go to https://www.foodcoop.com/.

11. Available at http://cultivate.coop/wiki/Consumer_cooperative#Europe.

12. Most consumer co-ops require a payment but not a time donation (e.g., Eroski, REI).

13. Social reproduction involves those practices that preserve and cultivate the conditions necessary for the generational continuance of persons. This entails the carrying out of cultural practices that enable livelihoods that are meaningful, dignified, and economically adequate relative to the norms of the community. On my view, social reproduction is necessarily ecological (here I follow Mies and S-PD) and this is also the case with SCCCU. See also Chapter 1 on S-PD.

14. Available at http://community-wealth.org/content/seikatsu-club-consumers-co-operative-union. "Worker co-operative" is not a legally recognized form of enterprise in Japan, so those who work in them have their earnings taxed as wage income (Marshall 2006, 168).

15. Available at http://seikatsuclub.coop/about/rengo_about_e.html.

16. On Minamata disease from a social reproduction participatory democracy frame (S-PD), see Mies and Shiva 1993, 83, 260, 305.

17. The rise of the corporate state and its negative impacts on democracy is a well-studied theme, but PD works that focus on this particular configuration of issues and the food system include Patel (2007, especially 31–63); Bookchin (1964), Bennholdt-Thomsen, Faraclas, and von Werlhof (2001). See also my Chapter 1.

18. Even PD progressives such as Schweickart endorse a version of this story (Schweickart 2011, 166–171).

19. The concept of the "megamachine" is developed with great insight and controversy by Mumford in his 1974 work. See also Bookchin 1964.

20. See also http://seikatsuclub.coop/about/introduction_e.html.

21. On Slow Food and time, see Patel 2007, 281–287.

22. On their organic practices, see AsiaDHRRA 2006, 7.

23. The SCCCU's "10 principles on safety, health and the environment": "1. Pursuit of safety for consumer materials; 2. Raising self-sufficiency in food; 3. Reduction of harmful substances; 4. Sustainable use of natural resources; 5. Reduction of waste and promotion of reuse; 6. Reduction of energy use; 7. Reduction of risk; 8. Information disclosure; 9. Independent control and auditing; 10. Mass participation." Available at: http://seikatsuclub.coop/about/introduction_e.html.

24. In this they are similar to PB NYC's budget delegates who do not formulate proposals but develop them into projects that can efficaciously address residents' needs. See Chapter 2.

25. Since its inception, advertising and labeling practices have been rife with deception and manipulation not just to trick consumers but to foster an antidemocratic mass politics (Mattson 1998, 129–130; see also, Busch 2013, 175–177).

26. Available at http://seikatsuclub.coop/about/20120801_e_activity2.html.

27. Available at http://seikatsuclub.coop/about/economy_e.html.

28. "Seikatsu Club co-ops are independent organizations in each prefecture, managing and operating their movements and business. Furthermore, members' autonomous organizations at local authority level make decisions and operate their daily activities. These Seikatsu Club co-ops form Seikatsu Club Union as an entity for collective purchase and development of new goods. Local Seikatsu Club co-ops also hand over to Seikatsu Club Union work to improve efficiency, such as ordering and distribution systems, IT systems, etc. Seikatsu Club Union is run by a general assembly and board of directors, meeting in participation with affiliated local Seikatsu Club co-ops." Available at http://seikatsuclub.coop/about/introduction_e.html.

29. The milk co-op was financed by six of the consumer co-ops for about US$6 million. Each of these six consumer co-ops has shares in the worker co-op. See http://seikatsuclub.coop/about/rengo_about_e.html.

30. Available at http://community-wealth.org/content/seikatsu-club-consumers-co-operative-union.

31. Similar types of research centers are also utilized as a best practice in participatory budgeting (see my Chapter 2) and the Mondragon Corporation (Chapter 3) and I argue are critical for the PD transformation of the economy, politics and society (see Conclusion).

32. Available at http://seikatsuclub.coop/about/economy_e.html.

33. An exception is Maria Mies who discussed the housewife throughout her work. For her structuralist understanding of the housewife, see Mies [1986] 1999, 74–104.

34. The ownership gap is globally common but does vary considerably by country and region. There are also controversies about the data. See http://oxfamblogs.org/fp2p/killer-factcheck-women-own-2-of-land-not-true-what-do-we-really-know-about-women-and-land/.

35. Available at http://seikatsuclub.coop/about/rengo_about_e.html.

36. Available at http://www.seikatsuclub.coop/about/20131022activity_e.html. SCCCU opposed GMOs from the start.

37. For Spain, see Ness and Azzelini 2011. For Japan, see Anderson 2005, 6–7, 208.

38. Available at http://www.seikatsuclub.coop/about/economy_e.html.

39. See, for example, Lisa Newton's (2003) excellent articulation of a virtue ethics view re: the environment and Menser 2013a.

40. What is less clear though is if SCCCU is a fully Environmental Justice-PD. Although SCCCU addresses the needs of some vulnerable populations (children and the elderly in Japan; less developed countries abroad), it is not so clear how consistently SCCCU addresses class and racial issues despite their general affinity with the EJ approach toward pollution and collective determination.

41. For more on a "community economy" approach to development that links economistic worker co-op efforts with more ethical consumption oriented ones, see Healy and Graham 2008.

42. Many go to Basque Country to take the tour of the MC facilities and see firsthand how the federation operates. Such visits have been crucial for empowering groups around the world to launch their own econD projects, including the Evergreen Model based in Cleveland. See my Conclusion.

CHAPTER 6

1. All of these have some kind of benefit for wide sections of the populace, though not all are deeply PD. See Malleson for a consideration of social democratic policies from a PD perspective (Malleson 2014, 117–124).

2. By community members I mean that they are not elected officials or governmental officials.

3. In this regard they are similar to MSCs who allow for nonworkers on the board but the board is still dominated by workers. See Chapter 4.

4. In the case of the civil society framework, the Forest Stewardship Council (see my Chapter 3) is closer to the social-public model because there are representatives from relevant communities and workers and they have more than advisory power in the organization. But the FSC like other NGOs does not have control over a state budget or asset. However, if one did, and its process was PD, then it would be social-public.

5. Why did the unions agree not only to take the financial hit but also implement their own oppression? One way of reading Moody's account is that teachers took on the subject position of FIRE: that is, they started to think like investors. They put up their pensions to buy the paper; they now started to relate to the city not as workers, but as investors. After all, didn't the workers benefit from and to some extent even control part of the surplus? Didn't cutting their wages increase the value of their pensions? In some ways this was true. Kelly talks about this 401K mind-set in her (2001). Although it appears as if ownership were democratized through such stockholdings, for most they are truly trickle-down crumbs (Kelly 2001, 5). So though they were in some sense "investor-workers," they lacked the power of the worker-owners of Mondragon. Mondragon's "cooperators" set the priorities and formulate the policies. NYC unions did not set the agenda, they capitulated to FIRE (Fitch 1993; Harvey 2005, 75–76; Moody 2007; J. Freeman 2000, 256–287).

6. For a history of these kinds of events and neoliberal responses to them, see Klein 2007.

7. This shifting of powers is further evidence of what I called the "internal heterogeneity of the state." If all aspects and components of the state followed the same logic, then why do so many bemoan these changes?

8. On the growth of private authority in the national-global frame, see Sassen 2006, 192.

9. In all these cases/modalities of privatization, the state has not "withdrawn" from the economic realm, nor from the private sector. Even in cases of deregulation, the state

is active. It draws up and enforces contracts, taxes, grants subsidies, fines or waves fines, builds infrastructure, makes changes to workforce development and education, regulates, and so on. In other worlds, the state has not vacated the scene, rather, its role has changed (Sassen 2006, 187–203).

10. For an ecological Marxist structural critique of the unsustainability of the capitalist state, see O'Connor (1998). This is not the kind of critique I am referring to here, however. Like Eckersley, I believe that critique of the state to be "overly deterministic" (2004, 61). Like Eckersley, and others, I think that states have more power to determine how they respond to specific economic forces and events. Indeed, comparatively stronger states often shape these forces, events, and organizations (Eckersley 2004, 67, 60–67). Also, and unlike Eckersley, I believe, following the work of Gibson-Graham and others, that there is much more nontrivial economic diversity as well. (See Chapter 3.) However, unlike all of those just mentioned, but with Sassen, I argue that there is organizational diversity within the state bureaucracy itself. To be fair, however, Eckersley does describe specific programs that the state could engage in in order to promote ecological justice. She calls this model of governance the "green state." And she considers the ways in which this would change the conception of sovereignty and the framework for the interstate system. Her focus is on the precautionary principle and liability (2004, 138–141) but she does not entertain the notion that there is bureaucratic diversity within the state. Nor does she open up parts of the state to reclamation by the social. However, she does say, "Rather than defend an abstract global, cosmopolitan democracy of the kind envisaged by David Held, I have suggested that it is more desirable and feasible to transnationalize democracy in piecemeal, experimental, consensual and domain-driven ways." (248) But here she remains within a state-based *deliberative* model rather than a participatory social-public model (Eckersley 2004, 133–134, 160–163, 202).

11. Although less prevalent since the fall of the Soviet Union, the situation with public service delivery in socialist countries is still relevant, but the literature is not so helpful. McDonald and Ruiters write, "The historical reviews in this literature tend to be broad and cursory, and although much of it argues that socialist states generally offered good-quality, universal, and affordable services in the past, there is a tendency to either dismiss these systems out of hand as too hierarchical, nontransparent, and inefficient [. . .] or to uncritically celebrate them with little analysis as to how (and if) they could be reproduced today" (McDonald and Ruiters 2012c, 172).

12. For an ecological critique of state rationality, see Eckersley 2004, 88–93. For a case study (involving the U.S. Army Corps of Engineers), see Morgan 1971, and with respect to the U.S. environmental movements' resurgence amid state regulatory failures in the 1970s, see Cronin and Kennedy 1997. For more on the limits of state socialism and democratic socialism, see Cumbers 2012 and Malleson 2014.

13. I also consider some commoning and cybercommons perspectives below. For recent theoretical treatments, see Federici 2011, Caffentzis 2013, and Caffentzis and Federici 2013. Hardt and Negri (2009, 151–159) offer much conceptual articulation of the commons relative to work and life but do not deal with the actual institutional contexts or the corresponding literature. Harvey (2012) forwards the notion of the urban commons but gives no examples that explain how they function or are regulated.

14. Note that this (rules for punishment and by whom) is an addition to our previous articulations of both PD and maxD. See also Ostrom 1990, 94–102.

15. See my discussion of Schumpeter's view in Chapter 1 and Orlie 2001.

16. We laid the groundwork for this view in Chapter 4 in the discussion of MSCs and in Chapter 5 on SCCCU's conception of anticonsumerist consumption.

17. Key texts for reinventing the commons from an S-PD perspective are Bennholdt-Thomsen and Mies 2000, Federici 2011, Caffentzis 2013, and Caffentzis and Federici 2013. Hardt and Negri (2009) do so more from an A-PD frame. An excellent historical treatment that is highly relevant for this chapter's focus is Linebaugh 2008.

18. If the state enacts the proposals then the PB community, a non-state-public sphere according to some, is autonomous. If the state does not enact the projects, or even if the state only enacts some, then the PB community is NOT autonomous, because the mayor's office (e.g., state) has not respected the agenda of the PB community (social).

19. If the state sets the rules, then there is no commons; it's more of a traditional public space.

20. A fascinating attempt at the instantiation of the social-public and econD model was forwarded by U.S. Forestry Service manager Robert Marshall (Gottlieb 1993, 16–17).

21. In this regard, the ouvidoria is functionally similar to Mondragon's "social council." (See my Chapter 3.)

22. Available at http://www.nytimes.com/2015/03/15/nyregion/the-wet-wipes-box-says-flush-but-the-new-york-city-sewer-system-says-dont.html?_r=0.

23. See the remarkable work of Patricia Johanson, especially the Dallas Fair Park Lagoon, and the Ellis Creek Water Recycling Facility (Johanson 2016).

24. Available at http://observer.com/2008/07/a-cleaner-and-even-swimmable-hudson-river/.

25. For a relevant and detailed historical and political philosophical understanding of the Internet and the "free software" framework, see Chopra and Dexter 2008, especially chapters 1 and 5.

26. Restakis also writes about cases discussed in my book including worker cooperatives such as Mondragon and the SCCCU in his 2010.

27. Some are paid in this "click economy" but not very well (Scholz 2016) even though the sector is growing. Bauwens writes, "A study by the Computer and Communications Industry Association estimates that the US 'fair use' economy, based on shared, 'balanced copyright' knowledge, already employs 17.5 million people and accounted for one sixth of GDP in 2007" (Bauwens 2012).

28. I discussed B corps in Chapter 4 in the case of CHCA.

29. Other econD justifications and institutional contexts for BIG are discussed in Malleson 2014, 18, 42, 202–203 and in my Chapter 3.

30. FLOSS are different from B corps because the former are nonprofit.

31. See Fattori, available at http://blog.p2pfoundation.net/the-public-commons-partnership-and-the-commonification-of-that-which-is-public/2012/08/14.

CONCLUSION

1. By "cross platform" I mean that it can operate in varying institutional types (household, university, firm, municipality) and different sectors (political, economic, manufacturing, health care).

2. Esteva (2006, 2010) is a great PD place to start on the Oaxaca Commune and Peller (2016) offers an excellent analysis from an explicitly S-PD perspective.

3. This could further build on the efforts of Participedia.org and P2Pfoundation.net and their archives of past and present PD practices.

4. The spread of co-ops in the United States has been greatly assisted by the work done by the Ohio Employee Ownership Center at Kent State University (e.g., Lund

2011), the Center for Cooperatives at the University of Wisconsin, and the Democracy Collaborative. (See below).

5. For a thoroughly entertaining and inspiring science fiction account of how to do a climate resilient PD takeover of NYC read Robinson's (2017) strikingly insightful and creative *2140: a Novel*.

6. Anchor institutions are large-scale operations that have major impacts on their surroundings as landlords, employers, and purchasers of services. Because it is difficult for them to move and they often receive considerable government funding, they are long-term clients and inclined to support enterprises that contribute to the overall stability of their area.

7. See the Democracy Collaborative site for numerous reports and media accounts on this "anchor institution" "community wealth building" model: available at http://community-wealth.org/content/cleveland-model-how-evergreen-cooperatives-are -building-community-wealth. For a critical take on what is an evolving situation, see Posey 2014.

8. The grassroots alliance of organizations The Right to the City has worked on this especially since the fiscal crisis. See http://righttothecity.org/about/mission-history/.

9. In some ways this is what has happened to Porto Alegre. Many innovations, yes, but still under the thumb of the state both in terms of money and authority. Should it secede? And join with whom? Cleveland? For thoughts about a more PD polylateralism across borders, see Barber 2013 on the city-to-city possibilities and Quilligan 2010.

10. Available at https://policy.m4bl.org/.

References

Abers, Rebecca Neaera, and Margaret E. Keck. 2013. *Practical Authority: Agency and Institutional Change in Brazilian Water Politics*. New York: Oxford University Press.

Ackerman, Bruce, Ann Alstott, and Philippe van Parijs. 2006. *Redesigning Distribution: Basic Income and Stakeholder Grants as Cornerstones of a More Egalitarian Capitalism*. Vol. 5. Real Utopias Project Series. London: Verso.

Akhter, Farida. 2001. "Resisting 'Technology' and Defending Subsistence in Bangladesh: Nayakrishi Andolon and the Movement for a Happy Life." In *There Is an Alternative: Subsistence and Worldwide Resistance to Corporate Globalization*, ed. Veronika Bennholdt-Thomsen, Nicholas Faraclas, and Claudia von Werlhof, 167–177. New York: Zed Books.

Albert, Michael. 1997. *Thinking Forward: Learning to Conceptualize Economic Vision*. Winnipeg: Arbeiter Ring Publishing Books.

———. 2004. *Parecon: Life after Capitalism*. New York: Verso.

Albert, Michael, and David Schweickart. 2008. "There Is an Alternative: Economic Democracy and Participatory Economics, a Debate." In *Solidarity Economy: Building Economic Alternatives*, ed. Jenna Allard, Carl Davidson, and Julie Matthaei, 47–82. Chicago: ChangeMaker Publications.

Allard, Jenna, Carl Davidson, and Julie Matthaei, eds. 2008. *Solidarity Economy: Building Economic Alternatives*. Papers and Proceedings from the U.S. Social Forum 2007. Chicago: ChangeMaker Publications.

Allard, Jenna, and Julie Matthaei. 2008. "Introduction." In *Solidarity Economy: Building Economic Alternatives*, ed. Jenna Allard, Carl Davidson, and Julie Matthaei, 1–18. Chicago: ChangeMaker Publications.

Alliance for a Just Rebuilding. 2013. "Weathering the Storm." Available at http://www.rebuildajustny.org/weathering-the-storm-rebuilding-a-more-resilient-nycha-post-sandy/.

Alperovitz, Gar. 2012. *What Then Must We Do?* White River Junction, VT: Chelsea Green.

Alperovitz, Gar, and Lew Daly. 2008. *Unjust Desserts*. New York: New Press.

Anderson, Benedict. 2005. *Under Three Flags: Anarchism and the Anti-colonial Imagination*. New York: Verso.

Andrée, Peter, Jeffrey Ayres, Michael J. Bosia, and Marie-Josée Massicotte. 2014. *Globalization and Food Sovereignty: Global and Local Change in the New Politics of Food*. Toronto: University of Toronto Press.

Angotti, Tom. 2008. *New York for Sale: Community Planning Confronts Global Real Estate*. Cambridge, MA: MIT Press.

———. 2013. "Rethinking the Luxury City." *The Indypendent* 192, December 17. Available at https://indypendent.org/2013/12/rethinking-the-luxury-city/.

Ansell, Chris. 2000. "The Networked Polity: Regional Development in Western Europe." *Governance* 13: 303–333.

Arando, Saioa, Fred Freundlich, Monica Gago, Derek C. Jones, and Takao Kato. 2010. "Assessing Mondragon: Stability and Managed Change in the Face of Globalization." William Davidson Institute Working Paper 1003. November.

Arendt, Hannah. 1963. *On Revolution*. New York: Penguin.

Aristotle. 1981. *The Politics,* trans. T. A. Sinclair. New York: Penguin.

Arnstein, S. R. 1969. "A Ladder of Citizen Participation." *Journal of the American Institute of Planners* 35, 4: 216–224.

AsiaDHRRA. 2006. "Initiatives on Pro–Small Farmer Trade." Manila, Philippines: AsiaDHRRA and AFA. Available at www.asiadhrra.org.

Audi, Robert. 2009. *Business Ethics and Ethical Business*. Oxford: Oxford University Press.

Avritzer, Leonardo. 2009. *Participatory Institutions in Democratic Brazil*. Baltimore: Johns Hopkins University Press.

Azzellini, Dario. 2009. "Venezuela's Solidarity Economy: Collective Ownership, Expropriation, and Workers Self-Management." *Working USA: The Journal of Labor and Society* 12, 2 (June): 171–191.

Azzellini, Dario, and Immanuel Ness, eds. 2011. *Ours to Master and to Own: Workers' Control from the Commune to the Present*. Chicago: Haymarket Books.

Bachrach, Peter, and Aryeh Botwinick. 1992. *Power and Empowerment: A Radical Theory of Participatory Democracy*. Philadelphia: Temple University Press.

Baez, Nancy, and Andreas Hernandez. 2012. "Participatory Budgeting in the City: Challenging NYC's Development Paradigm from the Grassroots." *Interface: A Journal for and about Social Movements* 4, 1: 316–326.

Baierle, Sergio. 2005. "The Case of Porto Alegre: The Politics and Background." In *Participatory Democracy: Prospects for Democratizing Democracy*, ed. Dimitrios Roussopoulos and C. George Benello, 270–286. Montreal: Black Rose Books.

Baiocchi, Gianpaolo. 2003. "Participation, Activism, and Politics: The Porto Alegre Experiment." In *Deepening Democracy*, ed. Archon Fung and Eric Olin Wright, 45–76. New York: Verso.

———. 2005. *Militants and Citizens*. Stanford, CA: Stanford University Press.

———. 2006. "The Citizens of Porto Alegre." *Boston Review*, March 1. Available at http://bostonreview.net/gianpaolo-baiocchi-the-citizens-of-porto-alegre.

Baiocchi, Gianpaolo, Einar Braathen, and Ana Claudia Teixeira. 2012. "Transformation Institutionalized? Making Sense of Participatory Democracy in the Lula Era." In

Democratization in the Global South: The Importance of Transformative Politics, ed. Kristian Stokke and Olle Törnquist, 217–239. London: Palgrave McMillan.

Baiocchi, Gianpaolo, and Sofia Checa. 2009. "Cities as New Spaces for Citizenship Claims: Globalization, Urban Politics, and Civil Society in Brazil, Mexico, and South Africa in the 1990s." In *Democracy, States and the Struggle for Global Justice*, ed. Heather Gautney, Omar Dahbour, Ashley Dawson, and Neil Smith, 131–151. New York: Routledge.

Baiocchi, Gianpaolo, Patrick Heller, and Marcelo Silva. 2011. *Bootstrapping Democracy: Transforming Local Governance and Civil Society in Brazil*. Stanford, CA: Stanford University Press.

Baird, Kate Shea. 2016. "The Disobedient City and the Stateless Nation." *ROAR* 1, March 8: 9. Available at https://roarmag.org/magazine/the-disobedient-city-and-the-stateless-nation/.

Balanyá, Belén, Brid Brennan, Olivier Hoedeman, Satoko Kishimoto, and Philipp Terhorst, eds. 2005. *Reclaiming Public Water: Achievements, Struggles and Visions from Around the World*. Amsterdam: TNI/Corporate Europe Observatory.

Barber, Benjamin. (1984) 2003. *Strong Democracy: Participatory Politics for a New Age*. Berkeley, CA: University of California Press.

———. 2013. *If Mayors Ruled the World*. New Haven, CT: Yale University Press.

Barclay, Harold. (1982) 1990. *People without Government: An Anthropology of Anarchy*. London: Kahn and Averill.

Bauwens, Michel. 2012. "Peer-to-Peer Production and the Coming of the Commons." *Red Pepper*, July. Available at http://www.redpepper.org.uk/by/michel-bauwens.

Bauwens, Michel (with John Restakis). 2014. "Introducing the New Configuration between State, Civil Society and the Market." P2P. Available at http://p2pfoundation.net/Commons_Transition_Plan.

Beauchamp, Tom L., and Norman E. Bowie, eds. 1997. *Ethical Theory and Business*. 5th ed. Upper Saddle River, NJ: Prentice-Hall.

Becker, Carol Jean. 2010. "Self-Determination, Accountability Mechanisms, and Quasi-Governmental Status of Business Improvement Districts in the United States." *Public Performance and Management Review* 33, 3 (March): 413–435.

Benhabib, Seyla, ed. 1996. *Democracy and Difference: Contesting the Boundaries of the Political*. Princeton, NJ: Princeton University Press.

Bennholdt-Thomsen, Veronika, and Maria Mies. 2000. *The Subsistence Perspective: Beyond the Globalised Economy*. New York: Zed.

Bennholdt-Thomsen, Veronika, Nicholas Faraclas, and Claudia von Werlhof. 2001. *There Is an Alternative: Subsistence and Worldwide Resistance to Corporate Globalization*. New York: Zed Books.

Berry, Jeffrey M., Kent E. Portney, and Ken Thomson. 1993. *The Rebirth of Urban Democracy*. Washington, DC: Brookings Institution.

Bohman, James. 1998. "Survey Article: The Coming of Age of Deliberative Democracy." *Journal of Political Philosophy* 6, 4: 400–425.

Bookchin, Murray. (1964) 1966. "Ecology and Revolutionary Thought." By Lewis Herber (pseudonym for Murray Bookchin). *Anarchy* 69, 6 (1966): 18.

———. 1982. *The Ecology of Freedom*. Palo Alto, CA: Cheshire Books.

———. 1994. *To Remember Spain: The Anarchist and Syndicalist Revolution of 1936*. Oakland, CA: AK Press.

———. (1992) 1995. *From Urbanization to Cities*. Rev. ed. London: Cassel.

Bouchard, Marie, ed. 2013. *Innovation and the Social Economy.* Toronto: Toronto University Press.

Bouchard, Stephanie. 2012a. "Home Care Franchises Are Hot, Hot, Hot." *Healthcare Finance,* July 12. Available at http://www.healthcarefinancenews.com/news/home-care-franchises-are-hot-hot-hot.

———. 2012b. "Seeking an Edge, Two Home Care Agencies Become Certified B Corps." *Healthcare Finance,* December 13. Available at http://www.healthcarefinancenews.com/news/seeking-an-edge-home-care-agencies-differentiate-themselves.

Bowles, Sam, and Herbert Gintis. 1999. *Recasting Egalitarianism: New Rules for Accountability and Equity in Markets, States and Communities.* Vol. III. Real Utopias Project Series. London: Verso.

Brenna, Brid, Bernhard Hack, Olivier Hoedeman, Satoko Kishimoto, and Philipp Terhorst. 2004. "Reclaiming Public Water! Participatory Alternatives to Privatization." TNI Briefing Series 2004/7. Amsterdam: Transnational Institute.

Brennan, Timothy, and Keya Ganguly. 2009. "Crude Wars." In *Democracy, States and the Struggle for Global Justice,* ed. Heather Gautney, Omar Dahbour, Ashley Dawson, and Neil Smith, 31–44. New York: Routledge.

Bryan, Frank M. 2004. *Real Democracy: The New England Town Hall Meeting and How It Works.* Chicago: Chicago University Press.

Bullard, Robert D., ed. 2007. *Growing Smarter: Achieving Livable Communities, Environmental Justice, and Regional Equity.* Cambridge, MA: MIT Press.

Busch, Lawrence. 2013. *Standards: Recipes for Reality.* Cambridge, MA: MIT Press.

Cabannes, Yves. 2004. "Participatory Budgeting: A Significant Contribution to Participatory Democracy." *Environment and Urbanization* 16: 27–46.

———. 2014. "20 Cities." Working paper. September 2014. International Institute for Environment and Development (IIED). Available at www.iied.org/pubs.

Cabannes, Yves, and Zhuang Ming. 2013. "Participatory Budgeting at Scale and Bridging the Rural-Urban Divide in Chengdu." *Environment and Urbanization* 26, 1: 257–275.

Caffentzis, George. 2013. *In Letters of Blood and Fire: Work, Machines and Value.* Oakland, CA: PM Press/Common Notions/Autonomedia.

Caffentzis, George, and Silvia Federici. 2013. "Commons against and beyond Capitalism," *Upping the Anti: A Journal of Theory and Action* 15 (September): 83–97.

Carlsson, Chris. 2008. *Nowtopia.* Oakland, CA: AK Press.

Center for Advances in Public Engagement. 2008. "Essentials #1: Public Engagement: A Primer from Public Agenda." New York: Public Agenda. Available at www.publicagenda.org/.../public_engagement_primer.pdf.

Chavez, Daniel. 2004. *Polis and Demos: The Left in Municipal Governance in Montevideo and Porto Alegre.* Maastricht: Shaker Publishing.

Chew, Sing P. 2001. *Worldwide Ecological Degradation.* New York: Rowman and Littlefield.

Chopra, Samir, and Scott Dexter. 2008. *Decoding Liberation.* Cambridge, MA: MIT Press.

Clark, Anna. 2014. "Is Participatory Democracy Real Democracy?" *Next City,* April 28. Accessed April 22, 2015. Available at http://nextcity.org/features/view/is-participatory-budgeting-real-democracy-chicago.

Cleaver, Harry. 2000. *Reading Capital Politically.* 2nd ed. London: AK Press.

Cohen, Jean, and Andrew Arato. 1992. *Civil Society and Political Theory.* Cambridge, MA: MIT Press.

Cohen, Joshua. 1996. "Procedure and Substance in Deliberative Democracy." In *Democracy and Difference: Contesting the Boundaries of the Political*, ed. Seyla Benhabib, 95–119. Princeton, NJ: Princeton University Press.

Cohen, Joshua, and Joel Rogers 1995. "Secondary Associations and Democratic Governance." In *Associations and Democracy*, ed. Erik Olin Wright, 7–98. Vol. 1. Real Utopias Project Series. London: Verso.

Cole, G.D.H. 1920a. *Guild Socialism Restated*. London: Leonard Parsons.

———. 1920b. *The Social Theory*. London: Methuen.

Community Development Project. 2015. "A People's Budget: A Research and Evaluation Report on Participatory Budgeting in New York City, Cycle 4: Key Research Findings." New York: Urban Justice Center with PBNYC Research Team.

Compa, Lance. 2008. "Corporate Social Responsibility and Workers Rights." *Comparative Labor Law and Policy Journal* 30, 1: 1–10.

Cook, Terrence E., and Patrick M. Morgan, eds. 1971. *Participatory Democracy*. San Francisco: Canfield Press.

Corntassel, Jeff. 2008. "Toward Sustainable Self-Determination: Rethinking the Contemporary Indigenous-Rights Discourse." *Alternatives* 33: 105–132.

Council of Europe (COE). 2013. *Living in Dignity in the 21st Century*. Paris: Council of Europe.

Cronin, John, and Robert F. Kennedy Jr. 1997. *The Riverkeepers*. New York: Scribner.

Cumbers, Andrew. 2012. *Reclaiming Public Ownership*. London: Zed.

———. 2013. "Making Space for Public Ownership: The Re-municipalisation of Public Services through Grassroots Struggle and Local State Action." *Planning Theory and Practice* 14, 4: 547–551.

Cunningham, Frank. 2001. *Theories of Democracy: A Critical Introduction*. Routledge: New York.

Curl, John. 2012. *For All the People*. 2nd ed. Oakland, CA: PM Press.

Dahl, Robert. (1967) 1971. "The City in the Future of Democracy." In *Participatory Democracy*, ed. Terrence E. Cook and Patrick M. Morgan. San Francisco: Canfield Press.

———. 1985. *A Preface to Economic Democracy*. Berkeley, CA: California University Press.

———. 1989. *Democracy and Its Critics*. New Haven, CT: Yale University Press.

Dahlsrud, Alexander. 2008. "How Corporate Social Responsibility Is Defined: An Analysis of 37 Definitions." *Corporate Social Responsibility and Environmental Management* 15: 1–13.

Dalla Costa, Maria, and Selma James. 1972. *The Power of Women and the Subversion of Community*. Bristol, U.K.: Falling Wall Press.

Dallmayr, Fred R. 1987. "Democracy and Postmodernism." *Human Studies* 10, 1: 143–170.

Davis, James. 2002. "This Is What Bureaucracy Looks Like: NGOs and Anti-capitalism." In *The Battle of Seattle: The New Challenge to Capitalist Globalization*, ed. Eddie Yuen, George Katsiaficas, and Daniel Burton Rose, 175–182. New York: Soft Skull Press.

Dawson, Ashley. 2010. "Climate Justice: The Emerging Movement against Green Capitalism." *South Atlantic Quarterly* 109, 2 (Spring): 313–338.

Day, Richard J. F. 2005. *Gramsci Is Dead: Anarchist Currents in the Newest Social Movements*. Ann Arbor, MI: Pluto Press.

De Angelis, Massimo. 2010. "The Production of Commons and the 'Explosion' of the Middle Class." *Antipode* 42, 4: 954–977.

Dé Ishtar, Zoe. 1994. *Daughters of the Pacific*. Melbourne: Spinifex Press.

Dejardins, Joseph. 2011. *An Introduction to Business Ethics*. 4th ed. New York: McGraw Hill.

Dewey, John. 1927. *The Public and Its Problems*. Athens, OH: Ohio University Press.

Diamond, Jared. 2005. *Collapse*. New York: Penguin.

Dirlik, Arif. 1993. *Anarchism in the Chinese Revolution*. Berkeley, CA: University of California Press.

Dryzek, John S. 2005. *The Politics of the Earth*. 2nd ed. New York: Oxford University Press.

Dubb, Steve. 2012. "C-W Interview: Seikatsu Club Consumers' Co-operative Union." College Park, MD: The Democracy Collaborative at the University of Maryland.

Dubois, W.E.B. 1907. *Economic Cooperation among Negro Americans*. Atlanta, GA: The Atlanta University Press.

Durose, Catherine, and Liz Richardson, eds. 2016. *Designing Public Policy for Co-production*. Chicago, IL: Policy Press.

Durrenberger, E. Paul, and Judith E. Marti, eds. 2006. *Labor in Cross-Cultural Perspective*. Lanham, MD: AltaMira Press.

Eckersley, Robyn. 2004. *The Green State: Rethinking Democracy and Sovereignty*. Cambridge, MA: MIT Press.

Egels-Zanden, Niklas, and Peter Hyllman. 2007. "Evaluating Strategies for Negotiating Workers' Rights in Transnational Corporations: The Effects of Codes of Conduct and Global Agreements on Workplace Democracy." *Journal of Business Ethics* 76: 207–223.

Eichner, Carolyn J. 2004. *Surmounting the Barricades: Women in the Paris Commune*. Bloomington, IN: Indiana University Press.

Ellerman, David. 1990. *The Democratic Corporation*. Washington, DC: The World Bank.

———. 1992. *Property and Contract in Economics: The Case of Economic Democracy*. Cambridge, MA: Basil Blackwell Inc.

———. 2010. "Marxism as Capitalist Tool." *Journal of Socio-Economics* 39, 6 (December): 696–700.

———. 2013. "Three Themes about Democratic Enterprises: Capital Structure, Education, and Spin-offs." In *Sharing Ownership, Profits and Decision-Making in the 21st Century: Advances in the Economic Analysis of Participatory and Labor-Managed Firms*, ed. Douglas Kruse, 329–355. Bingley, U.K.: Emerald Group.

———. 2015. "Does Classical Liberalism Imply Democracy?" *Ethics and Global Politics*, 8. Available at http://dx.doi.org/10.3402/egp.v8.29310.

Esteva, Gustavo. 2007. "Oaxaca: The Path of Radical Democracy." *Socialism and Democracy* 21, 2, 74–96.

———. 2010. "The Oaxaca Commune and Mexico's Coming Insurrection," *Antipode* 42, 4: 978–993.

Esteva, Gustavo, and Madhu Suri Prakash. 1998. *Grassroots Postmodernism: Remaking the Soil of Cultures*. London: Zed Books.

Estey, Ken. 2011. "Domestic Workers and Cooperatives: Beyond Care Goes beyond Capitalism, A Case Study in Brooklyn New York." *Working USA* 14, 3: 347–365.

Evanoff, Richard. 1998. "A Look inside Japan's Seikatsu Club Consumers' Cooperative." *Social Anarchism* 26. Available at http://www.socialanarchism.org/mod/magazine/display/84/index.php.

———. 2011. *Bioregionalism and Global Ethics: A Transactional Approach to Achieving Ecological Sustainability, Social Justice, and Human Well-Being*. New York: Routledge.

FCC. 2014. "Net Neutrality." Available at http://www.fcc.gov/openinternet.

Featherstone, Liza, and United Students against Sweatshops. 2002. *Students against Sweatshops*. New York: Verso.

Federici, Silvia. 2004. *Caliban and the Witch: Women, the Body and Primitive Accumulation*. Brooklyn, NY: Autonomedia.

———. 2011. "Feminism and the Politics of the Common." *The Commoner* 14: 1–14. Available at http://www.commoner.org.uk/?p=113.

Fitch, Robert. 1993. *The Assassination of New York*. New York: Verso.

Flanders, Laura. 2014. "How America's Largest Worker Owned Co-op Lifts People Out of Poverty." *YES! Magazine*, August 14. Available at http://www.yesmagazine.org /issues/the-end-of-poverty/how-america-s-largest-worker-owned-co-op-lifts-people -out-of-poverty.

Florence, Namulundah. 2014. *Wangari Maathai: Visionary, Environmental Leader, Political Activist*. New York: Lantern Books.

Flynn, Sean, and Kathryn Boudouris. 2005. "Democratising the Regulation and Governance of Water in the US." In *Reclaiming Public Water: Achievements, Struggles and Visions from Around the World*, ed. Belén Balanyá, Brid Brennan, Olivier Hoedeman, Satoko Kishimoto, and Philipp Terhorst, 73–84. Amsterdam: TNI/Corporate Europe Observatory.

Font, Joan, Donatella Della Porta, and Yves Sintomer, eds. 2014. *Participatory Democracy in Southern Europe*. New York: Rowman Littlefield.

Foster, Sheila R., and Christian Iaione. 2016. "The City as a Commons." *Yale Law & Policy Review* 34, 2 (Article 2): 281–349.

Fotopoulos, Takis. 1998. *Towards an Inclusive Democracy*. London: Bloomsbury Academic.

Fox, Michael. 2006. "CECOSESOLA: Four Decades of Independent Struggle for a Venezuelan Cooperative." June 19. Available at https://venezuelanalysis.com /analysis/1793.

Freeman, Joshua B. 2000. *Working Class New York: Life and Labor since World War II*. New York: The New Press.

Freeman, R. Edward. 1984a. "A Stakeholder Theory of the Modern Corporation." In *Ethical Theory and Business*, ed. Tom Beauchamp and Norman Bowie, 38–48. Upper Saddle River, NJ: Prentice-Hall.

———. 1984b. *Strategic Management: A Stakeholder Approach*. Boston: Pitman.

Freeman, R. Edward, Jeffrey S. Harrison, Andrew C. Wicks, Bidhan L. Parmar, and Simone De Colle. 2010. *Stakeholder Theory: The State of the Art*. Cambridge: Cambridge University Press.

Friedman, Milton. (1970) 1997. "The Social Responsibility of Business Is to Increase Its Profits." In *Ethical Theory and Business*, ed. Tom Beauchamp and Norman Bowie, 58–65. Upper Saddle River, NJ: Prentice-Hall.

Friedman, Thomas. 1999. *The Lexus and the Olive Tree*. New York: Farrar Straus and Giroux.

Fung, Archon. 2003. "Deliberative Democracy and International Labor Standards." *Governance: An International Journal of Policy, Administration, and Institutions* 16, 1 (January): 51–71.

Fung, Archon, and Eric Olin Wright, eds. 2003a. *Deepening Democracy: Institutional Innovations in Empowered Participatory Governance*. New York: Verso.

———, eds. 2003b. "Thinking about Empowered Participatory Governance." In *Deepening Democracy*, ed. Archon Fung and Eric Olin Wright, 3–42. New York: Verso.

Fung, Brian. 2014. "Comcast, Charter and Time Warner Cable All Say Obama's Net Neutrality Plan Shouldn't Worry Investors." *The Washington Post*, December 16.

Gautney, Heather, Omar Dahbour, Ashley Dawson, and Neil Smith. 2009. *Democracy, States and the Struggle for Global Justice*. New York: Routledge.

Gibson-Graham, J-K. 1996. *The End of Capitalism (As We Knew It)*. Malden, MA: Blackwell Publishers.

———. 2003. "Enabling Ethical Economies: Cooperativism and Class." *Critical Sociology* 29, 2 (March): 123–161.

Gilens, Martin, and Benjamin I. Page. 2014. "Testing Theories of American Politics: Elites, Interest Groups, and Average Citizens." *Perspectives on Politics* 12, 3 (September): 564–581.

Gilman, Hollie Russon. 2012. "Transformative Deliberations: Participatory Budgeting in the United States." *Journal of Public Deliberation* 8, 2 (Article 11). Available at http://www.publicdeliberation.net/jpd/vol8/iss2/art11.

Goldfrank, Benjamin. 2012. "The World Bank and the Globalization of Participatory Budgeting." *Journal of Public Deliberation* 8, 2, Article 7. Available at http://www.publicdeliberation.net/jpd/vol8/iss2/art7.

Gómez, Luis Sánchez, and Philipp Terhorst. 2004. "Cochabamba, Bolivia: Public-Collective Partnership after the Water War." In *Reclaiming Public Water: Achievements, Struggles and Visions from Around the World*, ed. Belén Balanyá, Brid Brennan, Olivier Hoedeman, Satoko Kishimoto, and Philipp Terhorst, 121–130. Amsterdam: TNI/Corporate Europe Observatory.

Gordon Nembhard, Jessica. 2014. *Collective Courage: a History of African American Cooperative Thought and Practice*. University Park, PA: Penn State Press.

———. 2015. "Thinking about a Next System with W.E.B. Dubois and Fannie Lou Hamer," The Next System Project. Available at http://thenextsystem.org/thinking-about-a-next-system-with-w-e-b-du-bois-and-fannie-lou-hamer/.

Gottlieb, Robert. 1993. *Forcing the Spring: The Transformation of the American Environmental Movement*. Washington, DC: Island Press.

Gould, Carol. 1988. *Rethinking Democracy*. New York: Cambridge University Press.

———. 2004. *Globalization and Human Rights*. New York: Cambridge University Press.

———. 2014. *Interactive Democracy*. New York: Cambridge University Press.

Graeber, David. 2001. *Toward an Anthropological Theory of Value: The False Coin of Our Own Dreams*. New York: Palgrave.

———. 2013. *The Democracy Project*. New York: Spiegel and Grau.

———. 2015. *The Utopia of Rules: On Technology, Stupidity, and the Secret Joys of Bureaucracy*. Brooklyn, NY: Melville House.

Green, Philip, and Drucilla Cornell. 2005. "Rethinking Democratic Theory: The American Case." *Journal of Social Philosophy* 36, 4 (Winter): 517–535.

Grinde Jr., Donald A., and Bruce E. Johansen. (1982) 1991. *Exemplar of Liberty: Native America and the Evolution of Democracy*. Los Angeles, CA: American Indian Studies Center, University of California.

Grubacic, Andrej. 2010. *Don't Mourn, Balkanize!* Oakland, CA: PM Press.

Gutierrez-Aguilar, Raquel. 2004. "The Coordinadora: One Year after the Water War." In *¡Cochabamba!: Water War in Bolivia*, ed. Oscar Olivera (with Tom Lewis), 53–64. Cambridge, MA: South End Press.

Gutmann, Amy, and Dennis Thompson. 1996. *Democracy and Disagreement: Why Moral Conflict Cannot Be Avoided in Politics, and What Should Be Done about It*. Cambridge, MA: Harvard University Press.

Habermas, Jurgen. 1996. *Between Facts and Norms*. Cambridge, MA: MIT Press.

Hagelskamp, Carolin, Chloe Rinehart, Rebecca Silliman, and David Schleifer. 2016. *Public Spending by the People: Participatory Budgeting in the United States and Canada in 2014–15*. New York: Public Agenda. Available at http://www.publicagenda.org/media/public-spending-by-the-people.

Hall, David. 2015. *Why Public-Private Partnerships Don't Work: The Many Advanatges of the Public Alternative*. Greenwich, U.K.: Public Services International Research Unit.

Hammond, Tim, and Elizabeth Angell. 2013. "Is Everywhere Taksim?: Public Space and Possible Publics." Jadaliyya, June 9. Available at http://www.jadaliyya.com/pages/index/12143/is-everywhere-taksim_public-space-and-possible-pub.

Hardt, Michael, and Antonio Negri. 2004. *Multitude*. New York: Penguin.

———. 2009. *Commonwealth*. Cambridge, MA: Harvard University Press.

Harvey, David. 2005. *A Brief History of Neoliberalism*. Oxford: Oxford University Press.

———. 2012. *Rebel Cities*. London: Verso.

Hasan, Rafeeq. 2015. "Rawls on Meaningful Work and Freedom." *Social Theory and Practice* 41, 3: 477–504.

Hauptmann, Emily. 2001. "Can Less Be More? Leftist Deliberative Democrats' Critique of Participatory Democracy." *Polity* 33, 3 (Spring): 397–421.

Hayden, Tom. (1962) 2005. *The Port Huron Statement*. New York: Thunder's Mouth Press.

Healy, Stephen, and Julie Graham. 2008. "Building Community Economies: A Post-capitalist Project of Sustainable Development." In *Economic Representations: Academic and Everyday*, ed. David F. Ruccio, 291–314. New York: Routledge.

Held, David. 2006. *Models of Democracy*. 3rd ed. Stanford, CA: Stanford University Press.

Heller-Wagner, Eric. 1995. "Radical Religion and Civil Society: The Unitarians of South Africa." In *Religion and the Reconstruction of Civil Society: Papers from the Founding Congress of the South African Academy of Religion*, ed. J. W. De Gruchy and Steve Martin, 125–151. Pretoria: University of South Africa.

Hilmer, Jeffrey. 2010. "The State of Participatory Democratic Theory." *New Political Science* 32, 1 (March): 43–63.

Hirst, Paul. 1994. *Associative Democracy*. Amherst, MA: University of Massachusetts Press.

———. 1997. *From Statism to Pluralism*. London: UCL Press.

Hogness, Peter. 2012. "Faculty Pan Pathways at Public Hearing, Plan to Develop Alternative." *The Clarion,* August 2012.

Hooghe, Liesbet, and Gary Marks. 2003. "Unraveling the Central State, But How? Types of Multilevel Governance." *American Political Science Review* 977, 2 (May): 233–243.

Holloway, John. (2002) 2005. *How to Change the World without Taking Power*. Ann Arbor, MI: Pluto Press.

———. 2010. *Crack Capitalism*. New York: Pluto Press.

Hourdequin, Marion, and David G. Havlick. 2011. "Ecological Restoration in Context: Ethics and the Naturalization of Former Military Lands." *Ethics, Policy, and Environment* 14, 1: 69–89.

Howard, Ted, Steve Dubb, and Sarah McKinley. 2014. "Economic Democracy." In *Achieving Sustainability: Visions, Principles and Practices,* ed. Debra Rowe. New York: MacMillan.

Hsieh, Nien-he. 2005. "Rawlsian Justice and Workplace Republicanism." *Social Theory and Practice* 31, 1: 115–142.

Huet, Tim. 1997. "Can Co-ops Go Global? Mondragon Is Trying." *Dollars and Sense* (November/December).

Hunold, Christian, and Iris Marion Young. 1998. "Justice, Democracy, and Hazardous Siting." *Political Studies* XLVI: 82–95.

Immerwahr, John, Carolin Hagelskamp, Christopher DiStasi, and Jeremy Hess. 2013. "Beyond Business as Usual: Leaders of California's Civic Organizations Seek New Ways to Engage the Public in Local Governance." New York: Public Agenda. Available at http://www.ca-ilg.org/sites/main/files/file-attachments/beyondbusinessasusual_publicagenda_2013.pdf.

INCITE! Women of Color against Violence, eds. 2009. *The Revolution Will Not Be Funded: Beyond the Non-Profit Industrial Complex.* Boston: South End Press.

Isakhan, Benjamin, and Stephen Stockwell, eds. 2012. *The Secret History of Democracy.* New York: Palgrave Macmillan.

Jamali, Dima. 2008. "A Stakeholder Approach to Corporate Social Responsibility: A Fresh Perspective into Theory and Practice." *Journal of Business Ethics* 82, 1 (September): 213–231.

Jefferson, Thomas. (1813) 1905. "Letter to John Adams." In *The Works of Thomas Jefferson*, ed. Paul L. Ford, 13: 400. Vol XII. New York: G. P. Putnam's Sons.

Johansen, Bruce E. 1982. *Forgotten Founders: How the American Indian Helped Shape Democracy.* Boston: Harvard Common Press.

Johansen, Bruce E., and Donald A. Grinde Jr. 2003. "Reaching the Grassroots: The Worldwide Diffusion of Iroquois Democratic Traditions." *American Indian Culture and Research Journal* 27, 2: 77–91.

Johanson, Patricia. 2016. "Reimagining Infrastructure." Center for Humans and Nature. Available at http://www.humansandnature.org/patricia-johanson.

John, Richard R. 1998. *Spreading the News: The American Postal System from Franklin to Morse.* Cambridge, MA: Harvard University Press.

Kamieniecki, Sheldon, and Margaret Scully Granzeier. 1998. "Eco-cultural Security and Indigenous Self-Determination: Moving toward a New Conception of Sovereignty." In *The Greening of Sovereignty in World Politics*, ed. Karen T. Litfin, 257–270. Cambridge, MA: MIT Press.

Kant, Immanuel. (1785) 1987. *Fundamental Principles of the Metaphysics of Morals.* Buffalo, NY: Prometheus Books.

Kasdan, Alexa, and Lindsay Cattell. 2012. "A People's Budget: A Research and Evaluation Report on the Pilot Year of Participatory Budgeting in New York City." Community Development Project at the Urban Justice Center with the PBNYC Research Team. Available at http://www.urbanjustice.org/.

Kasdan Alexa, Erin Markman, and Pat Convey. 2014. "A People's Budget: A Research and Evaluation Report on Participatory Budgeting in New York City Cycle 3." Community Development Project at the Urban Justice Center with the PBNYC Research Team. Available at http://cdp.urbanjustice.org/cdp-reports.

Kasmir, Sharryn. 1996. *The Myth of Mondragon.* Albany: State University of NY Press.

———. 2015. "Mondragón Co-ops and the Anthropological Imagination." June 29. Available at http://www.focaalblog.com/2015/06/29/sharryn-kasmir-mondragon-coops-and-the-anthropological-imagination/#sthash.Y0BVqGRp.dpuf.

Katsiaficas, George. 1983. *The Imagination of the New Left: A Global Analysis of 1968.* Boston: South End Press.

———. (1997) 2006. *The Subversion of Politics: European Autonomous Social Movements and the Decolonization of Everyday Life.* Oakland, CA: AK Press.

———. 2004. "Seattle Was Not the Beginning." In *The Battle of Seattle: The New Challenge to Capitalist Globalization*, ed. Eddie Yuen, George Katsiaficas, and Daniel Burton Rose, 69–72. New York: Soft Skull Press.

———. 2012. *Asia's Unknown Uprisings*. Vol. 1. Oakland, CA: PM Press.

Kaufman, Arnold. (1960) 1969a. "Human Nature and Participatory Democracy." In *The Bias of Pluralism*, ed. William Connolly, 178–200. New York: Atherton Press.

———. 1969b. "Participatory Democracy: Ten Years Later." In *The Bias of Pluralism*, ed. William Connolly, 201–211. New York: Atherton Press.

Keane, John. 2009. *The Life and Death of Democracy*. New York: W.W. Norton.

Keck, Marcus, and Patrick Sakdapolrak. 2013. "What is Social Resilience? Lessons Learned and Ways Forward." *Erkunde*, 67, 1: 5–19.

Kelly, Marjorie. 2001. *The Divine Right of Capital*. San Francisco: Berrett-Koehler Publishers.

Kelly, Marjorie, and Sarah McKinley. 2015. *Cities Building Community Wealth*. Democracy Collaborative. Available at http://democracycollaborative.org/cities.

Kemmis, Douglas. 1992. *Community and the Politics of Place*. Norman, OK: University of Oklahoma Press.

Keng, Cameron. 2014. "If Apple Were a Worker Cooperative, Each Employee Would Earn at Least $403K." *Forbes*, December 18. Available at http://www.forbes.com /sites/cameronkeng/2014/12/18/if-apple-was-a-worker-cooperative-each-employee -would-earn-at-least-403k/.

Kishimoto, Satoko. 2006. "Public Water Services." May 1, 2007. Accessed April 28, 2015. Available at http://www.tni.org/archives/act/1842.

Kishimoto, Satoko, Emanuele Lobina, and Olivier Petitjean. 2015. *Our Public Water Future*. Amsterdam: TNI.

Klein, Naomi. 2001. *No Logo*. London: Harper Collins.

———. 2007. *The Shock Doctrine*. New York: Metropolitan Books.

———. 2014. *This Changes Everything: Capitalism vs the Climate*. New York: Simon and Schuster.

Konczal, Mike, and Bryce Covert. 2014. "Socialize Uber: It's Easier Than You Think." *The Nation*, December 29. Available at https://www.thenation.com/article/socialize -uber/.

Kohn, Margaret. 2016. *The Death and Life of the Urban Commonwealth*. Oxford: Oxford University Press.

Kropotkin, Peter. (1902) 1976. *Mutual Aid: A Factor in Evolution*. Boston: Porter Sargant.

Lacey, Robert J. 2008. *American Pragmatism and Democratic Faith*. DeKalb, IL: Northern Illinois University Press.

Lawson, Bill. 2008. "The Value of Environmental Justice." *Environmental Justice* 1, 3 (December): 155–158.

Lee, Min-Dong Paul, 2008. "A Review of the Theories of Corporate Social Responsibility: Its Evolutionary Path and the Road Ahead." *International Journal of Management Reviews* 10, 1 (March): 53–73.

Lerner, Josh. 2014a. *Making Democracy Fun*. Cambridge, MA: MIT Press.

———. 2014b. *Everyone Counts*. Ithaca, NY: Cornell Press.

Lessig, Lawrence. 2011. *Republic, Lost: How Money Corrupts Congress--and a Plan to Stop It*. New York: Twelve/Hachette.

Lévesque, Benoît. 2013. "How the Social Economy Won Recognition in Québec at the End of the Twentieth Century." In *Innovation and the Social Economy: The Québec Experience*, ed. Marie J. Bouchard. Toronto: University of Toronto Press.

Lewis, Michael, and Pat Conaty. 2012. *The Resilience Imperative: Cooperative Transitions to a Steady-State Economy*. Gabriola Island, BC: New Society Publishers.

Lewis, Michael, and Dan Swinney. 2008. "Social Economy and Solidarity Economy: Transformative Concepts for Unprecedented Times?" In *Solidarity Economy: Building Alternatives for People and Planet*, ed. Jenna Allard, Carl Davidson, and Julie Matthaei, 28–41. Chicago, IL: ChangeMaker Publications.

Linebaugh, Peter. 2008. *The Magna Carta Manifesto: Liberties and Commons for All*. Berkeley, CA: University of California Press.

Litfin, Karen, ed. 1998. *The Greening of Sovereignty in World Politics*. Cambridge, MA: MIT Press.

Litfin, Karen T. 2000. "Environment, Wealth, and Authority: Global Climate Change and Emerging Modes of Legitimation." *International Studies Review* 2, 2 (Summer): 119–148.

Lobina, Emanuele, Satoko Kishimoto, and Olivier Petitjean. 2014. "Here to Stay: Water Remunicipalisation as a Global Trend." Amsterdam: Public Services International Research Unit (PSIRU), Multinational Observatory and Transnational Institute.

Lund, Margaret. 2011. "Solidarity as a Business Model: A Multi-Stakeholder Cooperative Manual." Kent, OH: Cooperative Development Center at Kent State University. Available at http://www.uwcc.wisc.edu/pdf/multistakeholder%20coop%20manual.pdf.

Lynd, Staughton. 1971. "Bicameralism from Below." In *Participatory Democracy*, ed. Terrence E. Cook and Patrick M. Morgan, 134–142. San Francisco: Canfield Press.

Lynd, Staughton, and Andrej Grubacic. 2008. *Wobblies and Zapatistas*. Oakland, CA: PM Press.

Maathai, Wangari. (1985) 2006. *The Green Belt Movement*. New York: Lantern Books.

Macpherson, C. B. 1977. *The Life and Times of Liberal Democracy*. Oxford: Oxford University Press.

Malleson, Tom. 2014. *After Occupy: Economic Democracy for the 21st Century*. Oxford: Oxford University Press.

Maltz, Helio. 2005. "Porto Alegre's Water: Public and for All." In *Reclaiming Public Water: Achievements, Struggles and Visions from Around the World*, ed. Belén Balanyá, Brid Brennan, Olivier Hoedeman, Satoko Kishimoto, and Philipp Terhorst, 29–36. Amsterdam: TNI/Corporate Europe Observatory.

Mann, Barbara Alice. 2000. *Iroquoian Women: The Gantowisas*. New York: Peter Lang.

Manno, Jack. 2013. "Imagining Governance to Save the Planet? Try the Great Law of Peace as a Model of Covenantal Leadership." *Minding Nature* 6, 2 (May): 26–32.

Mansbridge, Jane. 1980. *Beyond Adversary Democracy*. New York: Basic Books.

Mansbridge, Jane, James Bohman, Simone Chambers, David Estlund, Andreas Føllesdal, Archon Fung, Christina Lafont, Bernard Manin, and José Luis Marti. 2010. "The Place of Self-Interest and the Role of Power in Deliberative Democracy." *Journal of Political Philosophy* 18, 1: 64–100.

Marcuse, Herbert. 1941. *Reason and Revolution*, 2nd ed. London: Routledge, Kegan and Paul.

Marshall, Bob. 2006. "Japan's Worker Cooperative Movement into the 21st Century." *The Asia-Pacific Journal: Japan Focus* 4, 6: 1–17.

Mattson, Kevin. 1998. *Creating a Democratic Public: The Struggle for Urban Participatory Democracy during the Progressive Era*. University Park, PA: Penn State Press.

May, Todd. 1994. *The Political Philosophy of Poststructuralist Anarchism*. University Park, PA: Penn State Press.

———. 2010. *Contemporary Political Movements and the Thought of Jacques Rancière: Equality in Action*. Edinburgh: Edinburgh University Press.

Mayer, Robert. 2001. "Robert Dahl and the Right to Workplace Democracy." *The Review of Politics* 63: 221–247.

Mazzucato, Mariana. 2014. *The Entrepreneurial State: Debunking Public vs. Private Sector Myths*. New York: Anthem Press.

McDonald, David A., and Greg Ruiters, eds. 2012a. *Alternatives to Privatization: Public Options for Essential Services in the Global South*. New York: Routledge.

———, eds. 2012b. "Introduction: In Search of Alternatives to Privatization." In *Alternatives to Privatization: Public Options for Essential Services in the Global South*, ed. David McDonald and Greg Ruiters, 1–15. New York: Routledge.

———, eds. 2012c. "Careful What You Ask For: State-led Alternatives to Privatization." In *Alternatives to Privatization: Public Options for Essential Services in the Global South*, ed. David McDonald and Greg Ruiters 157–182. New York: Routledge.

McNulty, Stephanie L. 2015. "Barriers to Participation: Exploring Gender in Peru's Participatory Budget Process." *The Journal of Development Studies* 51, 11: 1–15.

Medearis, John. 2004. "Lost or Obscured? How V. I. Lenin, Joseph Schumpeter, and Hannah Arendt Misunderstood the Council Movement." *Polity* 36, 3 (April): 447–476.

Mendel-Reyes, Meta. 1995. *Reclaiming Democracy: The Sixties in Politics and Memory*. New York: Routledge.

Menser, Michael. 2005. "The Global Social Forum Movement, Porto Alegre's 'Participatory Budget,' and the Maximization of Democracy." *Situations: A Journal of the Radical Imagination* 1, 1: 87–108.

———. 2008. "Transnational Democracy in Action: The Case of La Via Campesina." *Journal of Social Philosophy* 39, 1 (Spring): 20–41.

———. 2009. "Disarticulate the State! Maximizing Democracy in 'New' Autonomous Movements in the Americas." In *Democracy, States and the Struggle for Global Justice*, ed. Neil Smith, Omar Dahbour, Heather Gautney, and Ashley Dawson, 251–272. New York: Routledge.

———. 2013a. "The Bioregion and Social Difference: Learning from Young's Metropolitan Regionalism." *Environmental Ethics* 35, 4: 439–459.

———. 2013b. "The Participatory Metropolis, or Resilience Requires Democracy." Center for Humans and Nature. Available at http://www.humansandnature.org/democracy-michael-menser.

———. 2014. "The Territory of Self-Determination: Social Reproduction, Agro-Ecology and the Role of the State." In *Globalization and Food Sovereignty: Global and Local Change in the New Politics of Food*, ed. Peter Andrée, Jeffrey Ayres, Michael J. Bosia, and Marie-Josée Massicotte, 53–83. Toronto: University of Toronto Press.

Mentinis, Mihalis. 2006. *Zapatistas: The Chiapas Revolt and What It Means for Radical Politics*. Ann Arbor, MI: Pluto.

Michaelson, Marc. 1994. "Wangari Maathai and Kenya's Green Belt Movement: Exploring the Evolution and Potentialities of Consensus Movement Mobilization." *Social Problems* 41, 4 (November): 540–561.

Mies, Maria. (1986) 1999. *Patriarchy and Accumulation on a World Scale*. London: Zed.

Mies, Maria, and Veronica Bennholdt-Thomsen. 1999. *The Subsistence Perspective*. London: Zed.

Mies, Maria, and Vandana Shiva. 1993. *Ecofeminism*. New York: Palgrave.

Mill, John Stuart. (1848) 1909. *The Principles of Political Economy with Some of Their Applications to Social Philosophy.* London: Longmans, Green and Co.

———. (1859) 2001. *On Liberty.* London: Batoche Books.

Miller, James. 1987. *Democracy Is in the Streets.* New York: Simon and Schuster.

Mills, Charles, and Carole Pateman, 2007. *Contract and Domination.* Cambridge: Polity.

Monasterio, Jose Mari Luzarraga, Dionisio Aranzadi Telleria, and Iñazio Irizar Etxebarria. 2007. "Understanding Mondragon Globalization Process: Local Job Creation through Multi- Localization." Oñati and Bilbao: Spain Mondragón Unibertsitatea and Universidad de Deusto. Available at http://www.community-wealth.org /articles/outside-us.html.

Moody, Kim. 2007. *From Welfare State to Real Estate.* New York: New Press.

Morgan, Arthur E. 1971. *Dams and Other Disasters: A Century of the Army Corps of Engineers in Civil Works.* Boston: Porter Sargent.

Mueller, Carol. 1993. "Ella Baker and the Origins of 'Participatory Democracy.'" In *Women in the Civil Rights Movement: Trailblazers and Torchbearers, 1941–1965*, ed. Vicki L. Crawford, Jacqueline Anne Rouse, and Barbara Woods, 51–70. Bloomington, IN: Indiana University Press.

Mumford, Lewis. 1974. *The Pentagon of Power: The Myth of the Machine*, Vol. 2. Harcourt Brace Jovanovich: New York.

Munthu, Sankar. 2003. *Enlightenment Against Empire.* Princeton, NJ: Princeton University Press.

Muñoz Ramirez, Gloria. 2008. *The Fire and the Word.* San Francisco: City Lights.

Mutz, Diana. 2006. *Hearing the Other Side.* New York: Cambridge University Press.

Nabatchi, Tina, and Matt Leighninger. 2015. *Public Participation for 21st Century Democracy.* New York: Jossey-Bass.

National Environmental Justice Advisory Council Public Participation and Accountability Subcommittee and U.S. EPA Office of Environmental Justice. 1996. *The Model Plan for Public Participation.* Washington, DC: U.S. Environmental Protection Agency Office of Environmental Justice.

Navarro, Vincent. 2014. "The Case of Mondragon." *CounterPunch*, April 30. Available at http://www.counterpunch.org/2014/04/30/the-case-of-mondragon/.

Neamtan, Nancy. 2008. "Chantier de l'Économie Sociale: Building Solidarity Economy in Quebec." In *Solidarity Economy: Building Economic Alternatives*, ed. Jenna Allard, Carl Davidson, and Julie Matthaei, 268–276. Chicago: ChangeMaker Publications.

Ness, Immanuel, and Dario Azzelini. 2011. *Ours to Master and Own: Workers' Control from the Commune to the Present.* Chicago: Haymarket Books.

Newton, Lisa H. 1989. "Chainsaws of Greed." *Business & Professional Ethics Journal* 8, 3 (Fall): 29–61.

———. 2003. *Ethics and Sustainability.* Fairfield, CT: Prentice Hall.

Notes from Nowhere, ed. 2003. *We Are Everywhere: The Irresistible Rise of Global Anti-Capitalism.* London: Verso.

O'Connor, James. 1998. *Natural Causes.* New York: Guilford Press.

Olivera, Oscar, ed. (with Tom Lewis). 2004. ¡Cochabamba!: Water War in Bolivia. Cambridge, MA: South End Press.

Orlie, Melissa A. 2001. "Political Capitalism and the Consumption of Democracy." In *Democracy and Vision: Sheldon Wolin and the Vicissitudes of the Political*, ed. William E. Connolly and Aryeh Botwinick, 138–160. Princeton, NJ: Princeton University Press.

Ostrom, Elinor. 1990. *Governing the Commons*. Cambridge: Cambridge University Press.

Paget-Clarke, Nic. 1998. "Interview with Japanese Farmers' and Consumer Cooperatives' Representatives." *In Motion Magazine*, August 15. Available at http://www.inmotionmagazine.com/jfcg.html.

Palazzo, Guido, and Andreas Georg Scherer. 2006. "Corporate Legitimacy as Deliberation: A Communicative Framework." *Journal of Business Ethics* 66: 71–88.

Panayotakis, Costas. 2011. *Remaking Scarcity: From Capitalist Inefficiency to Economic Democracy*. Ann Arbor, MI: Pluto.

Paraprofessional Health Institute. 2013. "Facts 3: America's Direct Care Workforce." November. Available at www.PHInational.org.

———. 2014. "Facts 5: Home Care Aides at a Glance." December. Available at www.PHInational.org.

Parenti, Christian. 2011. *Tropic of Chaos*. New York: Nation Books.

Patel, Raj. 2007. *Stuffed and Starved*. New York: Melville House.

———. 2010. *The Value of Nothing*. New York: Picador.

Pateman, Carole. 1970. *Participation and Democratic Theory*. Cambridge: Cambridge University Press.

———. (1979) 1985. *The Problem of Political Obligation: A Critique of Liberal Theory*. Berkeley, CA: University of California Press.

———. 1989. *The Disorder of Women*. Stanford, CA: Stanford University Press.

———. 2012. "Participatory Democracy Revisited: APSA President Address." *Perspectives on Politics* 10, 1 (March): 7–19.

Pavel, M. Paloma, ed. 2009. *Breakthrough Communities: Sustainability and Justice in the Next American Metropolis*. Cambridge, MA: MIT Press.

Peller, Barucha. 2016. "Self Reproduction and the Oaxaca Commune." *ROAR* 1 (March 18): 7.

Perkins, Ellie, and Edith Kuiper et al. 2005. "Explorations: Feminist Ecological Economics." *Feminist Economics* 11, 3 (November): 107–150.

Petitjean, Olivier. 2015. "Taking Stock of Remunicipalisation in Paris: A Conversation with Anne Le Strat." In *Our Public Water Future: The Global Experience with Remunicipalisation*, ed. Satoko Kishimoto, Emanuele Lobina, and Olivier Petitjean, 66–72. Amsterdam: TNI.

Polletta, Francesca. 2002. *Freedom Is an Endless Meeting*. Chicago: University of Chicago Press.

Poirier, Yves. 2008. "Linking the Global and Local: Seikatsu's Vision." GEO 2 (II). Available at http://www.geo.coop/taxonomy/term/124.

Posey, Sean. 2014. "Learning from the Cleveland Model: Notes on the Next American Revolution." The Hampton Institute, November 12. Available at http://www.hamptoninstitution.org/cleveland-model.html#.V82mS7V3-9U.

Pratt, Scott. 2002. *Native Pragmatism*. Bloomington, IN: Indiana University Press.

Priest, Dana, and William M. Arkin. 2010. "Top Secret America: The Rise of the New Security State." *The Washington Post*, July 19, 2010.

Quilligan, James Bernard. 2010. "The Commons of Mind, Life and Matter: Toward a Non-Polar Framework for Global Negotiations." *Kosmos* (Spring/Summer): 41–47.

Ramasubramanian, Laxmi, Mike Menser, Erin Reiser, Leah Feder, Raquel Forrester, Robin Leichenko, Shorna Allred, Gretchen Ferenz, Mia Brezin, Jennifer Bolstad, Walter Meyer, and Keith Tidball. 2016. "Chapter 11: Strategies for Community Resilience Practice for the Jamaica Bay Watershed," In *Prospects for Resilience: Insights from New York City's Jamaica Bay*, ed. Eric Sanderson, William Solecki, John Waldman, and Adam Parris, 241–252. Washington: Island Press.

Reed, Mark. 2008. "Stakeholder Participation for Environmental Management: A Literature Review." *Biological Conservation* 141, 2417–2431.

Restakis, John. 2010. *Humanizing the Economy: Co-operatives in the Age of Capital*. Gabriola Island, BC: New Society Publishers.

Robinson, Kim Stanley. 2017. *2140: A Novel*. New York: Orbit.

Rockhill, Gabriel, and Philip Watts. 2009. *Jacques Rancière: History, Politics, Aesthetics*. Durham, NC: Duke University Press.

Roemer, John, and Erik Olin Wright, eds. 1996. *Equal Shares: Making Market Socialism Work*. Vol. 2. Real Utopias Project Series. London: Verso.

Rogers, Dallas. 2013. "REDWatch: Monitory Democracy as a Radical Approach to Citizen Participation in Planning." *Planning Theory and Practice* 14, 4: 542–546.

Rossi, Federico M. 2015. "Building Factories without Bosses: The Movement of Worker-Managed Factories in Argentina." *Social Movement Studies* 14, 1: 98–107.

Roussopoulos, Dimitrios I., and C. George Benello, eds. 2005. *Participatory Democracy: Prospects for Democratizing Democracy*. Montreal: Black Rose Press.

Royle, Tony. 2005. "Realism or Idealism? Corporate Social Responsibility and the Employee Stakeholder in the Global Fast-Food Industry." *Business Ethics: A European Review* 14, 1: 42–55.

Ruggie, John Gerard. 1993. "Territoriality and Beyond: Problematizing Modernity in International Relations." *International Organization* 47, 1 (Winter): 139–174.

Sachs, Jeffrey. 2008. *Commonwealth*. New York: Penguin.

Sakolsky, Ron, and James Koehnline (eds). 1993. *Gone to Croatan: Origins of North American Dropout Culture*. Brooklyn, NY: Autonomedia.

Sangha, Soni. 2012. "Putting in Their 2 Cents." *New York Times*, March 30.

Santos, Boaventura de Sousa. 2004. "The World Social Forum: Toward a Counter-Hegemonic Globalisation (Part I)." In *World Social Forum: Challenging Empires*, ed. Jai Sen and Peter Waterman, 233–245. Montreal: Black Rose Books.

———, ed. 2005a. *Democratizing Democracy: Beyond the Liberal Democratic Canon*. New York: Verso.

———. 2005b. "General Introduction: Reinventing Social Emancipation: Toward New Manifestos." In *Democratizing Democracy: Beyond the Liberal Democratic Canon*, ed. Boaventura de Sousa Santos, xvii–xxxiii. New York: Verso.

———. 2005c. "Participatory Budgeting in Porto Alegre: Toward a Redistributive Democracy." In *Democratizing Democracy: Beyond the Liberal Democratic Canon*, ed. Boaventura de Sousa Santos, 307–376. New York: Verso.

———. 2006a. *Another Production Is Possible*. New York: Verso.

———. 2006b. *The Rise of the Global Left: The World Social Forum and Beyond*. New York: Zed.

Santos, Boaventura de Sousa, and Leonardo Avritzer. 2005. "Introduction: Opening up the Canon of Democracy." In *Democratizing Democracy: Beyond the Liberal Democratic Canon*, ed. Boaventura de Sousa Santos, xxxiv–lxxiv. New York: Verso.

Sassen, Saskia. 2006. *Territory, Authority, Rights: From Medieval to Global Assemblages*. Princeton, NJ: Princeton University Press.

Scherer, Andreas Georg, and Guido Palazzo. 2007. "Towards a Political Concpetion of Corporate Responsibility: Business and Socieity Seen from a Habermasian Perspective." *Academy of Management Review* 32, 4: 1096–1120.

Schlosberg, David. 1999. *Environmental Justice and the New Pluralism: The Challenge of Difference for Environmentalism*. Oxford: Oxford University Press.

Schlosberg, David, and David Carruthers. 2010. "Indigenous Struggles, Environmental Justice, and Community Capabilities." *Global Environmental Politics* 10, 4 (November): 12–35.

Scholz, Trebor. 2016. "Platform Cooperativism: Challenging the Corporate Sharing Economy." New York: Rosa Luxemburg Stifttung. January. Available at http://www.rosalux-nyc.org/platform-cooperativism-2/.

Schumpeter, Joseph. (1942) 1950. *Capitalism, Socialism and Democracy*. 3rd ed. New York: Harper and Row.

Schwarzenbach, Sibyl A. 2009. *On Civic Friendship: Including Women in the State*. New York: Columbia University Press.

Schweickart, David. 1980. *Capitalism or Worker Control? An Ethical and Economic Appraisal*. New York: Praeger.

———. 2002. *After Capitalism*. New York: Rowman and Littlefield.

———. 2011. *After Capitalism*. 2nd ed. New York: Rowman and Littlefield.

Scott, James. 2009. *The Art of Not Being Governed*. New Haven, CT: Yale University Press.

Selee, Andrew, and Enrique Peruzzotti, eds. 2009. *Participatory Innovation and Representative Democracy in Latin America*. Baltimore, MD: Johns Hopkins University Press.

Sensat, Julius. 1983. "Review of *Capitalism or Worker Control?* by David Schweickart." *The Philosophical Review* 92 (October): 622–625.

Shaffer, Jack. 1999. *Historical Dictionary of the Cooperative Movement*. Lanham, MD: Scarecrow Press.

Shah, Anwar. 2007. *Participatory Budgeting. Public Sector Governance and Accountability*. Washington, DC: World Bank.

Shapiro, Ian. 2003. *The State of Democratic Theory*. Princeton, NJ: Princeton University Press.

Shiva, Vandana. 1989. *Staying Alive: Women, Ecology and Development*. London: Zed Books.

———. 1993. *Monocultures of the Mind*. London: Zed Books.

———. 2002. *Water Wars*. Cambridge, MA: South End Press.

———. 2005. *Earth Democracy*. Cambridge, MA: South End Press.

Shrader-Frechette, Kristin. 2002. *Environmental Justice: Creating Equality Reclaiming Democracy*. New York: Oxford University Press.

Sintomer, Yves, Carsten Herzberg, Giovanni Allegretti (with Anja Röcke and Mariana Alves). 2013. *Participatory Budgeting Worldwide*—Updated Version. Dialog Global Series, no. 25. Bonn: Engagement Global Service Agency Communities in One World.

Sintomer, Yves, Carsten Herzberg, Anja Röcke, and Giovanni Allegretti. 2012. "Transnational Models of Citizen Participation: The Case of Participatory Budgeting." *The Journal of Public Deliberation* 8, 2 (Article 9). Available at http://www.publicdeliberation.net/cgi/viewcontent.cgi?article=1234&context=jpd.

Sitrin, Marina. 2006. *Horizontalism*. Oakland, CA: AK Press.

———. 2012. *Everyday Revolutions: Horizontalism and Autonomy in Argentina*. New York: Zed Books.

———. 2015. "With and Beyond Left Governments." *ZNet*, April 21. Available at https://zcomm.org/znetarticle/with-and-beyond-left-governments/.

Smith, Neil. 2009. "Introduction: Altered States." In *Democracy, States and the Struggle for Global Justice*, ed. Neil Smith, Omar Dahbour, Heather Gautney, and Ashley Dawson, 1–16. New York: Routledge.

Spronk, Susan. 2007. "Bolivia: A Movement Toward or Beyond Statism?" *Monthly Review*, March 29.

Spronk, Susan, and Jeffery R. Webber. 2007. "Struggles against Accumulation by Dispossession in Bolivia: The Political Economy of Natural Resource Contention." *Latin American Perspectives* 34, 2: 31–47.

Standing, Guy. 2014. "The Precariat and Class Struggle." [Published as "O precariado e a luta de classes."] *Revista Crítica de Ciências Sociais* 103 (May): 9–24.

Stiglitz, Joseph. 2008. "Foreword." In *Privatization: Successes and Failures*, ed. Gérard Roland, ix–xix. New York: Columbia University Press.

———. 2015. *Rewriting the Rules of the American Economy: An Agenda for Growth and Shared Prosperity.* New York: Roosevelt Institute.

Stikkers, Kenneth W. 2009. "Dewey, Economic Democracy, and the Mondragon Cooperatives." *European Kournal of Pragmatism and American Philosophy* 3, 2: 186–199.

Stortone, Stefano. 2010. "Participatory Budgeting: Heading Towards a 'Civil Democracy'?" In *A Panacea for all Seasons? Civil Society and Governance in Europe*, ed. Matthias Freise, Miikka Pyykkönen, and Eglè Vaidelytè, 99–121. Baden Baden: Nomos.

Su, Celina. 2012. "Whose Budget? Our Budget? Broadening Political Stakeholdership via Participatory Budgeting." *Journal of Public Deliberation* 8, 2: 1–14.

Taylor, Bron. 2013. "Kenya's Greenbelt Movement." In *Civil Society in the Age of Monitory Democracy*, ed. Lars Trägårdh, Nina Witoszek, and Bron Taylor, 180–207. Oxford: Berghahn Books.

Thompson, David. 2001. "Mondragon's Eroski as Mass Retailer." *Cooperative Grocer Network* 97 (November–December). Available at http://www.grocer.coop/articles/mondragons-eroski-mass-retailer.

Thompson, Paul. 1995. *Spirit of the Soil: Agriculture and Environmental Ethics*. London: Routledge.

Tokatlian, Juan Gabriel. 2008. "America the Breakup Artist: US Support for Partition Movements Is Opening a Can of Worms." *Christian Science Monitor*, June 3.

Touchton, Michael, and Brian Wampler. 2014, "Improving Social Well Being through Democratic Institutions." *Comparative Political Studies* 47, 10: 1442–1469.

Tremlett, Giles. 2013. "Mondragon: Spain's Giant Cooperative Where Times Are Hard but Few Go Bust." *The Guardian*, March 7. Available at https://www.theguardian.com/world/2013/mar/07/mondragon-spains-giant-cooperative.

Trucost. 2013. "Natural Capital at Risk: The Top 100 Externalities of Business." April. Available at www.trucost.com.

Turner, Terisa E., and Leigh S. Brownhill. 2001. "'Women Never Surrendered': The Mau Mau and Globalization from Below in Kenya 1980–2000." In *There Is an Alternative: Subsistence and Worldwide Resistance to Corporate Globalization*, ed. Veronika Bennholdt-Thomsen, Nicholas Faraclas, and Claudia von Werlhof, 106–132. New York: Zed Books.

Van Reybrouck, David. 2017. *Against Elections: The Case for Democracy.* Trans. Liz Walters. London: The Bodley Head.

Vargese, Sangeeth. 2010. "Free the Workplace!" *Forbes*, June 14. Accessed June 10, 2016. Available at http://www.forbes.com/2010/06/14/traci-fenton-democracy-leadership-governance-varghese.html.

Viero, Odete Maria, and Andre Passos Cordeiro. 2003. "New Rules, New Roles: Does PSP Benefit the Poor? The Case of Public Provisioning in Porto Alegre." London: WaterAid and TearFund.

Wainwright, Hilary. 2003. *Reclaim the State.* New York: Verso.

———. 2007. "The Commons, the State, and Transformative Politics." *Red Pepper*, December. Available at http://www.redpepper.org.uk/The-commons-the-state-and/.

———. 2013. "Participatory Alternatives to Privatisation." Speech delivered to social movements in Greece, February 2013. Available at https://www.tni.org/en/briefing/participatory-alternatives-privatisation.

———. 2014. "The Tragedy of the Private: The Potential of the Public." Amsterdam: Public Services International and Transnational Institute.

Wainwright, Hilary (with Mathew Little). 2009. *Public Service Reform . . . But Not as We Know It!* Hove, U.K.: Picnic Publishing.

Walker, Gordon. 2012. *Environmental Justice: Concepts, Evidence, and Politics.* Abingdon, U.K.: Routledge.

Wampler, Brian. 2007. *Participatory Budgeting in Brazil.* University Park, PA: Penn State Press.

Warren, Mark. 1996. "What Should We Expect from More Democracy? Radically Democratic Reponses to Politics." *Political Theory* 24, 2: 241–270.

———. 2000. *Democracy and Association.* Princeton, NJ: Princeton University Press.

Weinstock, Daniel M. 2006. "The Real World of (Global) Democracy." *Journal of Social Philosophy* 37, 1 (Spring): 6–20.

Whitman, Elizabeth. 2012. "PB hits NYC." *The Nation*, April 16. Available at http://www.thenation.com/article/167406/participatory-budgeting-hits-new-york-city#.

Whyte, Kyle Pows. 2011. "The Recognition Dimensions of Environmental Justice in Indian Country." *Environmental Justice*, 4, 4: 199–205.

———. 2013. "Justice Forward: Tribes, Climate Adaptation and Responsibility." *Climatic Change* 120, 3: 517–530.

———. 2014. "Renewing Relatives: Nmé Stewardship in a Shared Watershed." December 1. Available at http://hfe-observatories.org/project/renewing-relatives-nme-stewardship-in-a-shared-watershed/.

———. 2016. "Is It Colonial Déjà Vu? Indigenous Peoples and Climate Injustice." In *Humanities for the Environment: Integrating Knowledges, Forging New Constellations of Practice*, ed. Joni Adamson and Michael Davis, 88–104. New York: Routledge.

Whyte, William Foote, and Kathleen Whyte. (1988) 1991. *Making Mondragon.* Ithaca, NY: ILR Press.

Wilentz, Sean. 2005. *The Rise of American Democracy.* New York: W. W. Norton.

Wilson, James. 1999. *The Earth Shall Weep: A History of Native America.* New York: Grove Press.

Wolin, Sheldon. 1996. "Fugitive Democracy." In *Democracy and Difference: Contesting the Boundaries of the Political*, ed. Seyla Benhabib, 31–45. Princeton, NJ: Princeton University Press.

Wolff, Richard D. 2012. *Democracy at Work: A Cure for Capitalism.* Chicago: Haymarket.

World Bank. 2004. *State-Society Synergy for Accountability.* Washington DC: The World Bank.

Wright, Erik. 2010. *Envisioning Real Utopias.* London: Verso.

Young, Iris Marion. 1990. *Justice and the Politics of Difference.* Princeton, NJ: Princeton University Press.

———. 2000. *Inclusion and Democracy.* New York: Oxford University Press.

———. 2004. "Responsibility and Global Labor Justice." *Journal of Political Philosophy* 12, 4: 365–388.

———. 2007. "Hybrid Democracy: Iroquois Federalism and the Postcolonial Project." In *Global Challenges: War, Self-determination and Responsibility for Justice*. Malden, MA: Polity.

Yuen, Eddie, Lisa J. Bunin, and Tim Stroshane. 1997. "Multicultural Ecology: An Interview with Carl Anthony." *Nature, Ecology, Society* 8, 3 (September): 41–62.

Yuen, Eddie, Daniel Burton-Rose, and George N. Katsiaficas, eds. 2004. *Confronting Capitalism: Dispatches from a Global Movement*. Brooklyn, NY: Soft Skull Press.

Zibechi, Raul. August 2004. "Worker-Run Factories: From Survival to Economic Solidarity." Americas Program, Interhemispheric Resource Center (IRC). Citizen Action in the Americas, No. 12. Available at www.americaspolicy.org.

———. 2005. "Subterranean Echoes: Resistance and Politics 'Desde el Sótano.'" *Socialism and Democracy* 19, 3: 13–39.

———. 2010. *Dispersing Power*. Trans. Ramor Ryan. Oakland, CA: AK Press.

———. 2012. *Territories in Resistance*. Trans. Ramor Ryan. Oakland, CA: AK Press.

Zimmerman, Joseph F. 1986. *Participatory Democracy*. Westport, CT: Praeger.

Index

Michael Menser is Assistant Professor of Philosophy and Urban Sustainability Studies at Brooklyn College and Assistant Professor of Earth and Environmental Sciences and Environmental Psychology at the City University of New York Graduate Center. He is co-founder of the Participatory Budgeting Project and co-editor of *Technoscience* and *Cyberculture*.

www.ingramcontent.com/pod-product-compliance
Lightning Source LLC
Chambersburg PA
CBHW050807270326

41926CB00026B/4590